Narrative/Theory

David H. Richter
Queens College

Longman *Publishers USA*

Narrative/Theory
Copyright © 1996 by Longman Publishers USA.
All rights reserved.
No part of this publication may be reproduced,
stored in a retrieval system, or transmitted
in any form or by any means, electronic, mechanical,
photocopying, recording, or otherwise,
without the prior permission of the publisher.

Longman, 10 Bank Street, White Plains, N.Y. 10606

Associated companies:
Longman Group Ltd., London
Longman Cheshire Pty., Melbourne
Longman Paul Pty., Auckland
Copp Clark Longman Ltd., Toronto

Acquisitions editor: Virginia L. Blanford
Assistant editor: Chris Konnari
Production editor: Dee Josephson
Cover design: Betty Sokol
Cover illustration: © 1996 Al Held/Licensed by VAGA, New York, NY.
    Courtesy Andre Emmerich Gallery, New York, NY
Compositor: The Composing Room of Michigan
Text credits appear on pp. xi–xii.

Library of Congress Cataloging-in-Publication Data
Narrative/theory / edited by David H. Richter.
        p. cm.
    Includes bibliographical references and index.
    ISBN 0-8013-1610-3
    1. Fiction—History and criticism—Theory, etc.   I. Richter,
David H.
PN3331.N27   1996
809.3—dc20   95-21302
                                                     CIP

1 2 3 4 5 6 7 8 9 10-MA-9998979695

To my wife, Golde

Contents

Part III   IDEOLOGIES   243

Preface

When I first started teaching at Queens College twenty-five years ago, we were going through one of our periodic self-fashionings, and the fashion in refashioning back then, in the wake of the Sixties, was to ditch all required courses. Students who had previously been forced to take introductions to drama and fiction and many other subjects as well, now had only a single freshman composition course followed by four years of electives. My own department, following the same trend, stripped down its gateway requirements to a single course in poetry. This had to stay because poetry was special: there were terms of art, like trochaic tetrameter or metonymy or villanelle, that had to be learned, and techniques of close reading that had to be acquired.

The novel, along with prose narrative in general, was left to shift for itself. Most of my colleagues weren't upset because everybody knew how to read fiction: you just read stories and discussed their themes. Since the narrative we studied in those days was quintessentially high modernist fiction, since the art of fiction was deemed to have already reached its pinnacle in stories such as Conrad's "Heart of Darkness," Joyce's "The Dead," Woolf's "Kew Gardens," and Hemingway's "In Another Country," one didn't need much more than the techniques of close reading—the thematic analysis already learned from Brooks' and Warren's *Understanding Poetry*—to explicate the tangle of symbols and motifs. There was no need for special tools to understand narrative.

It wasn't true even then, of course. Even in those far simpler days when the New Criticism dominated critical practice, rhetorical theorists like Wayne Booth and Seymour Chatman had developed sophisticated vocabularies for analyzing narrative. The questions they were beginning to open out—the relation of the story to the discourse, the agents to the narrator, the teller to the tale, the involvement and disengagement of the audience—genuinely enriched our formal understanding of how narrative worked. And as we learned about the artistic choices involved in narrative technique, it became harder to maintain the provincial prejudice that whatever was not high modernist fiction was either primitive (like Defoe and Fielding), crude (like Zola and Wolfe), or obscure (like Robbe-Grillet and Nabokov).

Ironically, an excellent choice of textbooks was available twenty-five years ago for the course in the critical analysis of fiction we didn't have, including Robert Scholes's *Approaches to the Novel*, Calderwood and Behrens's *Perspectives on Fiction*, and Philip Stevick's *Theory of the Novel*. These books brought together some of the most interesting current essays on plot and character, theme and symbol, and point of view. Needless to say, these anthologies are long out of print. Although some of the essays they reprinted are still required reading, the collections themselves cannot be resuscitated because the assumptions under which they were structured are no longer current.

A generation ago it was generally assumed that literary works at their best were supreme and universal expressions of the human spirit, and that students read these profound works to broaden and deepen their own humanity. The works to be studied had been sifted by time: only the greatest and the most universal had survived; students reading these texts were connected with the truest and most permanent criterion of taste, the collective applause of humankind. It was presumed that literary meaning was more complicated than the meaning of "everyday" language, that literary texts were ambiguous or indeed bore multiple levels of meaning, each of which needed to be explored. Nevertheless, it was taken as given that this complex of meaning was not a private meaning subjectively produced by the operations of a specific reader, but a public meaning objectively available to any seeker.

At present, however, there is no working consensus about what literature is and what it is good for. Literature departments are characteristically split between those who continue to think of themselves as humanists analyzing the masterpieces of Western culture and as those who think of themselves as experts in the semiotic and cultural significance of texts whose definition as "literature" is up for grabs. Part of the split is over the literary canon: whether we believe in the idea of a slowly evolving, collectively determined group of classics, whether we should massively expand the "canon" to include more works by women and minorities, or whether the whole idea of a "canon"—a group of works representing "the best that has been known and thought in the world"—may no longer work. Part of the split is over how we read literature, about whether readers are formed by the text, or whether we "perform" texts as quasi-independent interpreters, or, as Stanley Fish has insisted, whether for all practical purposes we write them ourselves.

Now more than ever it seems clear that teaching a course in narrative or prose fiction—from a sophomore Introduction to Fiction class for nonmajors to a graduate seminar in narratology—requires that we ground students in the rudiments of theory. And the easiest way to do this is to use a collection of original essays that brings up the most important issues and sets them into their contexts, either as background reading or as the primary focus of the course. But to be useful to today's students, any contemporary collection of readings on narrative theory needs to be centered in the decentered world we now inhabit, to reflect the desperate questions of the present day rather than the suave certainties of the past.

The most obvious change is that the canon of the narrative we study has drastically shifted. Today it seems almost embarrassing to think how seriously we once took the debate over F. R. Leavis's vision of the "great tradition" of the novel—a pantheon running from Austen through Eliot and Conrad to D. H. Lawrence. Lawrence's realism now looks a lot like that of the other high modernists, and modernism itself no longer seems the goal of history it once did. Since Lawrence and Hemingway, we have played the postmodern games of Nabokov and Calvino, and slid on to the dirty realism of Carver and the magical realism of Garcia Marquez. Nor does contemporary anglophone culture any longer seem to contain the world: my students are often more excited by the recent novels of Naguib Mahfouz and Milan Kundera, or by exotic antiques like *The Tale of Genji* or *The Story of the Stone*. They are as likely to do their masters theses on Nella Larsen, Kazuo Ishiguro, or Amy Tan as on Dickens, Hawthorne, or Joyce.

If the idea of the canon as a closed club primarily for white heterosexual males has given way to an expanded (and still expanding) definition of the textual and the literary, we have just begun to think about how being different or Other affects the creative process and the literature that is created. These sorts of extra-formal issues were just starting to be raised about narrative texts a generation ago. They appear in the third section of *Narrative/Theory*, titled "Ideologies."

The formal analysis of narrative itself—once the exclusive focus of anthologies of theory—has been equally affected by the waves of theory that have broken over the last two decades. The formal analysis of narrative has run along two major tracks, and the reader will find most of the major players in both camps gathered in the second section of *Narrative/Theory*, entitled "Elements of Narrative." The first methodology to develop historically was the *structuralist-semiotic* branch of narratology, which takes meaning to be something that comes out of the decipherment of linguistic codes. Its origins are in the Russian formalist criticism that flourished in the 1920s, and whose ideas spread via Czechoslovakia (the "Prague Linguistic Circle") to France, where they have flourished since the 1960s, and from there to the rest of the world. The other track—with roots that go back to Aristotle and Longinus—began in Chicago in the 1940s, where R. S. Crane developed a *rhetorical poetics* of narrative (along with other genres of literature) that has evolved and complicated over the last fifty years. Space doesn't permit a full discussion of these literary theories here, but briefly one could contrast them by saying that structural narratology is concerned, first and foremost, with what narrative *is*, while rhetorical narratology is concerned with what it *does* or how it *works*.

It would be nice to be able to divide "form" and "content" so neatly. But two decades of theory have also led us to question the binary opposition of formal "technique" and raw "content": we understand, with Fredric Jameson, that the content too has its semiotic form, and the form its ideological content. Two of the essays in the "Ideologies" section have strong formal implications: Jameson's own essay analyzing the ideological implications of a single paragraph of Flaubert's *A Simple Heart* and Peter Brooks's analysis of the psychoanalytical underpinnings of narrative plot structures. These essays demonstrate the way in which both Marxist and Freudian ideas about narrative, once crudely attached to the sociological or psychic "content" brought by the author to the text, now view social and psychological forces as intimately engaged in the aesthetic realizations of narrative. Similarly, several essays in the "Elements of Narrative" section have strong extra-formal implications: Mikhail Bakhtin's prosaics of narrative, written partly in response to the Russian formalists, insists upon the ways in which the "dialects" of social life are held in suspension within prose narratives, quoted, parodied, reaccented, within the dialogical framework of fiction. And Susan Lanser's *Fictions of Authority* is an attempt, operating beyond feminism as such, to incorporate gender as a formal narratological category.

Finally, students need to see narrative theory as part of an ongoing struggle, not only by readers but by writers of narrative to clear away or reject practices they loathed, or to define more positively the space in which they wanted to operate. Before the beginning of this century at least, novelists enjoyed a monopoly on literary theory, and they still write some of the best expositions of their craft as manifestos. Students need to see this sort of writing as well, partly because theory always seems more "authentic" and authoritative when it is provided by the voice of practical experience, partly because these essays, starting with Henry Fielding's in the mid-eighteenth century, constitute a form of historical encounter with the way narrative has defined itself. An entire book the size of this one could have been filled with selections of this sort, and I had to limit this section to illustrative apologies for eighteenth-century epic, the Victorian novel, realism, naturalism, modernism, postmodernism, and magical realism, with regrets for not being able to include the myriad other articulate spokespeople from Clara Reeve to Alain Robbe-Grillet.

In this first section of *Narrative/Theory*, titled "Manifestos," as in the other two, I have tried wherever possible to give the authors space and to avoid the "slice and dice" approach to the art of anthology. Seventeen of the thirty-one selections in the book are complete essays, and most of the rest represent discrete sections or chapters from books. In the few places where I have regretfully had to abridge an essay, I indicate elisions with a row of stars and, where necessary, indicate in a footnote what has been elided. Brief introductions to each of the three sections place the essays into the context of the ongoing conversations of which they were a part and attempt to indicate what is at stake in the theoretical positions. Brief biographical headnotes to the writers will indicate something about their histories and interests. A glossary of narratological terms, appended, will help the beginner avoid getting stuck in the unfamiliar language of theory. Here as elsewhere, the aim is to provide the sort of background that will give the student a prospective sense of the sorts of questions and issues that the instructor is going to raise. Taken together, the essays in *Narrative/Theory* constitute a short course in the theory of fiction representing most of the current perspectives in the contemporary conversation about narrative, literary and otherwise. It could be used as a primary text in a course in the theory of fiction—for which no currently adequate textbook exists; but we expect the book to find its widest use as an ancillary text for courses in the novel, the short story, and film, where it can be used to enrich and deepen students' understanding of the concepts involved in the analysis of narrative.

The impetus for this book came from my students at Queens College in the "Fiction in Theory and Practice" course required for creative writers, who let me know candidly what worked and didn't in the readings I force-fed them. But it would not have come into existence without the faith and prodding of Ginny Blanford of Longman, who signed it up, and her able assistant Chris Konnari. Thanks too to Esther Silverman, my copy editor at Longman, and the production editor, Dee Josephson, who turned my messy manuscript into the attractive and readable object you have in your hands. I am grateful too for the comments of my reviewers who controlled my quirks of taste and donated wonderful constructive criticism: they include Janet Aikins of the University of New Hampshire; Ann Ardis of the University of Delaware; Jamie Barlowe of the University of Toledo; Beth Boehm of the University of Louisville; Gerry Butler of San Diego State University; Janice Carlisle of Tulane University; Robert Caserio of Temple University; Bob Merrill of University of Nevada at Reno; William Monroe of University of Houston; Gregory Scholtz of Wartburg College; Robyn Warhol of the University of Vermont; and Patti White of Ball State University. I particularly want to thank Laura Wadenpfuhl of the Graduate School, City University of New York, who contributed gratis the narratological glossary she devised for her study of narrative in the romances and sonnet sequences of Sir Philip Sidney and Lady Mary Wroth; I have adulterated it with a few terms peculiar to the texts collected here. Finally, this book belongs to all those—especially Ralph and Wayne, Jim and Peter and Mike—whose conversations about theory, narrative, and real life, our shared stories and discourses, sustain me in a community of scholars and friends.

CREDITS

General Introduction

His cruelty proved at last fatal to himself. He had shed with impunity the noblest blood of Rome; he perished as soon as he was dreaded by his own domestics. Marcia his favorite concubine ... seized the occasion of presenting a draught of wine to her lover, after he had fatigued himself with hunting some wild beasts. Commodus retired to sleep; but whilst he was labouring with the effects of poison and drunkenness, a robust youth, by profession a wrestler, entered his chamber and strangled him without resistance.

————Edward Gibbon: *Decline and Fall of the Roman Empire*

Isabel had seen the world. She had passed two years at one of the first boarding schools in London, had spent a fortnight at Bath, and had supped one night in Southampton. "Beware, my Laura," she would often say, "beware of the insipid vanities and idle dissipation of the Metropolis of England; beware of the unmeaning luxuries of Bath and of the stinking fish of Southampton." "Alas," exclaimed I, "how am I to avoid those evils I shall never be exposed to? ... I, who am doomed to waste my days of youth and beauty in an humble cottage in the Vale of Usk." Ah! little did I then think I was ordained so soon to quit that humble cottage for the deceitful pleasures of the world.

————Jane Austen: *Love and Freindship*

Fourscore and seven years ago, our forefathers brought forth upon this continent a new nation, conceived in liberty and dedicated to the proposition that all men are created equal. Now we are engaged in a great civil war testing whether that nation, or any nation so conceived and dedicated, can long endure.

————Abraham Lincoln: Gettysburg Address

There's a line drive through the gap down in right center field that gets down and rolls out to the warning track and on to the wall. In to score Walton. Sandberg has a double; he's gonna go for third. Here's the relay from Thompson and tags him out. Sandberg gets an RBI double and then is thrown out trying to stretch it to a triple.

————John Rooney: CBS Broadcast of Cubs-Giants Playoff Game,
October 7, 1989

1

THE UBIQUITY OF NARRATIVE

Although a few people may have managed to escape altogether from fiction—
particularly from the varieties of literary fiction that can be viewed as a form of high
art—narrative is an unavoidable part of everyday life, arguably the single most
important way we come to understand the world we live in. On the most basic
level, we tell stories to each other, true or with "stretchers," about the events of our
day, and get impatient with those people who can't tell them interestingly or
coherently. Written down in the papers, or shown with moving pictures and sound
on television, the news of the world comes to us in the form of framed narratives.
Viewed on MTV, a heavy metal band produces a filmed story of provocation and
betrayal. Unseen and unscripted on the radio, the fast-paced drama of a baseball
game rides into our minds as an elliptical narrative in the present tense, in which we
can be made to vividly imagine a number of events as occurring simultaneously
although—owing to the limitations of language—they have to be told sequentially.[1]

But narrative also enters into areas of life where description or argumentation
would be expected. History, of course, is fundamentally a narrative form of
discourse, despite our contemporary fascination with statistics and charts, and
historical writers such as Gibbon can betray a novelist's sensitivity to the power of
irony and a weakness for heavy-handed symbolism, aesthetic choices that impinge
on the vision of real events within his representation. Orators too wind up telling
stories: even so puny a specimen for its times as Abraham Lincoln's 287-word
address on the significance of Gettysburg required him to situate the carnage within
a historical process, a plot of testing, begun in the past and continuing into the
future. So do economists. Adam Smith's explication in *The Wealth of Nations* of the
efficiencies of the division of labor invites us to imagine a sequence in the making
of a single pin where "one man draws out the wire, another straights it, a third cuts
it, a fourth points it, a fifth grinds it at the top for receiving the head." Today's
economists, whether monetarists or Keynesians, develop macroeconomic
explanations in terms of narratives about what industrialists did in the face of rising
oil prices, or what small investors are going to do when interest rates fall, and
quarrel explicitly with the narratives their adversaries create.

Narrative can be appealed to in even less probable aspects of human life. It has
become conventional for chemists to cast complex reactions as abstract little
narratives with active and passive agents of molecular change, just as biologists do
with the sequences of evolution or the activities of antibodies. Even those experts
who analyze paintings and sculptures turn the viewing of these entirely static works
of art into narratives by telling stories, not only narratives about the pictorial scene
that may be represented there or about the artists' relationships with the subjects of
their representations, but ones about the interactions of the viewer's eyes with the
masterpiece, the way in which one is held by one detail, repelled by another, the

---

[1] In the example above, we are simultaneously (and effortlessly) following the ball in flight, the batter and
the runner both advancing along the base path, and the outfielder throwing to the third baseman.

gaze sliding from one aspect of the picture or statue to the next. Perhaps what should be surprising is not how pervasive narrative is but that we can convey and explain things in any other way.

The lure of narrative begins long before that of literature, starting probably with a mother's or father's bedside "once upon a time," but the appeal of literature at all ages and levels of artistry is that of being able to turn on the stream of story for ourselves. Even children who have not yet learned their first letters enjoy reading picture books by themselves, interpreting a sequence of illustrations as a satisfying narrative. Those of us who go on to Proust began here and graduated through courses of cheap comic books whose sometimes startling artistry of spatial form Proust himself might have appreciated. And the cinema and television programs, to which I am as addicted as my grade-school-aged children, despite their "dramatic" use of live actors, have their main appeal as narrative and require an analytic vocabulary about point of view, focalization, and voice, similar in many respects to that of prose fiction.

As theorists such as Wolfgang Iser and Robert Scholes have suggested, the key to the "narrativity" of a sequence of events, our desire to cast it or to read it as a narrative, is not the completeness and smoothness of the sequence from beginning through middle to end, but rather the gaps in its structure, which involve the audience, giving rise retrospectively to curiosity (as when we wonder how a state of affairs came to be) or prospectively to desire (as when we foresee possible favorable or unfavorable outcomes). But those gaps and discontinuities that produce curiosity and desire can be almost entirely abstract, as in a musical composition that "skips" a tone in a scale passage only to come back to it later, or one that boldly announces a theme but interrupts its development with other material, creating a sense of unfinished business that the composer will have to assuage before the piece can arrive at its denouement.

This book is about narrative as a human science—so far as we know, no other species of animal tells stories—and as an art form that has been studied and theorized about for at least 300 years. It is an attempt to collect some of the most interesting ideas, mostly from the present and the recent past, about how narratives are constructed and how they work on readers. For the most part, these ideas have come from literary theorists whose models of narrative have come from prose fiction.

NARRATIVE TRUTH AND FICTION

One of the motives for the theoretical analysis of narrative fiction has been the gnarled relation between truth and fiction. From the first days of literary criticism, when Plato exiled the poets from the Republic for telling attractive lies about gods and men, it has been necessary to defend the writing and reading of nonfactual narrative. One possible reply was that of Philip Sidney, whose poets in effect take the fifth amendment: they are not liars because "the poet never affirmeth": storytellers tell stories all right, but at least they do not tell them for true.

But if they do not tell the truth, then what do they tell? Aristotle, in the generation after Plato, had defended epic and tragedy not merely as refusing any claim to factual and circumstantial truth. He argued further that literature was both nobler and more philosophical than the factual narrative of history, because its plots conformed to "the law of the necessary and the probable," representing what would happen in life purified from the dross of the accidental and the incidental. Although Aristotle's defense is geared to the notion that fictions are more probable and thus in a sense truer than real life, he nevertheless suggests late in the *Poetics* that the stories of poets can follow a probability scheme different from that of ordinary contemporary reality. Poets can represent with an equivalent verisimilitude not merely "the way things are" but "the way things used to be" or "the way things are thought to be" or "the way things used to be thought to be"—so that beliefs about the supernatural, or even superstitions in which people no longer believe, can work in a plot. This makes sense: without believing in ghosts or vampires, we have no trouble following the plots of *Hamlet* or *Dracula*.

A more general statement of this might take the form of viewing fiction as hypotheticals, existing in a separate "possible world" where some of the facts of life or even of the laws of nature we normally recognize are suspended.[2] We require such hypothetical worlds to be consistent (that is, rules like "vampires can be killed by pounding a wooden stake through their heart" should work all the time if they work at all) and coherent (a world in which people can become vampires after death must also be one in which the soul survives the mortal body). These possible worlds of fiction can resemble the world we live in or can be very different. A "conservative" bias is implicit in the reading process, though, since we readers generally try to minimize the adjustments we make, naturalizing the "possible world" in terms of the world we live in till that becomes impossible. And authors usually cooperate with this, since the less the worlds they create resemble the one we live in, the more difficult it is going to be for them to give us a lively sense of the values and the rules by which things happen. As a result, even science fiction stories set far in the future or among strange extraterrestrials seldom change more than a few of the routine scripts about the contemporary world.

The difference between hypothetical stories and narratives claiming falsely to be a factual account of something that actually occurred is a distinction that gets ingrained into us from early childhood. My seven-year-old daughter has long known the difference, not only between truth and falsehood, but between falsehood and "once upon a time." She is even savvy to more complicated hybrids of lies and "once upon a time," like myths: those stories—like the tooth fairy's nocturnal substitution of coin of the realm for deciduous teeth—that adults pretend to believe for ritual purposes while knowing them to be false.

---

[2] Theorists of narrative sometimes differ in the degree to which they are willing to problematize the notion of the "real world" against which we naturalize the "possible worlds" of fiction. Umberto Eco exteriorizes the "real world" as a set of scripts in which that world is represented; he calls those scripts "the encyclopedia" and allows for the fact that his own encyclopedia is likely to differ from other people's. Mary-Laure Ryan, to the contrary, takes the "real world" as something to which all of us have equal and common access.

If works of fiction were all pure hypotheticals like fairy tales and fantasies, truth and fiction would be mutually exclusive. There would be one large category of stories that made claims to be true about the actual world (which would include both true stories and lies) and there would be another category of stories that were hypothetically but not actually or factually true. But of course it isn't that simple. Fiction includes allegories and fables, in which impossible events—like a goose that lays golden eggs—can be represented as a way of inculcating homely truths about the real world—like the fact that excessive greed can cause one to lose everything. It includes satires such as Swift's *Gulliver's Travels* and Orwell's *Animal Farm,* in which comic caricatures are meant to represent public figures like Sir Robert Walpole or Joseph Stalin, and historical novels such as *Ivanhoe* and *War and Peace,* in which real-life figures like Richard the Lion Heart and Napoleon can influence the action and its outcome for Scott and Tolstoy's imagined characters.

Even more confusingly, the novel includes texts such as Defoe's *Moll Flanders* that are read as "false true stories,"[3] a sort of lie, rather than "let's pretend." And on the other hand, it includes texts like Joyce's *Portrait of the Artist as a Young Man* and Woolf's *To the Lighthouse* that are aesthetically designed simulations of real life, autobiographies presented in the form of fiction. In contrast to Defoe's "false true stories," these are "true fictions" about the contingent real worlds that Joyce and Woolf grew up in and whose meaning they did not have to invent. But in both cases an autobiographical character within the novel—Stephen Dedalus and Lily Briscoe—discovers that the need to comprehend and to master that contingent world can be fulfilled only within the symbolic triumph of successful artistic representation.[4]

But factual narrative can also be described in such honorific terms as the "triumph of successful artistic representation." Many critics have judged *In Cold Blood,* Truman Capote's narrative about Perry Smith and Steve Hickock, the two murderers of the Clutter family in Kansas, as more powerfully written than any of his fictions. It can be studied as a work of literature, because, like other factual texts that have become literature—such as Boswell's *Life of Johnson*—it is a work of the

---

[3] Although we all know, with one part of our minds, that *Moll Flanders* is by Daniel Defoe, the experience of reading the text doesn't convey that fact, not even covertly. (In a few spots there are signs of Defoe's authorship, but they are signs rather than signals, inadvertent traces rather than messages to the reader.) The experience is close to that of reading a genuine autobiography by a naive and inexperienced author, partly because of the skill of Defoe's impersonation, partly because he carefully avoids any sense of a structured consequential plot. For an analysis of this phenomenon, see Ralph Wilson Rader, "Defoe, Richardson, Joyce," in *The Critical Tradition* (Boston: Bedford, 1989), pp. 828-46.

[4] Similarly, Woolf appears in *To the Lighthouse* as both the object and subject of representation, as Cam Ramsay and as Lily Briscoe. On the other side, the usual sort of autobiographical novel, such as *David Copperfield,* presents selected elements of the life of the author within the hypothetical probability scheme of the novel's possible world. It is interesting to know that Dickens actually pasted labels in a blacking factory the way David does wine labels at the warehouse of Murdstone & Grinby, but it isn't essential to understanding the story, because every character is invented to play his or her role in David's odyssey. *Portrait of the Artist,* like true stories, includes characters (like Dante Riordan and Mr. Casey) and actions (like Stephen's bed-wetting) whose existence derives from an uninvented reality outside the fiction, and whose introduction would make no sense except that they were true.

imagination. As we know from their notes and diaries, Capote and Boswell were able to discover within themselves what it was like to be Perry Smith or Samuel Johnson, down to their physical bodily feelings, with the minuteness that we ordinarily think possible only of pure hypothetical creations. Nevertheless, as readers we have no trouble differentiating fictions that take their shape from real life from the biographies, histories, and "factions" that make a claim to historical veracity.

LITERATURE AND NARRATIVE

As with narrative and fiction, narrative and literature are partially overlapping categories: some literature is narrative in form and some is dramatic or lyric; and some narrative qualifies as literature and some doesn't. Unlike fiction, literature is one of those value-laden categories that provoke disagreement more often than not. Whatever we call literature we are asserting to have aesthetic and intellectual significance. "You call *that* literature? I call it trash!" I remember my mother asking about some novel I was reading that had words in it she didn't like to hear me say— Joyce's *Ulysses,* I think. My mother was entitled to her opinion, even though no less an authority than the Supreme Court of United States had in 1933 officially declared it literature, and so lifted a customs contraband order barring its import as a pornographic book.

Societies have collective opinions on what constitutes literature, and the boundaries vary widely from century to century. Familiarity is a key issue: generally whatever forms are new and popular are deemed subliterary. In the early seventeenth century, poetry was literature but the drama was outside the boundaries: Ben Jonson was ridiculed for publishing his plays as his "works." (We can applaud his arrogance since it was only after he did so that Shakespeare's surviving partners decided to publish his plays in an expensive folio.) In the eighteenth century, the novel wasn't literature, though it was one of the best-selling genres of the day. Till well into the nineteenth century, the periodical book reviews listed "Literature" as a separate category from "Novels." "Literature" included poetry, essays on the classical authors, works of history—a grab bag of disparate genres— but novels were outside the pale until after Walter Scott's prestige as a romantic poet rubbed off on his *Waverley* novels. These days "the novel" as such is definitely literature, even though some of the most popular forms of fiction from horror stories to Harlequin Romances may not qualify.

Cinematic narrative, just entering its second century, has even more recently become literature in the honorific sense, assisted by university film studies programs and the learned studies they generate. Screenplays of classic films by Ford, Welles, Bergman, and Kurosawa are often published; though most routine films are "reprinted" and collected today as VCR tapes. In some ways—including the use of live actors—film seems to be most like the drama, but the camera creates a subjective "point of view" effect that is more like the novel. The tension we sometimes experience between two simultaneous perspectives—the one implied by the image we see on the screen and the one implied by the voice we hear narrating the story—has no counterpart in drama but is equivalent to the relation between voice and focalization in prose fiction.[5] Many of the discussions of fictional elements in this book apply fairly closely to corresponding elements of film narrative.

On the other side of the Mason-Dixon line between literature and non-literature are other forms of popular narrative: comic books, cartoons, MTV videos, television series programs. Whether the boundary is correctly positioned is impossible to say. Although some forms of popular culture are repetitive and moribund, some of the freshest and most interesting examples of narrative, now as in former centuries, are officially "non-literature." The only thing we can be sure of—as might be suggested by the acclaim awarded to Art Spiegelman's cartoon novel about the Holocaust, *Maus,* and by the reprinting here as well as in England of the teleplays of the British TV writer Dennis Potter—is that the boundary is constantly in motion.

FORM, IDEOLOGY, HISTORY

The theories collected in this book about narrative, primarily fictional literary narrative, have been divided into three sections. The second, "Elements of Fiction," is about narrative as a way of using language that can be studied either by an analysis of sign systems and the way they work (the new science of semiotics) or by a study of affective communication between authors and audiences (the old art of rhetoric). In a sense these essays contribute to a "formal" understanding of narrative, providing us with tools for analyzing narrative, with ways of thinking about action and character and other matters that get represented in narratives, and about the techniques writers have developed for representing them. Here is where we can get clear about the relation between the flesh-and-blood authors who write narratives and the narrators who are created to mediate the telling, and about the audiences that are implicit within narratives and their relation to the flesh-and-blood people who actually read them.

Most of the previously published collections of narrative theory I know have consisted solely of essays taking up the rhetoric or the poetics of fiction, arranged under rubrics like "plot," "characterization," "point of view," "symbolism," and so forth. This was an apt method for a formalist age that believed in human universality rather than cultural difference, that ignored as unimportant or at least bracketed as unanalyzable the individual disparities between the ways writing and reading is done by men and women, or whites and blacks, or gays and straights. Although some of us today may be in danger of overemphasizing difference, of presuming that

---

[5] In a study of film noir (with its frequent voice-over effects) Robert Caserio concluded that "voice" and "focalization" work in opposite ways in prose fiction and in film: in a film (such as "Sunset Boulevard") it is the voice we hear that "focalizes" the narrative, establishing a point of view, while the picture we see may give us information technically unavailable to the central consciousness. In prose fiction (such as Faulkner's short story "Barn Burning") the focalizing perspective may rest with the child, Sartie Snopes, but the story is voiced in an educated adult language that Sartie could not comprehend.

white males like me cannot read Toni Morrison's *Beloved* and understand the life of Sethe, it seems clear that none of us leaves our genetic origin and environmental acquisitions behind when we pick up a book. Those key issues of class, race, gender, and sexual orientation are always with us, influencing how readers read as well as how writers write. The final section of the book, titled "Ideologies," theorizes about these aspects of our encounters with narrative.

The third dimension of literary theory is history. Narrative is surely nearly as old as human language, and even literary fiction has a history nearly as long as the written word. But "the novel" was invented all over Europe during the eighteenth century and relatively quickly, within a century or so, went from a despised subliterary form to the central place in the ordering of the arts. A genuine poetics of the novel was even later in developing: Henry James began writing about the novel as an art form late in the nineteenth century. But all during its evolution the novel evolved through a series of style systems and conventions, so that novelists— whether or not they had any ambition to contribute to the poetics of the form— were nevertheless interested in defending the innovations they were making in narrative, or in attacking the older forms of the novel they hoped to displace. The opening section of this book, titled "Manifestos," collects a sampling of texts by canonical novelists ranging from Henry Fielding in the mid-eighteenth century (who traced his own artistic lineage back to Homer and Cervantes) to the contemporary magical realist writer Milan Kundera, who traces his own lineage back to—well, back to Cervantes. As a group these essays constitute a fragmented and discontinuous history, if not exactly of literary narrative, of the style systems in which narrative has been written, and of our ideas about what narrative was and ought to be.

If narrative is the way we learn about our world, narrative theory is the way we learn about narrative, about how and why it affects us as it does. Some of the issues raised are technical questions about precisely whose vision and what language are used to tell a story; others engage the subjects closest to our sense of personal identity: race, class, gender, and sexual orientation, and the unconscious drives in whose fulfillment we are driven to act or go still. Stories tell us: We become the stories we tell and are told. In understanding narrative we can come to understand who we are and how we were made that way.

part I

Manifestos

ROMANCE AND ANTI-ROMANCE: THE NOVEL BEFORE THE NOVEL

The relationship between the domain of "literature" and that of "prose fiction" or "the novel" has been an uneasy one from the beginning. As far back as the fourth century B.C., Aristotle apparently knew of an "art that imitates by words alone in prose" but it had no name in his own time, and apart from this brief mention in the *Poetics,* he himself ignored it. These texts were perhaps ancestors of the "Alexandrian romances" that flourished in the second and third centuries A.D., such as the *Aethiopica* of Heliodorus or Longus's *Daphnis and Chloe,* tales of the struggles and adventures of separated lovers, often grotesquely gnarled and complicated by loosely connected episodes and digressions and filled with idealized characters—stereotyped heroes and villains—and perfumed language. These texts in the high style were balanced by others in a low style, Varronian or Menippean satires like the *Golden Ass* of Apuleius, or the *Satyricon* of Petronius, or even by parodic romances such as the *Leucippe and Clitophon* of Achilles Tatius. Romance was an ambiguous genre: poetry, in the form of lyric, epic, and poetic drama, was "literature"; prose fiction was relegated to the fringes of the literary. The serious romance was a ne'er-do-well younger brother of the epic, but the comic anti-romance had an even baser muse.

In the Middle Ages, the same pattern can be found: prose fiction used for Romance in Wolfram von Eschenbach's *Parzifal,* or Thomas Malory's *Morte d'Arthur* (published 1485). During the English Renaissance there was a genuine flowering of Elizabethan prose fiction but it nevertheless did not produce anything remotely like the eighteenth century novel. One strand is the knightly romance, often medleys mixing prose and poetry like Philip Sidney's *Arcadia* and Mary Wroth's *Urania.* Shorter and less elaborate versions of prose romance were the sources of Shakespeare's comedies, like Thomas Lodge's lyrical *Rosalind,* which became *As You Like It,* and Robert Greene's acerbic *Pandosto: The Triumph of Time,* which became *The Winter's Tale.* And countering the romance we again find the anti-romance, which takes a variety of different shapes throughout the period: one "low" tradition went back to the Spanish picaresque in *La vida de Lazarillo de Tormes* and *Guzman de Alfarache,* which inspired Deloney's *Thomas of Reading* and Thomas Nashe's *Unfortunate Traveler*—possibly the most readable of the Elizabethan novellas today. Another version of the anti-romance descended from the Roman satire was Rabelais' *Gargantua and Pantagruel,* a learned and witty parody of the conventions of chivalric and romantic literature.

WANTED: A POETICS

The romantic and antiromantic traditions were in a sort of dialectical opposition until they were combined in Cervantes' *Don Quixote* (1607, translated into English by 1612). This is a key text: its synthesis of romance and anti-romance was to have a far-reaching influence on the history of the novel. But in fact, it is interesting how little Cervantes directly affects the course of prose fiction in English until the era of Henry Fielding over a century later. Fielding's audience was aware of a still viable tradition of romance—translations and imitations of seventeenth-century romances such as *Le grand Cyrus* of Madeleine de Scudéry, complicated fantastical confections involving proud disdainful princesses and long-suffering heroic lovers. But there was also a newer tradition of realism originating in popular journalism that reached an artistic acme in the pseudo-factual fictions of Defoe. Like his rival Richardson, though by very different techniques, Fielding was to synthesize the textures of realism with the affective structures of romance in launching the genre that within another century would move from the outer suburbs to the center of the literary arts. Fielding's own best novels, *Joseph Andrews* and *Tom Jones,* flatter Cervantes by including at their centers an absurd quest punctuated by narrative digressions. In the next decade Charlotte Lennox (in *The Female Quixote*) and Tobias Smollett (in *Launcelot Greaves*) were to adapt Cervantes even more directly.

Until Fielding's day, a poetics of the novel would have been an impertinence; the form had not yet taken shape. Fielding, a classically trained author, instantly set out to provide one, published primarily in the prefatory chapters of *Joseph Andrews* and *Tom Jones.* Fielding does not attempt to invent the wheel: his prefaces base themselves on Aristotle's strictures on epic form in the *Poetics,* which Fielding applies directly to the novel. Thus the novel should not be a loose biography of a fictional character but must recount a single unified action from beginning through middle to end. One of Fielding's motives may be defining his own comic forms against Defoe's pseudo-autobiographies, and even against the novels of Richardson (whose 1741 continuation of *Pamela* may have suggested the possibility of a formless never-to-be-concluded river of prose); but his major impulse was to locate the novel somewhere within the ordering of the arts by establishing it as governed by aesthetic rules. Fielding supplies in the preface to *Joseph Andrews* his Augustan version of the lost Aristotelian poetics of comedy, with ridicule taking the place of *katharsis* as the end result of the action, and the representation of affectation and hypocrisy replacing the pitiable and the fearful as the formal means to that end. Later in *Joseph Andrews,* introducing Book III, Fielding presents his version of Aristotle's insistence that the artist represents universal traits in all of us rather than imitating particular people. And the prefatory chapters of *Tom Jones* include essays on other Aristotelian and Horatian topics including the use of traditional plot materials, literary probability, and characterization. The one thing obviously missing from Fielding's poetics was any attempt to understand the role of the narrator relative to his characters: the novel was analyzed as though it were a form of drama.

MAKING SPACE

By the middle of the nineteenth century, the novel had achieved a legitimate place in the ordering of the arts, owing partly to the respectability conferred by Walter Scott's *Waverley* series of historical romances, but it had also become a growing site of the market for popular entertainment, owing to the widespread literacy in both England and America. Like videos today, novels were rented to fans who planned to read them and forget them rather than bind them in leather for their libraries.[1] Many of the most interesting theoretical essays of this period are by serious novelists whose main interest was in making space for their own productions.

Thus Melville's 1850 essay, "Hawthorne and His Mosses," is more than an appreciative essay in the prevailing romantic mode[2] on the Sage of Salem, with whom Melville had lately become acquainted. It insists on reading Hawthorne in a certain way, and in valorizing one side of Hawthorne—the author of "Young Goodman Brown" and "My Kinsman, Major Molineux" and "Rappaccini's Daughter"—at the expense of the author of "Little Annie's Ramble" and other quaint, anodyne stories that were demonstrably more popular at the time. Melville's Hawthorne is the author whose "power of blackness . . . derives its force from . . . that Calvinistic sense of Innate Depravity and Original Sin, from whose visitations, in some shape or other, no deeply thinking mind is always and wholly free." It is true that Melville's Hawthorne is *our* Hawthorne: the essay looks forward to contemporary criticism that has emphasized Hawthorne's Puritan themes and tragic vision. But it is equally obvious that Melville's Hawthorne is also Melville's *Melville* as well—he is implicitly recommending the power of blackness in himself that had

---

[1] The "three-decker" novel of the Victorian period was primarily a product of the rental market. Mudie's Library, a nineteenth-century franchise, allowed clients to borrow one volume per annual subscription, so that readers who wanted to borrow all three volumes at once (to make sure they could read the middle and end of their book) had to take out three subscriptions. To enforce the three-subscription norm, Mudie's avoided works that didn't fit the preferred format.

[2] Like romantic critics beginning with Wordsworth (or even back to Immanuel Kant), Melville insists on the quality of Hawthorne's writing as being—like that of Shakespeare—a measure of the writer's soul or spirit of genius, the latter being expressed into the former.

just published *White-Jacket,* and was soon to create *Moby-Dick,* "Benito Cereno," *The Confidence-Man* and *Billy Budd, Sailor.* "Hawthorne and His Mosses" makes space for Melville in another way too, of course, through its lashing criticism of most of his contemporary novelists as flunkeys, Anglophile wannabes that "furnish an appendix to Goldsmith" instead of giving artistic definition to "that unshackled democratic spirit" of America.

Like Herman Melville, George Eliot's "Silly Novels by Lady Novelists" (1856) works by clearing space for her own serious novels by attacking the entertainments with which it was in competition. (Her first novel, *Adam Bede,* which I suspect no one has ever called silly, was to appear in 1859.) One of her issues is the curious paradox in the way novels by women were evaluated: by and large, she felt male reviewers were harsh and cold to novelists such as Charlotte Brontë and Elizabeth Gaskell who were in genuine competition with masters such as Dickens and Thackeray; but reviewers were warm in their praise of precisely those women whose mediocre works reinforced male prejudices about female creativity. To this one needs to add, however, that many of the silly novels Eliot attacks here are not much sillier than those of eminently respectable male authors writing at the time, from Thomas Lister, of the silver-fork school, to the mystical productions of Edward Bulwer-Lytton. By clearing the ground, she makes room for her own rich realism, which attempted to create a social world denser and richer than that of the decadent descendents of Walter Scott and a moral seriousness even more respectable.

By 1884, Henry James, an American transplanted to England, was able to take the space-clearing strictures of writers like Melville and Eliot and incorporate them into a new poetics. A title like "The Art of Fiction" seems to promise a compendium of techniques, but that is just what James is least willing to provide. The title isn't even James's own: it is taken from Walter Besant, who had lectured that "laws of fiction may be laid down and taught with as much precision and exactness as the laws of harmony, perspective and proportion." Trained as a painter himself before becoming a novelist, James disagreed: "If there are exact sciences, there are also exact arts, and the grammar of painting is so much more definite" than that of fiction "that it makes the difference." But if James rejects all of Besant's particular recommendations, he agrees that fiction is indeed an art. Today, after Eliot, Woolf, and James himself, this contention needs no proof. But the Victorian novel had been created by entertainers who made few claims for their trade, and the public was used to retreating into three-volume narratives that guaranteed adventure and escape, a love story with a happy ending, and poetic justice for all. Like Eliot, James positions himself against this stultifying formula as a way of championing his own style of fiction, which was more subtle and inward than was common. But he insists that novelists unlike himself be granted the freedom to experiment, not just with subject matter and point of view, but with moral issues that disturb and disquiet. And like Melville, James insists on a postromantic, expressive theory of fiction as art: "the deepest quality of a work of art will always be the quality of the mind of the producer. In proportion as that intelligence is fine will the novel . . . partake of the substance of beauty and truth."

MODERN LIFE

In James's critical ideas one can see not only the fruition of George Eliot's notions about realism but also the lineaments of modernism just coming to birth. In Virginia Woolf, those ideas finally take on their classic features. Like George Eliot, Woolf defines herself against her contemporaries, and the specific objects of her loathing are the Georgian triumvirate of H. G. Wells, Arnold Bennett, and John Galsworthy. In these Georgians, Woolf criticized a documentary realism (which had been one of George Eliot's lesser attainments) that had run itself into the ground in chronicling the material lives of trivial people. "Is life like this?" she asked; "Must novels be like this?" For Woolf, real human life is not defined by the solid structures given by society but the evanescent impressions of the sensibility: "The mind receives a myriad impressions. . . . From all sides they come, an incessant shower of innumerable atoms, and as they fall, as they shape themselves into the life of Monday or Tuesday, the accent falls differently from of old." Bennett and Galsworthy know too much and tell too much of what they know. Novels like her own, or like those of Joyce, convey only discordant, disparate impressions and leave it to the reader to synthesize their spiritual significance. (The modernist reader, it is clear to see, works much harder than his or her ancestors, since the text's significance is not given but created in the reading process.) Whereas Woolf's manifesto aligns itself with Anglophone writers such as Hardy and Conrad, her principal heroes are the Russians. In Tolstoy, Dostoevsky, and Chekhov, Woolf found another triumvirate, one that had exposed the anatomy of the human spirit without ignoring its material life.

WRITING BLACK

Melville's essay and Eliot's were written from the perspective of oppressed groups: American literature, in Melville's time, was very much on the defensive against British cultural imperialism, while Eliot's essay expresses the anxiety of a sex presumed to be "weaker" in perspicacity and talent as well as upper body strength. A century later, Richard Wright and Ralph Ellison were attempting to define politically and personally what it means to write as an African American. Wright's manifesto is the more obviously political, because he insists on turning around the audience of "Negro writing." Instead of addressing themselves primarily to white America, either as an explicit plea for racial justice or as evidence of the cultural achievement of the white man's former slaves, Wright wants his fellow African Americans to forge in the smithies of their souls the as-yet uncreated consciousness of their race. As a Marxist, Wright views that consciousness as a social consciousness first and foremost, and he is suspicious as to whether a writer can see the individual's place within society clearly without the tools of dialectical materialism, to cut through the false consciousness of ideology so as to make his brethren understand the relationship between "a Negro woman hoeing cotton in the South and the men who loll in swivel chairs in Wall Street and take the fruits of her toil." In this sense, Wright is in reaction against the modernist writers of the Harlem Renaissance (such as Langston Hughes and Zora Neale Hurston), whose psychological density and stylistic brilliance sacrificed the clarity of social vision Wright demanded.

Ralph Ellison, though confessedly at one time a disciple of Richard Wright's, takes a very different position, one closer perhaps to that of Henry James. For Ellison, a man's personal suffering or the suffering of his group may be the raw material of his art, but the quality of that art has nothing intrinsically to do with the raw material. "The process of making artistic forms . . . helps give meaning to the experience of the group. And it is the process of mastering the discipline, the techniques, the fortitude, the culture . . . that constitutes the writer's real experience as *writer,* as artist." Ellison views fictional technique as something more than an artistic tool: it becomes for him what Marxist analysis was for Wright, "a way of feeling, of seeing, and of expressing one's sense of life," a way of cutting through received ideas and getting a true perspective on being a human being and an American.

LOST IN THE FUNHOUSE; FUN IN THE LOST HOUSE

Goals like Ellison's were, in a way, a slightly modified version of Woolf's: the creation of a fully dramatized subjective narrative that would represent adequately the perceived texture of life itself. Many writers today certainly still pursue these goals, but *post*modern writers such as John Barth or Robert Coover in the United States, or Samuel Beckett and Alain Robbe-Grillet in France, while retaining the technical innovations of modernism, have rejected the vision behind the technique. The limits of modernism have been reached: for a book to imitate life no longer seems worth doing. Postmodernism produces hyperrealist texts in which technique becomes the vehicle for exploring the limits and paradoxes of storytelling itself: the postmodern novel announces itself as nothing more—or less—than a book.

John Barth's "Literature of Exhaustion" is one manifesto seeking rejuvenation for literature at the modernist dead end, when "the novel, if not narrative literature generally, if not the printed word altogether, has by this hour of the world just about shot its bolt." The author of *End of the Road* sees a rejuvenation for the word in Jorge Luis Borges, the Argentinian postmodernist whose works consist of a few lapidary short stories made up, as Barth puts it, of "algebra and fire." Borges's stories typically present an *idea* rather than a narrative: "Tlön, Uqbar, Orbis Tertius" invites us to construct a world whose material reality resembles Plato's heaven of forms; "The Garden of Forking Paths" is about the idea of infinite narratives; "Pierre Menard, Author of the *Quixote,*" plays with the idea of our reinscribing the classics today, verbatim—as new works rejuvenated by the ironic consciousness with which we would have to reproduce their ideas. The dryness of Borges's wit is precisely what Barth feels is needed to water the modernist wasteland: "[Borges'] artistic victory . . . is that he confronts an intellectual dead end and employs it against itself to accomplish new human work. . . . It's a matter of every moment throwing out the bath water without for a moment losing the baby." Narratives about narrative is a very postmodern idea, but, as Pierre Menard knew better than any of us, it is also a very ancient one. The genre of prose fiction could be said to have begun "with *Quixote* imitating *Amadis of Gaul,* Cervantes pretending to be Cid Hamete Benengeli (and Alonso Quijano pretending to be Don Quixote)."

Cervantes is also the key figure for the Czech-born magical realist Milan Kundera, though, for Kundera, the importance of the *Quixote* is not its technical innovation as a text about textuality. For Kundera, the *Quixote* is narrative as "inquiry," an emblem of Cartesian Man heroically seeking meaning in a world without lights, where there are no answers, only questions. In the four centuries since the *Quixote,* however, Kundera views society as having become hostile to freedom of inquiry: it has created institutions, ideologies, totalizing politics of various sorts, all leading to a "no exit," a horror without escape. Kundera loves the serene modernists, Joyce, Woolf, and Proust, who worked in London and Paris, providing a record of the journeys of their spirits. But for him the more apt vision of the generation was provided by the modernists from Central Europe—Kafka and Musil, Broch and Hašek—who envisioned modern life as an absurd theatre of cruelty from which Cartesian logic had been banished. To Kundera, the one antidote to modernity at the end of the road is the spirit of the novel, its appeals to play, to dream, to thought. A veteran of the Prague Spring of 1968, which crushed the Czech renaissance, Kundera has renounced his allegiance to God and country, the people and the individual, and puts his faith only in "the depreciated legacy of Cervantes."

From Fielding to Barth and Kundera, we have come full circle, beginning with a self-conscious imitator of Cervantes and ending with two imitators of Cervantean self-consciousness, beginning with a subliterary genre seeking a secure place in history and ending with a quintessentially literary genre seeking to escape the dead end to which history had apparently consigned it. In each of these cases, and in all those in between, theorizing about narrative is a way of pushing the envelope, of opening out possibilities for writing, of making space for one's own stories.

Henry Fielding

Henry Fielding was born in 1707 at Sharpham Park, a country estate in Gloucestershire, eldest son to an impecunious general with aristocratic connections. He got his classical education at Eton College and the University of Leyden, then struck out for London, where in his twenties he became the star playwright specializing in political satire and burlesque farce. When the Walpole government put an end to Fielding's career by establishing a prior censorship of the stage, he supported himself through journalism while reading for the bar. Fielding began writing novels almost by accident, stung by what he considered the hypocritical immorality of Samuel Richardson's best-seller *Pamela* (1740). Fielding replied first with a broad parodic pastiche (*Shamela,* 1741), and the next year with *Joseph Andrews* (1742), a comic novel that begins with a satire on Richardson but quickly turns into a high-hearted adaptation of Cervantes' *Don Quixote*. During the 1740s Fielding continued his journalism in parallel with a legal career, the two converged when, in gratitude for articles in support of the Hanoverian monarchy and the Whig government at the time of the Jacobite revolt of 1745, he was rewarded with a post as judge in the criminal court of central London, later extended to all of Middlesex county. Busy with two careers and heartbroken at the death of his wife, he nevertheless worked on his epic masterpiece, *Tom Jones* (1749). While writing his flawed last novel, *Amelia* (1751), Fielding continued to combat casual and organized crime from his chambers in Bow Street, organizing the first official detective force. In his mid-forties Fielding's health broke; he resigned his magistracy in favor of his half-brother John Fielding. In 1754 he voyaged to Portugal in search of a healthier climate but died soon after his arrival in a town outside Lisbon.

Preface to *Joseph Andrews*

As it is possible the mere *English* Reader may have a different Idea of Romance with the Author of these little Volumes; and may consequently expect a kind of Entertainment, not to be found, nor which was even intended, in the following Pages; it may not be improper to premise a few Words concerning this kind of Writing, which I do not remember to have seen hitherto attempted in our Language.

The Epic as well as the Drama is divided into Tragedy and Comedy. *Homer,* who was the Father of this Species of Poetry, gave us a Pattern of both these, tho' that of the latter kind is entirely lost;[1] which *Aristotle* tells us, bore the same relation to Comedy which his *Iliad* bears to Tragedy. And perhaps, that we have no more Instances of it among the Writers of Antiquity, is owing to the Loss of this great Pattern, which, had it survived, would have found its Imitators equally with the other Poems of this great Original.

---

[1] Homer's comic epic, now lost, was called the *Margites. Ed.*

And farther, as this Poetry may be Tragic or Comic, I will not scruple to say it may be likewise either in Verse or Prose: for tho' it wants one particular, which the Critic enumerates in the constituent Parts of an Epic Poem, namely Metre; yet, when any kind of Writing contains all its other Parts, such as Fable, Action, Characters, Sentiments, and Diction, and is deficient in Metre only; it seems, I think, reasonable to refer it to the Epic; at least, as no Critic hath thought proper to range it under any other Head, nor to assign it a particular Name to itself.

Thus the *Telemachus* of the Arch-Bishop of *Cambray*[2] appears to me of the Epic Kind, as well as the *Odyssey of Homer;* indeed, it is much fairer and more reasonable to give it a Name common with that Species from which it differs only in a single Instance, than to confound it with those which it resembles in no other. Such are those voluminous Works commonly called *Romances,* namely, *Clelia, Cleopatra, Astraea, Cassandra,* the *Grand Cyrus,* and innumerable others which contain, as I apprehend, very little Instruction or Entertainment.

Now a comic Romance is a comic Epic-Poem in Prose; differing from Comedy, as the serious Epic from Tragedy: its Action being more extended and comprehensive; containing a much larger Circle of Incidents, and introducing a greater Variety of Characters. It differs from the serious Romance in its Fable and Action, in this; that as in the one these are grave and solemn, so in the other they are light and ridiculous: it differs in its Characters, by introducing Persons of inferiour Rank, and consequently of inferiour Manners, whereas the grave Romance, sets the highest before us; lastly in its Sentiments and Diction, by preserving the Ludicrous instead of the Sublime. In the Diction I think, Burlesque itself may be sometimes admitted; of which many Instances will occur in this Work, as in the Descriptions of the Battles, and some other Places, not necessary to be pointed out to the Classical Reader; for whose Entertainment those Parodies or Burlesque Imitations are chiefly calculated.

But tho' we have sometimes admitted this in our Diction, we have carefully excluded it from our Sentiments and Characters: for there it is never properly introduced, unless in Writings of the Burlesque kind, which this is not intended to be. Indeed, no two Species of Writing can differ more widely than the Comic and the Burlesque: for as the latter is ever the Exhibition of what is monstrous and unnatural, and where our Delight, if we examine it, arises from the surprizing Absurdity, as in appropriating the Manners of the highest to the lowest, or *è converso;*[3] so in the former, we should ever confine ourselves strictly to Nature from the just Imitation of which, will flow all the Pleasure we can this way convey to a sensible Reader. And perhaps, there is one Reason, why a Comic Writer should of all others be the least excused for deviating from Nature, since it may not be always so easy for a serious Poet to meet with the Great and the Admirable; but Life every where furnishes an accurate Observer with the Ridiculous.

I have hinted this little, concerning Burlesque; because, I have often heard that Name given to Performances, which have been truly of the Comic kind, from the Author's having sometimes admitted it in his Diction only; which as it is the Dress of Poetry, doth like the Dress of Men establish Characters, (the one of the whole Poem, and

---

[2] François de Fénélon (1651–1715). *Ed.*
[3] Vice versa. *Ed.*

the other of the whole Man,) in vulgar Opinion, beyond any of their greater Excel-
lencies: But surely, a certain Drollery in Style, where the Characters and Sentiments
are perfectly natural, no more constitutes the Burlesque, than an empty Pomp and Dignity of Words, where every thing else is mean and low, can entitle any Performance to
the Appellation of the true Sublime.

And I apprehend, my Lord *Shaftesbury's* Opinion of mere Burlesque agrees with
mine, when he asserts, 'There is no such Thing to be found in the Writings of the
Antients.' But perhaps, I have less Abhorrence than he professes for it: and that not because I have had some little Success on the Stage this way; but rather, as it contributes
more to exquisite Mirth and Laughter than any other; and these are probably more
wholesome Physic for the Mind, and conduce better to purge away Spleen, Melancholy
and ill Affections, than is generally imagined. Nay, I will appeal to common Observation, whether the same Companies are not found more full of Good-Humour and
Benevolence, after they have been sweeten'd for two or three Hours with Entertainments of this kind, than when soured by a Tragedy or a grave Lecture.

But to illustrate all this by another Science, in which, perhaps, we shall see the
Distinction more clearly and plainly: Let us examine the Works of a Comic History-
Painter,[4] with those Performances which the *Italians* call *Caricatura;* where we shall
find the true Excellence of the former, to consist in the exactest copying of Nature;
insomuch, that a judicious Eye instantly rejects any thing *outré;* any Liberty which the
Painter hath taken with the Features of that *Alma Mater.*—Whereas in the *Caricatura*
we allow all Licence. Its Aim is to exhibit Monsters, not Men; and all Distortions and
Exaggerations whatever are within its proper Province.

Now what *Caricatura* is in Painting, Burlesque is in Writing; and in the same manner the Comic Writer and Painter correlate to each other. And here I shall observe,
that as in the former, the Painter seems to have the Advantage; so it is in the latter infinitely on the side of the Writer: for the *Monstrous* is much easier to paint than describe, and the *Ridiculous* to describe than paint.

And tho' perhaps this latter Species doth not in either Science so strongly affect
and agitate the Muscles as the other; yet it will be owned, I believe, that a more rational and useful Pleasure arises to us from it. He who should call the Ingenious *Hogarth*
a Burlesque Painter, would, in my Opinion, do him very little Honour: for sure it is
much easier, much less the Subject of Admiration, to paint a Man with a Nose, or any
other Feature of a preposterous Size, or to expose him in some absurd or monstrous
Attitude, than to express the Affections of Men on Canvas. It hath been thought a vast
Commendation of a Painter, to say his Figures *seem to breathe;* but surely, it is a much
greater and nobler Applause, *that they appear to think.*

But to return—The Ridiculous only, as I have before said, falls within my Province
in the present Work.—Nor will some Explanation of this Word be thought impertinent
by the Reader, if he considers how wonderfully it hath been mistaken, even by Writers who have profess'd it: for to what but such a Mistake, can we attribute the many
Attempts to ridicule the blackest Villanies; and what is yet worse, the most dreadful
Calamities? What could exceed the Absurdity of an Author, who should write *the Com-*

---

[4] William Hogarth (1697–1764), a close friend of Fielding's, was the artist-engraver of "comic histories" like
The Rake's Progress. Ed.

edy of Nero, *with the merry Incident of ripping up his Mother's Belly;* or what would give a greater Shock to Humanity, than an Attempt to expose the Miseries of Poverty and Distress to Ridicule? And yet, the Reader will not want much Learning to suggest such Instances to himself.

Besides, it may seem remarkable, that *Aristotle,* who is so fond and free of Definitions, hath not thought proper to define the Ridiculous. Indeed, where he tells us it is proper to Comedy, he hath remarked that Villany is not its Object: but he hath not, as I remember, positively asserted what is. Nor doth the *Abbé Bellegarde,* who hath writ a Treatise on this Subject, tho' he shews us many Species of it, once trace it to its Foundation.[5]

The only Source of the true Ridiculous (as it appears to me) is Affectation. But tho' it arises from one Spring only, when we consider the infinite Streams into which this one branches, we shall presently cease to admire at the copious Field it affords to an Observer. Now Affectation proceeds from one of these two Causes, Vanity, or Hypocrisy: for as Vanity puts us on affecting false Characters, in order to purchase Applause; so Hypocrisy sets us on an Endeavour to avoid Censure by concealing our Vices under an Appearance of their opposite Virtues. And tho' these two Causes are often confounded, (for there is some Difficulty in distinguishing them) yet, as they proceed from very different Motives, so they are as clearly distinct in their Operations: for indeed, the Affectation which arises from Vanity is nearer to Truth than the other; as it hath not that violent Repugnancy of Nature to struggle with, which that of the Hypocrite hath. It may be likewise noted, that Affectation doth not imply an absolute Negation of those Qualities which are affected: and therefore, tho', when it proceeds from Hypocrisy, it be nearly allied to Deceit; yet when it comes from Vanity only, it partakes of the Nature of Ostentation: for instance, the Affectation of Liberality in a vain Man, differs visibly from the same Affectation in the Avaricious; for tho' the vain Man is not what he would appear, or hath not the Virtue he affects, to the degree he would be thought to have it; yet it sits less aukwardly on him than on the avaricious Man, who *is* the very Reverse of what he would *seem* to be.

From the Discovery of this Affectation arises the Ridiculous—which always strikes the Reader with Surprize and Pleasure; and that in a higher and stronger Degree when the Affectation arises from Hypocrisy, than when from Vanity: for to discover any one to be the exact Reverse of what he affects, is more surprizing, and consequently more ridiculous, than to find him a little deficient in the Quality he desires the Reputation of. I might observe that our *Ben Johnson,* who of all Men understood the *Ridiculous* the best, hath chiefly used the hypocritical Affectation.

Now from Affectation only, the Misfortunes and Calamities of Life, or the Imperfections of Nature, may become the Objects of Ridicule. Surely he hath a very ill-framed Mind, who can look on Ugliness, Infirmity, or Poverty, as ridiculous in themselves: nor do I believe any Man living who meets a dirty Fellow riding through the Streets in a Cart, is struck with an Idea of the Ridiculous from it; but if he should see the same Figure descend from his Coach and Six, or bolt from his Chair with his Hat under his Arm, he would then begin to laugh, and with justice. In the same manner,

---

[5] Bellegarde wrote "Reflections on the Ridiculous and the Ways to Avoid It" (1696). *Ed.*

were we to enter a poor House, and behold a wretched Family shivering with Cold and languishing with Hunger, it would not incline us to Laughter, (at least we must have very diabolical Natures, if it would:) but should we discover there a Grate, instead of Coals, adorned with Flowers, empty Plate or China Dishes on the Side-board, or any other Affectation of Riches and Finery either on their Persons or in their Furniture; we might then indeed be excused, for ridiculing so fantastical an Appearance. Much less are natural Imperfections the Objects of Derision: but when Ugliness aims at the Applause of Beauty, or Lameness endeavours to display Agility; it is then that these unfortunate Circumstances, which at first moved our Compassion, tend only to raise our Mirth.

The Poet carries this very far;

None are for being what they are in Fault,
But for not being what they would be thought.[6]

Where if the Metre would suffer the Word *Ridiculous* to close the first Line, the Thought would be rather more proper. Great Vices are the proper Objects of our Detestation, smaller Faults of our Pity: but Affectation appears to me the only true Source of the Ridiculous.

But perhaps it may be objected to me, that I have against my own Rules introduced Vices, and of a very black Kind into this Work. To which I shall answer: First, that it is very difficult to pursue a Series of human Actions and keep clear from them. Secondly, That the Vices to be found here, are rather the accidental Consequences of some human Frailty, or Foible, than Causes habitually existing in the Mind. Thirdly, That they are never set forth as the Objects of Ridicule but Detestation. Fourthly, That they are never the principal Figure at that Time on the Scene; and lastly, they never produce the intended Evil.

Having thus distinguished *Joseph Andrews* from the Productions of Romance Writers on the one hand, and Burlesque Writers on the other, and given some few very short Hints (for I intended no more) of this Species of writing, which I have affirmed to be hitherto unattempted in our Language; I shall leave to my good-natur'd Reader to apply my Piece to my Observations, and will detain him no longer than with a Word concerning the Characters in this Work.

And here I solemnly protest, I have no Intention to vilify or asperse any one: for tho' every thing is copied from the Book of Nature, and scarce a Character or Action produced which I have not taken from my own Observations and Experience, yet I have used the utmost Care to obscure the Persons by such different Circumstances, Degrees, and Colours, that it will be impossible to guess at them with any degree of Certainty; and if it ever happens otherwise, it is only where the Failure characterized is so minute, that it is a Foible only which the Party himself may laugh at as well as any other.

As to the Character of *Adams,* as it is the most glaring in the whole, so I conceive

---

[6] From William Congreve's poem "Of Pleasing." *Ed.*

it is not to be found in any Book now extant. It is designed a Character of perfect Simplicity; and as the Goodness of his Heart will recommend him to the Good-natur'd; so I hope it will excuse me to the Gentlemen of his Cloth; for whom, while they are worthy of their sacred Order, no Man can possibly have a greater Respect. They will therefore excuse me, notwithstanding the low Adventures in which he is engaged, that I have made him a Clergyman; since no other Office could have given him so many Opportunities of displaying his worthy Inclinations.

Herman Melville

Herman Melville was born in New York City in 1819. For various brief spans, Melville went to school, worked in a bank, studied surveying and engineering, and served as a schoolmaster. At twenty, he went off to sea and spent most of the next five years aboard ships—a merchant vessel, several whalers, and a man-of-war. During this time he learned the skills and endured the ongoing tedium of a sailor's life, but he jumped ship on a Pacific island, lived among cannibals, escaped, was imprisoned in Tahiti for participation in a mutiny and released to comb the beaches, and finally returned home on an American frigate. On his return, Melville began writing about his adventures, and his first efforts, *Typee* (1846) and *Omoo* (1847) were wildly successful with both critics and the general public. But with his darker studies of innocence and evil beginning with *Mardi* (1849) and *White-Jacket* (1850), Melville began to challenge and alienate his readers. It seems no accident that Melville's 1850 review of his new friend Hawthorne, reprinted below, celebrates and defends the "power of blackness" their work had in common. In 1851, Melville published his masterpiece, *Moby-Dick,* and if its genius was recognized by some reviewers, it was reviled by others and was not a popular success. Melville's reputation went into a quick decline, hastened by *Pierre* (1852), a gothic study of sin, madness, and death that was greeted by an orgy of abuse. After the failure of *The Confidence-Man* (1857), which was considered merely indigestible rather than immoral or mad, Melville ceased writing novels, drifting from one job to another and writing poetry until he was appointed a customs inspector for New York, a position he filled with conspicuous probity for over twenty years. In the latter half of his life, Melville wrote the epic-length poem *Clarel* (1876), two more volumes of poetry, and a second masterpiece, *Billy Budd, Sailor,* left in manuscript at his death in 1891 and not published until 1924. By then, a Melville revival had begun, which has continued unabated until the present when, more than a century after his death, he is considered one of the greatest novelists of his own or indeed of any time.

Hawthorne and His Mosses

By a Virginian Spending July in Vermont

A papered chamber in a fine old farm-house—a mile from any other dwelling, and dipped to the eaves in foliage—surrounded by mountains, old woods, and Indian ponds,—this, surely, is the place to write of Hawthorne. Some charm is in this northern air, for love and duty seem both impelling to the task. A man of a deep and noble nature has seized me in this seclusion. His wild, witch voice rings through me; or, in softer cadences, I seem to hear it in the songs of the hill-side birds, that sing in the larch trees at my window.

Would that all excellent books were foundlings, without father or mother, that so it might be, we could glorify them, without including their ostensible authors. Nor would any true man take exception to this;—least of all, he who writes,—"When the Artist rises high enough to achieve the Beautiful, the symbol by which he makes it perceptible to mortal senses becomes of little value in his eyes, while his spirit possesses itself in the enjoyment of the reality."[1]

But more than this. I know not what would be the right name to put on the title-page of an excellent book, but this I feel, that the names of all fine authors are fictitious ones, far more so than that of Junius,[2]—simply standing, as they do, for the mystical, ever-eluding Spirit of all Beauty, which ubiquitously possesses men of genius. Purely imaginative as this fancy may appear, it nevertheless seems to receive some warranty from the fact, that on a personal interview no great author has ever come up to the idea of his reader. But that dust of which our bodies are composed, how can it fitly express the nobler intelligences among us? With reverence be it spoken, that not even in the case of one deemed more than man, not even in our Saviour, did his visible frame betoken anything of the augustness of the nature within. Else, how could those Jewish eyewitnesses fail to see heaven in his glance.

It is curious, how a man may travel along a country road, and yet miss the grandest, or sweetest of prospects, by reason of an intervening hedge, so like all other hedges, as in no way to hint of the wide landscape beyond. So has it been with me concerning the enchanting landscape in the soul of this Hawthorne, this most excellent Man of Mosses. His "Old Manse" has been written now four years, but I never read it till a day or two since. I had seen it in the book-stores—heard of it often—even had it recommended to me by a tasteful friend, as a rare, quiet book, perhaps too deserving of popularity to be popular. But there are so many books called "excellent", and so much unpopular merit, that amid the thick stir of other things, the hint of my tasteful friend was disregarded and for four years the Mosses on the old Manse never refreshed me with their perennial green. It may be, however, that all this while, the book, like wine, was only improving in flavor and body. At any rate, it so chanced that this long procrastination eventuated in a happy result. At breakfast the other day, a mountain girl, a cousin of mine, who for the last two weeks has every morning helped me to

---

[1] Hawthorne himself in "The Artist of the Beautiful." *Ed.*

[2] Pseudonymous English writer of political essays (1769–1772). *Ed.*

strawberries and raspberries,—which, like the roses and pearls in the fairy-tale, seemed to fall into the saucer from those strawberry-beds her cheeks,—this delightful creature, this charming Cherry says to me—"I see you spend your mornings in the hay-mow; and yesterday I found there 'Dwight's Travels in New England.' Now I have something far better than that,—something more congenial to our summer on these hills. Take these raspberries, and then I will give you some moss."—"Moss!" said I.— "Yes, and you must take it to the barn with you, and good-bye to 'Dwight'."

With that she left me, and soon returned with a volume, verdantly bound, and garnished with a curious frontispiece in green,—nothing less, than a fragment of real moss cunningly pressed to a fly-leaf.—"Why this," said I spilling my raspberries, "this is the 'Mosses from an Old Manse'." "Yes" said cousin Cherry "yes, it is that flowery Hawthorne."—"Hawthorne and Mosses" said I "no more: it is morning: it is July in the country: and I am off for the barn."

Stretched on that new mown clover, the hill-side breeze blowing over me through the wide barn door, and soothed by the hum of the bees in the meadows around, how magically stole over me this Mossy Man! and how amply, how bountifully, did he redeem that delicious promise to his guests in the Old Manse, of whom it is written— "Others could give them pleasure, or amusement, or instruction—these could be picked up anywhere—but it was for me to give them rest. Rest, in a life of trouble! What better could be done for weary and world-worn spirits? What better could be done for anybody, who came within our magic circle, than to throw the spell of a magic spirit over him?"—So all that day, half-buried in the new clover, I watched this Hawthorne's "Assyrian dawn, and Paphian sunset and moonrise, from the summit of our Eastern Hill."

The soft ravishments of the man spun me round about in a web of dreams, and when the book was closed, when the spell was over, this wizard "dismissed me with but misty reminiscences, as if I had been dreaming of him."

What a mild moonlight of contemplative humor bathes that Old Manse!—the rich and rare distilment of a spicy and slowly-oozing heart. No rollicking rudeness, no gross fun fed on fat dinners, and bred in the lees of wine,—but a humor so spiritually gentle, so high, so deep, and yet so richly relishable, that it were hardly inappropriate in an angel. It is the very religion of mirth; for nothing so human but it may be advanced to that. The orchard of the Old Manse seems the visible type of the fine mind that has described it. Those twisted, and contorted old trees, "that stretch out their crooked branches, and take such hold of the imagination, that we remember them as humorists, and odd-fellows." And then, as surrounded by these grotesque forms, and hushed in the noon-day repose of this Hawthorne's spell, how aptly might the still fall of his ruddy thoughts into your soul be symbolized by "the thump of a great apple, in the stillest afternoon, falling without a breath of wind, from the mere necessity of perfect ripeness"! For no less ripe than ruddy are the apples of the thoughts and fancies in this sweet Man of Mosses.

"Buds and Bird-voices"—What a delicious thing is that!—"Will the world ever be so decayed, that Spring may not renew its greenness?"—And the "Fire-Worship." Was ever the hearth so glorified into an altar before? The mere title of that piece is better than any common work in fifty folio volumes. How exquisite is this:—"Nor did it lessen the charm of his soft, familiar courtesy and helpfulness, that the mighty spirit, were opportunity offered him, would run riot through the peaceful house, wrap its inmates in his terrible embrace, and leave nothing of them save their whitened bones. This possibility of mad destruction only made his domestic kindness the more beautiful and touching. It was so sweet of him, being endowed with such power, to dwell, day after day, and one long, lonesome night after another, on the dusky hearth, only now and then betraying his wild nature, by thrusting his red tongue out of the chimney-top! True, he had done much mischief in the world, and was pretty certain to do more, but his warm heart atoned for all. He was kindly to the race of man."

But he has still other apples, not quite so ruddy, though full as ripe;—apples, that have been left to wither on the tree, after the pleasant autumn gathering is past. The sketch of "The Old Apple Dealer" is conceived in the subtlest spirit of sadness; he whose "subdued and nerveless boyhood prefigured his abortive prime, which, likewise, contained within itself the prophecy and image of his lean and torpid age." Such touches as are in this piece can not proceed from any common heart. They argue such a depth of tenderness, such a boundless sympathy with all forms of being, such an omnipresnet love, that we must needs say, that this Hawthorne is here almost alone in his generation,—at least, in the artistic manifestation of these things. Still more. Such touches as these,—and many, very many similar ones, all through his chapters— furnish clews, whereby we enter a little way into the intricate, profound heart where they originated. And we see, that suffering some time or other and in some shape or other,—this only can enable any man to depict it in others. All over him, Hawthorne's melancholy rests like an Indian Summer, which though bathing a whole country in one softness, still reveals the distinctive hue of every towering hill, and each far-winding vale.

But it is the least part of genius that attracts admiration. Where Hawthorne is known, he seems to be deemed a pleasant writer, with a pleasant style,—a sequestered, harmless man, from whom any deep and weighty thing would hardly be anticipated:—a man who means no meanings. But there is no man, in whom humor and love, like mountain peaks, soar to such a rapt height, as to receive the irradiations of the upper skies;—there is no man in whom humor and love are developed in that high form called genius; no such man can exist without also possessing, as the indispensable complement of these, a great, deep intellect, which drops down into the universe like a plummet. Or, love and humor are only the eyes, through which such an intellect views this world. The great beauty in such a mind is but the product of its strength. What, to all readers, can be more charming than the piece entitled "Monsieur du Miroir"; and to a reader at all capable of fully fathoming it, what, at the same time, can possess more mystical depth of meaning?—Yes, there he sits, and looks at me,— this "shape of mystery," this "identical Monsieur du Miroir."—"Methinks I should tremble now, were his wizard power of gliding through all impediments in search of me, to place him suddenly before my eyes."

How profound, nay appalling, is the moral evolved by the "Earth's Holocaust"; where—beginning with the hollow follies and affectations of the world,—all vanities and empty theories and forms, are, one after another, and by an admirably graduated, growing comprehensiveness, thrown into the allegorical fire, till, at length, nothing is left but the all-engendering heart of man; which remaining still unconsumed, the great conflagration is nought.

Of a piece with this, is the "Intelligence Office," a wondrous symbolizing of the secret workings in men's souls. There are other sketches, still more charged with ponderous import.

"The Christmas Banquet," and "The Bosom Serpent" would be fine subjects for a curious and elaborate analysis, touching the conjectural parts of the mind that produced them. For spite of all the Indian-summer sunlight on the hither side of Hawthorne's soul, the other side—like the dark half of the physical sphere—is shrouded in a blackness, ten times black. But this darkness but gives more effect to the ever-moving dawn, that forever advances through it, and circumnavigates his world. Whether Hawthorne has simply availed himself of this mystical blackness as a means to the wondrous effects he makes it to produce in his lights and shades; or whether there really lurks in him, perhaps unknown to himself, a touch of Puritanic gloom,—this, I cannot altogether tell. Certain it is, however, that this great power of blackness in him derives its force from its appeals to that Calvinistic sense of Innate Depravity and Original Sin, from whose visitations, in some shape or other, no deeply thinking mind is always and wholly free. For, in certain moods, no man can weigh this world, without throwing in something, somehow like Original Sin, to strike the uneven balance. At all events, perhaps no writer has ever wielded this terrific thought with greater terror than this same harmless Hawthorne. Still more: this black conceit pervades him, through and through. You may be witched by his sunlight,—transported by the bright gildings in the skies he builds over you;—but there is the blackness of darkness beyond; and even his bright gildings but fringe, and play upon the edges of thunder-clouds.—In one word, the world is mistaken in this Nathaniel Hawthorne. He himself must often have smiled at its absurd misconception of him. He is immeasurably deeper than the plummet of the mere critic. For it is not the brain that can test such a man; it is only the heart. You cannot come to know greatness by inspecting it; there is no glimpse to be caught of it, except by intuition; you need not ring it, you but touch it, and you find it is gold.

Now it is that blackness in Hawthorne, of which I have spoken, that so fixes and fascinates me. It may be, nevertheless, that it is too largely developed in him. Perhaps he does not give us a ray of his light for every shade of his dark. But however this may be, this blackness it is that furnishes the infinite obscure of his back-ground,—that back-ground, against which Shakespeare plays his grandest conceits, the things that have made for Shakespeare his loftiest, but most circumscribed renown, as the profoundest of thinkers. For by philosophers Shakespeare is not adored as the great man of tragedy and comedy.—"Off with his head! so much for Buckingham!" this sort of rant, interlined by another hand, brings down the house,—those mistaken souls, who dream of Shakespeare as a mere man of Richard-the-Third humps, and Macbeth daggers. But it is those deep far-away things in him; those occasional flashings-forth of the intuitive Truth in him; those short, quick probings at the very axis of reality;—these are the things that make Shakespeare, Shakespeare. Through the mouths of the dark characters of Hamlet, Timon, Lear, and Iago, he craftily says, or sometimes insinuates the things, which we feel to be so terrifically true, that it were all but madness for any good man, in his own proper character, to utter, or even hint at them. Tormented into desperation, Lear the frantic King tears off the mask, and speaks the sane madness of vital truth. But, as I before said, it is the least part of genius that attracts admiration. And so, much of the blind, unbridled admiration that has been heaped upon Shakespeare, has been lavished upon the least part of him. And few of his endless commentators and critics seem to have remembered, or even perceived, that the immediate products of a great mind are not so great, as that undeveloped, (and sometimes undevelopable) yet dimly-discernable greatness, to which these immediate products are but the infallible indices. In Shakespeare's tomb lies infinitely more than Shakespeare ever wrote. And if I magnify Shakespeare, it is not so much for what he did do, as for what he did not do, or refrained from doing. For in this world of lies, Truth is forced to fly like a scared white doe in the woodlands; and only by cunning glimpses will she reveal herself, as in Shakespeare and other masters of the great Art of Telling the Truth,—even though it be covertly, and by snatches.

But if this view of the all-popular Shakespeare be seldom taken by his readers, and if very few who extol him, have ever read him deeply, or, perhaps, only have seen him on the tricky stage, (which alone made, and is still making him his mere mob renown)—if few men have time, or patience, or palate, for the spiritual truth as it is in that great genius;—it is, then, no matter of surprise that in a contemporaneous age, Nathaniel Hawthorne is a man, as yet, almost utterly mistaken among men. Here and there, in some quite arm-chair in the noisy town, or some deep nook among the noiseless mountains, he may be appreciated for something of what he is. But unlike Shakespeare, who was forced to the contrary course by circumstances, Hawthorne (either from simple disinclination, or else from inaptitude) refrains from all the popularizing noise and show of broad farce, and blood-besmeared tragedy; content with the still, rich utterances of a great intellect in repose, and which sends few thoughts into circulation, except they be arterialized at his large warm lungs, and expanded in his honest heart.

Nor need you fix upon that blackness in him, if it suit you not. Nor, indeed, will all readers discern it, for it is, mostly, insinuated to those who may best understand it, and account for it; it is not obtruded upon every one alike.

Some may start to read of Shakespeare and Hawthorne on the same page. They may say, that if an illustration were needed, a lesser light might have sufficed to elucidate this Hawthorne, this small man of yesterday. But I am not, willingly, one of those, who, as touching Shakespeare at least, exemplify the maxim of Rochefoucault, that "we exalt the reputation of some, in order to depress that of others";—who, to teach all noble-souled aspirants that there is no hope for them, pronounce Shakespeare absolutely unapproachable. But Shakespeare has been approached. There are minds that have gone as far as Shakespeare into the universe. And hardly a mortal man, who, at some time or other, has not felt as great thoughts in him as any you will find in Hamlet. We must not inferentially malign mankind for the sake of any one man, whoever he may be. This is too cheap a purchase of contentment for conscious mediocrity to make. Besides, this absolute and unconditional adoration of Shakespeare has grown to be a part of our Anglo Saxon superstitions. The Thirty Nine articles are now Forty. Intolerance has come to exist in this matter. You must believe in Shakespeare's unapproachability, or quit the country. But what sort of a belief is this for an American, a man who is bound to carry republican progressiveness into Literature, as well as into Life? Believe me, my friends, that Shakespeares are this day being born on the banks of the Ohio. And the day will come, when you shall say who reads a book by an Englishman that is a modern? The great mistake seems to be, that even with those Americans who look forward to the coming of a great literary genius among us, they somehow fancy he will come in the costume of Queen Elizabeth's day,—be a writer of dramas founded upon old English history, or the tales of Boccaccio. Whereas, great geniuses are parts of the times; they themselves are the times; and possess a correspondent coloring. It is of a piece with the Jews, who while their Shiloh[3] was meekly walking in their streets, were still praying for his magnificent coming; looking for him in a chariot, who was already among them on an ass. Nor must we forget, that, in his own lifetime, Shakespeare was not Shakespeare, but only Master William Shakespeare of the shrewd, thriving, business firm of Condell, Shakespeare & Co., proprietors of the Globe Theatre in London; and by a courtly author, of the name of Greene, was hooted at, as an "upstart crow" beautified "with other birds' feathers." For, mark it well, imitation is often the first charge brought against real originality. Why this is so, there is not space to set forth here. You must have plenty of sea-room to tell the Truth in; especially, when it seems to have an aspect of newness, as America did in 1492, though it was then just as old, and perhaps older than Asia, only those sagacious philosophers, the common sailors, had never seen it before; swearing it was all water and moonshine there.

Now, I do not say that Nathaniel of Salem is a greater than William of Avon, or as great. But the difference between the two men is by no means immeasurable. Not a very great deal more, and Nathaniel were verily William.

This, too, I mean, that if Shakespeare has not been equalled, he is sure to be surpassed, and surpassed by an American born now or yet to be born. For it will never do for us who in most other things out-do as well as out-brag the world, it will not do for us to fold our hands and say, In the highest department advance there is none. Nor will it at all do to say, that the world is getting grey and grizzled now, and has lost that fresh charm which she wore of old, and by virtue of which the great poets of past times made themselves what we esteem them to be. Not so. The world is as young today, as when it was created; and this Vermont morning dew is as wet to my feet, as Eden's dew to Adam's. Nor has Nature been all over ransacked by our progenitors, so that no new charms and mysteries remain for this latter generation to find. Far from it. The trillionth part has not yet been said; and all that has been said, but multiplies the avenues to what remains to be said. It is not so much paucity, as superabundance of material that seems to incapacitate modern authors.

Let America then prize and cherish her writers; yea, let her glorify them. They are not so many in number, as to exhaust her good-will. And while she has good kith and kin of her own, to take to her bosom, let her not lavish her embraces upon the household of an alien. For believe it or not England, after all, is, in many things, an alien to

---

[3] Messiah: the metaphor derives from Shiloh's status as the resting place of the Ark of the Covenant before the building of Solomon's Temple. *Ed.*

us. China has more bowels of real love for us than she. But even were there no Hawthorne, no Emerson, no Whittier, no Irving, no Bryant, no Dana, no Cooper, no Willis (not the author of the "Dashes," but the author of the "Belfry Pigeon")[4]—were there none of these, and others of like calibre among us, nevertheless, let America first praise mediocrity even, in her own children, before she praises (for everywhere, merit demands acknowledgment from every one) the best excellence in the children of any other land. Let her own authors, I say, have the priority of appreciation. I was much pleased with a hot-headed Carolina cousin of mine, who once said,—"If there were no other American to stand by, in Literature,—why, then, I would stand by Pop Emmons and his 'Fredoniad,'[5] and till a better epic came along, swear it was not very far behind the Iliad." Take away the words, and in spirit he was sound.

Not that American genius needs patronage in order to expand. For that explosive sort of stuff will expand though screwed up in a vice, and burst it, though it were triple steel. It is for the nation's sake, and not for her authors' sake, that I would have America be heedful of the increasing greatness among her writers. For how great the shame, if other nations should be before her, in crowning her heroes of the pen. But this is almost the case now. American authors have received more just and discriminating praise (however loftily and ridiculously given, in certain cases) even from some Englishmen, than from their own countrymen. There are hardly five critics in America; and several of them are asleep. As for patronage, it is the American author who now patronizes his country, and not his country him. And if at times some among them appeal to the people for more recognition, it is not always with selfish motives, but patriotic ones.

It is true, that but few of them as yet have evinced that decided originality which merits great praise. But that graceful writer, who perhaps of all Americans has received the most plaudits from his own country for his productions,—that very popular and amiable writer, however good, and self-reliant in many things, perhaps owes his chief reputation to the self-acknowledged imitation of a foreign model, and to the studied avoidance of all topics but smooth ones.[6] But it is better to fail in originality, than to succeed in imitation. He who has never failed somewhere, that man can not be great. Failure is the true test of greatness. And if it be said, that continual success is a proof that a man wisely knows his powers,—it is only to be added, that, in that case, he knows them to be small. Let us believe it, then, once for all, that there is no hope for us in these smooth pleasing writers that know their powers. Without malice, but to speak the plain fact, they but furnish an appendix to Goldsmith, and other English authors. And we want no American Goldsmiths; nay, we want no American Miltons. It were the vilest thing you could say of a true American author, that he were an American Tompkins.[7] Call him an American, and have done; for you can not say a nobler

---

[4] Nathaniel Parker Willis (1806-1867), author of the poem "The Belfry Pigeon" (1831) and *Dashes at Life with a Free Pencil* (1845). *Ed.*

[5] Richard Emmons, author of *The Fredoniad* (1827) epic of the War of 1812. *Ed.*

[6] Melville is probably alluding to American essayist and fiction-writer Washington Irving (1783-1859). *Ed.*

[7] Byword for a flunkey. *Ed.*

thing of him.—But it is not meant that all American writers should studiously cleave to nationality in their writings; only this, no American writer should write like an Englishman, or a Frenchman; let him write like a man, for then he will be sure to write like an American. Let us away with this Bostonian leaven of literary flunkeyism towards England. If either must play the flunkey in this thing, let England do it, not us. And the time is not far off when circumstances may force her to it. While we are rapidly preparing for that political supremacy among the nations, which prophetically awaits us at the close of the present century; in a literary point of view, we are deplorably unprepared for it; and we seem studious to remain so. Hitherto, reasons might have existed why this should be; but no good reason exists now. And all that is requisite to amendment in this matter, is simply this: that, while freely acknowledging all excellence, everywhere, we should refrain from unduly lauding foreign writers and, at the same time, duly recognize the meritorious writers that are our own;—those writers, who breathe that unshackled, democratic spirit of Christianity in all things, which now takes the practical lead in this world, though at the same time led by ourselves—us Americans. Let us boldly contemn all imitation, though it comes to us graceful and fragrant as the morning; and foster all originality, though, at first, it be crabbed and ugly as our own pine knots. And if any of our authors fail, or seem to fail, then, in the words of my enthusiastic Carolina cousin, let us clap him on the shoulder, and back him against all Europe for his second round. The truth is, that in our point of view, this matter of a national literature has come to such a pass with us, that in some sense we must turn bullies, else the day is lost, or superiority so far beyond us, that we can hardly say it will ever be ours.

And now, my countrymen, as an excellent author, of your own flesh and blood,—an unimitating, and, perhaps, in his way, an inimitable man—whom better can I commend to you, in the first place, than Nathaniel Hawthorne. He is one of the new, and far better generation of your writers. The smell of your beeches and hemlocks is upon him; your own broad prairies are in his soul; and if you travel away inland into his deep and noble nature, you will hear the far roar of his Niagara. Give not over to future generations the glad duty of acknowledging him for what he is. Take that joy to your self, in your own generation; and so shall he feel those grateful impulses in him, that may possibly prompt him to the full flower of some still greater achievement in your eyes. And by confessing him, you thereby confess others; you embrace the whole brotherhood. For genius, all over the world, stands hand in hand, and one shock of recognition runs the whole circle round.

In treating of Hawthorne, or rather of Hawthorne in his writings (for I never saw the man; and in the chances of a quiet plantation life, remote from his haunts, perhaps never shall) in treating of his works, I say, I have thus far omitted all mention of his "Twice Told Tales," and "Scarlet Letter." Both are excellent; but full of such manifold, strange and diffusive beauties, that time would all but fail me, to point the half of them out. But there are things in those two books, which, had they been written in England a century ago, Nathaniel Hawthorne had utterly displaced many of the bright names we now revere on authority. But I am content to leave Hawthorne to himself, and to the infallible finding of posterity; and however great may be the praise I have bestowed upon him, I feel, that in so doing, I have more served and honored myself, than him.

For, at bottom, great excellence is praise enough to itself; but the feeling of a sincere and appreciative love and admiration towards it, this is relieved by utterance; and warm, honest praise ever leaves a pleasant flavor in the mouth; and it is an honorable thing to confess to what is honorable in others.

But I cannot leave my subject yet. No man can read a fine author, and relish him to his very bones, while he reads, without subsequently fancying to himself some ideal image of the man and his mind. And if you rightly look for it, you will almost always find that the author himself has somewhere furnished you with his own picture.—For poets (whether in prose or verse), being painters of Nature, are like their brethren of the pencil, the true portrait-painters, who, in the multitude of likenesses to be sketched, do not invariably omit their own; and in all high instances, they paint them without any vanity, though, at times, with a lurking something, that would take several pages to properly define.

I submit it, then, to those best acquainted with the man personally, whether the following is not Nathaniel Hawthorne;—and to himself, whether something involved in it does not express the temper of his mind,—that lasting temper of all true, candid men—a seeker, not a finder yet:—

> "A man now entered, in neglected attire, with the aspect of a thinker, but somewhat too rough-hewn and brawny for a scholar. His face was full of sturdy vigor, with some finer and keener attribute beneath; though harsh at first, it was tempered with the glow of a large, warm heart, which had force enough to heat his powerful intellect through and through. He advanced to the Intelligencer, and looked at him with a glance of such stern sincerity, that perhaps few secrets were beyond its scope.
>
> "'I seek for truth', said he."[8]

Twenty four hours have elapsed since writing the foregoing. I have just returned from the hay mow, charged more and more with love and admiration of Hawthorne. For I have just been gleaning through the Mosses, picking up many things here and there that had previously escaped me. And I found that but to glean after this man, is better than to be in at the harvest of others. To be frank (though, perhaps, rather foolish) notwithstanding what I wrote yesterday of these Mosses, I had not then culled them all; but had, nevertheless, been sufficiently sensible of the subtle essence, in them, as to write as I did. To what infinite height of loving wonder and admiration I may yet be borne, when by repeatedly banquetting on these Mosses, I shall have thoroughly incorporated their whole stuff into my being,—that, I can not tell. But already I feel that this Hawthorne has dropped germinous seeds into my soul. He expands and deepens down, the more I contemplate him; and further, and further, shoots his strong New-England roots into the hot soil of my Southern soul.

By careful reference to the "Table of Contents," I now find, that I have gone through all the sketches; but that when I yesterday wrote, I had not at all read two particular pieces, to which I now desire to call special attention,—"A Select Party," and

---

[8] From Hawthorne's "The Intelligence Office." *Ed*.

"Young Goodman Brown." Here, be it said to all those whom this poor fugitive scrawl of mine may tempt to the perusal of the "Mosses," that they must on no account suffer themselves to be trifled with, disappointed, or deceived by the trivality of many of the titles of these Sketches. For in more than one instance, the title utterly belies the piece. It is as if rustic demijohns containing the very best and costliest of Falernian and Tokay, were labelled "Cider," "Perry," and "Elderberry wine." The truth seems to be, that like many other geniuses, this Man of Mosses takes great delight in hoodwinking the world,—at least, with respect to himself. Personally, I doubt not, that he rather prefers to be generally esteemed but a so-so sort of author; being willing to reserve the thorough and acute appreciation of what he is, to that party most qualified to judge—that is, to himself. Besides, at the bottom of their natures, men like Hawthorne, in many things, deem the plaudits of the public such strong presumptive evidence of mediocrity in the object of them, that it would in some degree render them doubtful of their own powers, did they hear much and vociferous braying concerning them in the public pastures. True, I have been braying myself (if you please to be witty enough, to have it so) but then I claim to be the first that has so brayed in this particular matter; and therefore, while pleading guilty to the charge still claim all the merit due to originality.

But with whatever motive, playful or profound, Nathaniel Hawthorne has chosen to entitle his pieces in the manner he has, it is certain, that some of them are directly calculated to deceive—egregiously deceive, the superficial skimmer of pages. To be downright and candid once more, let me cheerfully say, that two of these titles did dolefully dupe no less an eagle-eyed reader than myself; and that, too, after I had been impressed with a sense of the great depth and breadth of this American man. "Who in the name of thunder" (as the country-people say in this neighborhood) "who in the name of thunder," would anticipate any marvel in a piece entitled "Young Goodman Brown"? You would of course suppose that it was a simple little tale, intended as a supplement to "Goody Two Shoes." Whereas, it is deep as Dante; nor can you finish it, without addressing the author in his own words—"It is yours to penetrate, in every bosom, the deep mystery of sin." And with Young Goodman, too, in allegorical pursuit of his Puritan wife, you cry out in your anguish,—

> "'Faith!' shouted Goodman Brown, in a voice of agony and desperation; and the echoes of the forest mocked him, crying—'Faith! Faith!' as if bewildered wretches were seeking her all through the wilderness."

Now this same piece, entitled "Young Goodman Brown," is one of the two that I had not all read yesterday; and I allude to it now, because it is, in itself, such a strong positive illustration of that blackness in Hawthorne, which I had assumed from the mere occasional shadows of it, as revealed in several of the other sketches. But had I previously perused "Young Goodman Brown," I should have been at no pains to draw the conclusion, which I came to, at a time, when I was ignorant that the book contained one such direct and unqualified manifestation of it.

The other piece of the two referred to, is entitled "A Select Party," which, in my first simplicity upon originally taking hold of the book, I fancied must treat of some pumpkin-pie party in Old Salem, or some chowder party on Cape Cod. Whereas, by all the gods of Peedee! it is the sweetest and sublimest thing that has been written since Spencer wrote. Nay, there is nothing in Spencer that surpasses it, perhaps, nothing that equals it. And the test is this: read any canto in "The Faery Queen," and then read "A Select Party," and decide which pleases you the most,—that is, if you are qualified to judge. Do not be frightened at this; for when Spencer was alive, he was thought of very much as Hawthorne is now,—was generally accounted just such a "gentle" harmless man. It may be, that to common eyes, the sublimity of Hawthorne seems lost in his sweetness,—as perhaps in this same "Select Party" of his; for whom, he has builded so august a dome of sunset clouds, and served them on richer plate, than Belshazzar's when he banquetted his lords in Babylon.

But my chief business now, is to point out a particular page in this piece, having reference to an honored guest, who under the name of "The Master Genius" but in the guise of "a young man of poor attire, with no insignia of rank or acknowledged eminence," is introduced to the Man of Fancy, who is the giver of the feast. Now the page having reference to this "Master Genius," so happily expresses much of what I yesterday wrote, touching the coming of the literary Shiloh of America, that I cannot but be charmed by the coincidence; especially, when it shows such a parity of ideas, at least in this one point, between a man like Hawthorne and a man like me.

And here, let me throw out another conceit of mine touching this American Shiloh, or "Master Genius," as Hawthorne calls him. May it not be, that this commanding mind has not been, is not, and never will be, individually developed in any one man? And would it, indeed, appear so unreasonable to suppose, that this great fullness and overflowing may be, or may be destined to be, shared by a plurality of men of genius? Surely, to take the very greatest example on record, Shakespeare cannot be regarded as in himself the concretion of all the genius of his time; nor as so immeasurably beyond Marlow, Webster, Ford, Beaumont, Jonson, that those great men can be said to share none of his power? For one, I conceive that there were dramatists in Elizabeth's day, between whom and Shakespeare the distance was by no means great. Let anyone, hitherto little acquainted with those neglected old authors, for the first time read them thoroughly, or even read Charles Lamb's Specimens of them, and he will be amazed at the wondrous ability of those Anaks[9] of men, and shocked at this renewed example of the fact, that Fortune has more to do with fame than merit,—though, without merit, lasting fame there can be none.

Nevertheless, it would argue too illy of my country were this maxim to hold good concerning Nathaniel Hawthorne, a man, who already, in some few minds, has shed "such a light, as never illuminates the earth, save when a great heart burns as the household fire of a grand intellect."

The words are his,—in the "Select Party"; and they are a magnificent setting to a coincident sentiment of my own, but ramblingly expressed yesterday, in reference to himself. Gainsay it who will, as I now write, I am Posterity speaking by proxy—and after times will make it more than good, when I declare—that the American, who up to

---

[9] Giants, in the book of Numbers 13:33. *Ed.*

the present day, has evinced, in Literature, the largest brain with the largest heart, that man is Nathaniel Hawthorne. Moreover, that whatever Nathaniel Hawthorne may hereafter write, "The Mosses from an Old Manse" will be ultimately accounted his masterpiece. For there is a sure, though a secret sign in some works which prove the culmination of the powers (only the developable ones, however) that produced them. But I am by no means desirous of the glory of a prophet. I pray Heaven that Hawthorne may *yet* prove me an impostor in this prediction. Especially, as I somehow cling to the strange fancy, that, in all men, hiddenly reside certain wondrous, occult properties— as in some plants and minerals—which by some happy but very rare accident (as bronze was discovered by the melting of the iron and brass in the burning of Corinth) may chance to be called forth here on earth; not entirely waiting for their better discovery in the more congenial, blessed atmosphere of heaven.

Once more—for it is hard to be finite upon an infinite subject, and all subjects are infinite. By some people, this entire scrawl of mine may be esteemed altogether unnecessary, inasmuch, "as years ago" (they may say) "we found out the rich and rare stuff in this Hawthorne, whom you now parade forth, as if only *yourself* were the discoverer of this Portuguese diamond in our Literature."—But even granting all this; and adding to it, the assumption that the books of Hawthorne have sold by the five-thousand,—what does that signify?—They should be sold by the hundred-thousand; and read by the million; and admired by every one who is capable of admiration.

George Eliot

Mary Anne Evans, who wrote under the name George Eliot, was born in 1819, the youngest daughter of an agricultural estate manager in Warwickshire. She was rigorously self-educated, reading widely in literature, philosophy, and theology and absorbing the important modern languages. Her first works were translations from the German of free-thinking theological works such as David Friedrich Strauss's *Life of Jesus* (1846) and essays and reviews for John Chapman's *Westminster Review,* where "Silly Novels by Lady Novelists" appeared in 1856. Eliot began to write fiction herself soon thereafter, beginning with the short *Scenes from Clerical Life* (1857). *Adam Bede* (1859), her first novel, established her in the forefront of literature. Her later works include *The Mill on the Floss* (1860), the historical novel *Romola* (1861), *Felix Holt the Radical* (1866), and her two late masterpieces *Middlemarch* (1871-1872) and *Daniel Deronda* (1874-1876). In 1878 George Lewes, her partner for life, died—they had lived together unmarried for nearly twenty-five years because he was unable to obtain a legal divorce— and Eliot the following year married John Cross, her financial advisor. She died in 1880.

Silly Novels by Lady Novelists

WESTMINSTER REVIEW, LXVI (OCTOBER, 1856), 442–461

. . .

Silly novels by Lady Novelists are a genus with many species, determined by the particular quality of silliness that predominates in them—the frothy, the prosy, the pious, or the pedantic. But it is a mixture of all these—a composite order of feminine fatuity, that produces the largest class of such novels, which we shall distinguish as the *mind-and-millinery* species. The heroine is usually an heiress, probably a peeress in her own right, with perhaps a vicious baronet, an amiable duke, and an irresistible younger son of a marquis as lovers in the foreground, a clergyman and a poet sighing for her in the middle distance, and a crowd of undefined adorers dimly indicated beyond. Her eyes and her wit are both dazzling; her nose and her morals are alike free from any tendency to irregularity; she has a superb *contralto* and a superb intellect; she is perfectly well-dressed and perfectly religious; she dances like a sylph, and reads the Bible in the original tongues. Or it may be that the heroine is not an heiress—that rank and wealth are the only things in which she is deficient; but she infallibly gets into high society, she has the triumph of refusing many matches and securing the best, and she wears some family jewels or other as a sort of crown of righteousness at the end. Rakish men either bite their lips in impotent confusion at her repartees, or are touched to penitence by her reproofs, which, on appropriate occasions, rise to a lofty strain of rhetoric; indeed, there is a general propensity in her to make speeches, and to rhapsodize at some length when she retires to her bedroom. In her recorded conversations she is amazingly eloquent, and in her unrecorded conversations, amazingly witty. She is understood to have a depth of insight that looks through and through the shallow theories of philosophers, and her superior instincts are a sort of dial by which men have only to set their clocks and watches, and all will go well. The men play a very subordinate part by her side. You are consoled now and then by a hint that they have affairs, which keeps you in mind that the working-day business of the world is somehow being carried on, but ostensibly the final cause of their existence is that they may accompany the heroine on her 'starring' expedition through life. They see her at a ball, and are dazzled; at a flower-show, and they are fascinated; on a riding excursion, and they are witched by her noble horsemanship; at church, and they are awed by the sweet solemnity of her demeanour. She is the ideal woman in feelings, faculties, and flounces. For all this, she as often as not marries the wrong person to begin with, and she suffers terribly from the plots and intrigues of the vicious baronet; but even death has a soft place in his heart for such a paragon, and remedies all mistakes for her just at the right moment. The vicious baronet is sure to be killed in a duel, and the tedious husband dies in his bed requesting his wife, as a particular favour to him, to marry the man she loves best, and having already dispatched a note to the lover informing him of the comfortable arrangement. Before matters arrive at this desirable issue our feelings are tried by seeing the noble, lovely, and gifted heroine pass through many *mau-*

vais moments, but we have the satisfaction of knowing that her sorrows are wept into embroidered pocket-handkerchiefs, that her fainting form reclines on the very best upholstery, and that whatever vicissitudes she may undergo, from being dashed out of her carriage to having her head shaved in a fever, she comes out of them all with a complexion more blooming and locks more redundant than ever.

We may remark, by the way, that we have been relieved from a serious scruple by discovering that silly novels by lady novelists rarely introduce us into any other than very lofty and fashionable society. We had imagined that destitute women turned novelists, as they turned governesses, because they had no other 'lady-like' means of getting their bread. On this supposition, vacillating syntax and improbable incident had a certain pathos for us, like the extremely supererogatory pincushions and ill-devised nightcaps that are offered for sale by a blind man. We felt the commodity to be a nuisance, but we were glad to think that the money went to relieve the necessitous, and we pictured to ourselves lonely women struggling for a maintenance, or wives and daughters devoting themselves to the production of 'copy' out of pure heroism,—perhaps to pay their husband's debts, or to purchase luxuries for a sick father. Under these impressions we shrank from criticising a lady's novel: her English might be faulty, but, we said to ourselves, her motives are irreproachable; her imagination may be uninventive, but her patience is untiring. Empty writing was excused by an empty stomach, and twaddle was consecrated by tears. But no! This theory of ours, like many other pretty theories, has had to give way before observation. Women's silly novels, we are now convinced, are written under totally different circumstances. The fair writers have evidently never talked to a tradesman except from a carriage window; they have no notion of the working-classes except as 'dependents'; they think five hundred a-year a miserable pittance; Belgravia and 'baronial halls' are their primary truths; and they have no idea of feeling interest in any man who is not at least a great landed proprietor, if not a prime minister. It is clear that they write in elegant boudoirs, with violet-coloured ink and a ruby pen; that they must be entirely indifferent to publishers' accounts, and inexperienced in every form of poverty except poverty of brains. It is true that we are constantly struck with the want of verisimilitude in their representations of the high society in which they seem to live; but then they betray no closer acquaintance with any other form of life. If their peers and peeresses are improbable, their literary men, tradespeople, and cottagers are impossible; and their intellect seems to have the peculiar impartiality of reproducing both what they *have* seen and heard, and what they have *not* seen and heard, with equal unfaithfulness.

. . .

Writers of the mind-and-millinery school are remarkably unanimous in their choice of diction. In their novels, there is usually a lady or gentleman who is more or less of a upas tree: the lover has a manly breast; minds are redolent of various things; hearts are hollow; events are utilized; friends are consigned to the tomb; infancy is an engaging period; the sun is a luminary that goes to his western couch, or gathers the rain-drops into his refulgent bosom; life is a melancholy boon; Albion and Scotia are conversational epithets. There is a striking resemblance, too, in the character of their moral comments, such, for instance, as that 'It is a fact, no less true than melancholy, that all people, more or less, richer or poorer, are swayed by bad example;' that 'Books, however trivial, contain some subjects from which useful information may be drawn;' that 'Vice can too often borrow the language of virtue;' that 'Merit and nobility of nature must exist, to be accepted, for clamour and pretension cannot impose upon those too well read in human nature to be easily deceived;' and that, 'In order to forgive, we must have been injured.' There is, doubtless, a class of readers to whom these remarks appear peculiarly pointed and pungent; for we often find them doubly and trebly scored with the pencil, and delicate hands giving in their determined adhesion to these hardy novelties by a distinct *très vrai,*[1] emphasized by many notes of exclamation. The colloquial style of these novels is often marked by much ingenious inversion, and a careful avoidance of such cheap phraseology as can be heard every day. Angry young gentlemen exclaim—''Tis ever thus, methinks;' and in the half-hour before dinner a young lady informs her next neighbour that the first day she read Shakespeare she 'stole away into the park, and beneath the shadow of the greenwood tree, devoured with rapture the inspired page of the great magician.' But the most remarkable efforts of the mind-and-millinery writers lie in their philosophic reflections. The authoress of 'Laura Gay,' for example, having married her hero and heroine, improves the event by observing that 'if those sceptics, whose eyes have so long gazed on matter that they can no longer see aught else in man, could once enter with heart and soul into such bliss as this, they would come to say that the soul of man and the polypus are not of common origin, or of the same texture.' Lady novelists, it appears, can see something else besides matter; they are not limited to phenomena, but can relieve their eyesight by occasional glimpses of the *noumenon,*[2] and are, therefore, naturally better able than any one else to confound sceptics, even of that remarkable, but to us unknown school, which maintains that the soul of man is of the same texture as the polypus.

The most pitiable of all silly novels by lady novelists are what we may call the *oracular* species—novels intended to expound the writer's religious, philosophical, or moral theories. There seems to be a notion abroad among women, rather akin to the superstition that the speech and actions of idiots are inspired, and that the human being most entirely exhausted of common sense is the fittest vehicle of revelation. To judge from their writings, there are certain ladies who think that an amazing ignorance, both of science and of life, is the best possible qualification for forming an opinion on the knottiest moral and speculative questions. Apparently, their recipe for solving all such difficulties is something like this: Take a woman's head, stuff it with a smattering of philosophy and literature chopped small, and with false notions of society baked hard, let it hang over a desk a few hours every day, and serve up hot in feeble English, when not required. You will rarely meet with a lady novelist of the oracular class who is diffident of her ability to decide on theological questions,—who has any suspicion that she is not capable of discriminating with the nicest accuracy between the good and evil in all church parties,—who does not see precisely how it is that men have gone wrong hitherto,—and pity philosophers in general that they have not had the opportunity of consulting her. Great writers, who have modestly contented themselves with putting their experience into fiction, and have thought it quite

---

[1] "Very true!" *Ed.*

[2] In Kant's philosophy, the realty that underlies our perceptions of things. *Ed.*

a sufficient task to exhibit men and things as they are, she sighs over as deplorably deficient in the application of their powers. 'They have solved no great questions'—and she is ready to remedy their omission by setting before you a complete theory of life and manual of divinity, in a love story, where ladies and gentlemen of good family go through genteel vicissitudes, to the utter confusion of Deists, Puseyites, and ultra-Protestants, and to the perfect establishment of that particular view of Christianity which either condenses itself into a sentence of small caps, or explodes into a cluster of stars on the three hundred and thirtieth page. It is true, the ladies and gentlemen will probably seem to you remarkably little like any you have had the fortune or misfortune to meet with, for, as a general rule, the ability of a lady novelist to describe actual life and her fellow-men, is in inverse proportion to her confident eloquence about God and the other world, and the means by which she usually chooses to conduct you to true ideas of the invisible is a totally false picture of the visible.

As typical a novel of the oracular kind as we can hope to meet with, is 'The Enigma: a Leaf from the Chronicles of the Wolchorley House.' The 'enigma' which this novel is to solve, is certainly one that demands powers no less gigantic than those of a lady novelist, being neither more nor less than the existence of evil. The problem is stated, and the answer dimly foreshadowed on the very first page. The spirited young lady, with raven hair, says, 'All life is an inextricable confusion;' and the meek young lady, with auburn hair, looks at the picture of the Madonna which she is copying, and— '*There* seemed the solution of that mighty enigma.' The style of this novel is quite as lofty as its purpose; indeed, some passages on which we have spent much patient study are quite beyond our reach, in spite of the illustrative aid of italics and small caps; and we must await further 'development' in order to understand them. Of Ernest, the model young clergyman, who sets every one right on all occasions, we read, that 'he held not of marriage in the marketable kind, after a social desecration;' that, on one eventful night, 'sleep had not visited his divided heart, where tumultuated, in varied type and combination, the aggregate feelings of grief and joy;' and that, 'for the *marketable* human article he had no toleration, be it of what sort, or set for what value it might, whether for worship or class, his upright soul abhorred it, whose ultimatum, the self-deceiver, was to him THE *great spiritual lie,* "living in a vain show, deceiving and being deceived;" since he did not suppose the phylactery and enlarged border on the garment to be *merely* a social trick.' (The italics and small caps are the author's, and we hope they assist the reader's comprehension.) Of Sir Lionel, the model old gentleman, we are told that 'the simple ideal of the middle age, apart from its anarchy and decadence, in him most truly seemed to live again, when the ties which knit men together were of heroic cast. The first-born colours of pristine faith and truth engraven on the common soul of man, and blent into the wide arch of brotherhood, where the primæval law of *order* grew and multiplied, each perfect after his kind, and mutually inter-dependent.' You see clearly, of course, how colours are first engraven on a soul, and then blent into a wide arch, on which arch of colours—apparently a rainbow— the law of order grew and multiplied, each—apparently the arch and the law—perfect after his kind? If, after this, you can possibly want any further aid towards knowing what Sir Lionel was, we can tell you, that in his soul 'the scientific combinations of thought could educe no fuller harmonies of the good and the true, than lay in the primæval pulses which floated as an atmosphere around it!' and that, when he was sealing a letter, 'Lo! the responsive throb in that good man's bosom echoed back in simple truth the honest witness of a heart that condemned him, not, as his eye, bedewed with love, rested, too, with something of ancestral pride, on the undimmed motto of the family—"LOIAUTÉ".'

. . .

But, perhaps, the least readable of silly women's novels, are the *modern-antique* species, which unfold to us the domestic life of Jannes and Jambres, the private love affairs of Sennacherib, or the mental struggles and ultimate conversion of Demetrius the silversmith.[3] From most silly novels we can at least extract a laugh; but those of the modern antique school have a ponderous, a leaden kind of fatuity, under which we groan. What can be more demonstrative of the inability of literary women to measure their own powers, than their frequent assumption of a task which can only be justified by the rarest concurrence of acquirement with genius? The finest effort to reanimate the past is of course only approximative—is always more or less an infusion of the modern spirit into the ancient form,

Was ihr den Geist der Zeiten heisst,
Das ist im Grund der Herren eigner Geist,
In dem die Zeiten sich bespiegeln.[4]

Admitting that genius which has familiarized itself with all the relics of an ancient period can sometimes, by the force of its sympathetic divination, restore the missing notes in the 'music of humanity,'[5] and reconstruct the fragments into a whole which will really bring the remote past nearer to us, and interpret it to our duller apprehension,—this form of imaginative power must always be among the very rarest, because it demands as much accurate and minute knowledge as creative vigour. Yet we find ladies constantly choosing to make their mental mediocrity more conspicuous, by clothing it in a masquerade of ancient names; by putting their feeble sentimentality into the mouths of Roman vestals or Egyptian princesses, and attributing their rhetorical arguments to Jewish high-priests and Greek philosophers. A recent example of this heavy imbecility is, 'Adonijah, a Tale of the Jewish Dispersion,' which forms part of a series, 'uniting,' we are told, 'taste, humour, and sound principles.' 'Adonijah,' we presume, exemplifies the tale of 'sound principles;' the taste and humour are to be found in other members of the series. We are told on the cover, that the incidents of this tale are 'fraught with unusual interest,' and the preface winds up thus: 'To those who feel interested in the dispersed of Israel and Judea, these pages may afford, perhaps, information on an important subject, as well as amusement.' Since the 'impor-

---

[3] Obscure biblical characters: Jannes and Jambres were the names St. Paul gave to Pharaoh's magicians in 2 Timothy 3: 18; Sennacherib was the king of Assyria who failed to take the city of Jerusalem in 2 Kings 26; and Demetrius the silversmith is in Acts 19: 24. *Ed.*

[4] Goethe, *Faust I*, 'Nacht,' 577–579. *Au.* "What you call the spirit of the times is actually the spirit of the geniuses through whom the times are reflected." *Ed.*

[5] Wordsworth, "Tintern Abbey," 91. *Au.*

tant subject' on which this book is to afford information is not specified, it may possibly lie in some esoteric meaning to which we have no key; but if it has relation to the dispersed of Israel and Judea at any period of their history, we believe a tolerably well-informed school-girl already knows much more of it than she will find in this 'Tale of the Jewish Dispersion.' 'Adonijah' is simply the feeblest kind of love story, supposed to be instructive, we presume, because the hero is a Jewish captive, and the heroine a Roman vestal; because they and their friends are converted to Christianity after the shortest and easiest method approved by the 'Society for Promoting the Conversion of the Jews;' and because, instead of being written in plain language, it is adorned with that peculiar style of grandiloquence which is held by some lady novelists to give an antique colouring, and which we recognise at once in such phrases as these: 'the splendid regnal talents undoubtedly possessed by the Emperor Nero'—'the expiring scion of a lofty stem'—'the virtuous partner of his couch'—'ah, by Vesta!'—and 'I tell thee, Roman.' Among the quotations which serve at once for instruction and ornament on the cover of this volume, there is one from Miss Sinclair, which informs us that 'Works of imagination are *avowedly* read by men of science, wisdom, and piety'; from which we suppose the reader is to gather the cheering inference that Dr. Daubeny, Mr. Mill, or Mr. Maurice, may openly indulge himself with the perusal of 'Adonijah,' without being obligated to secrete it among the sofa cushions, or read it by snatches under the dinner table.

'Be not a baker if your head be made of butter,' says a homely proverb, which, being interpreted, may mean, let no woman rush into print who is not prepared for the consequences. We are aware that our remarks are in a very different tone from that of the reviewers who, with a perennial recurrence of precisely similar emotions, only paralleled, we imagine, in the experience of monthly nurses, tell one lady novelist after another that they 'hail' her productions 'with delight.' We are aware that the ladies at whom our criticism is pointed are accustomed to be told, in the choicest phraseology of puffery, that their pictures of life are brilliant, their characters well drawn, their style fascinating, and their sentiments lofty. But if they are inclined to resent our plainness of speech, we ask them to reflect for a moment on the chary praise, and often captious blame, which their panegyrists give to writers whose works are on the way to become classics. No sooner does a woman show that she has genius or effective talent, than she receives the tribute of being moderately praised and severely criticised. By a peculiar thermometric adjustment, when a woman's talent is at zero, journalistic approbation is at the boiling pitch; when she attains mediocrity, it is already at no more than summer heat; and if ever she reaches excellence, critical enthusiasm drops to the freezing point. Harriet Martineau, Currer Bell,[6] and Mrs. Gaskell have been treated as cavalierly as if they had been men. And every critic who forms a high estimate of the share women may ultimately take in literature, will, on principle, abstain from any exceptional indulgence towards the productions of literary women. For it must be plain to every one who looks impartially and extensively into feminine literature, that its greatest deficiencies are due hardly more to the want of intellectual power than to the want of those moral qualities that contribute to literary excellence—patient diligence,

---

[6] Pseudonym of the novelist Charlotte Brontë. *Ed.*

a sense of the responsibility involved in publication, and an appreciation of the sacredness of the writer's art. In the majority of women's books you see that kind of facility which springs from the absence of any high standard; that fertility in imbecile combination or feeble imitation which a little self-criticism would check and reduce to barrenness; just as with a total want of musical ear people will sing out of tune, while a degree more melodic sensibility would suffice to render them silent. The foolish vanity of wishing to appear in print, instead of being counter balanced by an consciousness of the intellectual or moral derogation implied in futile authorship, seems to be encouraged by the extremely false impression that to write *at all* is a proof of superiority in a woman. On this ground, we believe that the average intellect of women is unfairly represented by the mass of feminine literature, and that while the few women who write well are very far above the ordinary intellectual level of their sex, that many women who write ill are very far below it. So that, after all, the severer critics are fulfilling a chivalrous duty in depriving the mere fact of feminine authorship of any false prestige which may give it a delusive attraction, and in recommending women of mediocre faculties—as at least a negative service they can render their sex—to abstain from writing.

The standing apology for women who become writers without any special qualification is, that society shuts them out from other spheres of occupation. Society is a very culpable entity, and has to answer for the manufacture of many unwholesome commodities, from bad pickles to bad poetry. But society, like 'matter,' and Her Majesty's Government, and other lofty abstractions, has its share of excessive blame as well as excessive praise. Where there is one woman who writes from necessity, we believe there are three women who write from vanity; and, besides, there is something so antiseptic in the mere healthy fact of working for one's bread, that the most trashy and rotten kind of feminine literature is not likely to have been produced under such circumstances. 'In all labour there is profit;' but ladies' silly novels, we imagine, are less the result of labour than of busy idleness.

Happily, we are not dependent on argument to prove that Fiction is a department of literature in which women can, after their kind, fully equal men. A cluster of great names, both living and dead, rush to our memories in evidence that women can produce novels not only fine, but among the very finest;—novels, too, that have a precious speciality, lying quite apart from masculine aptitudes and experience. No educational restrictions can shut women out from the materials of fiction, and there is no species of art which is so free from rigid requirements. Like crystalline masses, it may take any form, and yet be beautiful; we have only to pour in the right elements—genuine observation, humour, and passion. But it is precisely this absence of rigid requirement which constitutes the fatal seduction of novel-writing to incompetent women. Ladies are not wont to be very grossly deceived as to their power of playing on the piano; here certain positive difficulties of execution have to be conquered, and incompetence inevitably breaks down. Every art which has its absolute *technique* is, to a certain extent, guarded from the intrusions of mere left-handed imbecility. But in novel-writing there are no barriers for incapacity to stumble against, no external criteria to prevent a writer from mistaking foolish facility for mastery. And so we have again and again the old story of La Fontaine's ass, who puts his nose to the flute, and, finding that he elicits some sound, exclaims, 'Moi, aussi, je joue de la flute;'[7] —a fable which we commend, at parting, to the consideration of any feminine reader who is in danger of adding to the number of 'silly novels by lady novelists.'

---

[7] "I too can play the flute." *Ed.*

Henry James

Henry James was born in New York City in 1843, and educated, together with his elder brother William James, at various schools in England, France, Switzerland, and Germany. He began publishing short stories in his twenties, but did not find his true voice until he left America permanently in 1875, first for Paris and then permanently for London. His early fiction centers on the "international theme" of the moral and spiritual gap between America and Europe. *The American* (1877), *Daisy Miller* (1878), and *The Portrait of a Lady* (1881) made James's reputation; today they seem to be in uneasy transition between the social chronicle of the mid-nineteenth century and the psychological realism that was to flourish after the turn of the century. The novels of James's middle years, *The Princess Casamassima* (1886) and *The Tragic Muse* (1890), were less successful, and James's attempt to conquer the London stage with *Guy Domville* (1895) ended in disaster. James withdrew to Lamb House near Rye, where he produced the three highly nuanced masterworks of his late period, *The Wings of the Dove* (1902), *The Ambassadors* (1903), and *The Golden Bowl* (1904). In his last decade, James turned to memoir, but the outbreak of World War I disturbed the quiet of memory. In solidarity with the British cause during the long period of American neutrality, James applied for citizenship (granted 1915) and worked at war relief, the exertions of which broke his own health. He died in 1916. "The Art of Fiction" was originally published in *Longman's Magazine* in 1884.

The Art of Fiction

I should not have affixed so comprehensive a title to these few remarks, necessarily wanting in any completeness upon a subject the full consideration of which would carry us far, did I not seem to discover a pretext for my temerity in the interesting pamphlet lately published under this name by Mr. Walter Besant.[1] Mr. Besant's lecture at the Royal Institution—the original form of his pamphlet—appears to indicate that many persons are interested in the art of fiction, and are not indifferent to such re-

---

[1] British novelist and man of letters (1836–1901). *Ed.*

marks, as those who practice it may attempt to make about it. I am therefore anxious not to lose the benefit of this favorable association, and to edge in a few words under cover of the attention which Mr. Besant is sure to have excited. There is something very encouraging in his having put into form certain of his ideas in the mystery of storytelling.

It is a proof of life and curiosity—curiosity on the part of the brotherhood of novelists as well as on the part of their readers. Only a short time ago it might have been supposed that the English novel was not what the French call *discutable.* It had no air of having a theory, a conviction, a consciousness of itself behind it—of being the expression of an artistic faith, the result of choice and comparison. I do not say it was necessarily the worse for that: it would take much more courage than I possess to intimate that the form of the novel as Dickens and Thackeray (for instance) saw it had any taint of incompleteness. It was, however, *naif* (if I may help myself out with another French word); and evidently if it be destined to suffer in any way for having lost its *naïveté* it has now an idea of making sure of the corresponding advantages. During the period I have alluded to there was a comfortable, good-humored feeling abroad that a novel is a novel, as a pudding is a pudding, and that our only business with it could be to swallow it. But within a year or two, for some reason or other, there have been signs of returning animation—the era of discussion would appear to have been to a certain extent opened. Art lives upon discussion, upon experiment, upon curiosity, upon variety of attempt, upon the exchange of views and the comparison of standpoints; and there is a presumption that those times when no one has anything particular to say about it, and has no reason to give for practice or preference, though they may be times of honor, are not times of development—are times, possibly even, a little of dullness. The successful application of any art is a delightful spectacle, but the theory too is interesting; and though there is a great deal of the latter without the former I suspect there has never been a genuine success that has not had a latent core of conviction. Discussion, suggestion, formulation, these things are fertilizing when they are frank and sincere. Mr. Besant has set an excellent example in saying what he thinks, for his part, about the way in which fiction should be written, as well as about the way in which it should be published; for his view of the "art," carried on into an appendix, covers that too. Other laborers in the same field will doubtless take up the argument, they will give it the light of their experience, and the effect will surely be to make our interest in the novel a little more what it had for some time threatened to fail to be—a serious, active, inquiring interest, under protection of which this delightful study may, in moments of confidence, venture to say a little more what it thinks of itself.

It must take itself seriously for the public to take it so. The old superstition about fiction being "wicked" has doubtless died out in England; but the spirit of it lingers in a certain oblique regard directed toward any story which does not more or less admit that it is only a joke. Even the most jocular novel feels in some degree the weight of the proscription that was formerly directed against literary levity: the jocularity does not always succeed in passing for orthodoxy. It is still expected, though perhaps people are ashamed to say it, that a production which is after all only a "make-believe" (for what else is a "story"?) shall be in some degree apologetic—shall renounce the pretension of attempting really to represent life. This, of course, any sensible, wide-awake story declines to do, for it quickly perceives that the tolerance granted to it on such a condition is only an attempt to stifle it disguised in the form of generosity. The old evangelical hostility to the novel, which was as explicit as it was narrow, and which regarded it as little less favorable to our immortal part than a stage play, was in reality far less insulting. The only reason for the existence of a novel is that it does attempt to represent life. When it relinquishes this attempt, the same attempt that we see on the canvas of the painter, it will have arrived at a very strange pass. It is not expected of the picture that it will make itself humble in order to be forgiven; and the analogy between the art of the painter and the art of the novelist is, so far as I am able to see, complete. Their inspiration is the same, their process (allowing for the different quality of the vehicle) is the same, their success is the same. They may learn from each other, they may explain and sustain each other. Their cause is the same, and the honor of one is the honor of another. The Mahometans think a picture an unholy thing, but it is a long time since any Christian did, and it is therefore the more odd that in the Christian mind the traces (dissimulated though they may be) of a suspicion of the sister art should linger to this day. The only effectual way to lay it to rest is to emphasize the analogy to which I just alluded—to insist on the fact that as the picture is reality, so the novel is history. That is the only general description (which does it justice) that we may give of the novel. But history also is allowed to represent life; it is not, any more than painting, expected to apologize. The subject matter of fiction is stored up likewise in documents and records, and if it will not give itself away, as they say in California, it must speak with assurance, with the tone of the historian. Certain accomplished novelists have a habit of giving themselves away which must often bring tears to the eyes of people who take their fiction seriously. I was lately struck, in reading over many pages of Anthony Trollope, with his want of discretion in the particular. In a digression, a parenthesis or an aside, he concedes to the reader that he and this trusting friend are only "making believe." He admits that the events he narrates have not really happened, and that he can give his narrative any turn the reader may like best.[2] Such a betrayal of a sacred office seems to me, I confess, a terrible crime; it is what I mean by the attitude of apology; and it shocks me every whit as much in Trollope as it would have shocked me in Gibbon or Macaulay. It implies that the novelist is less occupied in looking for the truth (the truth, of course I mean, that he assumes, the premises that we must grant him, whatever they may be) than the historian, and in doing so it deprives him at a stroke of all his standing room. To represent and illustrate the past, the actions of men, is the task of either writer, and the only difference that I can see is, in proportion as he succeeds, to the honor of the novelist, consisting as it does in his having more difficulty in collecting his evidence, which is so far from being purely literary. It seems to me to give him a great character, the fact that he has at once so much in common with the philosopher and the painter; this double analogy is a magnificent heritage.

It is of all this evidently that Mr. Besant is full when he insists upon the fact that fiction is one of the *fine* arts, deserving in its turn of all the honors and emoluments that have hitherto been reserved for the successful profession of music, poetry, paint-

---

[2] James may be alluding to the opening of Chapter 51 of Trollope's *Barchester Towers* (1857). *Ed.*

ing, architecture. It is impossible to insist too much on so important a truth, and the place that Mr. Besant demands for the work of the novelist may be represented, a trifle less abstractly, by saying that he demands not only that it shall be reputed artistic, but that it shall be reputed very artistic indeed. It is excellent that he should have struck this note, for his doing so indicates that there was need of it, that his proposition may be to many people a novelty. One rubs one's eyes at the thought; but the rest of Mr. Besant's essay confirms the revelation. I suspect in truth that it would be possible to confirm it still further, and that one would not be far wrong in saying that in addition to the people to whom it has never occurred that a novel ought to be artistic, there are a great many others who, if this principle were urged upon them, would be filled with an indefinable mistrust. They would find it difficult to explain their repugnance, but it would operate strongly to put them on their guard. "Art," in our Protestant communities, where so many things have got so strangely twisted about, is supposed in certain circles to have some vaguely injurious effect upon those who make it an important consideration, who let it weigh in the balance. It is assumed to be opposed in some mysterious manner to morality, to amusement, to instruction. When it is embodied in the work of the painter (the sculptor is another affair!) you know what it is: it stands there before you, in the honesty of pink and green and a gilt frame; you can see the worst of it at a glance, and you can be on your *guard*. But when it is introduced into literature it becomes more insidious—there is danger of its hurting you before you know it. Literature should be either instructive or amusing, and there is in many minds an impression that these artistic preoccupations, the search for form, contribute to neither end, interfere indeed with both. They are too frivolous to be edifying, and too serious to be diverting; and they are moreover priggish and paradoxical and superfluous. That, I think, represents the manner in which the latent thought of many people who read novels as an exercise in skipping would explain itself if it were to become articulate. They would argue, of course, that a novel ought to be "good," but they would interpret this term in a fashion of their own, which indeed would vary considerably from one critic to another. One would say that being good means representing virtuous and aspiring characters, placed in prominent positions; another would say that it depends on a "happy ending," on a distribution at the last of prizes, pensions, husbands, wives, babies, millions, appended paragraphs, and cheerful remarks. Another still would say that it means being full of incident and movement, so that we shall wish to jump ahead, to see who was the mysterious stranger, and if the stolen will was ever found, and shall not be distracted from this pleasure by any tiresome analysis or "description." But they would all agree that the "artistic" idea would spoil some of their fun. One would hold it accountable for all the description, another would see it revealed in the absence of sympathy. Its hostility to a happy ending would be evident, and it might even in some cases render any ending at all impossible. The "ending" of a novel is, for many persons, like that of a good dinner, a course of dessert and ices, and the artist in fiction is regarded as a sort of meddlesome doctor who forbids agreeable aftertastes. It is therefore true that this conception of Mr. Besant's of the novel as a superior form encounters not only a negative but a positive indifference. It matters little that as a work of art it should really be as little or as much of its essence to supply happy endings, sympathetic characters, and an objective tone, as if it were a work of mechanics: the association of ideas, however incongruous, might easily be too much for it if an eloquent voice were not sometimes raised to call attention to the fact that it is at once as free and as serious a branch of literature as any other.

Certainly this might sometimes be doubted in presence of the enormous number of works of fiction that appeal to the credulity of our generation, for it might easily seem that there could be no great character in a commodity so quickly and easily produced. It must be admitted that good novels are much compromised by bad ones, and that the field at large suffers discredit from overcrowding. I think, however, that this injury is only superficial, and that the superabundance of written fiction proves nothing against the principle itself. It has been vulgarized, like all other kinds of literature, like everything else today, and it has proved more than some kinds accessible to vulgarization. But there is as much difference as there ever was between a good novel and a bad one: the bad is swept with all the daubed canvases and spoiled marble into some unvisited limbo, or infinite rubbish yard beneath the back windows of the world, and the good subsists and emits its light and stimulates our desire for perfection. As I shall take the liberty of making but a single criticism of Mr. Besant, whose tone is so full of the love of his art, I may as well have done with it at once. He seems to me to mistake in attempting to say so definitely beforehand what sort of an affair the good novel will be. To indicate the danger of such an error as that has been the purpose of these few pages; to suggest that certain traditions on the subject, applied *a priori,* have already had much to answer for, and that the good health of an art which undertakes so immediately to reproduce life must demand that it be perfectly free. It lives upon exercise, and the very meaning of exercise is freedom. The only obligation to which in advance we may hold a novel, without incurring the accusation of being arbitrary, is that it be interesting. That general responsibility rests upon it, but it is the only one I can think of. The ways in which it is at liberty to accomplish this result (of interesting us) strike me as innumerable, and such as can only suffer from being marked out or fenced in by prescription. They are as various as the temperament of man, and they are successful in proportion as they reveal a particular mind, different from others. A novel is in its broadest definition a personal, a direct impression of life: that, to begin with, constitutes its value, which is greater or less according to the intensity of the impression. But there will be no intensity at all, and therefore no value, unless there is freedom to feel and say. The tracing of a line to be followed, of a tone to be taken, of a form to be filled out, is a limitation of that freedom and a suppression of the very thing that we are most curious about. The form, it seems to me, is to be appreciated after the fact: then the author's choice has been made, his standard has been indicated; then we can follow lines and directions and compare tones and resemblances. Then in a word we can enjoy one of the most charming of pleasures, we can estimate quality, we can apply the test of execution. The execution belongs to the author alone; it is what is most personal to him, and we measure him by that. The advantage, the luxury, as well as the torment and responsibility of the novelist, is that there is no limit to what he may attempt as an executant—no limit to his possible experiments, efforts, discoveries, successes. Here it is especially that he works, step by step, like his brother of the brush, of whom we may always say that he has painted his picture in a manner best known to himself. His manner is his secret, not necessarily a jealous one. He cannot disclose it as a general thing if he would; he would be at a loss to teach it to others. I say this with a due recollection of having insisted on the community of method of the artist who paints a picture and the artist who writes a novel. The painter *is* able to teach the rudiments of his practice, and it is possible, from the study of good work (granted the aptitude), both to learn how to paint and to learn how to write. Yet it remains true, without injury to the *rapprochement,* that the literary artist would be obligated to say to his pupil much more than the other, "Ah, well, you must do it as you can!" It is a question of degree, a matter of delicacy. If there are exact sciences, there are also exact arts, and the grammar of painting is so much more definite that it makes the difference.

I ought to add, however, that if Mr. Besant says at the beginning of his essay that the "laws of fiction may be laid down and taught with as much precision and exactness as the laws of harmony, perspective, and proportion," he mitigates what might appear to be an extravagance by applying his remark to "general" laws, and by expressing most of these rules in a manner with which it would certainly be unaccommodating to disagree. That the novelist must write from his experience, that his "characters must be real and such as might be met with in actual life"; that "a young lady brought up in a quiet country village should avoid descriptions of garrison life," and "a writer whose friends and personal experiences belong to the lower middle class should carefully avoid introducing his characters into society"; that one should enter one's notes in a common-place book;[3] that one's figures should be clear in outline; that making them clear by some trick of speech or of carriage is a bad method, and "describing them at length" is a worse one; that English fiction should have a "conscious moral purpose"; that "it is almost impossible to estimate too highly the value of careful workmanship—that is, of style"; that "the most important point of all is the story," that "the story is everything": these are principles with most of which it is surely impossible not to sympathize. That remark about the lower middle-class writer and his knowing his place is perhaps rather chilling; but for the rest I should find it difficult to dissent from any one of these recommendations. At the same time, I should find it difficult positively to assent to them, with the exception, perhaps, of the injunction as to entering one's notes in a common-place book. They scarcely seem to me to have the quality that Mr. Besant attributes to the rules of the novelist—the "precision and exactness" of "the laws of harmony, perspective, and proportion." They are suggestive, they are even inspiring, but they are not exact, though they are doubtless as much so as the case admits of: which is a proof of that liberty of interpretation for which I just contended. For the value of these different injunctions—so beautiful and so vague— is wholly in the meaning one attaches to them. The characters, the situation, which strike one as real will be those that touch and interest one most, but the measure of reality is very difficult to fix. The reality of Don Quixote or of Mr. Micawber is a very delicate shade; it is a reality so colored by the author's vision that, vivid as it may be, one would hesitate to propose it as a model: one would expose one's self to some very embarrassing questions on the part of a pupil. It goes without saying that you will not write a good novel unless you possess the sense of reality; but it will be difficult to give

---

[3] A notebook. *Ed.*

you a recipe for calling that sense into being. Humanity is immense, and reality has a myriad forms; the most one can affirm is that some of the flowers of fiction have the odor of it, and others have not; as for telling you in advance how your nosegay should be composed, that is another affair. It is equally excellent and inconclusive to say that one must write from experience; to our suppositious aspirant such a declaration might savor of mockery. What kind of experience is intended, and where does it begin and end? Experience is never limited, and it is never complete; it is an immense sensibility, a kind of huge spiderweb of the finest silken threads suspended in the chamber of consciousness, and catching every air-borne particle in its tissue. It is the very atmosphere of the mind; and when the mind is imaginative—much more when it happens to be that of a man of genius—it takes to itself the faintest hints of life, it converts the very pulses of the air into revelations. The young lady living in a village has only to be a damsel upon whom nothing is lost to make it quite unfair (as it seems to me) to declare to her that she shall have nothing to say about the military. Greater miracles have been seen than that, imagination assisting, she should speak the truth about some of these gentlemen. I remember an English novelist, a woman of genius,[4] telling me that she was much commended for the impression she had managed to give in one of her tales of the nature and way of life of the French Protestant youth. She had been asked where she learned so much about this recondite being, she had been congratulated on her peculiar opportunities. These opportunities consisted in her having once, in Paris, as she ascended a staircase, passed an open door where, in the household of a *pasteur*,[5] some of the young Protestants were seated at table round a finished meal. The glimpse made a picture; it lasted only a moment, but that moment was experience. She had got her direct personal impression, and she turned out her type. She knew what youth was, and what Protestantism; she also had the advantage of having seen what it was to be French, so that she converted these ideas into a concrete image and produced a reality. Above all, however, she was blessed with the faculty which when you give it an inch takes an ell, and which for the artist is a much greater source of strength than any accident of residence or of place in the social scale. The power to guess the unseen from the seen, to trace the implication of things, to judge the whole piece by the pattern, the condition of feeling life in general so completely that you are well on your way to knowing any particular corner of it—this cluster of gifts may almost be said to constitute experience, and they occur in country and in town, and in the most differing stages of education. If experience consists of impressions, it may be said that impressions *are* experience, just as (have we not seen it?) they are the very air we breathe. Therefore, if I should certainly say to a novice, "Write from experience and experience only," I should feel that this was rather a tantalizing monition if I were not careful immediately to add, "Try to be one of the people on whom nothing is lost!"

I am far from intending by this to minimize the importance of exactness—of truth of detail. One can speak best from one's own taste, and I may therefore venture to say that the air of reality (solidity of specification) seems to me to be the supreme virtue of a novel—the merit on which all its other merits (including that conscious moral

---

[4] The novelist is probably Anne Thackeray, Lady Ritchie, and the novel *The Story of Elizabeth*.
[5] Protestant minister.

purpose of which Mr. Besant speaks) helplessly and submissively depend. If it be not there, they are all as nothing, and if these be there, they owe their effect to the success with which the author has produced the illusion of life. The cultivation of this success, the study of this exquisite process, form, to my taste, the beginning and the end of the art of the novelist. They are his inspiration, his despair, his reward, his torment, his delight. It is here in very truth that he competes with life; it is here that he competes with his brother the painter in *his* attempt to render the look of things, the look that conveys their meaning, to catch the color, the relief, the expression, the surface, the substance of the human spectacle. It is in regard to this that Mr. Besant is well inspired when he bids him take notes. He cannot possibly take too many, he cannot possibly take enough. All life solicits him, and to "render" the simplest surface, to produce the most momentary illusion, is a very complicated business. His case would be easier, and the rule would be more exact, if Mr. Besant had been able to tell him what notes to take. But this, I fear, he can never learn in any manual; it is the business of his life. He has to take a great many in order to select a few, he has to work them up as he can, and even the guides and philosophers who might have most to say to him must leave him alone when it comes to the application of precepts, as we leave the painter in communion with his palette. That his characters "must be clear in outline," as Mr. Besant says—he feels that down to his boots; but how he shall make them so is a secret between his good angel and himself. It would be absurdly simple if he could be taught that a great deal of "description" would make them so, or that on the contrary the absence of description and the cultivation of dialogue, or the absence of dialogue and the multiplication of "incident," would rescue him from his difficulties. Nothing, for instance, is more possible than that he be of a turn of mind for which this odd, literal opposition of description and dialogue, incident and description, has little meaning and light. People often talk of these things as if they had a kind of internecine distinctness, instead of melting into each other at every breath, and being intimately associated parts of one general effort of expression. I cannot imagine composition existing in a series of blocks, nor conceive, in any novel worth discussing at all, of a passage of description that is not in its intention narrative, a passage of dialogue that is not in its intention descriptive, a touch of truth of any sort that does not partake of the nature of incident, or an incident that derives its interest from any other source than the general and only source of the success of a work of art—that of being illustrative. A novel is a living thing, all one and continuous, like any other organism, and in proportion as it lives will it be found, I think, that in each of the parts there is something of each of the other parts. The critic who over the close texture of a finished work shall pretend to trace a geography of items will mark some frontiers as artificial, I fear, as any that have been know to history. There is an old-fashioned distinction between the novel of character and the novel of incident which must have cost many a smile to the intending fabulist who was keen about his work. It appears to me as little to the point as the equally celebrated distinction between the novel and the romance—to answer as little to any reality. There are bad novels and good novels, as there are bad pictures and good pictures; but that is the only distinction in which I see any meaning, and I can as little imagine speaking of a novel of character as I can imagine speaking of a picture of character. When one says picture one says of character, when one says novel one says of incident, and the terms may be transposed at will. What is character but the determination of incident? What is incident but the illustration of character? What is either a picture or a novel that is *not* of character? What else do we seek in it and find in it? It is an incident for a woman to stand up with her hand resting on a table and look out at you in a certain way; or if it be not an incident I think it will be hard to say what it is. At the same time it is an expression of character. If you say you don't see it (character in *that—allons donc!),*[6] this is exactly what the artist who has reasons of his own for thinking he *does* see it undertakes to show you. When a young man makes up his mind that he has not faith enough after all to enter the church as he intended, that is an incident, though you may not hurry to the end of the chapter to see whether perhaps he doesn't change once more. I do not say that these are extraordinary or startling incidents. I do not pretend to estimate the degree of interest proceeding from them, for this will depend upon the skill of the painter. It sounds almost puerile to say that some incidents are intrinsically much more important than others, and I need not take this precaution after having professed my sympathy for the major ones in remarking that the only classification of the novel that I can understand is into that which has life and that which has it not.

The novel and the romance, the novel of incident and that of character—these clumsy separations appear to me to have been made by critics and readers for their own convenience, and to help them out of some of their occasional queer predicaments, but to have little reality or interest for the producer, from whose point of view it is of course that we are attempting to consider the art of fiction. The case is the same with another shadowy category which Mr. Besant apparently is disposed to set up— that of the "modern English novel"; unless indeed it be that in this matter he has fallen into an accidental confusion of standpoints. It is not quite clear whether he intends the remarks in which he alludes to it to be didactic or historical. It is as difficult to suppose a person intending to write a modern English as to suppose him writing an ancient English novel: that is a label which begs the question. One writes the novel, one paints the picture, of one's language and of one's time, and calling it modern English will not, alas! make the difficult task any easier. No more, unfortunately, will calling this or that work of one's fellow artist a romance—unless it be, of course, simply for the pleasantness of the thing, as for instance when Hawthorne gave this heading to his story of *Blithedale.* The French, who have brought the theory of fiction to remarkable completeness, have but one name for the novel, and have not attempted smaller things in it, that I can see, for that. I can think of no obligation to which the "romancer" would not be held equally with the novelist; the standard of execution is equally high for each. Of course it is of execution that we are talking—that being the only point of a novel that is open to contention. This is perhaps too often lost sight of, only to produce interminable confusions and cross purposes. We must grant the artist his subject, his idea, his *donnée.*[7] Our criticism is applied only to what he makes of it. Naturally I do not mean that we are bound to like it or find it interesting: in case we do not, our course is perfectly simple—to let it alone. We may believe that of a certain

---

[6] "Get out of here!" *Ed.*
[7] A starting point: literally, what is given. *Ed.*

idea even the most sincere novelist can make nothing at all, and the event may perfectly justify our belief; but the failure will have been a failure to execute, and it is in the execution that the fatal weakness is recorded. If we pretend to respect the artist at all, we must allow him his freedom of choice, in the fact, in particular cases, of innumerable presumptions that the choice will not fructify. Art derives a considerable part of its beneficial exercise from flying in the face of presumptions, and some of the most interesting experiments of which it is capable are hidden in the bosom of common things. Gustave Flaubert has written a story about the devotion of a servant girl to a parrot,[8] and the production, highly finished as it is, cannot on the whole be called a success. We are perfectly free to find it flat, but I think it might have been interesting; and I, for my part, am extremely glad he should have written it; it is a contribution to our knowledge of what can be done—or what cannot. Ivan Turgénieff has written a tale about a deaf and dumb serf and a lap dog,[9] and the thing is touching, loving, a little masterpiece. He struck the note of life where Gustave Flaubert missed it—he flew in the face of a presumption and achieved a victory.

Nothing, of course, will ever take the place of the good old fashion of "liking" a work of art or of not liking it: the most improved criticism will not abolish that primitive, that ultimate test. I mention this to guard myself from the accusation of intimating that the idea, the subject, of a novel or a picture, does not matter. It matters, to my sense, in the highest degree, and if I might put up a prayer it would be that artists should select none but the richest. Some, as I have already hastened to admit, are much more remunerative than others, and it would be a world happily arranged in which persons intending to treat them should be exempt from confusions and mistakes. This fortunate condition will arrive only, I fear, on the same day that critics become purged from error. Meanwhile, I repeat, we do not judge the artist with fairness unless we say to him, "Oh, I grant you your starting point, because if I did not I should seem to prescribe to you, and heaven forbid I should take that responsibility. If I pretend to tell you what you must not take, you will call upon me to tell you then what you must take; in which case I shall be prettily caught. Moreover, it isn't till I have accepted your data that I can begin to measure you. I have the standard, the pitch; I have no right to tamper with your flute and then criticize your music. Of course I may not care for your idea at all; I may think it silly, or stale, or unclean; in which case I wash my hands of you altogether. I may content myself with believing that you will not have succeeded in being interesting, but I shall, of course, not attempt to demonstrate it, and you will be as indifferent to me as I am to you. I needn't remind you that there are all sorts of tastes: who can know it better? Some people, for excellent reasons, don't like to read about carpenters; others, for reasons even better, don't like to read about courtesans. Many object to Americans. Others (I believe they are mainly editors and publishers) won't look at Italians. Some readers don't like quiet subjects; others don't like bustling ones. Some enjoy a complete illusion, others the consciousness of large concessions. They choose their novels accordingly, and if they don't care about your idea they won't, *a fortiori,* care about your treatment."

---

[8] *Un Coeur simple. Ed.*
[9] *Mumu. Ed.*

So that it comes back very quickly, as I have said, to the liking: in spite of M. Zola, who reasons less powerfully than he represents, and who will not reconcile himself to this absoluteness of taste, thinking that there are certain things that people ought to like, and that they can be made to like. I am quite at a loss to imagine anything (at any rate in this matter of fiction) that people *ought* to like or to dislike. Selection will be sure to take care of itself, for it has a constant motive behind it. That motive is simply experience. As people feel life, so they will feel that art that is most closely related to it. This closeness of relation is what we should never forget in talking of the effort of the novel. Many people speak of it as a factitious, artificial form, a product of ingenuity, the business of which is to alter and arrange the things that surround us, to translate them into conventional, traditional molds. This, however, is a view of the matter which carries us but a very short way, condemns the art to an eternal repetition of a few familiar *clichés*, cuts short its development, and leads us straight up to a dead wall. Catching the very note and trick, the strange irregular rhythm of life, that is the attempt whose strenuous force keeps Fiction upon her feet. In proportion as in what she offers us we see life *without* rearrangement do we feel that we are touching the truth; in proportion as we see it *with* rearrangement do we feel that we are being put off with a substitute, a compromise and convention. It is not uncommon to hear an extraordinary assurance of remark in regard to this matter of rearranging, which is often spoken of as if it were the last word of art. Mr. Besant seems to me in danger of falling into the great error with his rather unguarded talk about "selection." Art is essentially selection, but it is a selection whose main care is to be typical, to be inclusive. For many people art means rose-colored window-panes, and selection means picking a bouquet for Mrs. Grundy.[10] They will tell you glibly that artistic considerations have nothing to do with the disagreeable, with the ugly; they will rattle off shallow commonplaces about the province of art and the limits of art till you are moved to some wonder in return as to the province and the limits of ignorance. It appears to me that no one can ever have made a seriously artistic attempt without becoming conscious of an immense increase—a kind of revelation—of freedom. One perceives in that case—by the light of a heavenly ray—that the province of art is all life, all feeling, all observation, all vision. As Mr. Besant so justly intimates, it is all experience. That is a sufficient answer to those who maintain that it must not touch the sad things of life, who stick into its divine unconscious bosom little prohibitory inscriptions on the end of sticks, such as we see in public gardens—"It is forbidden to walk on the grass; it is forbidden to touch the flowers; it is not allowed to introduce dogs or to remain after dark; it is requested to keep to the right." The young aspirant in the line of fiction whom we continue to imagine will do nothing without taste, for in that case his freedom would be of little use to him; but the first advantage of his taste will be to reveal to him the absurdity of the little sticks and tickets. If he have taste, I must add, of course he will have ingenuity, and my disrespectful reference to that quality just now was not meant to imply that it is useless in fiction. But it is only secondary aid; the first is a capacity for receiving straight impressions.

---

[10] Personification of prudery. *Ed.*

Mr. Besant has some remarks on the question of "the story" which I shall not attempt to criticize, though they seem to me to contain a singular ambiguity, because I do not think I understand them. I cannot see what is meant by talking as if there were a part of a novel which is the story and part of it which for mystical reasons is not—unless indeed the distinction be made in a sense in which it is difficult to suppose that anyone should attempt to convey anything. "The story," if it represents anything, represents the subject, the idea, the *donnée* of the novel; and there is surely no "school"—Mr. Besant speaks of a school—which urges that a novel should be all treatment and no subject. There must assuredly be something to treat; every school is intimately conscious of that. This sense of the story being the idea, the starting point, of the novel, is the only one that I see in which it can be spoken of as something different from its organic whole; and since in proportion as the work is successful the idea permeates and penetrates it, informs and animates it, so that every word and every punctuation point contribute directly to the expression, in that proportion do we lose our sense of the story being a blade which may be drawn more or less out of its sheath. The story and the novel, the idea and the form, are the needle and thread, and I never heard of a guild of tailors who recommended the use of thread without the needle, or the needle without the thread. Mr. Besant is not the only critic who may be observed to have spoken as if there were certain things in life which constitute stories, and certain others which do not. I find the same odd implications in an entertaining article in the *Pall Mall Gazette,* devoted, as it happens, to Mr. Besant's lecture. "The story is the thing!" says this graceful writer, as if with a tone of opposition to some other idea. I should think it was, as every painter who, as the time for "sending in" his picture looms in the distance, finds himself still in quest of a subject—as every belated artist not fixed about his theme will heartily agree. There are some subjects which speak to us and others which do not, but he would be a clever man who should undertake to give a rule—an index expurgatorius—by which the story and the no-story should be known apart. It is impossible (to me at least) to imagine any such rule which shall not be altogether arbitrary. The writer in the *Pall Mall* opposes the delightful (as I suppose) novel of *Margot la Balafrée* to certain tales in which "Bostonian nymphs" appear to have "rejected English dukes for psychological reasons." I am not acquainted with the romance just designated, and can scarcely forgive the *Pall Mall* critic for not mentioning the name of the author, but the title appears to refer to a lady who may have received a scar in some heroic adventure. I am inconsolable at not being acquainted with this episode, but am utterly at a loss to see why it is a story when the rejection (or acceptance) of a duke is not, and why a reason, psychological or other, is not a subject when a cicatrix is.[11] They are all particles of the multitudinous life with which the novel deals, and surely no dogma which pretends to make it lawful to touch the one and unlawful to touch the other will stand for a moment on its feet. It is the special picture that must stand or fall, according as it seem to possess truth or to lack it. Mr. Besant

---

[11] *Margot la Balafrée* [*Scarred Margot,* 1884] is by Fortune de Boisgobey; the novel in which a Bostonian nymph rejects an English duke is James's own *An International Incident* (1879). The heroine of James's *Portrait of a Lady* (1881) also rejects an English lord "for psychological reasons." *Ed.*

does not, to my sense, light up the subject by intimating that a story must, under penalty of not being a story, consist of "adventures." Why of adventures more than of green spectacles? He mentions a category of impossible things, and among them he places "fiction without adventure." Why without adventure, more than without matrimony, or celibacy, or parturition, or cholera, or hydropathy, or Jansenism? This seems to me to bring the novel back to the hapless little role of being an artificial, ingenious thing—bring it down from its large, free character of an immense and exquisite correspondence with life. And what *is* adventure, when it comes to that, and by what sign is the listening pupil to recognize it? It is an adventure—an immense one—for me to write this little article; and for a Bostonian nymph to reject an English duke is an adventure only less stirring, I should say, than for an English duke to be rejected by a Bostonian nymph. I see dramas within dramas in that, and innumerable points of view. A psychological reason is, to my imagination, an object adorably pictorial; to catch the tint of its complexion—I feel as if that idea might inspire one to Titianesque efforts. There are few things more exciting to me, in short, than a psychological reason, and yet I protest, the novel seems to me the most magnificent form of art. I have just been reading, at the same time, the delightful story of *Treasure Island,* by Mr. Robert Louis Stevenson and, in a manner less consecutive, the last tale from M. Edmond de Goncourt, which is entitled *Chérie.* One of these works treats of murders, mysteries, islands of dreadful renown, hairbreadth escapes, miraculous coincidences, and buried doubloons. The other treats of a little French girl who lived in a fine house in Paris, and died of wounded sensibility because no one would marry her. I call *Treasure Island* delightful because it appears to me to have succeeded wonderfully in what it attempts; and I venture to bestow no epithet upon *Chérie,* which strikes me as having failed deplorably in what it attempts—that is, in tracing the development of the moral consciousness of a child. But one of these productions strikes me as exactly as much of a novel as the other, and as having a "story" quite as much. The moral consciousness of a child is as much a part of life as the islands of the Spanish Main, and the one sort of geography seems to me to have those "surprises" of which Mr. Besant speaks quite as much as the other. For myself (since it comes back in the last resort, as I say, to the preference of the individual), the picture of the child's experience has the advantage that I can at successive steps (in immense luxury, near to the "sensual pleasure" of which Mr. Besant's critic in the *Pall Mall* speaks) say Yes or No, as it may be, to what the artist puts before me. I have been a child in fact, but I have been on a quest for a buried treasure only in supposition, and it is a simple accident that with M. de Goncourt I should have for the most part to say No. With George Eliot, when she painted that country with a far other intelligence, I always said Yes.[12]

The most interesting part of Mr. Besant's lecture is unfortunately the briefest passage—his very cursory allusion to the "conscious moral purpose" of the novel. Here again it is not very clear whether he be recording a fact or laying down a principle; it is a great pity that in the latter case he should not have developed his idea. This branch

---

[12] James may be referring to Eliot's *Silas Marner* (1861). James was to brilliantly explore this territory himself in *What Maisie Knew* (1897). *Ed.*

of the subject is of immense importance, and Mr. Besant's few words point to consid-erations of the widest reach, not to be lightly disposed of. He will have treated the art of fiction but superficially who is not prepared to go every inch of the way that these considerations will carry him. It is for this reason that at the beginning of these re-marks I was careful to notify the reader that my reflections on so large a theme have no pretension to be exhaustive. Like Mr. Besant, I have left the question of the moral-ity of the novel till the last, and at the last I find I have used up my space. It is a ques-tion surrounded with difficulties, as witness the very first that meets us, in the form of a definite question, on the threshold. Vagueness, in such a discussion, is fatal, and what is the meaning of your morality and your conscious moral purpose? Will you not define your terms and explain how (a novel being a picture) a picture can be either moral or immoral? You wish to paint a moral picture or carve a moral statue: will you not tell us how you would set about it? We are discussing the Art of Fiction; questions of art are questions (in the widest sense) of execution; questions of morality are quite another affair, and will you not let us see how it is that you find it so easy to mix them up? These things are so clear to Mr. Besant that he has deduced from them a law which he sees embodied in English fiction, and which is "a truly admirable thing and a great cause for congratulation." It is a great cause for congratulation indeed when such thorny problems become as smooth as silk. I may add that in so far as Mr. Besant per-ceives that in point of fact English fiction has addressed itself preponderantly to these delicate questions he will appear to many people to have made a vain discovery. They will have been positively struck, on the contrary, with the moral timidity of the usual English novelist, with his (or with her) aversion to face the difficulties with which on every side the treatment of reality bristles. He is apt to be extremely shy (whereas the picture that Mr. Besant draws is a picture of boldness), and the sign of his work, for the most part, is a cautious silence on certain subjects. In the English novel (by which of course I mean the American as well), more than in any other, there is a traditional difference between that which people know and that which they agree to admit that they know, that which they see and that which they speak of, that which they feel to be a part of life and that which they allow to enter into literature. There is a great dif-ference, in short, between what they talk of in conversation and what they talk of in print. The essence of moral energy is to survey the whole field, and I should directly reverse Mr. Besant's remark and say not that the English novel has a purpose, but that it has a diffidence. To what degree a purpose in a work of art is a source of corruption I shall not attempt to inquire; the one that seems to me least dangerous is the purpose of making a perfect work. As for our novel, I may say lastly on this score that as we find it in England today it strikes me as addressed in a large degree to "young people," and that this in itself constitutes a presumption that it will be rather shy. There are cer-tain things which it is generally agreed not to discuss, not even to mention, before young people. That is very well, but the absence of discussion is not a symptom of the moral passion. The purpose of the English novel—"a truly admirable thing, and a great cause for congratulation"—strikes me therefore as rather negative.

There is one point at which the moral sense and the artistic sense lie very near together; that is in the light of the very obvious truth that the deepest quality of a work of art will always be the quality of the mind of the producer. In proportion as that intelligence is fine will the novel, the picture, the statue partake of the substance of beauty and truth. To be constituted of such elements is, to my vision, to have purpose enough. No good novel will ever proceed from a superficial mind; that seems to me an axiom which, for the artist in fiction, will cover all needful moral ground: if the youthful aspirant take it to heart it will illuminate for him many of the mysteries of "purpose." There are many other useful things that might be said to him, but I have come to the end of my article, and can only touch them as I pass. The critic in the *Pall Mall Gazette,* whom I have already quoted, draws attention to the danger, in speaking of the art of fiction, of generalizing. The danger that he has in mind is rather, I imagine, that of particularizing, for there are some comprehensive remarks which, in addition to those embodied in Mr. Besant's suggestive lecture, might without fear of misleading him be addressed to the ingenuous student. I should remind him first of the magnificence of the form that is open to him, which offers to sight so few restrictions and such innumerable opportunities. The other arts, in comparison, appear confined and hampered; the various conditions under which they are exercised are so rigid and definite. But the only condition that I can think of attaching to the composition of the novel is, as I have already said, that it be sincere. This freedom is a splendid privilege, and the first lesson of the young novelist is to learn to be worthy of it. "Enjoy it as it deserves," I should say to him; "take possession of it, explore it to its utmost extent, publish it, rejoice in it. All life belongs to you, and do not listen either to those who would shut you up into corners of it and tell you that it is only here and there that art inhabits, or to those who would persuade you that this heavenly messenger wings her way outside of life altogether, breathing a superfine air, and turning away her head from the truth of things. There is no impression of life, no manner of seeing it and feeling it, to which the plan of the novelist may not offer a place; you have only to remember that talents so dissimilar as those of Alexandre Dumas and Jane Austen, Charles Dickens and Gustave Flaubert have worked in this field with equal glory. Do not think too much about optimism and pessimism; try to catch the color of life itself. In France today we see a prodigious effort (that of Emile Zola, to whose solid and serious work no explorer of the capacity of the novel can allude without respect), we see an extraordinary effort vitiated by a spirit of pessimism on a narrow basis. M. Zola is magnificent, but he strikes an English reader as ignorant; he has an air of working in the dark; if he had as much light as energy, his results would be of the highest value. As for the aberrations of a shallow optimism, the ground (of English fiction especially) is strewn with their brittle particles as with broken glass. If you must indulge in conclusions, let them have the taste of a wide knowledge. Remember that your first duty is to be as complete as possible—to make as perfect a work. Be generous and delicate and pursue the prize."

Virginia Woolf

Virginia Woolf was born in London in 1882. Her father was Leslie Stephen, the Victorian scholar who edited the *Dictionary of National Biography*. Though she had no formal education, Woolf had in her father's library and friends resources equivalent to university training, of which she availed herself throughout childhood and adolescence. After her father's death, she moved in 1904 to Bloomsbury, the London district that houses the British Museum and National Library, where she and her sister Vanessa gathered about them the coterie of artists and intellectuals known as the "Bloomsbury Group." It included among others the economist John Maynard Keynes, historian Lytton Strachey, art critic Clive Bell (who married Vanessa), and novelist E. M. Forster. In 1912, she married the novelist and editor Leonard Woolf, with whom she founded the Hogarth Press, one of the distinguished small publishing firms of its day. Her three major novels, *Mrs. Dalloway* (1925), *To the Lighthouse* (1927), and *The Waves* (1931), are masterworks of literary modernism where plot and action become secondary to a lyrical treatment of consciousness. Her criticism appears in numerous essays, of which many of the best were collected in *The Common Reader* (1925), from which "Modern Fiction" is reprinted below. Her essay, *A Room of One's Own*, has become a central text of feminist literary criticism. Woolf had been subject to clinical depression since childhood and had had a serious psychotic break during World War I. When World War II came, she became terrified of relapsing into madness and, in March 1941, depressed after the publication of her last novel, *The Years*, she committed suicide by drowning in the Ouse River.

Modern Fiction

In making any survey, even the freest and loosest, of modern fiction it is difficult not to take it for granted that the modern practice of the art is somehow an improvement upon the old. With their simple tools and primitive materials, it might be said, Fielding did well and Jane Austen even better, but compare their opportunities with ours! Their masterpieces certainly have a strange air of simplicity. And yet the analogy between literature and the process, to choose an example, of making motor cars scarcely holds good beyond the first glance. It is doubtful whether in the course of the centuries, though we have learnt much about making machines, we have learnt anything about making literature. We do not come to write better; all that we can be said to do is to keep moving, now a little in this direction, now in that, but with a circular tendency should the whole course of the track be viewed from a sufficiently lofty pinnacle. It need scarcely be said that we make no claim to stand, even momentarily, upon that vantage ground. On the flat, in the crowd, half blind with dust, we look back with envy to those happier warriors, whose battle is won and whose achievements wear so serene an air of accomplishment that we can scarcely refrain from whispering that the fight was not so fierce for them as for us. It is for the historian of literature to decide; for him to say if we are now beginning or ending or standing in the middle of a great period of prose fiction, for down in the plain little is visible. We only know that certain gratitudes and hostilities inspire us; that certain paths seem to lead to fertile land, others to the dust and the desert; and of this perhaps it may be worth while to attempt some account.

Our quarrel, then, is not with the classics, and if we speak of quarrelling with Mr. Wells, Mr. Bennett, and Mr. Galsworthy it is partly that by the mere fact of their existence in the flesh their work has a living, breathing, every-day imperfection which bids us take what liberties with it we choose. But it is also true that, while we thank them for a thousand gifts, we reserve our unconditional gratitude for Mr. Hardy, for Mr. Conrad, and in a much lesser degree for the Mr. Hudson, of *The Purple Land, Green Mansions,* and *Far Away and Long Ago.* Mr. Wells, Mr. Bennett, and Mr. Galsworthy have excited so many hopes and disappointed them so persistently that our gratitude largely takes the form of thanking them for having shown us what they might have done but have not done; what we certainly could not do, but as certainly, perhaps, do not wish to do. No single phrase will sum up the charge or grievance which we have to bring against a mass of work so large in its volume and embodying so many qualities, both admirable and the reverse. If we tried to formulate our meaning in one word we should say that these three writers are materialists. It is because they are concerned not with the spirit but with the body that they have disappointed us, and left us with the feeling that the sooner English fiction turns its back upon them, as politely as may be, and marches, if only into the desert, the better for its soul. Naturally, no single word reaches the centre of three separate targets. In the case of Mr. Wells it falls notably wide of the mark. And yet even with him it indicates to our thinking the fatal alloy in his genius, the great clod of clay that has got itself mixed up with the purity of his inspiration. But Mr. Bennett is perhaps the worst culprit of the three, inasmuch as he is by far the best workman. He can make a book so well constructed and solid in its craftsmanship that it is difficult for the most exacting of critics to see through what chink or crevice decay can creep in. There is not so much as a draught between the frames of the windows, or a crack in the boards. And yet—if life should refuse to live there? That is a risk which the creator of *The Old Wives' Tale,* George Cannon, Edwin Clayhanger, and hosts of other figures, may well claim to have surmounted. His characters live abundantly, even unexpectedly, but it remains to ask how do they live, and what do they live for? More and more they seem to us, deserting even the well-built villa in the Five Towns, to spend their time in some softly padded first-class railway carriage, pressing bells and buttons innumerable; and the destiny to which they travel so luxuriously becomes more and more unquestionably an eternity of bliss spent in the very best hotel in Brighton. It can scarcely be said of Mr. Wells that he is a materialist in the sense that he takes too much delight in the solidity of his fabric. His mind is too generous in its sympathies to allow him to spend much time in making things shipshape and substantial. He is a materialist from sheer goodness of heart, taking upon his shoulders the work that ought to have been discharged by Government officials, and in the plethora of his ideas and facts scarcely having leisure to realise, or forgetting to think important, the crudity and coarseness of his human beings. Yet what more damaging criticism can there be both of his earth and of his Heaven than that they are to be inhabited here and here-after by his Joans and his Peters? Does not the inferiority of their natures tarnish whatever institutions and ideals may be provided for them by the generosity of their creator? Nor, profoundly though we respect the integrity and humanity of Mr. Galsworthy, shall we find what we seek in his pages.

If we fasten, then, one label on all these books, on which is one word, materialists, we mean by it that they write of unimportant things; that they spend immense skill and immense industry making the trivial and the transitory appear the true and the enduring.

We have to admit that we are exacting, and, further, that we find it difficult to justify our discontent by explaining what it is that we exact. We frame our question differently at different times. But it reappears most persistently as we drop the finished novel on the crest of a sigh—Is it worth while? What is the point of it all? Can it be that owing to one of those little deviations which the human spirit seems to make from time to time Mr. Bennett has come down with his magnificent apparatus for catching life just an inch or two on the wrong side? Life escapes; and perhaps without life nothing else is worth while. It is a confession of vagueness to have to make use of such a figure as this, but we scarcely better the matter by speaking, as critics are prone to do, of reality. Admitting the vagueness which afflicts all criticism of novels, let us hazard the opinion that for us at this moment the form of fiction most in vogue more often misses than secures the thing we seek. Whether we call it life or spirit, truth or reality, this, the essential thing, has moved off, or on, and refuses to be contained any longer in such ill-fitting vestments as we provide. Nevertheless, we go on perseveringly, conscientiously, constructing our two and thirty chapters after a design which more and more ceases to resemble the vision in our minds. So much of the enormous labour of proving the solidity, the likeness to life, of the story is not merely labour thrown away but labour misplaced to the extent of obscuring and blotting out the light of the conception. The writer seems constrained, not by his own free will but by some powerful and unscrupulous tyrant who has him in thrall to provide a plot, to provide comedy, tragedy, love, interest, and an air of probability embalming the whole so impeccable that if all his figures were to come to life they would find themselves dressed down to the last button of their coats in the fashion of the hour. The tyrant is obeyed; the novel is done to a turn. But sometimes, more and more often as time goes by, we suspect a momentary doubt, a spasm of rebellion, as the pages fill themselves in the customary way. Is life like this? Must novels be like this?

Look within and life, it seems, is very far from being "like this." Examine for a moment an ordinary mind on an ordinary day. The mind receives a myriad impressions—trivial, fantastic, evanescent, or engraved with the sharpness of steel. From all sides they come, an incessant shower of innumerable atoms; and as they fall, as they shape themselves into the life of Monday or Tuesday, the accent falls differently from of old; the moment of importance came not here but there; so that if a writer were a free man and not a slave, if he could write what he chose, not what he must, if he could base his work upon his own feeling and not upon convention, there would be no plot, no comedy, no tragedy, no love interest or catastrophe in the accepted style, and perhaps not a single button sewn on as the Bond Street tailors would have it. Life is not a series of gig lamps symmetrically arranged; but a luminous halo, a semi-transparent envelope surrounding us from the beginning of consciousness to the end. Is it not the task of the novelist to convey this varying, this unknown and uncircumscribed spirit, whatever aberration or complexity it may display, with as little mixture of the alien and external as possible? We are not pleading merely for courage and sincerity; we are suggesting that the proper stuff of fiction is a little other than custom would have us believe it.

It is, at any rate, in some such fashion as this that we seek to define the quality which distinguishes the work of several young writers, among whom Mr. James Joyce is the most notable, from that of their predecessors. They attempt to come closer to life, and to preserve more sincerely and exactly what interests and moves them, even if to do so they must discard most of the conventions which are commonly observed by the novelist. Let us record the atoms as they fall upon the mind in the order in which they fall, let us trace the pattern, however disconnected and incoherent in appearance, which each sight or incident scores upon the consciousness. Let us not take it for granted that life exists more fully in what is commonly thought big than in what is commonly thought small. Any one who has read *The Portrait of the Artist as a Young Man* or, what promises to be a far more interesting work, *Ulysses,*[1] now appearing in the *Little Review,* will have hazarded some theory of this nature as to Mr. Joyce's intention. On our part, with such a fragment before us, it is hazarded rather than affirmed; but whatever the intention of the whole there can be no question but that it is of the utmost sincerity and that the result, difficult or unpleasant as we may judge it, is undeniably important. In contrast with those whom we have called materialists Mr. Joyce is spiritual; he is concerned at all costs to reveal the flickerings of that innermost flame which flashes its messages through the brain, and in order to preserve it he disregards with complete courage whatever seems to him adventitious, whether it be probability, or coherence or any other of these signposts which for generations have served to support the imagination of a reader when called upon to imagine what he can neither touch nor see. The scene in the cemetery, for instance, with its brilliancy, its sordidity, its incoherence, its sudden lightning flashes of significance, does undoubtedly come so close to the quick of the mind that, on a first reading at any rate, it is difficult not to acclaim a masterpiece. If we want life itself here, surely we have it. Indeed, we find ourselves fumbling rather awkwardly if we try to say what else we wish, and for what reason a work of such originality yet fails to compare, for we must take high examples, with *Youth* or *The Mayor of Casterbridge*. It fails because of the comparative poverty of the writer's mind, we might say simply and have done with it. But it is possible to press a little further and wonder whether we may not refer our sense of being in a bright yet narrow room, confined and shut in, rather than enlarged and set free, to some limitation imposed by the method as well as by the mind. Is it the method that inhibits the creative power? Is it due to the method that we feel neither jovial nor magnanimous, but centered in a self which, in spite of its tremor of susceptibility, never embraces or creates what is outside itself and beyond? Does the em-

---

[1] Joyce's *Ulysses* (1922) had been appearing in installments before April 1919, when "Modern Fiction" was written. *Ed.*

phasis laid, perhaps didactically, upon indecency, contribute to the effect of something angular and isolated? Or is it merely that in any effort of such originality it is much easier, for contemporaries especially, to feel what it lacks than to name what it gives? In any case it is a mistake to stand outside examining "methods." Any method is right, every method is right, that expresses what we wish to express, if we are writers; that brings us closer to the novelist's intention if we are readers. This method has the merit of bringing us closer to what we were prepared to call life itself; did not the reading of *Ulysses* suggest how much of life is excluded or ignored, and did it not come with a shock to open *Tristram Shandy* or even *Pendennis* and be by them convinced that there are not only other aspects of life, but more important ones into the bargain.

However this may be, the problem before the novelist at present, as we suppose it to have been in the past, is to contrive means of being free to set down what he chooses. He has to have the courage to say that what interests him is no longer "this" but "that": out of "that" alone must he construct his work. For the moderns "that," the point of interest, lies very likely in the dark places of psychology. At once, therefore, the accent falls a little differently; the emphasis is upon something hitherto ignored; at once a different outline of form becomes necessary, difficult for us to grasp, incomprehensible to our predecessors. No one but a modern, perhaps no one but a Russian, would have felt the interest of the situation which Tchekov has made into the short story which he calls "Gusev." Some Russian soldiers lie ill on board a ship which is taking them back to Russia. We are given a few scraps of their talk and some of their thoughts; then one of them dies and is carried away; the talk goes on among the others for a time, until Gusev himself dies, and looking "like a carrot or a radish" is thrown overboard. The emphasis is laid upon such unexpected places that at first it seems as if there were no emphasis at all; and then, as the eyes accustom themselves to twilight and discern the shapes of things in a room we see how complete the story is, how profound, and how truly in obedience to his vision Tchekov has chosen this, that, and the other, and placed them together to compose something new. But it is impossible to say "this is comic," or "that is tragic," nor are we certain, since short stories, we have been taught, should be brief and conclusive, whether this, which is vague and inconclusive, should be called a short story at all.

The most elementary remarks upon modern English fiction can hardly avoid some mention of the Russian influence, and if the Russians are mentioned one runs the risk of feeling that to write of any fiction save theirs is waste of time. If we want understanding of the soul and heart where else shall we find it of comparable profundity? If we are sick of our own materialism the least considerable of their novelists has by right of birth a natural reverence for the human spirit. "Learn to make yourself akin to people. . . . But let this sympathy be not with the mind—for it is easy with the mind—but with the heart, with love towards them." In every great Russian writer we seem to discern the features of a saint, if sympathy for the sufferings of others, love towards them, endeavour to reach some goal worthy of the most exacting demands of the spirit constitute saintliness. It is the saint in them which confounds us with a feeling of our own irreligious triviality, and turns so many of our famous novels to tinsel and trickery. The conclusions of the Russian mind, thus comprehensive and compassionate, are inevitably, perhaps, of the utmost sadness. More accurately indeed we might speak of the inconclusiveness of the Russian mind. It is the sense that there is no answer, that if honestly examined life presents question after question which must be left to sound on and on after the story is over in hopeless interrogation that fills us with a deep, and finally it may be with a resentful, despair. They are right perhaps; unquestionably they see further than we do and without our gross impediments of vision. But perhaps we see something that escapes them, or why should this voice of protest mix itself with our gloom? The voice of protest is the voice of another and an ancient civilisation which seems to have bred in us the instinct to enjoy and fight rather than to suffer and understand. English fiction from Sterne to Meredith bears witness to our natural delight in humour and comedy, in the beauty of earth, in the activities of the intellect, and in the splendour of the body. But any deductions that we may draw from the comparison of two fictions so immeasurably far apart are futile save indeed as they flood us with a view of the infinite possibilities of the art and remind us that there is no limit to the horizon, and that nothing—no "method," no experiment, even of the wildest—is forbidden, but only falsity and pretence. "The proper stuff of fiction" does not exist; everything is the proper stuff of fiction, every feeling, every thought; every quality of brain and spirit is drawn upon; no perception comes amiss. And if we can imagine the art of fiction come alive and standing in our midst, she would undoubtedly bid us break her and bully her, as well as honour and love her, for so her youth is renewed and her sovereignty assured.

Richard Wright

Richard Wright was born on a farm near Natchez, Mississippi, in 1908, the son of a sharecropper who deserted his wife when Wright was five. Wright's mother became paralyzed in 1918, and he was raised in orphanages and by impoverished relatives. At fifteen, Wright struck out for Memphis, where he worked at unskilled jobs and as a postal clerk. During the Depression, he tramped around the country until he reached Chicago, where he became involved first with the labor movement and then the Communist Party, which he joined in 1936. A few talented poems got him onto the Federal Writers Project, which took Wright to New York, where he wrote a guide to Harlem. His first published short story, "Uncle Tom's Children," won him a major prize and a Guggenheim fellowship. This in turn enabled him to write his finest novel, *Native Son* (1940), a powerful naturalistic study that became a best seller. Like Clyde Griffiths in Dreiser's *An American Tragedy*—to which *Native Son* has been compared—Bigger Thomas kills, but is morally less guilty of murder than the society that produced him. Wright's later novels, *The Outsider* (1953) and *Savage Holiday* (1954), are not considered as forceful as his first. His stories, however, collected in *Uncle Tom's Children* (1938) and *Eight Men* (1961), are compelling, well-crafted works. Wright's autobiography, written just before he left the Party in 1946, is contained in *Black Boy* (1945). After World War II, Wright moved to France, where he wrote journalistic essays on racism and associated with the philosophers of the Left Bank. He died in Paris in 1960. "Blueprint for Negro Writing" was written in 1936 for the short-lived socialist magazine *New Challenge,* which Wright helped to edit.

Blueprint for Negro Writing

1. THE ROLE OF NEGRO WRITING: TWO DEFINITIONS

Generally speaking, Negro writing in the past has been confined to humble novels, poems, and plays, prim and decorous ambassadors who went a-begging to white America. They entered the Court of American Public Opinion dressed in the knee-pants of servility, curtsying to show that the Negro was not inferior, that he was human, and that he had a life comparable to that of other people. For the most part these artistic ambassadors were received as though they were French poodles who do clever tricks.

White America never offered these Negro writers any serious criticism. The mere fact that a Negro could write was astonishing. Nor was there any deep concern on the part of white America with the role Negro writing should play in American culture; and the role it did play grew out of accident rather than intent or design. Either it crept in through the kitchen in the form of jokes; or it was the fruits of that foul soil which was the result of a liaison between inferiority-complexed Negro "geniuses" and burntout white Bohemians with money.

On the other hand, these often technically brilliant performances by Negro writers were looked upon by the majority of literate Negroes as something to be proud of. At best, Negro writing has been something external to the lives of educated Negroes themselves. That the productions of their writers should have been something of a guide in their daily living is a matter which seems never to have been raised seriously.

Under these conditions Negro writing assumed two general aspects: (1) It became a sort of conspicuous ornamentation, the hallmark of "achievement." (2) It became the voice of the educated Negro pleading with white America for justice.

Rarely was the best of this writing addressed to the Negro himself, his needs, his sufferings, his aspirations. Through misdirection, Negro writers have been far better to others than they have been to themselves. And the mere recognition of this places the whole question of Negro writing in a new light and raises a doubt as to the validity of its present direction.

2. THE MINORITY OUTLOOK

Somewhere in his writings Lenin makes the observation that oppressed minorities often reflect the techniques of the bourgeoisie more brilliantly than some sections of the bourgeoisie themselves. The psychological importance of this becomes meaningful when it is recalled that oppressed minorities, and especially the petty bourgeois sections of oppressed minorities, strive to assimilate the virtues of the bourgeoisie in the assumption that by doing so they can lift themselves into a higher social sphere. But not only among the oppressed petty bourgeoisie does this occur. The workers of a minority people, chafing under exploitation, forge organizational forms of struggle to better their lot. Lacking the handicaps of false ambition and property, they have access to a wide social vision and a deep social consciousness. They display a greater freedom and initiative in pushing their claims upon civilization than even do the petty bourgeoisie. Their organizations show greater strength, adaptability, and efficiency than any other group or class in society.

That Negro workers, propelled by the harsh conditions of their lives, have demonstrated this consciousness and mobility for economic and political action there can be no doubt. But has this consciousness been reflected in the work of Negro writers to the same degree as it has in the Negro workers' struggle to free Herndon and the Scottsboro Boys,[1] in the drive toward unionism, in the fight against lynching? Have they as creative writers taken advantage of their unique minority position?

The answer decidedly is *no.* Negro writers have lagged sadly, and as time passes the gap widens between them and their people.

How can this hiatus be bridged? How can the enervating effects of this long-standing split be eliminated?

In presenting questions of this sort an attitude of self-consciousness and self-criticism is far more likely to be a fruitful point of departure than a mere recounting of past achievements. An emphasis upon tendency and experiment, a view of society as something becoming rather than as something fixed and admired is the one which points the way for Negro writers to stand shoulder to shoulder with Negro workers in mood and outlook.

3. A WHOLE CULTURE

There is, however, a culture of the Negro which is his and has been addressed to him; a culture which has, for good or ill, helped to clarify his consciousness and create emotional attitudes which are conducive to action. This culture has stemmed mainly from two sources: (1) the Negro church; and (2) the folklore of the Negro people.

It was through the portals of the church that the American Negro first entered the shrine of western culture. Living under slave conditions of life, bereft of his African heritage, the Negroes' struggle for religion on the plantations between 1820-60 as-

---

[1] The Scottsboro boys were nine young black men aged 12 to 19 who were tried in April 1931 for the alleged rape of two white girls in northern Alabama. After a perfunctory trial in which no lawyers were provided, all were convicted and eight of the nine sentenced to death. Nationwide protests resulted in the retrial and eventual release of all nine. A Supreme Court decision arising out of the trial, *Powell* v. *Alabama,* established the right to counsel in capital cases. In neighboring Georgia, Angelo Herndon (born 1913) led a protest march of over 1,000 unemployed blacks and whites to a county courthouse, and was tried and convicted of "attempting to incite an insurrection." The Georgia law was invalidated in 1937. *Ed.*

sumed the form of a struggle for human rights. It remained a relatively revolutionary struggle until religion began to serve as an antidote for suffering and denial. But even today there are millions of American Negroes whose only sense of a whole universe, whose only relation to society and man, and whose only guide to personal dignity comes through the archaic morphology of Christian salvation.

It was, however, in a folklore moulded out of rigorous and inhuman conditions of life that the Negro achieved his most indigenous and complete expression. Blues, spirituals, and folk tales recounted from mouth to mouth; the whispered words of a black mother to her black daughter on the ways of men, the confidential wisdom of a black father to his black son; the swapping of sex experiences on street corners from boy to boy in the deepest vernacular; work songs sung under blazing suns—all these formed the channels through which the racial wisdom flowed.

One would have thought that Negro writers in the last century of striving at expression would have continued and deepened this folk tradition, would have tried to create a more intimate and yet a more profoundly social system of artistic communication between them and their people. But the illusion that they could escape through individual achievement the harsh lot of their race swung Negro writers away from any such path. Two separate cultures sprang up: one for the Negro masses, unwritten and unrecognized; and the other for the sons and daughters of a rising Negro bourgeoisie, parasitic and mannered.

Today the question is: Shall Negro writing be for the Negro masses, moulding the lives and consciousness of those masses toward new goals, or shall it continue begging the question of the Negroes' humanity?

4. THE PROBLEM OF NATIONALISM
IN NEGRO WRITING

In stressing the difference between the role Negro writing failed to play in the lives of the Negro people, and the role it should play in the future of it is to serve its historical functions; in pointing out the fact that Negro writing has been addressed in the main to a small white audience rather than to a Negro one, it should be stated that no attempt is being made here to propagate a specious and blatant nationalism. Yet the nationalist character of the Negro people is unmistakable. Psychologically this nationalism is reflected in the whole of Negro culture, and especially in folklore.

In the absence of fixed and nourishing forms of culture, the Negro has a folklore which embodies the memories and hopes of his struggle for freedom. Not yet caught in paint or stone, and as yet but feebly depicted in the poem and novel, the Negroes' most powerful images of hope and despair still remain in the fluid state of daily speech. How many John Henrys have lived and died on the lips of these black people? How many mythical heroes in embryo have been allowed to perish for lack of husbanding by alert intelligence?

Negro folklore contains, in a measure that puts to shame more deliberate forms of Negro expression, the collective sense of Negro life in America. Let those who shy at the nationalist implications of Negro life look at this body of folklore, living and powerful, which rose out of a unified sense of a common life and a common fate. Here are those vital beginnings of a recognition of value in life as it is *lived,* a recognition that marks the emergence of a new culture in the shell of the old. And at the moment this process starts, at the moment when a people begin to realize a *meaning* in their suffering, the civilization that engenders that suffering is doomed.

The nationalist aspects of Negro life are as sharply manifest in the social institutions of Negro people as in folklore. There is a Negro church, a Negro press, a Negro social world, a Negro sporting world, a Negro business world, a Negro school system, Negro professions; in short, a Negro way of life in America. The Negro people did not ask for this, and deep down, though they express themselves through their institutions and adhere to this special way of life, they do not want it now. This special existence was forced upon them from without by lynch rope, bayonet and mob rule. They accepted these negative conditions with the inevitability of a tree which must live or perish in whatever soil it finds itself.

The few crumbs of American civilization which the Negro has got from the tables of capitalism have been through these segregated channels. Many Negro institutions are cowardly and incompetent; but they are all that the Negro has. And, in the main, any move, whether for progress or reaction, must come through these institutions for the simple reason that all other channels are closed. Negro writers who seek to mould or influence the consciousness of the Negro people must address their messages to them through the ideologies and attitudes fostered in this warping way of life.

5. THE BASIS AND MEANING OF NATIONALISM IN NEGRO WRITING

The social institutions of the Negro are imprisoned in the Jim Crow political system of the South, and this Jim Crow political system is in turn built upon a plantation-feudal economy. Hence, it can be seen that the emotional expression of group-feeling which puzzles so many whites and leads them to deplore what they call "black chauvinism" is not a morbidly inherent trait of the Negro, but rather the reflex expression of a life whose roots are imbedded deeply in Southern soil.

Negro writers must accept the nationalist implications of their lives, not in order to encourage them, but in order to change and transcend them. They must accept the concept of nationalism because, in order to transcend it, they must *possess* and *understand* it. And a nationalist spirit in Negro writing means a nationalism carrying the highest possible pitch of social consciousness. It means a nationalism that knows its origins, its limitations; that is aware of the dangers of its position; that knows its ultimate aims are unrealizable within the framework of capitalist America; a nationalism whose reason for being lies in the simple fact of self-possession and in the consciousness of the interdependence of people in modern society.

For purposes of creative expression it means that the Negro writer must realize within the area of his own personal experience those impulses which, when prefigured in terms of broad social movements, constitute the stuff of nationalism.

For Negro writers even more so than for Negro politicians, nationalism is a bewildering and vexing question, the full ramifications of which cannot be dealt with here. But among Negro workers and the Negro middle class the spirit of nationalism is rife in a hundred devious forms; and a simple literary realism which seeks to depict the lives of these people devoid of wider social connotations, devoid of the revolutionary significance of these nationalist tendencies, must of necessity do a rank injustice to the Negro people and alienate their possible allies in the struggle for freedom.

6. SOCIAL CONSCIOUSNESS AND RESPONSIBILITY

The Negro writer who seeks to function within his race as a purposeful agent has a serious responsibility. In order to do justice to his subject matter, in order to depict Negro life in all of its manifold and intricate relationships, a deep, informed, and complex consciousness is necessary; a consciousness which draws for its strength upon the fluid lore of a great people, and moulds this lore with the concepts that move and direct the forces of history today.

With the gradual decline of the moral authority of the Negro church, and with the increasing irresolution which is paralyzing Negro middle class leadership, a new role is devolving upon the Negro writer. He is being called upon to do no less than create values by which his race is to struggle, live and die.

By his ability to fuse and make articulate the experiences of men, because his writing possesses the potential cunning to steal into the inmost recesses of the human heart, because he can create the myths and symbols that inspire a faith in life, he may expect either to be consigned to oblivion, or to be recognized for the valued agent he is.

This raises the question of the personality of the writer. It means that in the lives of Negro writers must be found those materials and experiences which will create a meaningful picture of the world today. Many young writers have grown to believe that a Marxist analysis of society presents such a picture. It creates a picture which, when placed before the eyes of the writer, should unify his personality, organize his emotions, buttress him with a tense and obdurate will to change the world.

And, in turn, this changed world will dialectically change the writer. Hence, it is through a Marxist conception of reality and society that the maximum degree of freedom in thought and feeling can be gained for the Negro writer. Further, this dramatic Marxist vision, when consciously grasped, endows the writer with a sense of dignity which no other vision can give. Ultimately, it restores to the writer his lost heritage, that is, his role as a creator of the world in which he lives, and as a creator of himself.

Yet, for the Negro writer, Marxism is but the starting point. No theory of life can take the place of life. After Marxism has laid bare the skeleton of society, there remains the task of the writer to plant flesh upon those bones out of his will to live. He may, with disgust and revulsion, say *no* and depict the horrors of capitalism encroaching upon the human being. Or he may, with hope and passion, say *yes* and depict the faint stirrings of a new and emerging life. But in whatever social voice he chooses to speak, whether positive or negative, there should always be heard or *over*-heard his faith, his necessity, his judgment.

His vision need not be simple or rendered in primer-like terms; for the life of the Negro people is not simple. The presentation of their lives should be simple, yes; but all the complexity, the strangeness, the magic wonder of life that plays like a bright sheen over the most sordid existence, should be there. To borrow a phrase from the Russians, it should have a *complex simplicity*. Eliot, Stein, Joyce, Proust, Hemingway, and Anderson; Gorky, Barbusse, Nexo, and Jack London no less than the folklore of the Negro himself should form the heritage of the Negro writer. Every iota of gain in human thought and sensibility should be ready grist for his mill, no matter how far-fetched they may seem in their immediate implications.

7. THE PROBLEM OF PERSPECTIVE

What vision must Negro writers have before their eyes in order to feel the impelling necessity for an about face? What angle of vision can show them all the forces of modern society in process, all the lines of economic development converging toward a distant point of hope? Must they believe in some "ism"?

They may feel that only dupes believe in "isms"; they feel with some measure of justification that another commitment means only another disillusionment. But anyone destitute of a theory about the meaning, structure and direction of modern society is a lost victim in a world he cannot understand or control.

But even if Negro writers found themselves through some "ism," how would that influence their writing? Are they being called upon to "preach"? To be "salesmen"? To "prostitute" their writing? Must they "sully" themselves? Must they write "propaganda"?

No; it is a question of awareness, of consciousness; it is, above all, a question of perspective.

Perspective is that part of a poem, novel, or play which a writer never puts directly upon paper. It is that fixed point in intellectual space where a writer stands to view the struggles, hopes, and sufferings of his people. There are times when he may stand too close and the result is a blurred vision. Or he may stand too far away and the result is a neglect of important things.

Of all the problems faced by writers who as a whole have never allied themselves with world movements, perspective is the most difficult of achievement. At its best, perspective is a pre-conscious assumption, something which a writer takes for granted, something which he wins through his living.

A Spanish writer recently spoke of living in the heights of one's time. Surely, perspective means just *that*.

It means that a Negro writer must learn to view the life of a Negro living in New York's Harlem or Chicago's South Side with the consciousness that one-sixth of the earth surface belongs to the working class. It means that a Negro writer must create in his readers' minds a relationship between a Negro woman hoeing cotton in the South and the men who loll in swivel chairs in Wall Street and take the fruits of her toil.

Perspective for Negro writers will come when they have looked and brooded so hard and long upon the harsh lot of their race and compared it with the hopes and struggles of minority peoples everywhere that the cold facts have begun to tell them something.

8. THE PROBLEM OF THEME

This does not mean that a Negro writer's sole concern must be with rendering the social scene; but if his conception of the life of his people is broad and deep enough, if the sense of the *whole* life he is seeking is vivid and strong in him, then his writing will embrace all those social, political, and economic forms under which the life of his people is manifest.

In speaking of theme one must necessarily be general and abstract; the temperament of each writer moulds and colors the world he sees. Negro life may be approached from a thousand angles, with no limit to technical and stylistic freedom.

Negro writers spring from a family, a clan, a class, and a nation; and the social units in which they are bound have a story, a record. Sense of theme will emerge in Negro writing when Negro writers try to fix this story about some pole of meaning, remembering as they do so that in the creative process meaning proceeds *equally* as much from the contemplation of the subject matter as from the hopes and apprehensions that rage in the heart of the writer.

Reduced to its simplest and most general terms, theme for Negro writers will rise from understanding the meaning of their being transplanted from a "savage" to a "civilized" culture in all of its social, political, economic, and emotional implications. It means that Negro writers must have in their consciousness the foreshortened picture of the *whole,* nourishing culture from which they were torn in Africa, and of the long, complex (and for the most part, unconscious) struggle to regain in some form and under alien conditions of life a *whole* culture again.

It is not only this picture they must have, but also a knowledge of the social and emotional milieu that gives it tone and solidity of detail. Theme for Negro writers will emerge when they have begun to feel the meaning of the history of their race as though they in one life time had lived it themselves throughout all the long centuries.

9. AUTONOMY OF CRAFT

For the Negro writer to depict this new reality requires a greater discipline and consciousness than was necessary for the so-called Harlem school of expression. Not only is the subject matter dealt with far more meaningful and complex, but the new role of the writer is qualitatively different. The Negro writers' new position demands a sharper definition of the status of his craft, and a sharper emphasis upon its functional autonomy.

Negro writers should seek through the medium of their craft to play as meaningful a role in the affairs of men as do other professionals. But if their writing is demanded to perform the social office of other professions, then the autonomy of craft is lost and writing detrimentally fused with other interests. The limitations of the craft constitute some of its greatest virtues. If the sensory vehicle of imaginative writing is required to carry too great a load of didactic material, the artistic sense is submerged.

The relationship between reality and the artistic image is not always direct and simple. The imaginative conception of a historical period will not be a carbon copy of reality. Image and emotion possess a logic of their own. A vulgarized simplicity constitutes the greatest danger in tracing the reciprocal interplay between the writer and his environment.

Writing has its professional autonomy; it should complement other professions, but it should not supplant them or be swamped by them.

10. THE NECESSITY FOR COLLECTIVE WORK

It goes without saying that these things cannot be gained by Negro writers if their present mode of isolated writing and living continues. This isolation exists *among* Negro writers as well as *between* Negro and white writers. The Negro writers' lack of thorough integration with the American scene, their lack of a clear realization among themselves of their possible role, have bred generation after generation of embittered and defeated literati.

Barred for decades from the theater and publishing houses, Negro writers have been *made* to feel a sense of difference. So deep has this white-hot iron of exclusion been burnt into their hearts that thousands have all but lost the desire to become identified with American civilization. The Negro writers' acceptance of this enforced isolation and their attempt to justify it is but a defense-reflex of the whole special way of life which has been rammed down their throats.

This problem, by its very nature, is one which must be approached contemporaneously from *two* points of view. The ideological unity of Negro writers and the alliance of that unity with all the progressive ideas of our day is the primary prerequisite for collective work. On the shoulders of white writers and Negro writers alike rests the responsibility of ending this mistrust and isolation.

By placing cultural health above narrow sectional prejudices, liberal writers of all races can help to break the stony soil of aggrandizement out of which the stunted plants of Negro nationalism grow. And, simultaneously, Negro writers can help to weed out these choking growths of reactionary nationalism and replace them with hardier and sturdier types.

These tasks are imperative in light of the fact that we live in a time when the majority of the most basic assumptions of life can no longer be taken for granted. Tradition is no longer a guide. The world has grown huge and cold. Surely this is the moment to ask questions, to theorize, to speculate, to wonder out of what materials can a human world be built.

Each step along this unknown path should be taken with thought, care, self-consciousness, and deliberation. When Negro writers think they have arrived at something which smacks of truth, humanity, they should want to test it with others, feel it with a degree of passion and strength that will enable them to communicate it to millions who are groping like themselves.

Writers faced with such tasks can have no possible time for malice or jealousy. The conditions for the growth of each writer depend too much upon the good work of other writers. Every first rate novel, poem, or play lifts the level of consciousness higher.

Ralph Ellison

Ralph Waldo Ellison was born in Oklahoma City in 1914. He attended the Tuskegee Institute in Alabama until 1936 and then went on to New York, where he served on the Federal Writers Project and was an editor for *Negro Quarterly*. While serving in the Merchant Marine during World War II, Ellison conceived the idea for *Invisible Man* (1952), which he wrote with the aid of numerous literary fellowships and grants. This single work is the basis of Ellison's enduring reputation. It chronicles the odyssey of an intelligent but naively idealistic young African American from his Southern hometown, through his schooling at a renowned Negro college, his journey to the North, his involvement in union activities, the back-to-Africa movement, and the Communist Party, up to his moment of self-realization during a riot in Harlem. The hero's quest for identity and his continuing saga of disillusionments parallel Ellison's life, to an extent, but more important, form an epic of his race as a whole. Ellison's criticism and autobiographical essays appear in *Shadow and Act* (1964), from which the selection below is taken. Ellison served on the faculties of Columbia, Yale, the University of Chicago, and New York University. He died in New York City in 1994.

Hidden Name and Complex Fate

A Writer's Experience in the United States

In *Green Hills of Africa,* Ernest Hemingway reminds us that both Tolstoy and Stendhal had seen war, that Flaubert had seen a revolution and the Commune, that Dostoievsky had been sent to Siberia and that such experiences were important in shaping the art of these great masters. And he goes on to observe that "writers are forged in injustice as a sword is forged." He declined to describe the many personal forms which injustice may take in this chaotic world—who would be so mad as to try?—nor does he go into the personal wounds which each of these writers sustained. Now, however, thanks to his brother and sister, we do know something of the injustice in which he himself was forged, and this knowledge has been added to what we have long known of Hemingway's artistic temper.

In the end, however, it is the quality of his art which is primary. It is the art which allows the wars and revolutions which he knew, and the personal and social injustice which he suffered, to lay claims upon our attention; for it was through his art that they achieved their most enduring meaning. It is a matter of outrageous irony, perhaps, but in literature the great social clashes of history no less than the painful experience of the individual are secondary to the meaning which they take on through the skill, the talent, the imagination and personal vision of the writer who transforms them into art. Here they are reduced to more manageable proportions; here they are imbued with humane values; here, injustice and catastrophe become less important in themselves than what the writer makes of them. This is *not* true, however, of the writer's struggle with that recalcitrant angel called Art; and it was through *this* specific struggle that Ernest Hemingway became *Hemingway* (now refined to a total body of transcendent work, after forty years of being endlessly dismembered and resurrected, as it continues to be, in the styles, the themes, the sense of life and literature of countless other writers). And it was through this struggle with form that he became the master, the culture hero, whom we have come to know and admire.

It was suggested that it might be of interest if I discussed here this evening some of my notions of the writer's experience in the United States, hence I have evoked the name of Hemingway, not by way of inviting far-fetched comparisons but in order to establish a perspective, a set of assumptions from which I may speak, and in an attempt to avoid boring you by emphasizing those details of racial hardship which for some forty years now have been evoked whenever writers of my own cultural background have essayed their experience in public.

I do this *not* by way of denying totally the validity of these by now stylized recitals, for I have shared and still share many of their detailed injustices—what Negro can escape them?—but by way of suggesting that they are, at least in a discussion of a writer's experience, as *writer,* as artist, somewhat beside the point.

For we select neither our parents, our race nor our nation; these occur to us out of the love, the hate, the circumstances, the fate, of others. But we *do* become writers out of an act of will, out of an act of choice; a dim, confused and ofttimes regrettable choice, perhaps, but choice nevertheless. And what happens thereafter causes all those experiences which occurred before we began to function as writers to take on a special quality of uniqueness. If this does not happen then as far as writing goes, the experiences have been misused. If we do not make of them a value, if we do not transform them into forms and images of meaning which they did not possess before, then we have failed as artists.

Thus for a writer to insist that his personal suffering is of special interest in itself, or simply because he belongs to a particular racial or religious group, is to advance a claim for special privileges which members of his group who are not writers would be ashamed to demand. The kindest judgment one can make of this point of view is that it reveals a sad misunderstanding of the relationship between suffering and art. Thomas Mann and André Gide have told us much of this and there are critics, like Edmund Wilson, who have told of the connection between the wound and the bow.[1]

---

[1] Mann and Gide express the suffering and alienation of the artist in texts such as "Tonio Kröger" and *Lafcadio's Adventures.* Edmund Wilson's critical study *The Wound and the Bow* takes its title from the legendary Greek archer Philoctetes whose bow was invincible but whose body suffered from a suppurating wound: for Wilson, Philoctetes was a metaphor for the artist who redeems the society that rejects him. *Ed.*

As I see it, it is through the process of making artistic forms—plays, poems, novels—out of one's experience that one becomes a writer, and it is through this process, this struggle, that the writer helps give meaning to the experience of the group. And it is the process of mastering the discipline, the techniques, the fortitude, the culture, through which this is made possible that constitutes the writer's real experience as *writer*, as artist. If this sounds like an argument for the artist's withdrawal from social struggles, I would recall to you W. H. Auden's comment to the effect that:

> In our age, the mere making of a work of art is itself a political act. So long as artists exist, making what they please, and think they ought to make, even if it is not terribly good, even if it appeals to only a handful of people, they remind the Management of something managers need to be reminded of, namely, that the managed are people with faces, not anonymous members, that *Homo Laborans* is also *Homo Ludens*. . . .

Without doubt, even the most *engagé*[2] writer—and I refer to true artists, not to artists *manqués*[3]—begin their careers in play and puzzlement, in dreaming over the details of the world in which they become conscious of themselves.

Let Tar Baby, that enigmatic figure from Negro folklore, stand for the world. He leans, black and gleaming, against the wall of life utterly noncommittal under our scrutiny, our questioning, starkly unmoving before our naïve attempts at intimidation. Then we touch him playfully and before we can say *Sonny Liston!*[4] we find ourselves stuck. Our playful investigations become a labor, a fearful struggle, an *agon*.[5] Slowly we perceive that our task is to learn the proper way of freeing ourselves to develop, in other words, technique.

Sensing this, we give him our sharpest attention, we question him carefully, we struggle with more subtlety; while he, in his silent way, holds on, demanding that we perceive the necessity of calling him by his true name as the price of our freedom. It is unfortunate that he has so many, many "true names"—all spelling chaos; and in order to discover even one of these we must first come into the possession of our own names. For it is through our names that we first place ourselves in the world. Our names, being the gift of others, must be made our own.[6]

· · ·

At Tuskegee I had handled manuscripts which Prokofiev had given to Hazel Harrison, a Negro concert pianist who taught there and who had known him in Europe, and through Miss Harrison I had become aware of Prokofiev's symphonies. I had also become aware of the radical movement in politics and art, and in New York had begun reading the work of André Malraux, not only the fiction but chapters published from his *Psychology of Art*.[7] And in my search for an expression of modern sensibility in

---

[2] "Politically committed." *Ed.*

[3] "Would-be artists." *Ed.*

[4] Heavyweight boxing champion of the 1960s. *Ed.*

[5] "Tragic struggle." *Ed.*

[6] In the section omitted, Ellison discusses his name, his ancestry, and his young manhood. *Ed.*

[7] André Malraux (1901–1976), French novelist, art historian, and political leader wrote *Psychology of Art* (3 vols: 1947–1950). *Ed.*

the works of Negro writers I discovered Richard Wright. Shortly thereafter I was to meet Wright, and it was at his suggestion that I wrote both my first book review and my first short story. These were fatal suggestions.

For although I had tried my hand at poetry while at Tuskegee, it hadn't occurred to me that I might write fiction, but once he suggested it, it seemed the most natural thing to try. Fortunately for me, Wright, then on the verge of his first success, was eager to talk with a beginner and I was able to save valuable time in searching out those works in which writing was discussed as a craft. He guided me to Henry James' prefaces, to Conrad, to Joseph Warren Beach and to the letters of Dostoievsky. There were other advisers and other books involved, of course, but what is important here is that I was consciously concerned with the art of fiction, that almost from the beginning I was grappling quite consciously with the art through which I wished to realize myself. And this was not done in isolation; the Spanish Civil War was now in progress and the Depression was still on. The world was being shaken up, and through one of those odd instances which occur to young provincials in New York, I was to hear Malraux make an appeal for the Spanish Loyalists at the same party where I first heard the folk singer Leadbelly perform.[8] Wright and I were there seeking money for the magazine which he had come to New York to edit.

Art and politics; a great French novelist and a Negro folk singer; a young writer who was soon to publish *Uncle Tom's Children;* and I who had barely begun to study his craft. It is such accidents, such fortuitous meetings, which count for so much in our lives. I had never dreamed that I would be in the presence of Malraux, of whose work I became aware on my second day in Harlem when Langston Hughes suggested that I read *Man's Fate* and *Days of Wrath* before returning them to a friend of his. And it is this fortuitous circumstance which led to my selecting Malraux as a literary "ancestor," whom, unlike a relative, the artist is permitted to choose. There was in progress at the time all the agitation over the Scottsboro boys and the Herndon Case,[9] and I was aware of both. I had to be; I myself had been taken off a freight train at Decatur, Alabama, only three years before while on my way to Tuskegee. But while I joined in the agitation for their release, my main energies went into learning to write.

I began to publish enough, and not too slowly, to justify my hopes for success, and as I continued, I made a most perplexing discovery; namely, that for all his conscious concern with technique, a writer did not so much create the novel as he was created *by* the novel. That is, one did not make an arbitrary gesture when one sought to write. And when I say that the novelist is created by the novel, I mean to remind you that fictional techniques are not a mere set of objective tools, but something much more intimate: a way of feeling, of seeing, and of expressing one's sense of life. And the process of *acquiring* technique is a process of modifying one's responses, of learn-

---

[8] The "loyalists" were those favoring the Spanish Republic's Popular Front government when Fascist rebels supported by Nazi Germany attempted successfully to overthrow it during the Spanish Civil War (1936-1939). Leadbelly was the stage name of Huddie Ledbetter (1885-1949), black folk-blues singer and composer. *Ed.*

[9] See page 64, note 1. *Ed.*

ing to see and feel, to hear and observe, to evoke and evaluate the images of memory and of summoning up and directing the imagination; of learning to conceive of human values in the ways which have been established by the great writers who have developed and extended the art. And perhaps the writer's greatest freedom, as artist, lies precisely in his possession of technique; for it is through technique that he comes to possess and express the meaning of his life.

Perhaps at this point it would be useful to recapitulate the route—perhaps as mazelike as that of *Finnegans Wake*—which I have been trying to describe, that which leads from the writer's discovery of a sense of purpose, which is that of becoming a writer, and then the involvement in the passionate struggle required to master a bit of technique, and then, as this begins to take shape, the disconcerting discovery that it is *technique* which transforms the individual before he is able in turn to transform it. And in that personal transformation he discovers somethings else: he discovers that he has taken on certain obligations, that he must not embarrass his chosen form, and that in order to avoid this he must develop taste. He learns—and this is most discouraging—that he is involved with values which turn in their *own* way, and not in the way of politics, upon the central issues affecting his nation and his time. He learns that the American novel, from its first consciousness of itself as a literary form, has grappled with the meaning of the American experience; that it has been aware and has sought to define the nature of that experience by addressing itself to the specific details, the moods, the landscapes, the cityscapes, the tempo of American change. And that it has borne, at its best, the full weight of that burden of conscience and consciousness which Americans inherit as one of the results of the revolutionary circumstances of our national beginnings.

We began as a nation not through the accidents of race or religion or geography (Robert Penn Warren has dwelled on these circumstances) but when a group of men, *some* of them political philosophers, put down, upon what we now recognize as being quite sacred papers, their conception of the nation which they intended to establish on these shores. They described, as we know, the obligations of the state to the citizen, of the citizen to the state; they committed themselves to certain ideas of justice, just as they committed us to a system which would guarantee all of its citizens equality of opportunity.

I need not describe the problems which have arisen from these beginnings. I need only remind you that the contradiction between these noble ideals and the actualities of our conduct generated a guilt, an unease of spirit, from the very beginning, and that the American novel at its best has always been concerned with this basic moral predicament. During Melville's time and Twain's, it was an implicit aspect of their major themes; by the twentieth century and after the discouraging and traumatic effect of the Civil War and the Reconstruction it had gone underground, had become *understated.* Nevertheless it did not disappear completely and it is to be found operating in the work of Henry James as well as in that of Hemingway and Fitzgerald. And then (and as one who believes in the impelling moral function of the novel and who believes in the moral seriousness of the form) it pleases me no end that it comes into explicit statement again in the works of Richard Wright and William Faulkner, writers who lived close to moral and political problems which would not stay put underground.

I go into these details not to recapitulate the history of the American novel but to indicate the trend of thought which was set into motion when I began to discover the nature of that process with which I was actually involved. Whatever the opinions and decisions of critics, a novelist must arrive at his own conclusions as to the meaning and function of the form with which he is engaged, and these are, in all modesty, some of mine.

In order to orient myself I also began to learn that the American novel had long concerned itself with the puzzle of the one-and-the-many; the mystery of how each of us, despite his origin in diverse regions, with our diverse racial, cultural, religious backgrounds, speaking his own diverse idiom of the American in his own accent, is, nevertheless, American. And with this concern with the implicit pluralism of the country and with the composite nature of the ideal character called "the American," there goes a concern with gauging the health of the American promise, with depicting the extent to which it was being achieved, being made manifest in our daily conduct.

And with all of this there still remained the specific concerns of literature. Among these is the need to keep literary standards high, the necessity of exploring new possibilities of language which would allow it to retain that flexibility and fidelity to the common speech which has been its glory since Mark Twain. For me this meant learning to add to it the wonderful resources of Negro American speech and idiom and to bring into range as fully and eloquently as possible the complex reality of the American experience as it shaped and was shaped by the lives of my own people.

Notice that I stress as "fully" as possible, because I would no more strive to write great novels by leaving out the complexity of circumstances which go to make up the Negro experience and which alone go to make the obvious injustice bearable, than I would think of preparing myself to become President of the United States simply by studying Negro American history or confining myself to studying those laws affecting civil rights.

For it seems to me that one of the obligations I took on when I committed myself to the art and form of the novel was that of striving for the broadest range, the discovery and articulation of the most exalted values. And I must squeeze these from the life which I know best. (A highly truncated impression of that life I attempted to convey to you earlier.)

If all this sounds a bit heady, remember that I did not destroy that troublesome middle name of mine,[10] I only suppressed it. Sometimes it reminds me of my obligations to the man who named me.

It is our fate as human beings always to give up some good things for other good things, to throw off certain bad circumstances only to create others. Thus there is a value for the writer in trying to give as thorough a report of social reality as possible. Only by doing so may we grasp and convey the cost of change. Only by considering the broadest accumulation of data may we make choices that are based upon our own hard-earned sense of reality. Speaking from my own special area of American culture, I feel that to embrace uncritically values which are extended to us by others is to re-

---

[10] Waldo: Ellison's given names are those of the transcendentalist philosopher and poet Ralph Waldo Emerson (1803–1982).

ject the validity, even the sacredness, of our own experience. It is also to forget that the small share of reality which each of our diverse groups is able to snatch from the whirling chaos of history belongs not to the group alone, but to all of us. It is a property and a witness which can be ignored only to the danger of the entire nation.

I could suppress the name of my namesake out of respect for the achievements of its original bearer but I cannot escape the obligation of attempting to achieve some of the things which he asked of the American writer. As Henry James suggested, being an American is an arduous task, and for most of us, I suspect, the difficulty begins with the name.

John Barth

John Barth was born in Cambridge, Maryland, in 1930. He was educated at Johns Hopkins University, where, following other academic positions at Penn State and State University of New York at Buffalo, he is now Professor of English and Creative Writing. Barth's novels have always had a philosophical bent: His first two, *The Floating Opera* (1956) and *The End of the Road* (1958), used realistic seriocomic situations—a Baltimore attorney contemplating suicide amid ludicrous distractions, an academic sexual triangle—in order to explore the antinomies of existentialism, logical positivism, and philosophic pragmatism. His funniest novel, *The Sot-Weed Factor* (1960), used a pastiche of various seventeenth- and eighteenth-century narrative styles to explore the cultural narrative of the early colonies, particularly Barth's native Maryland. From the mid-sixties on, Barth took the turn toward postmodern narrative already implicit in his early work: starting with *Giles Goat-Boy* (1966) and continuing through is latest novel, *Once Upon a Time* (1994), his work has explored the metaphysics of fictionality itself, and the bewildering and paradoxical ways in which fiction mirrors and is mirrored by life. It was around the beginning of Barth's swerve into postmodernism that he expounded and defended this style system in "The Literature of Exhaustion," which appeared in *Atlantic* in 1967.

The Literature of Exhaustion

I want to discuss three things more or less together: first, some old questions raised by the new intermedia arts; second, some aspects of the Argentine writer Jorge Luis Borges,[1] whom I greatly admire; third, some professional concerns of my own, related

---

[1] Jorge Luis Borges (1899-1966) was an Argentine short story writer and poet. *Ed.*

to these other matters and having to do with what I'm calling "the literature of exhausted possibility"—or, more chicly, "the literature of exhaustion."

By "exhaustion" I don't mean anything so tired as the subject of physical, moral, or intellectual decadence, only the used-upness of certain forms or exhaustion of certain possibilities—by no means necessarily a cause for despair. That a great many Western artists for a great many years have quarreled with received definitions of artistic media, genres, and forms goes without saying: pop art, dramatic and musical "happenings," the whole range of "intermedia" or "mixed-means" art, bear recentest witness to the tradition of rebelling against Tradition. A catalogue I received some time ago in the mail, for example, advertises such items as Robert Filiou's *Ample Food for Stupid Thought,* a box full of postcards on which are inscribed "apparently meaningless questions," to be mailed to whomever the purchaser judges them suited for; Ray Johnston's *Paper Snake,* a collection of whimsical writings, "often pointed," once mailed to various friends (what the catalogue describes as The New York Correspondence School of Literature); and Daniel Spoerri's *Anecdoted Typography of Chance,* "on the surface" a description of all the objects that happen to be on the author's parlor table—"in fact, however . . . a cosmology of Spoerri's existence."

"On the surface," at least, the document listing these items is a catalogue of The Something Else Press, a swinging outfit. "In fact, however," it may be one of their offerings, for all I know: The New York Direct-Mail Advertising School of Literature. In any case, their wares are lively to read about, and make for interesting conversation in fiction-writing classes, for example, where we discuss Somebody-or-other's unbound, unpaginated, randomly assembled novel-in-a-box and the desirability of printing *Finnegans Wake* on a very long roller-towel. It's easier and sociabler to talk technique than it is to make art, and the area of "happenings" and their kin is mainly a way of discussing aesthetics, really; illustrating "dramatically" more or less valid and interesting points about the nature of art and the definition of its terms and genres.

One conspicuous thing, for example, about the "intermedia" arts is their tendency (noted even by *Life* magazine) to eliminate not only the traditional audience—"those who apprehend the artist's art" (in "happenings" the audience is often the "cast," as in "environments," and some of the new music isn't intended to be performed at all)—but also the most traditional notion of the artist: the Aristotelian conscious agent who achieves with technique and cunning the artistic effect; in other words, one endowed with uncommon talent, who has moreover developed and disciplined that endowment into virtuosity. It's an aristocratic notion on the face of it, which the democratic West seems eager to have done with; not only the "omniscient" author of older fiction, but the very idea of the controlling artist, has been condemned as politically reactionary, even fascist.

Now, personally, being of the temper that chooses to "rebel along traditional lines," I'm inclined to prefer the kind of art that not many people can *do:* the kind that requires expertise and artistry as well as bright aesthetic ideas and/or inspiration. I enjoy the pop art in the famous Albright-Knox connection, a few blocks from my house in Buffalo, like a lively conversation for the most part, but was on the whole more impressed by the jugglers and acrobats at Baltimore's old Hippodrome, where I used to go every time they changed shows: genuine *virtuosi* doing things that anyone can dream up and discuss but almost no one can do.

I suppose the distinction is between things worth remarking—preferably over beer, if one's of my generation—and things worth doing. "Somebody ought to make a novel with scenes that pop up, like the old children's books," one says with the implication that one isn't going to bother doing it oneself.

However, art and its forms and techniques live in history and certainly do change. I sympathize with a remark attributed to Saul Bellow, that to be technically up to date is the least important attribute of a writer, though I would have to add that this least important attribute may be nevertheless essential. In any case, to be technically *out* of date is likely to be a genuine defect: Beethoven's Sixth Symphony or the Chartres Cathedral if executed today would be merely embarrassing. A good many current novelists write turn-of-the-century-type novels, only in more or less mid-twentieth-century language and about contemporary people and topics; this makes them considerably less interesting (to me) than excellent writers who are also technically contemporary: Joyce and Kafka, for instance, in their time, and in ours, Samuel Beckett and Jorge Luis Borges. The intermedia arts, I'd say, tend to be intermediary too, between the traditional realms of aesthetics on the one hand and artistic creation on the other; I think the wise artist and civilian will regard them with quite the kind and degree of seriousness with which he regards good shoptalk: he'll listen carefully, if noncommittally, and keep an eye on his intermedia colleagues, if only the corner of his eye. They may very possibly suggest something usable in the making or understanding of genuine works of contemporary art.

The man I want to discuss a little here, Jorge Luis Borges, illustrates well the difference between a technically old-fashioned artist, a technically up-to-date civilian, and a technically up-to-date artist. In the first category I'd locate all those novelists who for better or worse write not as if the twentieth century didn't exist, but as if the great writers of the last sixty years or so hadn't existed (*nota bene* that our century's more than two-thirds done; it's dismaying to see so many of our writers following Dostoevsky or Tolstoy or Flaubert or Balzac, when the real technical question seems to me to be how to succeed not even Joyce and Kafka, but those who've *succeeded* Joyce and Kafka and are now in the evenings of their own careers). In the second category are such folk as an artist-neighbor of mine in Buffalo who fashions dead Winnies-the-Pooh in sometimes monumental scale out of oilcloth stuffed with sand and impaled on stakes or hung by the neck. In the third belong the few people whose artistic thinking is as hip as any French new-novelist's,[2] but who manage nonetheless to speak eloquently and memorably to our still-human hearts and conditions, as the great artists have always done. Of these, two of the finest living specimens that I know of are Beckett and Borges, just about the only contemporaries of my reading acquaintance mentionable

---

[2] The "new novel" or nouveau roman (so-called because of Alain Robbe-Grillet's 1963 manifesto, *Pour un nouveau roman*) was postmodern fiction pioneered by Michel Butor, Nathalie Sarraute, Robbe-Grillet himself, and others. *Ed.*

with the "old masters" of twentieth-century fiction. In the unexciting history of literary awards, the 1961 International Publishers' Prize, shared by Beckett and Borges, is a happy exception indeed.

One of the modern things about these two is that in an age of ultimacies and "final solutions"—at least *felt* ultimacies, in everything from weaponry to theology, the celebrated dehumanization of society, and the history of the novel—their work in separate ways reflects and deals with ultimacy, both technically and thematically, as, for example, *Finnegans Wake* does in its different manner. One notices, by the way, for whatever its symptomatic worth, that Joyce was virtually blind at the end, Borges is literally so, and Beckett has become virtually mute, musewise, having progressed from marvelously constructed English sentences through terser and terser French ones to the unsyntactical, unpunctuated prose of *Comment C'est* and "ultimately" to wordless mimes. One might extrapolate a theoretical course for Beckett: language, after all, consists of silence as well as sound, and the mime is still communication—"that nineteenth-century idea," a Yale student once snarled at me—but by the language of action. But the language of action consists of rest as well as movement, and so in the context of Beckett's progress immobile, silent figures still aren't altogether ultimate. How about an empty, silent stage, then, or blank pages[3]—a "happening" where nothing happens, like Cage's *4' 33"* performed in an empty hall?[4] But dramatic communication consists of the absence as well as the presence of the actors; "we have our exits and our entrances"; and so even that would be imperfectly ultimate in Beckett's case. Nothing at all, then, I suppose: but Nothingness is necessarily and inextricably the background against which Being et cetera; for Beckett, at this point in his career, to cease to create altogether would be fairly meaningful: his crowning work, his "last word." What a convenient corner to paint yourself into! "And now I shall finish," the valet Arsene says in *Watt*, "and you will hear my voice no more." Only the silence *Molloy* speaks of, "of which the universe is made."

After which, I add on behalf of the rest of us, it might be conceivable to rediscover validly the artifices of language and literature—such far-out notions as grammar, punctuation . . . even characterization! Even *plot!*—if one goes about it the right way, aware of what one's predecessors have been up to.

Now J. L. Borges is perfectly aware of all these things. Back in the great decades of literary experimentalism he was associated with *Prisma,* a "muralist" magazine that published its pages on walls and billboards; his later *Labyrinths and Ficciones* not only anticipate the farthest-out ideas of The Something-Else Press crowd—not a difficult thing to do—but being marvelous works of art as well, illustrate in a simple way the difference between the *fact* of aesthetic ultimacies and their artistic *use.* What it comes to is that an artist doesn't merely exemplify an ultimacy; he employs it.

Consider Borges' story "Pierre Menard, Author of the *Quixote*": the hero, an utterly sophisticated turn-of-the-century French Symbolist, by an astounding effort of

---

[3] An ultimacy already attained in the nineteenth century for that *avant-gardiste* of East Aurora, New York, Elbert Hubbard, in his *Essay on Silence. Au.*

[4] The avant-garde composition of John Cage (1912–1992), *4'33"* (1952), consisted of four minutes and 33 seconds of silence. *Ed.*

imagination, produces—not *copies* or *imitates,* mind, but *composes*—several chapters of Cervantes' novel.

> It is a revelation [Borges' narrator tells us] to compare Menard's *Don Quixote* with Cervantes'. The latter, for example, wrote (part one, chapter nine):
>
>> . . . truth, whose mother is history, rival of time, depository of deeds, witness of the past, exemplar and adviser to the present, the future's counselor.
>
> Written in the seventeenth century, written by the "lay genius" Cervantes, this enumeration is a mere rhetorical praise of history. Menard, on the other hand, writes:
>
>> . . . truth, whose mother is history, rival of time, depository of deeds, witness of the past, exemplar and adviser to the present, the future's counselor.
>
> History, the *mother* of truth: the idea is astounding. Menard, a contemporary of William James, does not define history as an inquiry into reality but as its origin. . . .

Et cetera. Now, this is an interesting idea, of considerable intellectual validity. I mentioned earlier that if Beethoven's Sixth were composed today, it would be an embarrassment; but clearly it wouldn't be, necessarily, if done with ironic intent by a composer quite aware of where we've been and where we are. It would have then potentially, for better or worse, the kind of significance of Warhol's Campbell's Soup ads, the difference being that in the former case a work of art is being reproduced instead of a work of non-art, and the ironic comment would therefore be more directly on the genre and history of the art than on the state of the culture. In fact, of course, to make the valid intellectual point one needn't even recompose the Sixth Symphony, any more than Menard really needed to re-create the *Quixote*. It would've been sufficient for Menard to have *attributed* the novel to himself in order to have a new work of art, from the intellectual point of view. Indeed, in several stories Borges plays with this very idea, and I can readily imagine Beckett's next novel, for example, as *Tom Jones,* just as Nabokov's last was that multivolume annotated translation of Pushkin. I myself have always aspired to write Burton's version of *The 1001 Nights,* complete with appendices and the like, in twelve volumes, and for intellectual purposes I needn't even write it. What evenings we might spend (over beer) discussing Saarinen's Parthenon, D. H. Lawrence's *Wuthering Heights,* or the Johnson Administration by Robert Rauschenberg!

The idea, I say, is intellectually serious, as are Borges' other characteristic ideas, most of a metaphysical rather than an aesthetic nature. But the important thing to observe is that Borges *doesn't* attribute the *Quixote* to himself, much less recompose it like Pierre Menard; instead, he writes a remarkable and original work of literature, the implicit theme of which is the difficulty, perhaps the unnecessity, of writing original works of literature. His artistic victory, if you like, is that he confronts an intellectual dead end and employs it against itself to accomplish new human work. If this corresponds to what mystics do—"every moment leaping into the infinite," Kierkegaard says, "and every moment falling surely back into the finite"—it's only one more aspect of that old analogy. In homelier terms, it's a matter of every moment throwing out the bath water without for a moment losing the baby.

Another way of describing Borges' accomplishment is in a pair of his own favorite terms, *algebra and fire.* In his most often anthologized story, "Tlön, Uqbar, Orbis Tertius," he imagines an entirely hypothetical world, the invention of a secret society of scholars who elaborate its every aspect in a surreptitious encyclopedia. This *First Encyclopaedia of Tlön* (what fictionist would not wish to have dreamed up the *Britannica?*) describes a coherent alternative to this world complete in every respect from its algebra to its fire, Borges tells us, and of such imaginative power that, once conceived, it begins to obtrude itself into and eventually to supplant our prior reality. My point is that neither the algebra nor the fire, metaphorically speaking, could achieve this result without the other. Borges' algebra is what I'm considering here—algebra is easier to talk about than fire—but any intellectual giant could equal it. The imaginary authors of the *First Encyclopaedia of Tlön* itself are not artists, though their work is in a manner of speaking fictional and would find a ready publisher in New York nowadays. The author of the story "Tlön, Uqbar, Orbis Tertius," who merely *alludes* to the fascinating *Encyclopaedia,* is an artist; what makes him one of the first rank, like Kafka, is the combination of that intellectually profound vision with great human insight, poetic power, and consummate mastery of his means, a definition which would have gone without saying, I suppose, in any century but ours.

Not long ago, incidentally, in a footnote to a scholarly edition of Sir Thomas Browne (*The Urn Burial,* I believe it was), I came upon a perfect Borges datum, reminiscent of Tlön's self-realization: the actual case of a book called *The Three Impostors,* alluded to in Browne's *Religio Medici* among other places. *The Three Impostors* is a non-existent blasphemous treatise against Moses, Christ, and Mohammed, which in the seventeenth century was widely held to exist, or to have once existed. Commentators attributed it variously to Boccaccio, Pietro Aretino, Giordano Bruno, and Tommaso Campanella,[5] and though no one, Browne included, had ever seen a copy of it, it was frequently cited, refuted, railed against, and generally discussed as if everyone had read it—until, sure enough, in the *eighteenth* century a spurious work appeared with a forged date of 1598 and the title *De Tribus Impostoribus.* It's a wonder that Borges doesn't mention this work, as he seems to have read absolutely everything, including all the books that don't exist, and Browne is a particular favorite of his. In fact, the narrator of "Tlön, Uqbar, Orbis Tertius" declares at the end:

---

[5] Giovanni Boccaccio (1313-1975), Florentine poet and scholar; Pietro Aretino (1492-1556), Florentine poet and satirist; Tommaso Campanella (1568-1639), Neapolitan poet and philosopher; and Giordano Bruno (1548-1600), Italian scientist burned at the stake for supporting the Copernican "heresy." Sir Thomas Browne (1605-1682) was an English physician and philosophical essayist best known for his *Religio Medici* (1642). *Ed.*

. . . English and French and mere Spanish will disappear from the globe. The world will be Tlön. I pay no attention to all this and go on revising, in the still days at the Adrogué hotel, an uncertain Quevedian translation (which I do not intend to publish) of Browne's *Urn Burial.*[6]

This "contamination of reality by dream," as Borges calls it, is one of his pet themes, and commenting upon such contaminations is one of his favorite fictional devices. Like many of the best such devices, it turns the artist's mode or form into a metaphor for his concerns, as does the diary-ending of *Portrait of the Artist As a Young Man* or the cyclical construction of *Finnegans Wake.* In Borges' case, the story "Tlön," etc., for example, is a real piece of imagined reality in our world, analogous to those Tlönian artifacts called *hrönir,* which imagine themselves into existence. In short, it's a paradigm of or metaphor for itself; not just the *form* of the story but the *fact* of the story is symbolic; "the medium is the message."

Moreover, like all of Borges' work, it illustrates in other of its aspects my subject: how an artist may paradoxically turn the felt ultimacies of our time into material and means for his work—*paradoxically* because by doing so he transcends what had appeared to be his refutation, in the same way that the mystic who transcends finitude is said to be enabled to live, spiritually and physically, in the finite world. Suppose you're a writer by vocation—a "print-oriented bastard," as the McLuhanites call us[7]— and you feel, for example, that the novel, if not narrative literature generally, if not the printed word altogether, has by this hour of the world just abut shot its bolt, as Leslie Fiedler and others maintain. (I'm inclined to agree, with reservations and hedges. Literary forms certainly have histories and historical contingencies, and it may well be that the novel's time as a major art form is up, as the "times" of classical tragedy, grand opera, or the sonnet sequence came to be. No necessary cause for alarm in this at all, except perhaps to certain novelists, and one way to handle such a feeling might be to write a novel about it. Whether historically the novel expires or persists seems immaterial to me; if enough writers and critics *feel* apocalyptical about it, their feeling becomes a considerable cultural fact, like the *feeling* that Western civilization, or the world, is going to end rather soon. If you took a bunch of people out into the desert and the world didn't end, you'd come home shamefaced, I imagine; but the persistence of an art form doesn't invalidate work created in the comparable apocalyptic ambience. That's one of the fringe benefits of being an artist instead of a prophet. There are others.) If you happened to be Vladimir Nabokov you might address that felt ultimacy by writing *Pale Fire:* a fine novel by a learned pedant, in the form of a pedantic commentary on a poem invented for the purpose. If you were Borges you might write

---

[6] Moreover, on rereading "Tlön," etc., I find now a remark I'd swear wasn't in it last year: that the eccentric American millionaire who endows the *Encyclopaedia* does so on condition that "the work will make no pact with the impostor Jesus Christ." *Au.*

[7] Marshall McLuhan (1911–1980), Canadian academic best known for *Understanding Media* (1964), which theorized about how mass media, such as television, and equipment, such as computers, change the face of Western culture. *Ed.*

Labyrinths: fictions by a learned librarian in the form of footnotes, as he describes them, to imaginary or hypothetical books.[8] And I'll add, since I believe Borges' idea is rather more interesting, that if you were the author of this paper, you'd have written something like *The Sot-Weed Factor* or *Giles Goat-Boy:* novels which imitate the form of the Novel, by an author who imitates the role of Author.

If this sort of thing sounds unpleasantly decadent, nevertheless it's about where the genre began, with *Quixote* imitating *Amadis of Gaul,* Cervantes pretending to be the Cid Hamete Benengeli (and Alonso Quijano pretending to be Don Quixote), or Fielding parodying Richardson. "History repeats itself as farce"—meaning, of course, in the form or mode of farce, not that history is farcical. The imitation (like the Dadaist echoes in the work of the "intermedia" types) is something new and *may be* quite serious and passionate despite its farcical aspect. This is the important difference between a proper novel and a deliberate imitation of a novel, or a novel imitative of other sorts of documents. The first attempts (has been historically inclined to attempt) to imitate actions more or less directly, and its conventional devices—cause and effect, linear anecdote, characterization, authorial selection, arrangement, and interpretation—can be and have long since been objected to as obsolete notions, or metaphors for obsolete notions: Robbe-Grillet's essays *For a New Novel* come to mind. There are replies to these objections, not to the point here, but one can see that in any case they're obviated by imitations-of-novels, which attempt to represent not life directly but a representation of life. In fact such works are no more removed from "life" than Richardson's or Goethe's epistolary novels are: both imitate "real" documents, and the subject of both, ultimately, is life, not the documents. A novel is as much a piece of the real world as a letter, and the letters in *The Sorrows of Young Werther* are, after all, fictitious.

One might imaginably compound this imitation, and though Borges doesn't, he's fascinated with the idea: one of his frequenter literary allusions is to the 602nd night of *The 1001 Nights,* when, owing to a copyist's error, Scheherezade begins to tell the King the story of the 1001 nights, from the beginning. Happily, the King interrupts; if he didn't there'd be no 603rd night ever, and while this would solve Scheherezade's problem—which is every storyteller's problem: to publish or perish—it would put the "outside" author in a bind. (I suspect that Borges dreamed this whole thing up: the business he mentions isn't in any edition of *The 1001 Nights* I've been able to consult. Not *yet,* anyhow: after reading "Tlön, Uqbar," etc., one is inclined to recheck every semester or so.)

Now Borges (whom someone once vexedly accused *me* of inventing) is interested in the 602nd Night because it's an instance of the story-within-the-story turned back upon itself, and his interest in such instances is threefold: first, as he himself declares, they disturb us metaphysically: when the characters in a work of fiction become readers or authors of the fiction they're in, we're reminded of the fictitious as-

---

[8] Borges was born in Argentina in 1899, educated in Europe, and for some years worked as director of the National Library in Buenos Aires, except for a period when Juan Perón demoted him to the rank of provincial chicken inspector as a political humiliation. Currently he's the *Beowulf*-man at the University of Buenos Aires. *Au.*

pect of our own existence, one of Borges' cardinal themes, as it was of Shakespeare, Calderón, Unamuno, and other folk. Second, the 602nd Night is a literary illustration of the *regressus in infinitum,*[9] as are almost all of Borges' principal images and motifs. Third, Scheherezade's accidental gambit, like Borges' other versions of the *regressus in infinitum*, is an image of the exhaustion, or attempted exhaustion, of possibilities—in this case literary possibilities—and so we return to our main subject.

What makes Borges' stance, if you like, more interesting to me than, say, Nabokov's or Beckett's, is the premise with which he approaches literature; in the words of one of his editors: "For [Borges] no one has claim to originality in literature; all writers are more or less faithful amanuenses of the spirit, translators and annotators of pre-existing archetypes." Thus his inclination to write brief comments on imaginary books: for one to attempt to add overtly to the sum of "original" literature by even so much as a conventional short story, not to mention a novel, would be too presumptuous, too naïve; literature has been done long since. A librarian's point of view! And it would itself be too presumptuous if it weren't part of a lively, passionately relevant metaphysical vision, and slyly employed against itself precisely to make new and original literature. Borges defines the Baroque as "that style which deliberately exhausts (or tries to exhaust) its possibilities and borders upon its own caricature." While his own work is *not* Baroque, except intellectually (the Baroque was never so terse, laconic, economical), it suggests the view that intellectual and literary history has been Baroque, and has pretty well exhausted the possibilities of novelty. His *ficciones* are not only footnotes to imaginary texts, but postscripts to the real corpus of literature.

This premise gives resonance and relation to all his principal images. The facing mirrors that recut in his stories are a dual *regressus*. The doubles that his characters, like Nabokov's, run afoul of suggest dizzying multiples and remind one of Browne's remark that "every man is not only himself . . . men are lived over again." (It would please Borges, and illustrate Browne's point, to call Browne a precursor of Borges. "Every writer," Borges says in his essay on Kafka, "creates his own precursors.") Borges' favorite third-century heretical sect is the Histriones—I think and hope he invented them—who believe that repetition is impossible in history and therefore live viciously in order to purge the future of the vices they commit: in other words, to exhaust the possibilities of the world in order to bring its end nearer.

The writer he most often mentions, after Cervantes, is Shakespeare; in one piece he imagines the playwright on his deathbed asking God to permit him to be one and himself, having been everyone and no one; God replies from the whirlwind that He is no one either; He has dreamed the world like Shakespeare, and including Shakespeare. Homer's story in Book IV of the *Odyssey,* of Menelaus on the beach at Pharos, tackling Proteus, appeals profoundly to Borges: Proteus is he who "exhausts the guides of reality" while Menelaus—who, one recalls, disguised his own identity in order to ambush him—holds fast. Zeno's paradox of Achilles and the Tortoise embodies a *regressus in infinitum* which Borges carries through philosophical history, pointing out that

---

[9] "Infinite regress"; usually pictorial, as in the Quaker Oats box on which a Quaker holds a smaller Quaker Oats box on which a Quaker holds a still smaller Quaker Oats box. . . . *Ed.*

Aristotle uses it to refute Plato's theory of forms, Hume to refute the possibility of cause and effect, Lewis Carroll to refute syllogistic deduction, William James to refute the notion of temporal passage, and Bradley to refute the general possibility of logical relations; Borges himself uses it, citing Schopenhauer, as evidence that the world is our dream, our idea, in which "tenuous and eternal crevices of unreason" can be found to remind us that our creation is false, or at least fictive.

The infinite library of one of his most popular stories is an image particularly pertinent to the literature of exhaustion; the "Library of Babel" houses every possible combination of alphabetical characters and spaces, and thus every possible book and statement, including your and my refutations and vindications, the history of the actual future, the history of every possible future, and, though he doesn't mention it, the encyclopedias not only of Tlön but of every imaginable other world—since, as in Lucretius' universe, the number of elements, and so of combinations, is finite (though very large), and the number of instances of each element and combination of elements is infinite, like the library itself.

That brings us to his favorite image of all, the labyrinth, and to my point. *Labyrinths* is the name of his most substantial translated volume, and the only full-length study of Borges in English, by Ana María Barrenechea, is called *Borges the Labyrinth-Maker.* A labyrinth, after all, is a place in which, ideally, all the possibilities of choice (of direction, in this case) are embodied, and—barring special dispensation like Theseus'—must be exhausted before one reaches the heart. Where, mind, the Minotaur waits with two final possibilities: defeat and death, or victory and freedom. Now, in fact, the legendary Theseus is non-Baroque; thanks to Ariadne's thread he can take a shortcut through the labyrinth at Knossos. But Menelaus on the beach at Pharos, for example, is genuinely Baroque in the Borgesian spirit, and illustrates a positive artistic morality in the literature of exhaustion. He is not there, after all, for kicks (any more than Borges and Beckett are in the fiction racket for their health): Menelaus is *lost,* in the larger labyrinth of the world, and has got to hold fast while the Old Man of the Sea exhausts reality's frightening guises so that he may extort direction from him when Proteus returns to his "true" self. It's a heroic enterprise, with salvation as its object—one recalls that the aim of the Histriones is to get history done with so that Jesus may come again the sooner, and that Shakespeare's heroic metamorphoses culminate not merely in a theophany but in an apotheosis.

Now, not just any old body is equipped for this labor, and Theseus in the Cretan labyrinth becomes in the end the aptest image for Borges after all. Distressing as the fact is to us liberal Democrats, the commonality, alas, will *always* lose their way and their souls: it's the chosen remnant, the virtuoso, the Thesean *hero,* who, confronted with Baroque reality, Baroque history, the Baroque state of his art, need *not* rehearse its possibilities to exhaustion, any more than Borges needs actually to *write* the *Encyclopaedia of Tlön* or the books in the Library of Babel. He need only be aware of their existence or possibility, acknowledge them, and with the aid of *very special* gifts—as extraordinary as saint- or hero-hood and not likely to be found in The New York Correspondence School of Literature—go straight through the maze to the accomplishment of his work.

Milan Kundera

Milan Kundera was born in 1929 at Brno in what is now the Czech Republic, the son of a concert pianist. He was educated at the Academy of Music and Dramatic Arts in Prague, where he studied film until 1956. He also taught film at the Academy until 1970. Kundera began his literary career with three volumes of poetry and several plays, which received numerous awards. His first novel, *The Joke,* was published in 1967, around the end of the "Prague Spring," the renaissance in Czech literature and film that briefly blossomed in response to the short-lived Dubček regime. After the 1968 invasion of Czechoslovakia by the USSR, a new highly repressive regime came to power. Kundera was fired from his teaching job and his books and plays were banned. He continued writing in Czech, then smuggled his work out of the country to be translated into French and English. This, at least, is how he published *Life Is Elsewhere, The Farewell Party,* and the stories of *Laughable Loves.* In 1975, Kundera managed to emigrate to France, where he lives in Paris and teaches at the University of Rennes. His works since then have included *The Book of Laughter and Forgetting, The Incredible Lightness of Being, Immortality,* and the literary criticism in *The Art of the Novel,* from which the following selection is taken.

The Depreciated Legacy of Cervantes

3.

As God slowly departed from the seat whence he had directed the universe and its order of values, distinguished good from evil, and endowed each thing with meaning, Don Quixote set forth from his house into a world he could no longer recognize. In the absence of the Supreme Judge, the world suddenly appeared in its fearsome ambiguity; the single divine Truth decomposed into myriad relative truths parceled out by men. Thus was born the world of the Modern Era, and with it the novel, the image and model of that world.

To take, with Descartes, the *thinking self* as the basis of everything, and thus to face the universe alone, is to adopt an attitude that Hegel was right to call heroic.

To take, with Cervantes, the world as ambiguity, to be obliged to face not a single absolute truth but a welter of contradictory truths (truths embodied in *imaginary selves* called characters), to have as one's only certainty the *wisdom of uncertainty,* requires no less courage.

What does Cervantes' great novel mean? Much has been written on the question. Some see in it a rationalist critique of Don Quixote's hazy idealism. Others see it as a celebration of that same idealism. Both interpretations are mistaken because they both seek at the novel's core not an inquiry but a moral position.

Man desires a world where good and evil can be clearly distinguished, for he has an innate and irrepressible desire to judge before he understands. Religions and ideologies are founded on this desire. They can cope with the novel only by translating its language of relativity and ambiguity into their own apodictic and dogmatic discourse. They require that someone be right: either Anna Karenina is the victim of a narrow-minded tyrant, or Karenin is the victim of an immoral woman; either K. is an innocent man crushed by an unjust Court, or the Court represents divine justice and K. is guilty.

The "either-or" encapsulates an inability to tolerate the essential relativity of things human, an inability to look squarely at the absence of the Supreme Judge. This inability makes the novel's wisdom (the wisdom of uncertainty) hard to accept and understand.

4.

Don Quixote set off into a world that opened wide before him. He could go out freely and come home as he pleased. The early European novels are journeys through an apparently unlimited world. The opening of *Jacques le Fataliste*[1] comes upon the two heroes in mid-journey; we don't know where they've come from or where they're going. They exist in a time without beginning or end, in a space without frontiers, in the midst of a Europe whose future will never end.

Half a century after Diderot, in Balzac, the distant horizon has disappeared like a landscape behind those modern structures, the social institutions: the police, the law, the world of money and crime, the army, the State. In Balzac's world, time no longer idles happily by as it does for Cervantes and Diderot. It has set forth on the train called History. The train is easy to board, hard to leave. But it isn't at all fearsome yet, it even has its appeal; it promises adventure to every passenger, and with it fame and fortune.

Later still, for Emma Bovary, the horizon shrinks to the point of seeming a barrier. Adventure lies beyond it, and the longing becomes intolerable. Within the monotony of the quotidian, dreams and daydreams take on importance. The lost infinity of the outside world is replaced by the infinity of the soul. The great illusion of the irreplaceable uniqueness of the individual—one of Europe's finest illusions—blossoms forth.

But the dream of the soul's infinity loses its magic when History (or what remains of it: the suprahuman force of an omnipotent society) takes hold of man. History no longer promises him fame and fortune; it barely promises him a land-surveyor's job. In the face of the Court or the Castle, what can K. do?[2] Not much. Can't he at least dream as Emma Bovary used to do? No, the situation's trap is too terrible, and like a

---

[1] Novel, written 1773 and published posthumously in 1796, by French philosopher and encyclopedist Denis Diderot (1713-1784). *Ed.*

[2] A protagonist called only "K." confronts the apparent arbitrary dictates of a legalistic Court (in *The Trial,* 1925) and an aristocratic Castle (in *The Castle,* 1926), both by Czech novelist Franz Kafka (1883-1924). *Ed.*

vacuum cleaner it sucks up all his thoughts and feelings: all he can think of is his trial, his surveying job. The infinity of the soul—if it ever existed—has become a nearly useless appendage.

5.

The path of the novel emerges as a parallel history of the Modern Era. As I look back over it, it seems strangely short and limited. Isn't that Don Quixote himself, after a three-hundred-year journey, returning to the village disguised as a land-surveyor? Once he had set out to seek adventures of his own choosing, but now in the village below the Castle he has no choice, the adventure is *imposed on him:* a petty squabble with the administration over a mistake in his file. So what, after three centuries, has happened to adventure, the first great theme of the novel? Has it become its own parody? What does that mean? That the path of the novel winds up in a paradox?

Yes, so it would seem. And that is by no means the only paradox. *The Good Soldier Schweik*[3] is perhaps the last great popular novel. Isn't it astonishing that this comic novel is also a war novel, whose action unfolds in the army and at the front? What has happened to war and its horrors if they've become laughing matters?

In Homer and in Tolstoy, war had a perfectly comprehensible meaning: people fought for Helen or for Russia. Schweik and his companions go to the front without knowing why and, what is even more shocking, without caring to know.

What, then, is the motor of war if not Helen or country? Sheer force that wills to assert itself as force? The "will to will" that Heidegger later wrote about? Yet hasn't that been behind all wars since the beginning of time? Yes, of course. But this time, in Hašek, it is stripped of any rational argument. No one believes in the drivel of the propaganda, not even those who manufacture it. Force is naked here, as naked as in Kafka's novels. Indeed, the Court has nothing to gain from executing K., nor has the Castle from tormenting the Land-Surveyor. Why did Germany, why does Russia today want to dominate the world? To be richer? Happier? Not at all. The aggressivity of force is thoroughly disinterested; unmotivated; it wills only its own will; it is pure irrationality.

Kafka and Hašek thus bring us face to face with this enormous paradox: In the course of the Modern Era, Cartesian rationality has corroded, one after the other, all the values inherited from the Middle Ages. But just when reason wins a total victory, pure irrationality (force willing only its will) seizes the world stage, because there is no longer any generally accepted value system to block its path.

This paradox, masterfully illuminated in Hermann Broch's *The Sleepwalkers,* is one of those I like to call *terminal.* There are others. For example: The Modern Era has nurtured a dream in which mankind, divided into its separate civilizations, would someday come together in unity and everlasting peace. Today, the history of the planet has finally become one indivisible whole, but it is war, ambulant and everlasting war,

---

[3] *The Good Soldier Schweik,* by satirical novelist Jaroslav Hašek (1883–1923) appeared in four volumes from 1920–1923. *Ed.*

that embodies and guarantees this long-desired unity of mankind. Unity of mankind means: No escape for anyone anywhere.

6.

Husserl's lectures on the European crisis and on the possible disappearance of European mankind were his philosophical testament. He gave those lectures in two capitals of Central Europe. This coincidence has a deep meaning: for it was in that selfsame Central Europe that, for the first time in its modern history, the West could see the death of the West, or, more exactly, the amputation of part of itself, when Warsaw, Budapest, and Prague were swallowed up by the Russian empire. This calamity was engendered by the First World War, which, unleashed by the Hapsburg empire, led to the end of that empire and unbalanced forever an enfeebled Europe.

The time was past when man had only the monster of his own soul to grapple with, the peaceful time of Joyce and Proust. In the novels of Kafka, Hašek, Musil,[4] Broch, the monster comes from outside and is called History; it no longer has anything to do with the train the adventurers used to ride; it is impersonal, uncontrollable, incalculable, incomprehensible—and it is inescapable. This was the moment (just after the First World War) when the pleiad of great Central European novelists saw, felt, grasped the *terminal paradoxes* of the Modern Era.

But it would be wrong to read their novels as social and political prophecies, as if they were anticipations of Orwell! What Orwell tells us could have been said just as well (or even much better) in an essay or pamphlet. On the contrary, these novelists discover "what only the novel can discover": they demonstrate how, under the conditions of the "terminal paradoxes," all existential categories suddenly change their meaning: What is *adventure* if a K.'s freedom of action is completely illusory? What is *future* if the intellectuals of *The Man Without Qualities* have not the slightest inkling of the war that will sweep their lives away the next day? What is *crime* if Broch's Huguenau not only does not regret but actually forgets the murder he has committed? And if the only great comic novel of the period, Hašek's *Schweik,* uses war as its setting, then what has happened to the *comic*? Where is the difference between *public* and *private* if K., even in bed with a woman, is never without the two emissaries of the Castle? And in that case, what is *solitude*? A burden, a misery, a curse, as some would have us believe, or on the contrary, a supremely precious value in the process of being crushed by the ubiquitous collectivity?

The periods of the novel's history are very long (they have nothing to do with the hectic shifts of fashion) and are characterized by the particular aspect of being on which the novel concentrates. Thus the potential of Flaubert's discovery of the quotidian was only fully developed seventy years later, in James Joyce's gigantic work. The

---

[4] Robert Musil (1880–1842), Austrian novelist, is best known for his witty, encyclopedic treatment of life at the close of the Habsburg Empire, *Der Mann ohne Eigenschaften* (*The Man Without Qualities;* 1930–1943). *Ed.*

period inaugurated seventy years ago by the pleiad of Central European novelists (the period of *terminal paradoxes*) seems to me far from finished.

7.

The death of the novel has been much discussed for a long time: notably by the Futurists, by the Surrealists, by nearly all the avant-gardes. They saw the novel dropping off the road of progress, yielding to a radically new future and an art bearing no resemblance to what had existed before. The novel was to be buried in the name of historical justice, like poverty, the ruling classes, obsolete cars, or top hats.

But if Cervantes is the founder of the Modern Era, then the end of his legacy ought to signify more than a mere stage in the history of literary forms; it would herald the end of the Modern Era. That is why the blissful smile that accompanies those obituaries of the novel strikes me as frivolous. Frivolous because I have already seen and lived through the death of the novel, a violent death (inflicted by bans, censorship, and ideological pressure), in the world where I spent much of my life and which is usually called totalitarian. At that time it became utterly clear that the novel was mortal; as mortal as the West of the Modern Era. As a model of this Western world, grounded in the relativity and ambiguity of things human, the novel is incompatible with the totalitarian universe. This incompatibility is deeper than the one that separates a dissident from an apparatchik, or a human-rights campaigner from a torturer, because it is not only political or moral but *ontological.* By which I mean: The world of one single Truth and the relative, ambiguous world of the novel are molded of entirely different substances. Totalitarian Truth excludes relativity, doubt, questioning; it can never accommodate what I would call the *spirit of the novel.*

But aren't there hundreds and thousands of novels published in huge editions and widely read in Communist Russia? Certainly; but these novels add nothing to the conquest of being. They discover no new segment of existence; they only confirm what has already been said; furthermore: in confirming what everyone says (what everyone must say), they fulfill their purpose, their glory, their usefulness to that society. By discovering nothing, they fail to participate in the *sequence of discoveries* that for me constitutes the history of the novel; they place themselves *outside* that history, or, if you like: they are *novels that come after the history of the novel.*

About half a century ago the history of the novel came to a halt in the empire of Russian Communism. That is an event of huge importance, given the greatness of the Russian novel from Gogol to Bely.[5] Thus the death of the novel is not just a fanciful idea. It has already happened. And we now know *how* the novel dies: it's not that it disappears; it falls away from its history. Its death occurs quietly, unnoticed, and no one is outraged.

---

[5] Nikolai Gogol (1809–1952), author of *Dead Souls* (1842), and Andrei Bely (pseudonym of Boris Nikolaievich Bugaev, 1880–1934), author of *St. Petersburg* (1913–1914), were the first and the last of the great Russian novelists who wrote in the century before the 1917 revolution. *Ed.*

8.

But hasn't the novel come to the end of the road by its own internal logic? Hasn't it already mined all its possibilities, all its knowledge, and all its forms? I've heard the history of the novel compared to a seam of coal long since exhausted. But isn't it more like a cemetery of missed opportunities, of unheard appeals? There are four appeals to which I am especially responsive.

The appeal of play: Laurence Sterne's *Tristram Shandy* and Denis Diderot's *Jacques le Fataliste* are for me the two greatest novelistic works of the eighteenth century, two novels conceived as grand games. They reach heights of playfulness, of lightness, never scaled before or since. Afterward, the novel got itself tied to the imperative of verisimilitude, to realistic settings, to chronological order. It abandoned the possibilities opened up by these two masterpieces, which could have led to a different development of the novel (yes, it's possible to imagine a whole other history of the European novel . . .).

The appeal of dream: The slumbering imagination of the nineteenth century was abruptly awakened by Franz Kafka, who achieved what the Surrealists later called for but never themselves really accomplished: the fusion of dream and reality. This was in fact a long-standing aesthetic ambition of the novel, already intimated by Novalis, but its fulfillment required a special alchemy that Kafka alone discovered a century later. His enormous contribution is less the final step in a historical development than an unexpected opening that shows that the novel is a place where the imagination can explode as in a dream, and that the novel can break free of the seemingly inescapable imperative of verisimilitude.

The appeal of thought: Musil and Broch brought a sovereign and radiant intelligence to bear on the novel. Not to transform the novel into philosophy, but to marshal around the story all the means—rational and irrational, narrative and contemplative—that could illuminate man's being; could make of the novel the supreme intellectual synthesis. Is their achievement the completion of the novel's history, or is it instead the invitation to a long journey?

The appeal of time: The period of *terminal paradoxes* incites the novelist to broaden the time issue beyond the Proustian problem of personal memory to the enigma of collective time, the time of Europe, Europe looking back on its own past, weighing up its history like an old man seeing his whole life in a single moment. Whence the desire to overstep the temporal limits of an individual life, to which the novel had hitherto been confined, and to insert in its space several historical periods (Aragon and Fuentes have already tried this).

But I don't want to predict the future paths of the novel, which I cannot know; all I mean to say is this: If the novel should really disappear, it will do so not because it has exhausted its powers but because it exists in a world grown alien to it.

part II
Form: Elements of Narrative

THE FORMS OF FORM

The essays contained in this section are by fifteen distinct individuals, each with his or her own views. Nevertheless one could say that the formal analysis of narrative has taken two major tracks, and both are well represented by the critics here gathered. The first to develop historically was the *structuralist-semiotic* branch of narratology, which begins with the Russian formalist critics who did most of their best work in the 1920s, and whose ideas spread via Czechoslovakia (the "Prague Linguistic Circle") to France, where they have flourished since the 1960s, and from there to the rest of the world. The other track—with roots that go back to Aristotle and Longinus—began in Chicago in the 1940s, where R. S. Crane developed a *rhetorical poetics* of narrative (along with other genres of literature) that has evolved and complicated over the last fifty years. Space doesn't permit a full discussion of these literary theories, but briefly one could contrast them by saying that structural narratology is concerned, first and foremost, with what narrative *is,* whereas rhetorical narratology is concerned with what it *does* or how it *works*.[1]

The structural narratologist starts with the premise that meaning comes out of the decipherment of codes, and that narrative is a second-order code imposed on the first-order code of language. Like sentences in a natural language, narratives are constructed according to a set of constitutive rules, which it is their aim to discover. There is a working assumption that, like languages, narratives have the elementary equivalent of "parts of speech"—paradigm categories whose members can be substituted for one another—and rules analogous to syntax for combining members of paradigm classes. Some narratologists, like Vladimir Propp, have tried to enumerate exhaustively the possible categories of agents and actions in simple

---

[1] Writing before either method of formal analysis was developed, Henry James and E. M. Forster nevertheless split along similar lines, James's prefaces generally tending to emphasize the rhetoric of fiction and Forster a formal poetics of the novel.

narratives (like the Russian folk tale). Similarly, the Italian semiotician Umberto Eco once analyzed the James Bond novels of Ian Fleming as a set of mix-and-match permutations of a small number of recurring elements. Point of view (which would be a syntactic or relational matter rather than a paradigm class) tends to be viewed in terms of its grammatical characteristics: whether the first or third person is used, whether the focus remains inside or outside the mind, whether that mind is the narrator's or that of another character, and so on. Essays included here that typify this perspective are by Bal, Banfield, Barthes, Cohn, Genette, and Prince.

The rhetorical narratologist starts with the premise that the narrative is from the outset an act of communication between author and reader. Here point of view concerns primarily the way in which the message is mediated or transmitted by surrogates the author creates (the "implied author" of the narrative, the narrator, the characters, the "narratee" within the tale, the narrative and authorial audiences). Basic units of structure such as plot devices and characters are viewed not as abstract possibilities but as elements constructed as part of the tenor of the message, not independent "parts of speech" but already elements of what the author is "trying to say." The essays by Crane, Booth, Phelan, Friedman, and Rabinowitz operate from this point of view.

STORY AND DISCOURSE

It's hard to know precisely where to start discussing narrative form, but the most common distinction—and there are variants that go back to Aristotle—is to separate the what from the how, the story that is told from the way that story is told. In his notebooks, Henry James called them the "story" and the "treatment"; the Russian Formalist critics of the 1920s used the terms *fabula* and *sjuzet;* French structuralists such as Claude Bremond used terms like *récit* and *raconte;* the closest translation (used by Seymour Chatman) is story and discourse. These represent two sets of choices the author makes: what shall happen in the story, and to whom, and why; and what sort of narrative that story will make.

One presumes that the story itself is given, but of course it is constructed, even when an author purloins a plot from some other text. When Thomas Mann novelized the story of Joseph and his brothers, he had to decide what to keep and what to leave, where to start and where to leave off, which of the book of Genesis's paradoxes and contradictions to highlight and which to be silent about. Similarly, it's easy to presume that there is a "natural" way of telling a story: "Begin at the beginning, go all the way through to the end, and then stop," says Humpty Dumpty to Alice, as though that were easy and natural. But of course it's not natural at all. The narratologist Mary-Laure Ryan has discovered that when ordinary people recount stories to each other, only the very short ones are told in perfect time-sequence. When we tell stories of any length we usually put in prolepses (flashbacks) and analepses (flash-forwards anticipating a future situation). And the places we start and end aren't natural either: they too are choices dictated by any number of considerations, all of which add to or subtract from the impact the story makes. We know that some stories have to begin before the beginning—to set a scene or set up an unusual character or situation—and that others make the strongest impression when we start in the middle and fill in the gaps later.

To appeal to "impact" or "strongest impression" is to ask, though, about ends rather than means. We need to begin by differentiating two sorts of purposes for which stories are told. We often ask our friends, "what is the point of that story?" as though all stories had a point to make. Some stories do: they are shaped to explain something, to lead the listener toward some specific or general truth about the real world, or specific observations about particular people or cases. Historical narratives tend to have a specific point, to tell us how Commodus dies or why Pickett's charge failed. But other stories have no point in this sense: we often tell our friends what happened during our day for the sake of its own inherent interest, for the sympathy or sorrow or laughter that it generates. Literary narratives that are designed to make a point are usually designed to say something more general about ethics or politics or the way the world works.[2] But more often than not, literary narratives are of the second group, stories that have no ulterior motive or exterior reference, stories told for their own sake.

STORY: PLOT AND CHARACTER

E. M. Forster once wrote that "The king died and then the queen died" is a story, a mere sequence of events, but "The king died and then the queen died of grief" is a plot with causal connections between the two events.[3] Aristotle said that a unified plot—as opposed to a series of unconnected episodes centering around a single character—is one with a beginning, middle, and end. The plot begins from an initially stable situation, then becomes unstable, undergoes further complications, and is finally resolved with the introduction of a new stability.

To take a familiar plot, that of *Great Expectations,* we would have to say that the plot begins when Pip is informed, through the lawyer Jaggers, that he is to be taken away from his brother-in-law Joe Gargery's forge and made into a gentleman, courtesy of an anonymous benefactor. In the "middle" the plot is complicated by Pip's shifting and equivocal relations with the eccentric heiress Miss Havisham— whom he mistakenly takes for that benefactor—and her circle, including his friend Herbert Pocket and his disdainful beloved Estella. It includes his partial corruption by the forces of money and snobbery, until his fantasies are snapped by the knowledge that the benefactor is actually Magwitch, a transported convict grown rich in Australia. The end involves the recrudescence of Pip's originally generous

---

[2] Literary satires are an exception: they are about the particular more often than the general. The episodes involving Flimnap in Book I of *Gulliver's Travels* are specifically designed to ridicule Robert Walpole in particular, not odious courtiers in general.

[3] For many of us, "The king died and then the queen died" would also be a plot, since we would infer a causal connection between events mentioned together.

and noble character, which we see in his rejection of the money and his heroic attempt to save Magwitch from the death prescribed for returned transportees. In a new stability, Pip becomes a bourgeois rather than a leisured gentleman, working for his living with his friend Pocket and married to Estella, who has also been humbled by fate.[4]

Such a plot *presupposes* events that precede the beginning: Pip's first encounter with Magwitch, which inspires the latter's generosity; his early meetings with Miss Havisham and Estella, which lead him to aspire above his working-class station in life. These events are necessary exposition. But the plot does not *include* those events. Without the lucky chance of Magwitch's new riches and the eccentric whim that leads him to settle those riches on Pip, Pip must have continued as an apprentice blacksmith at his brother-in-law Joe's forge. . . . The beginning of the plot is thus not the beginning of the story, and it is certainly not at the beginning of the discourse. The novel is about one fourth done, in fact, before the plot, properly speaking, begins. The economy of a Dickens novel, even a relatively short one like *Great Expectations,* allows for this sort of leisurely opening, with vast quantities of exposition whose relevance may not appear for hundreds of pages. Some Victorian novels (for example, Thackeray's *Vanity Fair*) include epilogue material—episodes from the lives of the main characters after the plot is over—that goes on for dozens of pages. In other eras, novels may have a very different sort of economy, and some modern novels—such as F. Scott Fitzgerald's *The Great Gatsby* and *Tender Is the Night*—begin in the middle of the plot and present the beginning by means of prolepses (flashbacks).

In a rhetorical poetics of fiction like that of R. S. Crane, only a fragment of which can be presented here, the end of any mimetic fiction[5] will be its power to produce in its audience a deterministic emotional effect. What determines this effect for Crane is largely the plot, broadly conceived as including elements of character and values. Here are three main factors:

- The moral quality of the protagonist(s) inspires us with more or less definite *desires;* depending on our degree of sympathy, we will wish the protagonist good or bad fortune, with greater or less ardor.
- The events of the plot set up lines of probability that lead us to form more or less definite *expectations* regarding the protagonist's fate. We expect him or her to have either good or bad fortune, in greater or less degree, temporarily or permanently. (We also may have indeterminate expectations, either because we are placed in suspense between two or more well-defined possible outcomes, or because the alternatives for the outcome are poorly defined.)
- The protagonist has a more or less definite degree of *responsibility* for what happens. We may be made to feel that he or she exercises definite control through conscious choice, or, on the other hand, that the outcome is the result of the actions of other agents, or of Chance, or Destiny. If the

---

[4] Or a contented bachelor *not* married to Estella, as in Dickens' first-conceived denouement.

[5] Fiction not constructed on didactic principles, such as allegories, fables, and fictional satires.

protagonist controls the outcome, then it matters whether he or she acts in full knowledge or as the result of a mistake of some sort.

These factors can lead us to make some of the usual large discriminations between types of plot and some fairly subtle ones. Tragedies differ from comedies by whether we are led to expect an unhappy or a happy ending; comedies are unlike melodramas that happen to end happily because in comedies we expect the happy ending from the outset, whereas the melodramas keep us in suspense. But the subtle emotional difference between two romantic comedies (Fielding's *Tom Jones* and Austen's *Pride and Prejudice,* for example) might be traced to the handling of the responsibility factor: Austen implicitly suggests that her heroine and hero, Lizzie and Darcy, create their own happiness by transforming themselves each into a suitable partner for the other; on the other hand Fielding insistently reminds us that Tom ends up as the heir to an estate and a lovely bride largely because of the favor of Fortune. In *Tom Jones,* in other words, our nose is rubbed in the fact that in the real world happiness is not always in the power of the innocent, the noble, and the good.[6]

These factors—our desires, expectations, sense of the protagonist's degree of responsibility for what happens—all refer to the protagonist's fate. In many, perhaps most, plots the fate of the protagonist is principally defined in terms of his or her fortunes or *circumstances*—life, health, social status, reputation, love relationships, and so on. But many plots define the fate of the protagonist in terms of a change in *consciousness.* Here the focus of our concern may be on the protagonist's developing capacity for making mature moral decisions (as in *Great Expectations*), or conversely on his or her ethical degeneration (as in Gide's *The Immoralist*). Or the protagonist may be tested by an extreme situation, so that we wonder whether he or she will take the easy way out, at the cost of self-contempt, or do the right thing and suffer the consequences (as in Hemingway's *Old Man and the Sea*). Sometimes the plot of consciousness will be concerned not with *character* but with *thought:* with whether the protagonist will make adequate and coherent sense of his or her life. The struggle may be successful (as in Bellow's *Herzog*) or unsuccessful (as in James's *Aspern Papers,* whose protagonist refuses the offered chance to enlarge his narrow world). Or in other plots learning may take the form of disillusionment, and the attitude we take will depend on whether the protagonist's romantic illusions are portrayed as nobler than the sordid realities he discovers (as in Fitzgerald's "Winter Dreams") or as follies he is better off without (as in Philip Roth's "Goodbye, Columbus").

Crane suggests in "The Concept of Plot" that any unified plot must have a single focus on action, character, or thought. Sometimes this focus is obvious. But in plots where the protagonist undergoes simultaneous or successive changes in fortune, character, and thought, such as Austen's *Pride and Prejudice* or James's *The Ambassadors,* we may find it difficult to determine which one is primary. Do we want Lizzie to conquer her character flaws or to marry a wealthy aristocrat? Is the

---

[6] Similarly there are strategies in which the protagonist's doom seems self-imposed (Hardy's *Mayor of Casterbridge*) and others where the protagonist seems an innocent victim (as in *Tess of the D'Urbervilles*).

focus of *The Ambassadors* on the disastrous result of the action on Strether's fortunes (he loses the confidence of his wealthy fiancée), on his ambiguous moral change (his new tolerance of what Americans would consider grossly immoral), or on his glorious new vision, his deepened and widened notion of life as an art?

James Phelan's approach to character also comes out of a similar theory of literature to that of Crane, but Phelan's approach implicitly concedes that texts may not be wholly unified and that authors often have more than one purpose in mind in creating narratives. For Phelan, all characters have multiple components and functions within the "progression"—or plot: these components and functions are "mimetic" (on which the story's verisimilitude depends) as well as "thematic" (when they represent or bring out ideas and values that give the narrative moral or intellectual significance). Furthermore, characters have "synthetic" components (when they help tell the story through narration, external and internal, and through quoted dialogue). Phelan's rhetorical analysis of character and progression works not only for the masterpieces of realism for which Crane's analysis was principally developed, but also for didactic and satirical works (where the thematic components and functions may overshadow the mimetic ones) and for postmodern texts (where the manipulation of the synthetic functions and components may be most important). It also can help us to understand certain difficulties in narratives: when we ask how the listeners in the yacht could possibly have sat still for the many hours it must have taken Marlow to narrate the story of *Heart of Darkness,* or how Clarissa and Lovelace could possibly have made the time to write the letters through which *Clarissa* is narrated, we are noting conflicts between the "mimetic" and "synthetic" functions of the characters.

STORY: PATTERN

Another aspect of the story is the patterns that plots make. Our aesthetic sense values clean beginnings and tidy endings, the shapeliness of a narrative—even as our sense of verisimilitude distrusts such clarity as an obvious sign of artifice. This is what E. M. Forster explores in "Pattern and Rhythm," in which he sees plot as taking the shape of an "hourglass" or a figure-X, and others that seem to be constructed as a chain, where the ending comes back to the beginning. Such patterns are more the rule than the exception. Although the neatness and rigor of the patterns made by Anatole France and Percy Lubbock may seem unusual, even the plots of apparently "loose and baggy" nineteenth-century novels either tend to circle back to beginnings (as *Great Expectations* insistently does) or, on the other hand, center on paired protagonists whose contrasting fates (one rising, the other falling) make an hourglass pattern (Thackeray's *Vanity Fair* or Dreiser's *Sister Carrie*).[7] Rhythm for Forster is a more minor version of pattern: it involves the thematic repetition (with

---

[7] The psychological significance of this sort of repetition is analyzed in the next section, in Peter Brooks's Freudian approach to fictional repetition in "Narrative Desire."

variations) of story elements like the musical theme from Vinteuil's sonata that haunts Swann in the first volume of Proust's *Á la récherche du temps perdu,* and which goes on to haunt the entire rest of the novel. While Proust's repetitions call insistent attention to the artifice that produced them, they can be made to seem natural, and indeed repetition is one of the chief ways expectations are generated in the audience. The increasingly tense deadlocks between Lovelace and his prisoner in *Clarissa* point the way to the climactic rape; the pattern of Tom Jones's getting in trouble through a magnanimous but imprudent act and then getting out of it again signals the reader that, since nothing terribly bad ever seems to happen as a result, nothing very bad ever will.

DISCOURSE: ORDER, DURATION, FREQUENCY

An obvious sign of the manipulation of "telling" is when the story is given to us out of order. Although, as has been noted, naive nonliterary narratives frequently include flashbacks (and even flashforwards), we assume that it is "natural" to tell a story in chronological order and that any deviation from that order is done for effect—minimally, the effect of clarifying the significance of the action in the present. What we learn first is viewed as a given, the status quo, the point from which change is registered. Scott Fitzgerald created an indelible sense of Gatsby as a man of mystery and glamour by introducing him near the end of his life's saga, and only much later allowing us to view, in a flashback, how he had been transformed into this icon of the jazz age from a midwestern country boy.

Gérard Genette's analysis of time in Proust, presented in part below, takes this sort of manipulation essentially for granted and concentrates more intensely on two other methods by which narrative can manipulate the sense of time. The second method, which Genette calls "duration" and which I should prefer to call pacing, refers to the relationship between story-time and reader-time and can be gauged by how many words in the narrative are used to convey how much plot-time. Years can pass in the course of a few sentences, whereas some of the soirees that Proust describes can take nearly as long to read as they must have taken to live through. (Others have manipulated pacing even more grossly: Laurence Sterne takes several chapters to describe Tristram Shandy's father and uncle descending a single flight of stairs, and Nicholson Baker, in a tour-de-force, has an entire novel take place during an escalator ride up from the lobby to the mezzanine floor of an office building.)

The sense of "frequency"—whether a particular action is performed once or habitually, over and over again, is a third way of manipulating the reader's time sense. "In the evening . . . the little Englishman, Hawkins, would light the lamp and bring out the cards," we are told at the start of Frank O'Connor's story "Guests of the Nation," and the use of the modal auxiliary "would" lets us know that the scene being set is a repetitive everyday occurrence, not an event that happened on a particular evening. (The latter would have been inscribed: "One evening, Hawkins lit the lamp. . . .") These temporal manipulations of "discourse" are often used together to strong effect: "Guests of the Nation," for example, uses the repetitive mode at the beginning of the story as a way of telescoping the time sense, of conveying in a few words the habits formed over months. Then the story goes on to recount the events leading to the execution of two British prisoners by their IRA guards, progressively slowing the pace as the moment of violence is approached in a way that intensifies the horror of the spectacle.

DISCOURSE: POINT OF VIEW, FOCALIZATION, AND VOICE

Beginning with Henry James, theorists of fiction have concerned themselves with the other all-important aspect of the "discourse," the "point of view" from which the story is told. It is conventional to describe narrative technique primarily in terms of the characteristics of the narrator, and to differentiate between first-person narrators telling their own stories (Genette terms this *autodiegesis*), first-person narrators telling other people's stories (*homodiegesis*) and third-person narrators (*heterodiegesis*).[8] First-person narrators can only tell us what they know or can find out; third-person narrators may have unlimited privilege (the so-called "omniscient" narrator), or they may be limited to knowing a single characters' inner life (selective omniscience), or may know a number of characters' inner states, each in turn (multiple selective omniscience), or may serve as a virtual camera eye objectively regarding the scene with no privilege to recount any character's thoughts and feelings.[9] As Wayne Booth insists in his classic essay, "Distance and Point of View," the "person" in which the story is told is far less important than the privilege the narrator is accorded to see into the characters' hearts (or to find them opaque), to know the end of the story at the beginning (or to come to each new event in surprise), to judge and comment on the agents and their acts.

Perhaps Booth's most celebrated distinction in that essay is between the narrator and the "implied author" whose presence and values we can reconstruct behind the narrative. A narrator whose norms differ from those of the implied author is often called an "unreliable narrator." Narrators are usually reliable reporters of the events of the story[10]; the deviation is more usually on the moral axis: the narrator's judgments are warped or self-serving or inconscient, like those of Jason Compson in *The Sound and the Fury*, or Lady Susan in Jane Austen's short novel of that name, requiring the reader to correct for the narrator's biases and blind spots.

---

[8] A small number of narratives are written in the second person, such as the novel *Bright Lights, Big City* by Jay McInerny. Usually the narrative "you" equates roughly to the autodiegetic narrator, but sometimes implicates the narratee and the audience in the tale.

[9] Even cameras sometimes take sides, of course. The narrator of Hemingway's "The Killers," who refrains from reporting the inner lives of any of the characters, immediately gives us the names of Nick and George, the denizens of Henry's Diner, but not those of the killers, Al and Max, whose names are withheld until they have addressed each other by name.

[10] Occasionally a mentally impaired narrator, such as Benjy Compson in Faulkner's *The Sound and the Fury*, may create difficulties for the audience in reconstructing the precise events of the story and their chronology.

In structural narratology, such as that of Mieke Bal, the distinctions included under "point of view" are split into the separate issues of "focalization" and "voice" roughly locating who sees and who speaks: the perspective from which the action is viewed and the language used to convey the action. The distinction is clearly important in any third-person narrative, where the language used may be similar to that which the center of consciousness would have used—or may be very different. Even in first-person narratives, like Joyce's "Araby," for example, the focalizing agent, a preadolescent boy, could hardly be responsible for the knotty syntax and difficult vocabulary in which the narrative is pitched. Critics have naturalized the difference between focalization and voice by suggesting that the story could be a retrospective narration by the adult into whom the boy grew up—but that is not a fact directly presented in the story.

The mode of narrative is clearly important in representations of consciousness, as Dorrit Cohn shows. The differences in effect can be quite significant between quoted interior monologue (where the words are the character's thoughts, in the first person: "I'm free!!"), narrated monologue (in the free indirect style, using the character's words but in the third person with the tense shifted: "He was free!!"), and psychonarration (the summary of the character's thoughts, in the author's words: "He rejoiced in his liberty"). The sympathy (or irony) with which a character is regarded often depends on the way his or her thoughts are framed. This framing varies, of course, from sentence to sentence, and even within sentences at times: the long strophe at the end of "Barn-Burning" in which Faulkner recounts Sartie Snopes's breathless vain race to warn his father of the doom about to overtake him flows in and out of Sartie's proper vocabulary, alternately conveying Sartie's own naive desperation and the narrator's more measured perspective on the death of the father.

DISCOURSE: VOICE AND LANGUAGE

The narrative voice may represent perspectives other than those of the characters of the fiction, as Mikhail Bakhtin suggests in "Discourse and the Novel." Analyzing the narrator's voice in Dickens' *Little Dorrit,* Bakhtin makes us aware that the "narrator" is not a single univocal speaker but embodies, parodically at times, various linguistic strata embedded in Victorian society, the jargons of various trades and professions, the chatter of particular segments of society, and so on. Within these "heteroglot" utterances may be included direct authorial discourse, though within a complex passage it may be impossible to say whether a particular phrase belongs to the author or to an Other whose language he is reaccenting—and it may indeed be both at once. Susan Sniader Lanser's "Feminist Poetics of Narrative Voice" takes up from Bakhtin's notion of heteroglossia, interrogating in particular the problems of establishing a female narrative voice within a patriarchal social milieu: having a strong authorial voice can be difficult in a society that denies women all *authority.* Sniader Lanser investigates three narrative stances taken up by women novelists—which she terms "authorial," "personal," and "communal"—to investigate the connection between what the novelists have had to say and the voice in which they have chosen to be heard.[11]

We think of language as belonging to the narrator or the characters, but language may, if Ann Banfield is correct, belong to no one at all, technically speaking. A linguist as much as a literary critic by trade, Banfield has examined the syntax of fiction and has concluded that certain sorts of sentences that appear in literary texts are literally "unspeakable"—usable in literary writing but not in speech. A sentence like: "Now she knew that she could never really possess him" is grammatically deviant in that the time deictic ("now") demands a verb in the present tense. The use of the "epic preterite," the special past tense in which narrative tends to be located, establishes the sentence as taking place in a hypothetical, fictional world, and within this eternal preterite such time-signals as "now," "then," and "soon" indicate the hypothetical present, past, and future. Banfield also speculates that the widespread use of these "unspeakable sentences" within free indirect discourse detached our sense of the subjective from the "I" whose subjectivity is the only one we can directly experience—and that this phenomenon may have been responsible, starting around the turn of the nineteenth century, for a new attitude toward the self. Banfield is not alone. Roland Barthes points out that in French the epic preterite (the *passé simple*) is used only in literary texts; the third-person narration, he argues, is in its own way equally unnatural (if not unspeakable), by effacing the perspective from which the narrative comes, making it collective and social, everyone's and no one's. "The Novel is a Death: it transforms life into destiny, a memory into a useful act, duration into an oriented and meaningful time. But this transformation can be accomplished only in the full view of society. It is society that imposes the Novel, that is a complex of signs, as a transcendence and as the History of a duration."

DISCOURSE: THE AUDIENCE

Although real authors and readers have lives outside their texts, there is also a sense in which the author and audience are also inscribed *within* the text. Whatever the real author is like, we acquire a sense of the author (Wayne Booth's "implied author") governing the world of the book and its norms, and in order to write the book the novelist has to have a sense of who we are. Each novel is written for an "implied reader"—which Peter Rabinowitz calls the "authorial audience"—who responds to the desires and expectations aroused by the text, which he or she is aware of as a text. The narrator, similarly, evokes a "narrative audience" who will be that narrator's receptor; being one level further in, the narrative audience must in effect believe as true whatever the text asserts. In any text there will be a difference between the authorial audience, which knows that it is reading a fiction, and the

---

[11] A debate between Lanser and Gerald Prince, on the proper place of categories such as gender in formalist/structuralist narratology, appears in the journal *Narrative* 3.1 (Fall 1994): 73-94.

narrative audience, which does not. In *Tom Jones,* the authorial audience knows that Tom will live happily every after, because it is aware that it is reading a text with comic signals, which implies that the characters' fates will accord with their deserts. But the narrative audience cannot be sure whether (say) Mr. Fitzpatrick will recover from his wound and Tom be released from Newgate Prison. Rabinowitz includes a fourth audience for texts with flagrantly unreliable narrators, the "ideal narrative audience," which believes, agrees with, and sympathizes with the narrator. In Ring Lardner's "Haircut," the narrative and the ideal narrative audiences will be at odds: the former will reject and the latter accept the values and understanding of "Whitey" the barber.

A diagram of the usual narrative situation would run as follows:

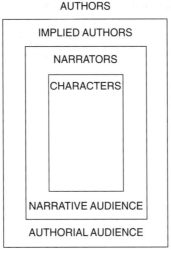

AUTHORS

IMPLIED AUTHORS

NARRATORS

CHARACTERS

NARRATIVE AUDIENCE

AUTHORIAL AUDIENCE

REAL READERS

Rabinowitz's model, derived from Wayne Booth, is based on rhetoric. Gerald Prince's somewhat different narratological perspective depends on a communications model. For Prince the central receptor is a figure he calls the narratee (*narrataire*) whose job it is to mediate between the narrator and the actual reader. "He constitutes a relay between the narrator and the reader, he helps establish the narrative framework, he emphasizes certain themes, he contributes to the development of the plot, he becomes the spokesman for the moral of the work." Minimally, the zero-degree narratee understands the language of the story and the objects and processes of its social world. This implicit receptor of the text knows what is assumed to be known and is ignorant of whatever needs to be explained. When Jake Barnes, in Hemingway's *The Sun Also Rises,* let us know that "Pernod is green imitation absinthe" or explains the order of events in a Spanish bullfight, that is because Hemingway's narratee does not know such things. Most narratees are negatively characterized in this way, but not always; sometimes without saying a word, the narratee can be a positively characterized individual within a story, like the Parisian attorney who listens to the monologue of Jean-Baptiste Clamence in Camus's *La chute,* or the former sailor who listens to Marlow's tale in *Lord Jim.* Prince's narratee is closest to Rabinowitz's "narrative audience," although, as Rabinowitz points out, there are subtle differences. Prince has other readers too: an "ideal reader" ("one who would understand perfectly the least of his words the most subtle of his intentions") who resembles Rabinowitz's "authorial audience"; and a "virtual reader" ("a certain type of reader" on whom the author bestows "certain qualities, faculties and inclinations according to his opinion of men in general") who corresponds to nothing in Rabinowitz's classification.

The two parallel essays by Prince and Rabinowitz, both attempting to classify the various versions of the reader within the narrative text, demonstrate that while there is a considerable degree of overlap between the structural and rhetorical approaches, they are fundamentally competing explanations based on disparate conceptions of what narratives are and how they work. Ultimately one's choice will be based on which set of tools fits best the curve of one's own mind, on which yields the most interesting insights about individual texts.

R. S. Crane

Ronald Salmon Crane was the leader and moving spirit of the Chicago school of neo-Aristotelian criticism. Born in 1886, Crane grew up in Michigan and was educated at the University of Michigan, Ann Arbor, and at the University of Pennsylvania, where he took his doctorate in 1911. Crane began teaching at Northwestern University, then moved in 1924 to the University of Chicago, where he became professor of English in 1925 and head of the department in 1935. Crane's interest in literary theory and his notion that criticism rather than historical scholarship was the best way of teaching literature, began in the 1930s during the implementation of the innovative Hutchins "great books" curriculum. Crane's 1952 manifesto was *Critics and Criticism,* a collection of essays by him and the other Chicago formalists (including Elder Olson, Norman Maclean, and the philosopher Richard Mc-Keon); the selection below is excerpted from Crane's final essay, "The Concept of Plot·and the Plot of *Tom Jones.*" His only critical book, *The Languages of Criticism and the Structure of Poetry,* was published the following year. Crane's major theoretical essays were published in two volumes as *The Idea of the Humanities* (1967).

The Concept of Plot and the Plot of *Tom Jones*

I shall assume that any novel or drama not constructed on didactic principles is a composite of three elements, which unite to determine its quality and effect—the things that are imitated (or "rendered") in it, the linguistic medium in which they are imitated, and the manner or technique of imitation; and I shall assume further that the things imitated necessarily involve human beings interacting with one another in ways determined by, and in turn affecting, their moral characters and their states of mind (i.e., their reasonings, emotions, and attitudes). If this is granted, we may say that the plot of any novel or drama is the particular temporal synthesis effected by the writer of the elements of action, character, and thought that constitute the matter of his invention. It is impossible, therefore, to state adequately what any plot is unless we include in our formula all three of the elements or causes of which the plot is the synthesis; and it follows also that plots will differ in structure according as one or another of the three causal ingredients is employed as the synthesizing principle. There are, thus, plots of action, plots of character, and plots of thought. In the first, the synthesizing principle is a completed change, gradual or sudden, in the situation of the protagonist, determined and effected by character and thought (as in *Oedipus* and *The Brothers Karamazov*); in the second, the principle is a completed process of change in the moral character of the protagonist, precipitated or molded by action, and made manifest both in it and in thought and feeling (as in James's *The Por-*

trait of a Lady); in the third, the principle is a completed process of change in the thought of the protagonist and consequently in his feelings, conditioned and directed by character and action (as in Pater's *Marius the Epicurean*). All these types of construction, and not merely the first, are plots in the meaning of our definition; and it is mainly, perhaps, because most of the familiar classic plots, including that of *Tom Jones,* have been of the first kind that so many critics have tended to reduce plot to action alone.[1]

If this is granted, we may go farther. For a plot, in the enlarged sense here given to the term, is not merely a particular synthesis of particular materials of character, thought, and action, but such a synthesis endowed necessarily, because it imitates in words a sequence of human activities, with a power to affect our opinions and emotions in a certain way. We are bound, as we read or listen, to form expectations about what is coming and to feel more or less determinate desires relatively to our expectations. At the very least, if we are interested at all, we desire to know what is going to happen or how the problems faced by the characters are going to be solved. This is a necessary condition of our pleasure in all plots, and there are many good ones—in the classics of pure detective fiction, for example, or in some modern psychiatric novels—the power of which depends almost exclusively on the pleasure we take in inferring progressively, from complex or ambiguous signs, the true state of affairs. For some readers and even some critics this would seem to be the chief source of delight in many plots that have obviously been constructed on more specific principles: not only *Tom Jones,* as we have seen, but *Oedipus* has been praised as a mystery story, and it is likely that much of Henry James's popularity is due to his remarkable capacity for provoking a superior kind of inferential activity. What distinguishes all the more developed forms of imitative literature, however, is that, though they presuppose this instinctive pleasure in learning, they go beyond it and give us plots of which the effects derive in a much more immediate way from the particular ethical qualities manifested in their agents' actions and thoughts vis-à-vis the human situations in which they are engaged. When this is the case, we cannot help becoming, in a greater or less degree, emotionally involved; for some of the characters we wish good, for others ill, and, depending on our inferences as to the events, we feel hope or fear, pity or satisfaction, or some modification of these or similar emotions. The peculiar power of any plot of this kind, as it unfolds, is a result of our state of knowledge at any point in complex interaction with our desires for the characters as morally differentiated beings; and we may be said to have grasped the plot in the full artistic sense only when we have analyzed this interplay of desires and expectations sequentially in relation to the incidents by which it is produced.

It is, of course, an essential condition of such an effect that the writer should so have combined his elements of action, character, and thought as to have achieved a

---

[1] This accounts in large part, I think, for the depreciation of "plot" in E. M. Forster's *Aspects of the Novel,* and for his notion of a rivalry between "plot" and "character," in which one or the other may "triumph." For a view much closer to that argued in this essay see Elizabeth Bowen, "Notes on Writing a Novel," *Orion,* II (1945), 18 ff. *Au.*

complete and ordered whole, with all the parts needed to carry the protagonist, by probable or necessary stages, from the beginning to the end of his change: we should not have, otherwise, any connected series of expectations wherewith to guide our desires. In itself, however, this structure is only the matter or content of the plot and not its form; the form of the plot—in the sense of that which makes its matter into a definite artistic thing—is rather its distinctive "working or power," as the form of the plot in tragedy, for example, is the capacity of its unified sequence of actions to effect through pity and fear a cartharsis of such emotions.

But if this is granted, then certain consequences follow for the criticism of dramas and novels. It is evident, in the first place, that no plot of this order can be judged excellent *merely* in terms of the unity of its action, the number and variety of its incidents, or the extent to which it produces suspense and surprise. These are but properties of its matter, and their achievement, even to a high degree, in any particular plot does not inevitably mean that the emotional effect of the whole will not still be diffused or weak. They are, therefore, necessary, but not sufficient, conditions of a good plot, the positive excellence of which depends upon the power of its peculiar synthesis of character, action, and thought, as inferable from the sequence of words, to move our feelings powerfully and pleasurably in a certain definite way.

But this power, which constitutes the form of the plot, is obviously, from an artistic point of view, the most important virtue any drama or novel can have; it is that, indeed, which most sharply distinguishes works of imitation from all other kinds of literary productions. It follows, consequently, that the plot, considered formally, of any imitative work is, in relation to the work as a whole, not simply a means—a "framework" or "mere mechanism"—but rather the final end which everything in the work, if that is to be felt as a whole, must be made, directly or indirectly, to serve. For the critic, therefore, the form of the plot is a first principle, which he must grasp as clearly as possible for any work he proposes to examine before he can deal adequately with the questions raised by its parts. This does not mean that we cannot derive other relevant principles of judgment from the general causes of pleasure operative in all artistic imitations, irrespective of the particular effect, serious or comic, that is aimed at in a given work. One of these is the imitative principle itself, the principle that we are in general more convinced and moved when things are "rendered" for us through probable signs than when they are given merely in "statement," without illusion, after the fashion of a scenario.[2] Critical judgments, valid enough if they are not taken absolutely, may also be drawn from considerations of the general powers of language as a literary medium, of the known potentialities or requirements of a given manner of representation (e.g., dramatic or narrative), and of the various conditions of suspense and surprise. We are not likely to feel strongly the emotional effect of a work in which the

---

[2] The meaning and force of this will be clear to anyone who has compared in detail the text of *The Ambassadors* with James's preliminary synopsis of the novel (*The Notebooks of Henry James* [New York, 1947], pp. 372-415). See also the excellent remarks of Allen Tate, apropos of *Madame Bovary,* in his "Techniques of Fiction" (*Forms of Modern Fiction,* ed. William Van O'Connor [Minneapolis, 1948], esp. pp. 37-45). *Au.*

worse rather than the better alternatives among these different expedients are con-sistently chosen or chosen in crucial scenes. The same thing, too, can be said of works in which the thought, however clearly serving an artistic use, is generally uninterest-ing or stale, or in which the characters of the agents, though right enough in concep-tion for the intended effect, are less than adequately "done" or fail to impress them-selves upon our memory and imagination, or in which we perceive that the most has not been made of the possibilities implicit in the incidents. And there is also a kind of judgment, distinct from any of these, the object of which is not so much the traits of a work that follow from its general character as an imitative drama or novel as the qualities of intelligence and moral sensibility in its author which are reflected in his conception and handling of its subject and which warrant us in ascribing "greatness," "seriousness," or "maturity" to some products of art and in denying these values to oth-ers no matter how excellent, in a formal sense, the latter may be.

Such criticism of parts in the light of general principles is indispensable, but it is no substitute for—and its conclusions, affirmative as well as negative, have constantly to be checked by—the more specific kind of criticism of a work that takes the form of the plot as its starting point and then inquires how far and in what way its peculiar power is maximized by the writer's invention and development of episodes, his step-by-step rendering of the characters of his people, his use and elaboration of thought, his handling of diction and imagery, and his decisions as to the order, method, scale, and point of view of his representation.

James Phelan

James Phelan was born in Flushing, New York, in 1951 and educated at Boston College and at the University of Chicago, where he completed his doctorate in English in 1977. Since that year he has taught in the English de-partment at The Ohio State University, where he currently serves as Chair. Rather than orienting his work around the texts of a given historical period, Phelan typically gravitates toward theoretical issues or problems and pur-sues them in texts from different periods. He has written about style in *Worlds from Words* (1983); about character and narrative progression in *Reading People, Reading Plots* (from which this excerpt is taken); and, most recently, about voice, homodiegetic narration, and audiences in *Narrative as Rhetoric*. He has also published the autobiographical journal *Beyond the Tenure Track: Fifteen Months in the Life of an English Professor* and has edited *Reading Narrative, Understanding Narrative* (with Peter J. Rabinowitz) and *The Adventures of Huckleberry Finn: Case Study in Cri-tical Controversy* (with Gerald Graff). The editor of the journal *Narrative*, Phelan is working on a study of narrative dynamics.

Functions of Character

I

Some twenty years ago, in a critical age more innocent than our own, David Lodge advanced the argument that everything in a novel could be explained by reference to an author's choice of language, and that therefore character is only a convenient abstraction from verbal signs. Part of Lodge's argument involved the following "watch, I'll-show-you" demonstration:

> If I wish to describe an actual person, Mr. Brown, I might be able to choose between calling him *tall* or *big, dark* or *swarthy*. . . . But I could never "choose" between calling him *tall* or *short, dark* or *fair*. If he is a character in a novel, however, I can choose to describe him as tall and fair, or short and dark, or short and fair, or tall and dark. I can also call him Mr. Green or Mr. Grey or by any other name. I could conceivably call him all these things for a special literary effect: *Mr. Brown, or Green as he was sometimes called, was short, but tall with it. His fair-complexioned face was swarthy. As one of his friends remarked, "Grey is a difficult man to pin down."*[1]

In an earlier book, I have argued at some length that Lodge's example actually works against his case because it shows that character cannot be fully explained by reference to language alone.[2] The passage describes a particular chameleon-like character, and though the character may still be in process (indeed he may always be in process), the representation of him in the first two sentences puts constraints on the language of the third. If that sentence is to remain a summary that also adds to the description, there are countless things the friend cannot say, including, for example, "Brown is an easy man to pin down." My claim in short is that Lodge's attempt to collapse character under language actually shows that character can put constraints on language.

Since in the earlier book my focus was on the role of language in fiction, I pursued those implications of the claim most relevant to my developing argument that language played a great variety of roles, ranging from the crucial to the incidental, in the achievement of fictional effects. Now I want to consider some other implications of Lodge's passage and my reading of it. What else can we conclude about character in imaginative literature besides the fact that it is or at least can be a nonlinguistic (or translinguistic) element? In one respect, of course, Lodge's commentary on his demonstration is very much on target: this description does not refer to a real person.[3] Fur-

---

[1] David Lodge, *Language of Fiction* (New York: Columbia University Press, 1966), pp. 63–64. *Au.*

[2] *Worlds from Words* (Chicago: University of Chicago Press, 1981), pp. 81–86. *Au.*

[3] I refrain from saying that the description absolutely *could not* refer to a real person because one could construct a plausible context for Lodge's sketch. But unless we had evidence to know that such an unusual context was operating, we would, by drawing on our conventional understanding of people in the real world, quickly conclude that the description was fictive discourse. For more on fictive discourse, see Barbara Herrnstein Smith, *On the Margins of Discourse* (Chicago: University of Chicago Press, 1978). *Au.*

thermore, Lodge's setup and execution of the description foreground its artificiality: Brown-Green-Grey is neither real nor the image of a real person but rather is a construct, designed as an amusing display of authorial ingenuity which will also make Lodge's argumentative point about the importance of language in fiction. Although our awareness of, say, Hamlet, or Huck Finn, or Clarissa Dalloway, as made-up is not foregrounded to the degree it is with Brown-Green-Grey, we can recognize that such an awareness is part of our apprehension of them as characters. Part of being a fictional character, in other words, is being artificial in this sense, and part of knowing a character is knowing that he/she/(it?)[4] is a construct. I will hereafter call the "artificial" component of character the *synthetic*.

Lodge's example, I think, gets its punch from the interaction of this synthetic component with something else, namely, Brown-Green-Grey's possession of recognizable traits: his being short, tall, swarthy, fair; his having surnames. In other words, the description creates its effect by playing off—and with—the way characters are images of possible people. Lodge gives Brown-Green-Grey traits that normally help us identify a person, but by giving this character two or three traits where one is usually present and by having the second and third contradict the first, Lodge takes away as he gives: this person is not really a person. To identify the concept implied in the phrase "this person," I propose that we recognize a second component of character, what I will hereafter call the *mimetic*.

If we were to abstract Lodge's example from its context, and ask what is the point of describing such a character, we could no doubt generate a variety of answers: it is a comment on the way the times require us to perform multiple social roles; it is a response to all those male poems about the inconstancy of women, suggesting that men are fickle through and through; it is a paean to the complexity of even the most ordinary individual. I am not interested here in choosing any of these answers as superior to the others, and, indeed, I shall later return to discuss why all in one important way miss the mark. But I am interested in what this ordinary ability to generate such answers suggests about literary character. The ability is no doubt connected with what Jonathan Culler has identified as that part of literary competence called "the rule of significance"—"read the poem as expressing a significant attitude concerning man and/or his relation to the universe."[5] (Thus, my later question will in effect be why we would be incompetent to follow that rule here.) More pertinent to my purposes here, the ability to generate such statements of significance reveals another component that character may have. In each statement, Brown-Green-Grey is taken as a representative figure, as standing for a class—the individual in modern society, men, the ordinary human, respectively—and his representativeness then supports some proposition or assertion allegedly made by Lodge through his text. This exercise suggests, then, that character also has a *thematic* component, while my claim that each of the three statements of significance somehow misses the mark suggests that his component may not always be developed.

---

[4] Joel Weinsheimer gets some useful mileage out of calling Jane Austen's protagonist "It" in "Theory of Character: *Emma*," *Poetics Today* 1, nos. 1–2 (1979): 185–211. *Au.*

[5] Jonathan Culler, *Structuralist Poetics: Structuralism, Linguistics, and the Study of Literature* (Ithaca, N.Y.: Cornell University Press, 1975), p. 115. *Au.*

In summary, this further consideration of Lodge's colorful creation indicates that character too can be multichromatic, that it is a literary element composed of three components, the mimetic, thematic, and synthetic, and that the mimetic and thematic components may be more or less developed, whereas the synthetic component, though always present, may be more or less foregrounded.[6] The logical next questions are whether the synthetic, by virtue of its ineradicable presence, ought to be privileged in our theoretical account of character and whether we can determine under what general conditions the mimetic and thematic components get more or less developed. Again it will be useful to work with a specific case in which the creation of a character is the focal point of the text. So I move from Lodge's Brown-Green-Grey to Browning's Duke of Ferrara, a more complex creation than our flexible friend.

In an essay on issues facing contemporary American criticism, Jonathan Culler offers in capsule form the structuralist view of character, one suggesting that critics

---

[6] Although Bernard J. Paris uses the terms *mimetic, thematic,* and *aesthetic* to talk about literary character, the eventual direction and emphasis of his studies of character are very different from my own. His schema is a prelude to his discussion of the mimetic component in the terms of third force psychology. See his *A Psychological Approach to Fiction* (Bloomington: Indiana University Press, 1974) and *Character and Conflict in Jane Austen's Fiction* (Detroit: Wayne State University Press, 1978). Much of my work on character in this book also has some point of contact with numerous other works on the subject (especially those done in the past ten years), but my argument typically leaves that common point and goes on to make its own different claims. Thus, I have typically found those works to be useful supplements or contrasts to mine but have not drawn on them in an extended way. The useful works include Mary Doyle Springer, *A Rhetoric of Literary Character* (Chicago: University of Chicago Press, 1978), Martin Price, *Forms of Life* (New Haven: Yale University Press, 1983), Thomas Docherty, *Reading (Absent) Character* (New York: Oxford University Press, 1983), Baruch Hochman, *Character in Literature* (Ithaca: Cornell University Press, 1985), and Robert Higbie, *Character and Structure in the English Novel* (Gainesville: University of Florida Press, 1984). See also the chapter-length discussions of character by Seymour Chatman in *Story and Discourse* (Ithaca: Cornell University Press, 1978) and by Alexander Gelley in *Narrative Crossings* (Baltimore: Johns Hopkins Press, 1987). In addition to the essay by Joel Weinsheimer cited in note 4 above, see the essay by Rawdon Wilson, "The Bright Chimera: Character as a Literary Term," *Critical Inquiry* 5 (1979): 725–49, and, for a strict structuralist account, A. J. Greimas, "Les actants, les acteurs, et les figures," in *Semiotique narrative et textuelle,* ed. C. Chabrol (Paris: Seuil, 1973). Before the proliferation of studies in the last ten years, the main book on character was Walter J. Harvey's *Character in the Novel* (Ithaca: Cornell University Press, 1965). And virtually all of these studies make reference to E. M. Forster's discussion of character in *Aspects of the Novel,* especially his famous distinction between "flat" and "round" characters.

Of these studies, Springer's shares more of my theoretical principles than any of the others, but my way of talking about character is quite different from her concern with "people like us" and my study has a much larger scope: she focuses on female characters in Henry James's novellas; I range from protagonists to minor characters in narratives from Austen to Calvino. I share Hochman's desire to defend the mimetic component, but again our studies move in different directions. Docherty provides the greatest contrast with my approach; he is far less accepting of the realist tradition in narrative and of the critical tradition of talking about the mimetic component of character. Higbie's thoughtful attempt to develop a "syncretic criticism" that can account for the psychological, structuralist, and sociohistorical elements of character has some affinities with my approach here, but there are many issues on which we part company, especially about the way in which character interacts with the other narrative elements. I have chosen not to discuss these alternative approaches to character at great length because, as will be noted later in this introduction, I felt that I could better indicate the implications and consequences of my approach by examining its consequences for issues in the interpretation of narrative that go beyond the element of character itself. I will, however, shortly compare my approach with one version of a strict structuralist approach. *Au.*

should turn away from what I have called the mimetic component of character and privilege the synthetic component: "The most intense and satisfying reading experiences may depend upon what we call involvement with characters, but successful critical investigation of the structure and effects of a novel, as a literary construct, may require thinking of characters as sets of predicates grouped under proper names."[7] Culler's discussion in *Structuralist Poetics* of Todorov's and Barthes' work on character clarifies this view by shedding light on what he means by predicates. Todorov, he says, "proposes to treat characters as proper names to which certain *qualities* are attached during the course of the narrative. Characters are not heroes, villains, or helpers; they are simply subjects of a group of predicates which the reader adds up as he goes along."[8] In *S/Z* Barthes treats Sarrasine as "the meeting place of turbulence, artistic ability, independence, violence, excess, femininity, etc."[9] Note first that Culler's conception of character as a collection of predicates does not go beyond interpretation—the predicates (or qualities) sometimes must be inferred from seeing a proper name associated with speech, thought, or action, or indeed, with speech associated with another proper name. By simultaneously depending at least in part on interpretation and denying any importance to the mimetic component, Culler does bring the thematic component of character (and then by extension of narrative in general) into an almost equal prominence with the synthetic. One consequence of Culler's conception is that it can resolve many critical disputes about particular characters by declaring that such disputes are themselves the result of a common category mistake. Applying Culler's conception to, say, the notorious dispute about whether the governess in *The Turn of the Screw* is sane or insane, we could conclude that the dispute stems from the mistaken assumption that the character is a representation of a possible person. Jettisoning that assumption, we could then more properly understand the character as the meeting place of both sane bravery and insane paranoia.

Applying this view to Browning's poem yields the following results. Through the use of pretended speech acts, Browning has made "Ferrara" the meeting place of many predicates or qualities: imperiousness, power, unscrupulousness ("I gave commands; Then all smiles stopped together"); vanity ("She thanked . . . as if she ranked/ My gift of a nine-hundred-years-old name/ With anybody's gift"); possessiveness ("None sets by/ That curtain I have drawn for you but I"); appreciation of beauty ("I call that piece a wonder now;" There she stands/ As if alive"). In addition, two rather incompatible qualities meet under "Ferrara": "mental instability," a quality inferred by concluding that the emissary from the Count is an inappropriate audience for the speech acts of the poem; and "boldness," a quality inferred by concluding that the emissary is an appropriate audience. Since the poem is Browning's creation of a character, this delineation of predicates gives us the major structural elements of the whole. The full structure results from the intersection of this larger set of predicates with a smaller set grouped under "my last duchess," a set whose most important members are friendliness, beauty, openness to pleasure. The poem reveals the character of the Duke by in-

---

[7] Jonathan Culler, "Issues in Contemporary American Criticism," in Ira Konigsberg (ed.) *American Criticism in the Poststructuralist Age* (Ann Arbor: University of Michigan Press, 1981), p. 5. *Au.*

[8] *Structuralist Poetics*, p. 235. *Au.*

[9] *Ibid.*, p. 236. *Au.*

dicating how the set of qualities associated with his name dominates over the set associated with "my last duchess."

If we analyze the poem according to a conception of character that gives weight to the mimetic component, we get markedly different results. As Ralph Rader has pointed out in an analysis that assumes the importance of the mimetic component, Browning's task is to create the *illusion* that we are not reading a poem but overhearing part of a conversation.[10] More specifically, Browning seeks to make the Duke's speech appear to be motivated entirely by the dramatic situation, even while it paints a complete portrait of him—complete, that is, within the limits of the implied dramatic situation. In sum, the Duke is a character whose mimetic component is overtly emphasized while his synthetic component, though present, remains covert. At this stage of the analysis, his thematic component does not figure prominently, but I will later discuss its place in the poem.

It may seem odd to argue that the synthetic remains covert when we are reading a poem written in rhymed couplets, but a short thought experiment suggested by Rader will help justify the point. Who is responsible for the rhymes, Browning or the Duke? The fact that we instinctively answer "Browning" indicates the kind of involvement with the Duke we have: we have only his voice but we do not hear *him* rhyming. The synthetic is there but it remains covert. To the more general question of whether a poem will always appear more synthetic than prose, I answer, not necessarily. Whenever we read a title page which tells us that the work is a novel, we know we are reading something as synthetic as any poem. But neither this knowledge nor our perception of line breaks, stanzas, and rhymes necessarily prevents our participating in the mimetic illusion. To participate in the illusion is to enter what Peter Rabinowitz has called the narrative audience; to remain covertly aware of the synthetic is to enter what Rabinowitz has called the authorial audience.[11] In other words, the authorial audience has the double consciousness of the mimetic and the synthetic, while the narrative audience has a single consciousness of the Duke as real. I will be discussing the nature of—and the relation between—these audiences in more detail in later chapters; for now let me just note that the authorial audience is the ideal audience that an author implicitly posits in constructing her text, the one which will pick up on all the signals in the appropriate way. When I speak about "our" responses in the pages that follow, I am referring to the responses of this audience. The narrative audience is that group of readers for whom the lyric, dramatic, or narrative situation is not synthetic but real. For the mimetic illusion to work, we must enter the narrative audience. To enter it in Browning's poem is to imagine oneself an invisible eavesdropper who hears and sees just this part of the interview between the Duke and the envoy.

---

[10] Ralph Rader, "The Dramatic Monologue and Related Lyric Forms," *Critical Inquiry* 3 (1976): 131–51. *Au.*

[11] Peter Rabinowitz, "Truth in Fiction: A Reexamination of Audiences," *Critical Inquiry* 4 (1977): 121–41. See also his "Assertion and Assumption: Fictional Patterns and the External World," *PMLA* 96 (1981): 408–19. Rabinowitz's book *Before Reading: Narrative Conventions and the Politics of Interpretation* (Ithaca: Cornell University Press, 1987) gives an account of the conventions of "authorial reading" that in many ways complements the analyses I undertake in this book. Although there are some important overlaps between Rabinowitz's work and mine, for the most part we are focusing on different problems: he is concerned with conventions that govern reading in advance of our encounters with narrative; I am concerned with the dynamics of those encounters themselves; in a sense, with how texts themselves tell us which conventions apply. *Au.*

Within the general conception of "My Last Duchess" sketched above, we must choose between the view of the Duke as mentally unstable and the view of him as extremely bold. Is the Duke's confession of his crime against his last duchess an unwitting self-revelation or a purposeful warning? I follow Rader in concluding that it is a purposeful warning whose purpose will be accomplished only if it does not appear to be a warning. The Duke must not appear to be warning for the same reason that he never openly objected to the frequent smiling of the duchess: "E'en then would be some stooping; and I choose/ Never to stoop." This hypothesis about the Duke's character is superior to one that says he is out-of-control for two main reasons, one general, the other specific. First, it gives a definite, positive motivation for this speech in this situation, whereas the alternative is a *faute de mieux* account (I can't see any reason why the Duke would say this to the envoy from the father of his next wife, so he must be crazy). Second, this conclusion more adequately explains the rather elaborate business the Duke goes through before the main revelation.

> I said
> "Fra Pandolf" by design, for never read
> Strangers like you that pictured countenance,
> The depth and passion of its earnest glance,
> But to myself they turned *(since none puts by*
> *The curtain I have drawn for you, but I)*
> *And seemed as they would ask me, if they durst,*
> How such a glance came there; so, *not the first*
> *Are you to turn and ask thus.*
>
> *(ll. 5–12; emphasis mine)*

The inference is that the Duke is acting with premeditation here: he is determined to make the envoy "sit and look at her" so that he can tell his story and thereby give his warning-sans-stooping.

Furthermore, this hypothesis, with its emphasis on the relation between the overt mimetic and covert synthetic components of the Duke, allows for some important insights about Browning's control of the whole, a control which is perhaps most impressive in the conclusion:

> Will't please you rise? We'll meet
> The company below then. I repeat,
> The Count your master's known munificence
> Is ample warrant that no just pretence
> Of mine for dowry will be disallowed;
> Though his fair daughter's self, as I avowed
> At starting, is my object. Nay, we'll go
> Together down, sir. Notice, Neptune, though
> Taming a sea-horse, thought a rarity,
> Which Claus of Innsbruck cast in bronze for me!
>
> *(ll. 47–56)*

It is here at the end that we learn for the first time that the Duke's auditor has come on business relating to the Duke's next marriage. This delayed disclosure is of course a direct consequence of the mimetic imperative: as the poem is constructed, any prior definition of the situation by the Duke would seem an obvious contrivance by Browning. As Browning follows the mimetic imperative, he also increases the effectiveness of the poem as a constructed object. The details illuminating the dramatic situation function not just as exposition but also as climactic strokes in the portrait of the character. The Duke's horrible imperiousness has been revealed in his account of how he handled the Duchess. But the sheer audacity that accompanies that imperiousness and adds substantially to its horror is made known only when we realize the audience and the occasion for the Duke's speech.[12] In addition to making this exposition an effective device for the achievement of completeness in the poem, Browning makes it contribute substantially to the arresting quality of the portrait he is drawing. Because the full dimensions of the Duke's character dawn upon us only gradually and only in retrospect, they dawn upon us more powerfully. Finally, these concluding realizations are brilliantly set off by the last two lines of the poem, in which the Duke symbolically encapsulates his purpose ("Neptune taming a seahorse"), even while, as Rader also points out, he seems to insist that he has been talking only about art throughout the whole monologue.

Comparing the analysis based on Culler's conception of character with the one based on a conception that gives weight to a mimetic component, we find some interesting results. Despite their considerable differences, both analyses offer worthwhile insights into the poem. Choosing between them is also a matter of choosing the kind of knowledge that one wants from a theory of character. Culler suggests that his conception will lead to a better understanding of the "structure and effect" of works. I think that the parallel analyses indicate that his claim is misleading. The structuralist analysis does not yield any substantial account of the effect of the poem and has little to say about the specific structure of the whole. Instead, it identifies the basic elements out of which the structure of both the text and the character are created; this identification of basic elements is both the weakness and the strength of the analysis. By identifying the basic elements, the structuralist can indicate something about the materials out of which the mimetic analyst will build his account, but such an indication comes at the price of failing to offer any well-developed interpretation of its own.

The mimetic analysis, on the other hand, commits one to developing an account of the structure and effect of a work. Judged by that shared criterion, it does offer a superior way of theorizing about character. But the differences in the results of the analyses suggest that, Culler's reference to structure and effect aside, the methods are not always competitive and that each could be used for a different critical purpose.

---

[12] In this connection, I find the crucial detail of the revelation to be a place where Browning can't help but let the seam between mimetic and synthetic components of the poem show. Although the Duke is someone concerned about relationships of power, his enunciating what he and the envoy both obviously know ("the Count *your master*") strikes me as motivated less by the dramatic situation and more by Browning's needs to get that information to the reader. But this rough spot makes the seamlessness of the rest of the poem even more striking. *Au.*

Where the structuralist analysis tends toward the inclusive (e.g., in its identification of semantically incompatible predicates), the mimetic tends toward the restrictive: it chooses among incompatible traits, it tries to build as precise a portrait of the character as possible. Where the structuralist remains suspicious of the emotional involvement that comes from viewing the character as a possible person, the mimetic analyst regards that involvement as crucial to the effect of the work. In short, where the structuralist seeks an objective view of the text, one which foregrounds the text as construct, the mimetic analyst takes a rhetorical view, one which foregrounds the text as communication between author and reader. Since I want my theory to account for the structure and effect of texts by accounting for such communication, I shall pursue the rhetorical (and mimetic) view here.

The consequences of choosing the rhetorical over the structuralist conception of character become even greater as we consider the role of the thematic component within the rhetorical conception of Browning's poem. Whereas the Duke has been defined for the structuralist as the meeting place of many thematic qualities, the rhetorical analysis to this point has neglected the thematic component of the Duke's character. Does the Duke have a role in the structure of the poem that leads to our abstracting thematic conclusions from it? The best answer, I think, is yes and no. On the one hand, it is fairly easy to construct thematic propositions that are implied or reinforced by Browning's creation of the Duke, propositions that would go right along with the structuralist conception of the character.[13] A partial list would include: to execute one's spouse for her friendliness is horrible; to possess beauty by killing it is reprehensible; power corrupts; men (frequently) treat women as possessions that exist for the sole purpose of giving them pleasure. On the other hand, these propositions are not conclusions that the poem itself leads one toward in the way that, say, Golding's *Lord of the Flies* tries to lead the reader toward the conclusion that humans are inherently evil. Instead, these propositions are in effect taken for granted by Browning. The powerful effect of his portrait does not depend on his demonstrating the truth of these assertions; rather these are general propositions whose truth Browning presumes independently of our reading the poem and on which he relies to make his portrait more arresting.

We can usefully distinguish between the thematic elements of a character like the Duke and of one like Jack in Golding's novel by making a distinction between a character's *dimensions* and his or her *functions*. A dimension is any attribute a character may be said to possess when that character is considered in isolation from the work in which he or she appears. A function is a particular application of that attribute made by the text through its developing structure. In other words, dimensions are converted into functions by the *progression* of the work. Thus, every function depends upon a dimension but not every dimension will necessarily correspond to a function. The Duke has many thematic dimensions (attributes that may be considered for their po-

---

13 Interestingly, however, many structuralists, including Culler, would want to resist any direct move from "work to world," any claim that the propositions had reference to the world beyond the text. For more on this point, see my "Thematic Reference, Literary Structure, and Fictive Character: An Examination of Interrelationships," *Semiotica* 48 3-4 (1984): 345-65, which also sets forth an early version of my account of "My Last Duchess." *Au.*

tential to contribute to thematic assertions) but essentially no thematic function: the work progresses not to make assertions but to reveal his character. Golding's Jack has many thematic dimensions—his lust for power, his willingness to destroy nature for his own advantage, his greater concern with short-term advantage than long-term good, and so on—that all contribute to his main thematic function of demonstrating the strength of inherent evil in humans. The distinction between dimensions and functions allows us to see why applying the rule of significance to the case of Mr. Brown-Green-Grey would be an act of literary incompetence. Lodge's character, like Browning's, has thematic dimensions—he is male and chameleon-like, he resists fixities, and so on—but no thematic function: the text achieves closure before it develops the thematic potentiality of these dimensions.

The distinction between dimensions and functions also applies to the mimetic and synthetic components of character, though, as we shall see, it has a greater relevance to the mimetic. Furthermore, it allows me to resituate the importance of the mimetic component within the general rhetorical approach to character I have been defining. The distinction between dimensions and functions is based on the principle that the fundamental unit of character is neither the trait nor the idea, neither the role nor the word, but rather what I will call the *attribute,* something that participates at least in potential form in the mimetic, thematic, and synthetic spheres of meaning simultaneously. Thus, the rhetorical theorist need not stipulate in advance that the characters in a given work will be represented people, or themes with legs, or obvious artificial constructs. The theorist only commits himself to the position that a character may come to perform any of these functions or indeed all three of them to varying degrees within the same narrative.

An analogy with the way speakers use utterances may clarify the distinction between dimensions and functions. Most utterances contain a potential for signification greater than the signification actualized, if only because most utterances do not take advantage of the signifying potential of the sounds used to make them. Nevertheless, a speaker may take advantage of this signifying potential by shaping his utterance in such a way that its sounds call attention to themselves. The teacher who bids good morning to his class in rhymed couplets conveys an attitude with those rhymes that is simply not present in a prosaic greeting. Or to take a more standard example, recall how Pope in "An Essay on Criticism" reinforces his dictum about sound echoing the sense by exemplifying his point in his own lines:

> Soft is the strain when Zephyr gently blows,
> And the smooth stream in smoother numbers flows;
> But when loud surges lash the sounding shore,
> The hoarse, rough verse should like the torrent roar.
> When Ajax strives some rock's vast weight to throw,
> The line too labors, and the words move slow.
>
> *(ll. 366-71)*

Similarly, when an author creates a character, she creates a potential for that character to participate in the signification of the work through the development of the character in three spheres of meaning; that potential may or may not be realized depending upon the way the whole work is shaped.

At the same time, we need to remember that, as we read, characters do not come to us first as attributes which we recognize as dimensions which then become transformed into functions as we look on in wonder, but that they come to us already in the process of being shaped into functions, or (especially within the mimetic sphere) as already functioning. When we read, "Miss Brooke had that sort of beauty that seemed to be set in relief by poor dress," or "Emma Woodhouse, handsome, clever, and rich, seemed to unite in her person the best blessings of existence," we are immediately encountering characters who are already performing mimetic functions. The point, in other words, is that my rhetorical theory of character is claiming to offer analytical distinctions that allow us to understand the principles upon which works are constructed rather than claiming to offer a blow-by-blow description of what happens when we read.[14]

II

This sketch of a framework for a rhetorical approach to character also indicates the conditions that must be satisfied for that sketch to develop into an adequate working theory of character in narrative. (1) We need to explore further the nature of the three components, including the relation between dimensions and functions. (2) We need to investigate the range of relations among the three different functions. (3) We need to investigate the nature and variety of narrative progression so that we can better understand the mechanisms by which dimensions get converted into functions. Fully satisfying these conditions will be the task of the later chapters, but here I can take some initial steps toward satisfying the first and third conditions.

---

[14] It will be obvious by now that my conception of a rhetorical theory of character—or of literature more generally—is sharply different from the rhetorical approach to literature taken by such deconstructive critics as J. Hillis Miller in *Fiction and Repetition* (Cambridge: Harvard University Press, 1982) and Paul de Man in *Allegories of Reading* (New Haven: Yale University Press, 1979). Although these critics have their differences from each other, they share the idea that a rhetorical approach involves the analysis of rhetorical figures and tropes implied in a text's use of language. Implicitly defining the text as a linguistic structure first and foremost, they cut the language of the text off from its author and its implied audience. They then scrutinize the figures and tropes of the text and typically show how the apparent logic behind the use of these figures and tropes undermines itself. By contrast, within my rhetorical approach I define the text as a communicative transaction between author and reader carried out through the various elements of the text (including such translinguistic ones as character and action) as these are shaped and designed for a particular purpose. In one sense, because the definitions of the text within these two rhetorical approaches are so different, their rivalry is not as intense as might first appear. In effect, one approach asks, what did the author mean to communicate through this language?; and the other asks, what can the language of this text, when viewed from the logic of figuration, be construed to mean? Each might say to the other than what the approach yields is valid, given its starting point. To argue over the starting point here would require me take a detour so wide that I might never get back to the main track of my investigation. I have decided, therefore, to stay on the main track and let my findings be a partial argument for the validity of my starting point. For an argument that directly takes up Miller's view of language and tries to indicate its deficiencies, see my *Worlds from Words,* Chap. 4. *Au.*

Mimetic dimensions, as we have seen, are a character's attributes considered as traits, e.g., the Duke's maleness, his position of power, his imperiousness, his boldness, and so on. Mimetic functions result from the way these traits are used together in creating the illusion of a plausible person and, for works depicting actions, in making particular traits relevant to later actions, including of course the development of new traits. In works where the traits fail to coalesce into the portrait of a possible person, e.g., Swift's creation of Gulliver, or some modern works intent on destroying the mimetic illusion, a character will have mimetic dimensions without a mimetic function. Moreover, within the creation of a possible person, a particular trait might serve only to identify that character, e.g., the detective who always eats junk food, and the trait might not (though it often will) have any consequences for his later actions—or for our understanding of them. In such a case, the character has a mimetic dimension that is incidental to his or her mimetic function: the plausibility of the portrait would remain without the trait and the rest of the work would be essentially unaffected by its absence.

Silently underlying this discussion of the mimetic component are some messy problems. First, all this talk about characters as plausible or possible persons presupposes that we know what a person is. But the nature of the human subject is of course a highly contested issue among contemporary thinkers. Although this study of character can have consequences for that debate, I shall not take it up directly here. Not only would such a discussion require lengthy excursions into biological, philosophical, sociological, and economic territories that would preclude the exploration I have just begun but, more important, such a discussion is not a necessary preliminary to the rhetorical study I am undertaking. For that to be justified, it is enough that authors write with some working notion of what a person is and with some belief that characters can (or indeed, cannot) represent persons and that as readers and critics we can discern these ideas in the work. At the same time, this principle means that for certain works we may need to invoke the findings of psychology, sociology, economics, biology, and/or philosophy because authors may be drawing on (or perhaps anticipating) these findings in their representations of the mimetic components of character. Thus, for example, it seems to me necessary to know something about the psychoanalytic understanding of character to enter the authorial audience of *Light in August:* certain features of the representation of Joe Christmas as a possible person that are rendered comprehensible by that knowledge remain virtually inscrutable without it. On the other hand, we do not need such an understanding to enter the authorial audience of, say, *Tom Jones* or *Pride and Prejudice:* the characters in these works, though perhaps susceptible to psychoanalytical interpretation, are constructed and offered to us on different principles.

The second problem is related to the first: how to specify adequately the criteria by which to judge a given representation of a character as plausible or not. For the most part, such a representation is a matter of conventions and the conventions change over time as both ideas about persons and fictional techniques for representing persons change. Modern readers may have a hard time finding Pamela Andrews a possible person but Richardson's contemporary readers (*pace* Henry Fielding) did not. Thus, I think that for my purposes flexible, shifting criteria are superior to fixed ones. Since my goal is to understand the principles upon which a narrative is constructed, I shall seek to make my judgments according to what I know or can infer about the conventions under which a given author is operating. Furthermore, we ought to recognize from the outset that it is very easy to call any character's plausibility into question by abstracting the character's behavior from the situations which influence it. Is it really plausible that a man who has been king all his life would be able to learn anything about himself by giving up his kingship and then hanging around on a heath in a storm with a fool, a disguised friend, and someone pretending to be mad? Come off it, Mr. Playwright. Finally, in addition to judging plausibility in connection with the whole web of circumstances surrounding a character's actions, I will out of respect for the variety of human behavior and experience seek to err on the side of generosity rather than of parsimony in judging plausibility: the dividends that might accrue to our remaining open to the idea that such and such a person could exist and behave in such and such a way in such and such a situation are more rewarding than the satisfaction we might get by initially questioning the plausibility of such a creation.

Thematic dimensions, as we have seen, are attributes taken individually or collectively, and viewed as vehicles to express ideas or as representative of a larger class than the individual character (in the case of satire the attributes will be representative of a person, group, or institution external to the work). Just as characters may be functioning mimetically from our first introduction to them, so too may they be functioning thematically, but just as the full mimetic function is often not revealed in the initial stages of a narrative, so too may thematic functions emerge more gradually. In works that strive to give characters a strong overt mimetic function, thematic functions develop from thematic dimensions as a character's traits and actions also demonstrate, usually implicitly, some proposition or propositions about the class of people or the dramatized ideas. Usually, the narrative will then use these functions to influence the way we respond to the actions of the character, and sometimes the progression may make these functions crucial to the work's final effect, even if the work is not organized to convince us of a particular proposition. We shall see an example of such a narrative shortly, when I turn to discuss Lardner's "Haircut." In works where the artificiality or the synthetic nature of characters is more overt, thematic dimensions get developed into functions somewhat differently: the representative quality of the traits or ideas will usually be explicitly revealed in the action or the narrative discourse. Golding's initial description of Jack connects Jack's physical appearance with the conventional image of Satan. Thus, Jack's physical attributes immediately give him a thematic dimension that is of course later converted into a thematic function.

The distinction between the mimetic and thematic components of character is a distinction between characters as individuals and characters as representative entities. In attaching the notion of "plausible person" to the mimetic component, I do not mean to imply that my own working concept of a person precludes representativeness. It seems to me that our understanding of people in life also commonly has a thematic component: we see the traits that others possess as defining a type of person or a set of ideas and attitudes that are not peculiarly their own. We say, "He's a sixties flower-child," or "She's a radical feminist," and imply that the identities of these people can be summed up by a set of ideas or values associated with those descriptions. At the same time, we (i.e., those of us sharing a fairly widespread, though less than universal, belief about how to treat other people) commonly regard ourselves as more enlightened, more open, more tolerant, if we refrain from making any quick leaps from traits to themes. Indeed, we label those who leap from skin color or sex to assumptions about a person as racist or sexist. As I have already suggested in the discussion of "My Last Duchess," we must also resist the automatic ascription of traits to themes in literature. In both cases, then, the problem arises not from thematizing itself but from doing so prematurely or carelessly, i.e., without sufficient attention to the relation of the trait to the rest of the person or character and the situation and actions in which he or she is engaged.

On the other side of this similarity between people and literary characters, there is, of course, a significant difference: however much we may wish that Ronald Reagan or Howard Cosell or the next door neighbor were just an artificial construct, each of them is undeniably organic, just as Elizabeth Bennet and Prince Hamlet of Denmark and Hester Prynne are undeniably synthetic. One consequence of the difference, I think, is that we are given a greater license for thematizing in literature; though we must remain wary of hasty jumps from trait to theme, we are likely to be invited to make more considered ones. Because literary characters are synthetic, their creators are likely to be doing something more than increasing the population, more than trying to bring another possible person into the world. They are likely to be increasing the population in order to show us something about the segment of the population to which the created member belongs.

As this point implies, the ineradicability of the synthetic component marks it off from the mimetic and thematic components: in the synthetic sphere dimensions are always also functions. Synthetic dimensions will always be synthetic functions because they will always have some role in the construction of the work; this role may be extraneous or disruptive, the character's other components may interfere with the success of the synthetic function, but the function cannot be eliminated. Furthermore, although every mimetic and thematic function implies a synthetic function, not every synthetic function implies a mimetic or thematic one. The unnamed emissary in "My Last Duchess" has a mimetic dimension by virtue of his status relative to both the Duke and the Count, but he has no functions other than the synthetic one of being the appropriate addressee for the Duke's veiled warning. (The Count, of course, is a character with mimetic and thematic dimensions but no corresponding functions.) Nevertheless, it does make sense to distinguish characters like the Duke of Ferrara whose synthetic status remains covert and those like Christian in *Pilgrim's Progress* whose synthetic status is foregrounded. Although this distinction is not strictly parallel to the distinction between dimensions and functions for the other two components, it does capture a similar phenomenon: the development of a potentiality in the character into an actuality. The means by which the synthetic component can be foregrounded are many and diverse, but one is especially noteworthy because it exploits the artificiality of the *material* out of which the character is made. An author can focus the reader's attention, through a narrator, another character's speech, or even an action, on the character's name or the descriptions of the character so that we regard the character as symbolic rather than natural. When I construct a narrative in which Smoothtalk meets Bumpkin on a bustling boulevard in Urbia, then I am inviting my readers, fit and few as the may be, to regard the characters as constructs designed for some thematic purpose.

E. M. Forster

Edward Morgan Forster was born in London in 1879. He was educated at snobbish preparatory schools at which he endured a period of misery that ended when he entered Kings College, Cambridge, at the age of seventeen. Here he studied classics and joined the "Apostles," an undergraduate society that included Bertrand Russell, Lytton Strachey, and Leonard Woolf. After graduating, Forster taught Latin at the Working-Men's College in Bloomsbury and lectured on art. In 1905 he published his first novel, *Where Angels Fear to Tread*, a subtle character study of the influence of Italy on the repressed English temperament, and followed up that success with *The Longest Journey* (1907) and *A Room with a View* (1908). His literary celebrity really began with *Howards End* (1910), a novel about class and culture in England. In 1912 Forster went to India, where he began his masterwork, *A Passage to India*. Not published until 1924, the novel manages to combine a political critique of British imperialism with a comedy of manners and metaphysical speculations on the nature of human interrelations. Forster published influential essays on the art of fiction—*Aspects of the Novel* (1926) from which the following chapter is taken—and on politics and culture—*Two Cheers for Democracy* (1951)—but his last two novels remained unpublished during his lifetime. *Maurice* (1971) and *The Life to Come* (1972) were withheld from print primarily because of their direct revelation of Forster's homosexual orientation. Forster died at Coventry, England, in 1970.

VIII

PATTERN AND RHYTHM

Our interludes, gay and grave, are over, and we return to the general scheme of the course. We began with the story, and having considered human beings, we proceeded to the plot which springs out of the story. Now we must consider something which springs mainly out of the plot, and to which the characters and any other element present also contribute. For this new aspect there appears to be no literary word—indeed the more the arts develop the more they depend on each other for definition. We will borrow from painting first and call it the pattern. Later we will borrow from music and call it rhythm. Unfortunately both these words are vague—when people apply rhythm or pattern to literature they are apt not to say what they mean and not to finish their sentences: it is, "Oh, but surely the rhythm . . ." or "Oh, but if you call that pattern . . ."

Before I discuss what pattern entails, and what qualities a reader must bring to its appreciation, I will give two examples of books with patterns so definite that a pictorial image sums them up: a book the shape of an hour-glass and a book the shape of a grand chain in that old-time dance, the Lancers.

Thais, by Anatole France, is the shape of an hour-glass.

There are two chief characters, Paphnuce the ascetic, Thais the courtesan. Paphnuce lives in the desert, he is saved and happy when the book starts. Thais leads a life of sin in Alexandria, and it is his duty to save her. In the central scene of the book they approach, he succeeds; she goes into a monastery and gains salvation, because she has met him, but he, because he has met her, is damned. The two characters converge, cross, and recede with mathematical precision, and part of the pleasure we get from the book is due to this. Such is the pattern of *Thais*—so simple that it makes a good starting-point for a difficult survey. It is the same as the story of *Thais,* when events unroll in their time-sequence, and the same as the plot of *Thais,* when we see the two characters bound by their previous actions and taking fatal steps whose consequence they do not see. But whereas the story appeals to our curiosity and the plot to our intelligence, the pattern appeals to our aesthetic sense, it causes us to see the book as a whole. We do not see it as an hour-glass—that is the hard jargon of the lecture room which must never be taken literally at this advanced stage of our enquiry. We just have a pleasure without knowing why, and when the pleasure is past, as it is now, and our minds are left free to explain it, a geometrical simile such as an hour-glass will be found helpful. If it was not for this hour-glass the story, the plot, and the characters of Thais and Paphnuce would none of them exert their full force, they would none of them breathe as they do. "Pattern," which seems so rigid is connected with atmosphere, which seems so fluid.

Now for the book that is shaped like the grand chain: *Roman Pictures* by Percy Lubbock.

Roman Pictures is a social comedy. The narrator is a tourist in Rome; he there meets a kindly and shoddy friend of his, Deering, who rebukes him superciliously for staring at churches and sets him out to explore society. This he does, demurely obedient; one person hands him on to another; café, studio, Vatican and Quirinal purlieus are all reached, until finally, at the extreme end of his career he thinks, in a most aristocratic and dilapidated palazzo, whom should he meet but the second-rate Deering; Deering is his hostess's nephew, but had concealed it owing to some backfire of snobbery. The circle is complete, the original partners have rejoined, and greet one another with mutual confusion which turns to mild laughter.

What is so good in *Roman Pictures* is not the presence of the "grand chain" pattern—any one can organize a grand chain—but the suitability of the pattern to the author's mood. Lubbock works all through by administering a series of little shocks, and by extending to his characters an elaborate charity which causes them to appear in a rather worse light than if no charity was wasted on them at all. It is the comic atmos-

phere, but sub-acid, meticulously benign. And at the end we discover to our delight
that the atmosphere has been externalized, and that the partners, as they click together in the marchesa's drawing-room, have done the exact thing which the book requires, which it required from the start, and have bound the scattered incidents together with a thread woven out of their own substance.

Thais and *Roman Pictures* provide easy examples of pattern; it is not often that
one can compare a book to a pictorial object with any accuracy, though curves, etc.,
are freely spoken of by critics who do not quite know what they want to say. We can
only say (so far) that pattern is an aesthetic aspect of the novel, and that though it may
be nourished by anything in the novel—any character, scene, word—it draws most of
its nourishment from the plot. We noted, when discussing the plot, that it added to itself the quality of beauty; beauty a little surprised at her own arrival: that upon its
neat carpentry there could be seen, by those who cared to see, the figure of the Muse;
that Logic, at the moment of finishing its own house, laid the foundation of a new one.
Here, here is the point where the aspect called pattern is most closely in touch with
its material; here is our starting point. It springs mainly from the plot, accompanies it
like a light in the clouds, and remains visible after it has departed. Beauty is sometimes
the shape of the book, the book as a whole, the unity, and our examination would be
easier if it was always this. But sometimes it is not. When it is not I shall call it rhythm.
For the moment we are concerned with pattern only.

Let us examine at some length another book of the rigid type, a book with a unity,
and in the sense an easy book, although it is by Henry James. We shall see in it pattern
triumphant, and we shall also be able to see the sacrifices an author must make if he
wants his pattern and nothing else to triumph.

The Ambassadors, like *Thais,* is the shape of an hour-glass. Strether and Chad,
like Paphnuce and Thais, change places, and it is the realization of this that makes the
book so satisfying at the close. The plot is elaborate and subtle, and proceeds by action or conversation or meditation through every paragraph. Everything is planned,
everything fits; none of the minor characters are just decorative like the talkative
Alexandrians at Nicias' banquet; they elaborate on the main theme, they work. The final effect is pre-arranged, dawns gradually on the reader, and is completely successful
when it comes. Details of intrigue, of the various missions from America, may be forgotten, but the symmetry they have created is enduring.

Let us trace the growth of this symmetry.

Strether, a sensitive middle-aged American, is commissioned by his old friend,
Mrs. Newsome, whom he hopes to marry, to go to Paris and rescue her son Chad, who
has gone to the bad in that appropriate city. The Newsomes are sound commercial
people, who have made money over manufacturing a small article of domestic utility.
Henry James never tells us what the small article is, and in a moment we shall understand why. Wells spits it out in *Tono Bungay,* Meredith reels it out in *Evan Harring-
ton,* Trollope prescribes it freely for Miss Dunstable, but for James to indicate how his
characters made their pile—it would not do. The article is somewhat ignoble and ludicrous—that is enough. If you choose to be coarse and daring and visualize it for yourself as, say, a button-hook, you can, but you do so at your own risk: the author remains
uninvolved.

Well, whatever it is, Chad Newsome ought to come back and help make it, and Strether undertakes to fetch him. He has to be rescued from a life which is both immoral and unremunerative.

Strether is a typical James character—he recurs in nearly all the books and is an essential part of their construction. He is the observer who tries to influence the action, and who through his failure to do so gains extra opportunities for observation. And the other characters are such as an observer like Strether is capable of observing—through lenses procured from a rather too first-class oculist. Everything is adjusted to his vision, yet he is not a quietist—no, that is the strength of the device; he takes us along with him, we move as well as look on.

When he lands in England (and a landing is an exalted and enduring experience for James, it is as vital as Newgate for Defoe; poetry and life crowd round a landing): when Strether lands, though it is only old England, he begins to have doubts of his mission, which increase when he gets to Paris. For Chad Newsome, far from going to the bad, has improved; he is distinguished, he is so sure of himself that he can be kind and cordial to the man who has orders to fetch him away; his friends are exquisite, and as for "women in the case" whom his mother anticipated, there is no sign of them whatever. It is Paris that has enlarged and redeemed him—and how well Strether himself understands this!

> His greatest uneasiness seemed to peep at him out of the possible impression that almost any acceptance of Paris might give one's authority away. It hung before him this morning, the vast bright Babylon, like some huge iridescent object, a jewel brilliant and hard, in which parts were not to be discriminated nor differences comfortably marked. It twinkled and trembled and melted together; and what seemed all surface one moment seemed all depth the next. It was a place of which, unmistakably, Chad was fond; wherefore, if he, Strether, should like it too much, what on earth, with such a bond, would become of either of them?

Thus, exquisitely and firmly, James sets his atmosphere—Paris irradiates the book from end to end, it is an actor though always unembodied, it is a scale by which human sensibility can be measured, and when we have finished the novel and allow its incidents to blur that we may see the pattern plainer, it is Paris that gleams at the centre of the hour-glass shape—Paris—nothing so crude as good or evil. Strether sees this soon, and sees that Chad realizes it better than he himself can; and when he has reached this stage of initiation the novel takes a turn: there is, after all, a woman in the case; behind Paris, interpreting it for Chad, is the adorable and exalted figure of Mme. de Vionnet. It is now impossible for Strether to proceed. All that is noble and refined in life concentrates in Mme. de Vionnet and is reinforced by her pathos. She asks him not to take Chad away. He promises—without reluctance, for his own heart has already shown him as much—and he remains in Paris not to fight it but to fight for it.

For the second batch of ambassadors now arrives from the New World. Mrs. Newsome, incensed and puzzled by the unseemly delay, has despatched Chad's sister, his brother-in-law, and Mamie, the girl whom he is supposed to marry. The novel now becomes, within its ordained limits, most amusing. There is a superb set-to between Chad's sister and Mme. de Vionnet, while as for Mamie—here is disastrous Mamie, seen as we see all things, through Strether's eyes.

> As a child, as a "bud," and then again as a flower of expansion, Mamie had bloomed for him, freely, in the almost incessantly open doorways of home; where he remembered her at first very forward, as then very backward—for he had carried on at one period, in Mrs. Newsome's parlours, a course of English literature reinforced by exams and teas—and once more, finally, as very much in advance. But he had kept no great sense of points of contact; it not being in the nature of things at Woollett that the freshest of the buds should find herself in the same basket with the most withered of the winter apples. . . . He none the less felt now, as he sat with the charming girl, the signal growth of a confidence. For she *was* charming, when all was said, and none the less so for the visible habit and practice of freedom and fluency. She was charming, he was aware, in spite of the fact that if he hadn't found her so he would have found her something he should have been in peril of expressing as "funny." Yes, she was funny, wonderful Mamie, and without dreaming it; she was bland, she was bridal—with never, that he could make out as yet, a bridegroom to support it; she was handsome and portly, and easy and chatty, soft and sweet and almost disconcertingly reassuring. She was dressed, if we might so far discriminate, less as a young lady than as an old one—had an old one been supposable to Strether as so committed to vanity; the complexities of her hair missed moreover also the looseness of youth; and she had a mature manner of bending a little, as to encourage and reward, while she held neatly in front of her a pair of strikingly polished hands: the combination of all of which kept up about her the glamour of her "receiving," placed her again perpetually between the windows and within sound of the ice cream plates, suggested the enumeration of all the names, gregarious specimens of a single type, she was happy to "meet."

Mamie! She is another Henry James type; nearly every novel contains a Mamie—Mrs. Gereth in *The Spoils of Poynton* for instance, or Henrietta Stackpole in *The Portrait of a Lady*. He is so good at indicating instantaneously and constantly that a character is second rate, deficient in sensitiveness, abounding in the wrong sort of worldliness; he gives such a character so much vitality that its absurdity is delightful.

So Strether changes sides and loses all hopes of marrying Mrs. Newsome. Paris is winning—and then he catches sight of something new. Is not Chad, as regards any fineness in him, played out? Is not Chad's Paris after all just a place for a spree? This fear is confirmed. He goes for a solitary country walk, and at the end of the day he comes across Chad and Mme. de Vionnet. They are in a boat, they pretend not to see him, because their relation is at bottom an ordinary liaison, and they are ashamed. They were hoping for a secret week-end at an inn while their passion survived; for it will not survive, Chad will tire of the exquisite Frenchwoman, she is part of his fling; he will go back to his mother and make the little domestic article and marry Mamie. They know all this, and it is revealed to Strether though they try to hide it; they lie, they are vulgar—even Mme. de Vionnet, even her pathos, once so exquisite, is stained with commonness.

It was like a chill in the air to him, it was almost appalling, that a creature so fine could be, by mysterious forces, a creature so exploited. For, at the end of all things, they *were* mysterious; she had but made Chad what he was—so why could she think she had made him infinite? She had made him better, she had made him best, she had made him anything one would; but it came to our friend with supreme queerness that he was none the less only Chad. The work, however admirable, was nevertheless of the strict human order, and in short it was marvellous that the companion of mere earthly joys, of comforts, aberrations—however one classed them—within the common experience, should be so transcendently prized.

She was older for him tonight, visibly less exempt from the touch of time; but she was as much as ever the finest and subtlest creature, the happiest apparition, it had been given him, in all his years, to meet; and yet he could see her there as vulgarly troubled, in very truth, as a maidservant crying for a young man. The only thing was that she judged herself as the maidservant wouldn't; the weakness of which wisdom too, the dishonour of which judgment, seemed but to sink her lower.

So Strether loses them too. As he says: "I have lost everything—it is my only logic." It is not that they have gone back. It is that he has gone on. The Paris they revealed to him—he could reveal it to them now, if they had eyes to see, for it is something finer than they could ever notice for themselves, and his imagination has more spiritual value than their youth. The pattern of the hour-glass is complete; he and Chad have changed places, with more subtle steps than Thais and Paphnuce, and the light in the clouds proceeds not from the well-lit Alexandria, but from the jewel which "twinkled and trembled and melted together, and what seemed all surface one moment seemed all depth the next."

The beauty that suffuses *The Ambassadors* is the reward due to a fine artist for hard work. James knew exactly what he wanted, he pursued the narrow path of æsthetic duty, and success to the full extent of his possibilities has crowned him. The pattern has woven itself with modulation and reservations Anatole France will never attain. Woven itself wonderfully. But at what sacrifice!

So enormous is the sacrifice that many readers cannot get interested in James, although they can follow what he says (his difficulty has been much exaggerated), and can appreciate his effects. They cannot grant his premise, which is that most of human life has to disappear before he can do us a novel.

He has, in the first place, a very short list of characters. I have already mentioned two—the observer who tries to influence the action, and the second-rate outsider (to whom, for example, all the brilliant opening of *What Maisie Knew* is entrusted). Then there is the sympathetic foil—very lively and frequently female—in *The Ambassadors*. Maria Gostrey plays this part; there is the wonderful rare heroine, whom Mme. de Vionnet approached and who is consummated by Milly in *The Wings of the Dove;* there is sometimes a villain, sometimes a young artist with generous impulses; and that is about all. For so fine a novelist it is a poor show.

In the second place, the characters, beside being few in number, are constructed on very stingy lines. They are incapable of fun, of rapid motion, of carnality, and of nine-tenths of heroism. Their clothes will not take off, the diseases that ravage them are anonymous, like the sources of their income, their servants are noiseless or resemble themselves, no social explanation of the world we know is possible for them, for there are no stupid people in their world, no barriers of language, and no poor. Even their sensations are limited. They can land in Europe and look at works of art and at each other, but that is all. Maimed creatures can alone breathe in Henry James's pages—maimed yet specialized. They remind one of the exquisite deformities who haunted Egyptian art in the reign of Akhenaton—huge heads and tiny legs, but nevertheless charming. In the following reign they disappear.

Now this drastic curtailment, both of the numbers of human beings and of their attributes, is in the interests of the pattern. The longer James worked, the more convinced he grew that a novel should be a whole—not necessarily geometric like *The Ambassadors,* but it should accrete round a single topic, situation, gesture, which should occupy the characters and provide a plot, and should also fasten up the novel on the outside—catch its scattered statements in a net, make them cohere like a planet, and swing through the skies of memory. A pattern must emerge, and anything that emerged from the pattern must be pruned off as wanton distraction. Who so wanton as human beings? Put Tom Jones or Emma or even Mr. Casaubon into a Henry James book, and the book will burn to ashes, whereas we could put them into one another's books and only cause local inflammation. Only a Henry James character will suit, and though they are not dead—certain selected recesses of experience he explores very well—they are gutted of the common stuff that fills characters in other books, and ourselves. And this castrating is not in the interests of the Kingdom of Heaven, there is no philosophy in the novels, no religion (except an occasional touch of superstition), no prophecy, no benefit for the superhuman at all. It is for the sake of a particular æsthetic effect which is certainly gained, but at this heavy price.

H. G. Wells has been amusing on this point, and perhaps profound. In *Boon*—one of his liveliest works—he had Henry James much upon his mind, and wrote a superb parody of him.

> James begins by taking it for granted that a novel is a work of art that must be judged by its oneness. Some one gave him that idea in the beginning of things and he has never found it out. He doesn't find things out. He doesn't even seem to want to find things out. He accepts very readily and then—elaborates. . . . The only living human motives left in his novels are a certain avidity and an entirely superficial curiosity. . . . His people nose out suspicions, hint by hint, link by link. Have you ever known living human beings

do that? The thing his novel is *about* is always there. It is like a church lit but with no congregation to distract you, with every light and line focussed on the high altar. And on the altar, very reverently placed, intensely there, is a dead kitten, an egg shell, a piece of string. . . . Like his *Altar of the Dead* with nothing to the dead at all. . . . For if there was, they couldn't all be candles, and the effect would vanish.

Wells sent *Boon* as a present to James, apparently thinking the master would be as much pleased by such heartiness and honesty as was he himself. The master was far from pleased, and a most interesting correspondence ensued. Each of the eminent men becomes more and more himself as it proceeds. James is polite, reminiscent, bewildered, and exceedingly formidable: he admits that the parody has not "filled him with a fond elation," and regrets in conclusion that he can sign himself "only yours faithfully, Henry James." Wells is bewildered too, but in a different way; he cannot understand why the man should be upset. And, beyond the personal comedy, there is the great literary importance of the issue. It is this question of the rigid pattern: hourglass or grand chain or converging lines of the Catherine wheel, or bed of Procrustes—whatever image you like as long as it implies unity. Can it be combined with the immense richness of material which life provides? Wells and James would agree it cannot, Wells would go on to say that life should be given the preference, and must not be whittled or distended for a pattern's sake. My own prejudices are with Wells. The James novels are a unique possession and the reader who cannot accept his premises misses some valuable and exquisite sensations. But I do not want more of his novels, especially when they are written by some one else, just as I do not want the art of Akhenaton to extend into the reign of Tutankhamen.

That then is the disadvantage of a rigid pattern. It may externalize the atmosphere, spring naturally from the plot, but it shuts the doors on life and leaves the novelist doing exercises, generally in the drawing-room. Beauty has arrived, but in too tyrannous a guise. In plays—the plays of Racine, for instance—she may be justified because beauty can be a great empress on the stage, and reconcile us to the loss of the men we knew. But in the novel, her tyranny as it grows powerful grows petty, and generates regrets which sometimes take the form of books like *Boon*. To put it in other words, the novel is not capable of as much artistic development as the drama: its humanity or the grossness of its material hinder it (use whichever phrase you like). To most readers of fiction the sensation from a pattern is not intense enough to justify the sacrifices that made it, and their verdict is "Beautifully done, but not worth doing."

Still this is not the end of our quest. We will not give up the hope of beauty yet. Cannot it be introduced into fiction by some other method than the pattern? Let us edge rather nervously towards the idea of "rhythm."

Rhythm is sometimes quite easy. Beethoven's Fifth Symphony, for instance, starts with the rhythm "diddidy dum," which we can all hear and tap to. But the symphony as a whole has also a rhythm—due mainly to the relation between its movements—which some people can hear but no one can tap to. This second sort of rhythm is difficult, and whether it is substantially the same as the first sort only a musician cold tell us. What a literary man wants to say though is that the first kind of rhythm, the did-didy dum, can be found in certain novels and may give them beauty. And the other rhythm, the difficult one—the rhythm of the Fifth Symphony as a whole—I cannot quote you any parallels for that in fiction, yet it may be present.

Rhythm in the easy sense, is illustrated by the work of Marcel Proust.

Proust's conclusion has not been published yet, and his admirers say that when it comes everything will fall into its place, times will be recaptured and fixed, we shall have a perfect whole. I do not believe this. The work seems to me a *progressive* rather than an æsthetic confession, and with the elaboration of Albertine the author was getting tired. Bits of news may await us, but it will be surprising if we have to revise our opinion of the whole book. The book is chaotic, ill constructed, it has and will have no external shape; and yet it hangs together because it is stitched internally, because it contains rhythms.

There are several examples (the photographing of the grandmother is one of them) but the most important from the binding point of view is his use of the "little phrase" in the music of Vinteuil. It does more than anything else—more even than the jealousy which successively destroys Swann, the hero, and Charlus—to make us feel that we are in a homogeneous world. We first hear Vinteuil's name in hideous circumstances. The musician is dead—an obscure little country organist, unknown to fame—and his daughter is defiling his memory. The horrible scene is to radiate in several directions, but it passes, we forget about it.

Then we are at a Paris salon. A violin sonata is performed and a little phrase from its andante catches the ear of Swann and steals into his life. It is always a living being, but takes various forms. For a time it attends his love for Odette. The love affair goes wrong, the phrase is forgotten, we forget it. Then it breaks out again when he is ravaged by jealousy, and now it attends his misery and past happiness at once, without losing its own divine character. Who wrote the sonata? On hearing it is by Vinteuil, Swann says, "I once knew a wretched little organist of that name—it couldn't be by him." But it is, and Vinteuil's daughter and her friend transcribed and published it.

That seems all. The little phrase crosses the book again and again, but as an echo, a memory; we like to encounter it, but it has no binding power. Then, hundreds and hundreds of pages on, when Vinteuil has become a national possession, and there is talk of raising a statue to him in the town where he has been so wretched and so obscure, another work of his is performed—a posthumous sextet. The hero listens—he is in an unknown rather terrible universe while a sinister dawn reddens the sea. Suddenly for him and for the reader too, the little phrase of the sonata recurs—half heard, changed, but giving complete orientation, so that he is back in the country of his childhood with the knowledge that it belongs to the unknown.

We are not obliged to agree with Proust's actual musical descriptions (they are too pictorial for my own taste): but what we must admire is his use of rhythm in literature, and his use of something which is akin by nature to the effect it has to produce—namely a musical phrase. Heard by various people—first by Swann, then by the hero—the phrase of Vinteuil is not tethered; it is not a banner such as we find

George Meredith using—double-blossomed cherry tree to accompany Clara Middle-ton, a yacht in smooth waters for Cecilia Halkett. A banner can only reappear, rhythm can develop, and the little phrase has a life of its own, unconnected with the lives of its auditors, as with the life of the man who composed it. It is almost an actor, but not quite, and that "not quite" means that its power has gone towards stitching Proust's book together from the inside, and towards the establishment of beauty and the rav-ishing of the reader's memory. There are times when the little phrase—from its gloomy inception, through the sonata into the sextet—means everything to the reader. There are times when it means nothing and is forgotten, and this seems to me the function of rhythm in fiction; not to be there all the time like a pattern, but by its lovely wax-ing and waning to fill us with surprise and freshness and hope.

Done badly, rhythm is most boring, it hardens into a symbol and instead of car-rying us on it trips us up. With exasperation we find that Galsworthy's spaniel John, or whatever it is, lies under the feet again; and even Meredith's cherry trees and yachts, graceful as they are, only open the window into poetry. I doubt that it can be achieved by the writers who plan their books beforehand, it has to depend on a local impulse when the right interval is reached. But the effect can be exquisite, it can be obtained without mutilating the characters and it lessens our need of an external form.

That must suffice on the subject of easy rhythm in fiction: which may be defined as repetition plus variation, and which can be illustrated by examples. Now for the more difficult question. Is there any effect in novels comparable to the effect of the Fifth Symphony as a whole, where, when the orchestra stops, we hear something that has never actually been played? The opening movement, the andante, and the trio-scherzo-trio-finale-trio finale that composes the third block, all enter the mind at once, and extend one another into a common entity. This common entity, this new thing, is the symphony as a whole, and it has been achieved mainly (though not entirely) by the relation between the three big blocks of sound which the orchestra has been play-ing. I am calling this relation "rhythmic." If the correct musical term is something else, that does not matter; what we have now to ask ourselves is whether there is any anal-ogy to it in fiction.

I cannot find any analogy. Yet there may be one; in music fiction is likely to find its nearest parallel.

The position of the drama is different. The drama may look towards the pictorial arts, it may allow Aristotle to discipline it, for it is not so deeply committed to the claims of human beings. Human beings have their great chance in the novel. They say to the novelist: "Recreate us if you like, but we must come in," and the novelist's prob-lem, as we have seen all along, is to give them a good run and to achieve something else at the same time. Whither shall he turn? not indeed for help but for analogy. Mu-sic, though it does not employ human beings, though it is governed by intricate laws, nevertheless does offer in its final expression a type of beauty which fiction might achieve in its own way. Expansion. That is the idea the novelist must cling to. Not com-pletion. Not rounding off but opening out. When the symphony is over we feel that the notes and tunes composing it have been liberated, they have found in the rhythm of the whole their individual freedom. Cannot the novel be like that? Is not there something of it in *War and Peace?*—the book with which we began and in which we must end. Such an untidy book. Yet, as we read it, do not great chords begin to sound behind us, and when we have finished does not every item—even the catalogue of strategies—lead a larger existence than was possible at the time?

Gérard Genette

Gérard Genette, founder of the structuralist journal *Poétique* and of structuralist narratology, was born in Paris in 1930 and educated at the École Normale Superieure, where he took his Agrégation de Lettres classiques in 1954. Genette taught in Le Mans before returning to Paris to teach at the Sorbonne in 1963. Since 1967 he has been at the elite institute of graduate study, the École des Hautes Études en Sciences Sociales. After taking his Doctorat ès lettres in 1972, Genette was appointed Directeur d'études at EHESS, combining this appointment with frequent visiting appointments at New York University and other American universities. Genette's publications include the three volumes of essays published as *Figures* (1966, 1969, 1972) from which English translations were made as *Narrative Discourse* (1980) and *Figures of Literary Discourse* (1982). He has recently published *L'oeuvre de l'art: immanence et transcendance* (1994); his most recent work in English is *Fiction and Diction* (1991, translated 1993).

"Order, Duration, Frequency"

I suggest a study of *narrative discourse* or, in a slightly different formulation, of *narrative (récit) as discourse (discours)*. As a point of departure, let us accept the hypothesis that all narratives, regardless of their complexity or degree of elaboration— and Proust's *A la recherche du temps perdu,* the text I shall be using as an example, reaches of course a very high degree of elaboration—can always be considered to be the development of a verbal statement such as "I am walking," or "He will come," or "Marcel becomes a writer." On the strength of this rudimentary analogy, the problems of narrative discourse can be classified under three main headings: the categories of *time* (temporal relationships between the narrative [story] and the "actual" events that are being told [history]); of *mode* (relationships determined by the distance and perspective of the narrative with respect to the history); and of *voice* (relationships between the narrative and the narrating agency itself: narrative situation, level of narration, status of the narrator and of the recipient, etc.). I shall deal only, and very sketchily, with the first category.

The time-category can itself be divided into three sections: the first concerned with the relationships between the temporal *order* of the events that are being told and the pseudo-temporal order of the narrative; the second concerned with the relationships between the *duration* of the events and the duration of the narrative; the third dealing with relationships of *frequency* of repetition between the events and the narrative, between history and story.

ORDER

It is well known that the folk-tale generally keeps a one-to-one correspondence between the "real" order of events that are being told and the order of the narrative, whereas literary narrative, from its earliest beginnings in Western literature, that is, in the Homeric epic, prefers to use the beginning *in medias res,* generally followed by an explanatory flashback. This chronological reversal has become one of the formal *topoi* of the epic genre. The style of the novel has remained remarkably close to its distant origin in this respect: certain beginnings in Balzac, as in the *Duchesse de Langeais* or *César Birotteau,* immediately come to mind as typical examples.

From this point of view, the *Recherche*—especially the earlier sections of the book—indicates that Proust made a much more extensive use than any of his predecessors of his freedom to reorder the temporality of events.

The first "time," dealt with in the six opening pages of the book, refers to a moment that cannot be dated with precision but that must take place quite late in the life of the protagonist: the time at which Marcel, during a period when, as he says, "he often used to go to bed early," suffered from spells of insomnia during which he relived his own past. The first moment in the organization of the narrative is thus far from being the first in the order of the reported history, which deals with the life of the hero.

The second moment refers to the memory relived by the protagonist during his sleepless night. It deals with his childhood at Combray, or, more accurately, with a specific but particularly important moment of this childhood: the famous scene that Marcel calls "the drama of his going to bed," when his mother, at first prevented by Swann's visit from giving him his ritualistic good-night kiss, finally gives in and consents to spend the night in his room.

The third moment again moves far ahead, probably to well within the period of insomnia referred to at the start, or a little after the end of this period: it is the episode of the *madeleine,* during which Marcel recovers an entire fragment of his childhood that had up till then remained hidden in oblivion.

This very brief third episode is followed at once by a fourth: a second return to Combray, this time much more extensive than the first in temporal terms since it covers the entire span of the Combray childhood. Time segment (4) is thus contemporary with time segment (2) but has a much more extensive duration.

The fifth moment is a very brief return to the initial state of sleeplessness and leads to a new retrospective section that takes us even further back into the past, since it deals with a love experience of Swann that took place well before the narrator was born.

There follows a seventh episode that occurs some time after the last events told in the fourth section (childhood at Combray): the story of Marcel's adolescence in Paris and of his love for Gilberte. From then on, the story will proceed in more closely chronological order, at least in its main articulations.

A la recherche du temps perdu thus begins with a zigzagging movement that could easily be represented by a graph and in which the relationship between the time of events and the time of the narrative could be summarized as follows:

N(arrative) 1 = H(istory) 4;   N2 = H2;   N3 = H4;   N4 = H2;   N5 = H4;
N6 = H1 (Swann's love);   N7 = H3.

We are clearly dealing with a highly complex and deliberate transgression of chronological order. I have said that the rest of the book follows a more continuous chronology in its main patterns, but this large-scale linearity does not exclude the presence of a great number of anachronisms in the details: *retrospections,* as when the story of Marcel's stay in Paris during the year 1914 is told in the middle of his later visit to Paris during 1916; or *anticipations,* as when, in the last pages of *Du Côté de chez Swann,* Marcel describes what has become of the Bois de Boulogne at a much later date, the very year he is actually engaged in writing his book. The transition from the *Côté des Guermantes* to *Sodome et Gomorrhe* is based on an interplay of anachronisms: the last scene of *Guermantes* (announcing the death of Swann) in fact takes place later than the subsequent first scene of *Sodome* (the meeting between Charlus and Jupien).

I do not intend to analyze the narrative anachronisms in detail but will point out in passing that one should distinguish between *external* and *internal* anachronisms, according to whether they are located without or within the limits of the temporal field defined by the main narrative. The external anachronisms raise no difficulty, since there is no danger that they will interfere with the main narrative. The internal anachronisms, on the contrary, create a problem of interference. So we must subdivide them into two groups, according to the nature of this relation. Some function to fill in a previous or later blank (ellipsis) in the narrative and can be called *completive* anachronisms, such as the retrospective story of Swann's death. Others return to a moment that has already been covered in the narrative: they are *repetitive* or apparently redundant anachronisms but fulfill in fact a very important function in the organization of the novel. They function as *announcements* (in the case of prospective anticipations) or as *recalls* (when they are retrospective). Announcements can, for example, alert the reader to the meaning of a certain event that will only later be fully revealed (as with the lesbian scene at Montjouvain that will later determine Marcel's jealous passion for Albertine). Recalls serve to give a subsequent meaning to an event first reported as without particular significance (as when we find that Albertine's belated response to a knock on the door was caused by the fact that she had locked herself in with Andrée), or serve even more often to alter the original meaning—as when Marcel discovers after more than thirty years' time that Gilberte was in love with him at Combray and that what he took to be a gesture of insolent disdain was actually meant to be an advance.

Next to these relatively simple and unambiguous retrospections and anticipations, one finds more complex and ambivalent forms of anachronisms: anticipations within retrospections, as when Marcel remembers what used to be his projects with regard to the moment that he is now experiencing; retrospections within anticipations, as when the narrator indicates how he will later find out about the episode he is now in the process of telling; "announcements" of events that have already been told anticipatively or "recalls" of events that took place earlier in the story but that have not yet been told; retrospections that merge seamlessly with the main narrative and make it impossible to identify the exact status of a given section, etc. Finally, I should mention what is perhaps the rarest but most specific of all instances: structures that could properly be called *achronisms,* that is to say, episodes entirely cut loose from any chronological situation whatsoever. These occurrences were pointed out by J. P. Houston in a very interesting study published in *French Studies,* January, 1962, entitled "Temporal Patterns in *À la recherche du temps perdu.*" Near the end of *Sodome et Gomorrhe,* as Marcel's second stay at Balbec draws to a close, Proust tells a sequence of episodes not in the order in which they took place but by following the succession of roadside-stops made by the little train on its journey from Balbec to La Raspelière. Events here follow a geographical rather than a chronological pattern. It is true that the sequence of places still depends on a temporal event (the journey of the train), but this temporality is not that of the "real" succession of events. A similar effect is achieved in the composition of the end of *Combray,* when the narrator successively describes a number of events that took place on the Méséglise way, at different moments, by following the order of their increasing distance from Combray. He follows the temporal succession of a walk from Combray to Méséglise and then, after returning to his spatial and temporal point of departure, tells a sequence of events that took place on the Guermantes way using exactly the same principle. The temporal order of the narrative is not that of the actual succession of events, unless it happens to coincide by chance with the sequence of places encountered in the course of the walk.

I have given some instances of the freedom that Proust's narrative takes with the chronological order of events, but such a description is necessarily sketchy and even misleading if other elements of narrative temporality such as duration and frequency are not also taken into account.

DURATION

Generally speaking, the idea of an isochrony between narrative and "history" is highly ambiguous, for the narrative unit which, in literature, is almost always a narrative text cannot really be said to possess a definite duration. One could equate the duration of a narrative with the time it takes to read it, but reading-times vary considerably from reader to reader, and an ideal average speed can only be determined by fictional means. It may be better to start out from a definition in the form of a relative quantity, and define isochrony as a uniform projection of historical time on narrative extension, that is, number of pages per duration of event. In this way, one can record variations in the speed of the narrative in relation to itself and measure effects of acceleration, deceleration, stasis, and ellipsis (blank spaces within the narrative while the flow of events keeps unfolding).

I have made some rather primitive calculations of the relative speed of the main narrative articulations, measuring on the one hand the narrative of the *Recherche* by number of pages and on the other hand the events by quantity of time. Here are the results.

The first large section, *Combray* or Marcel's childhood, numbers approximately

180 pages of the Pléiade edition and covers about ten years (let me say once and for all that I am defining the duration of events by general consensus, knowing that it is open to question on several points). The next episode, Swann's love-affair with Odette, uses approximately 200 pages to cover about two years. The Gilberte episode (end of *Swann*, beginning of *Jeunes filles en fleurs*) devotes 160 pages to a duration that can be evaluated at two or three years. Here we encounter an ellipsis involving two years of the protagonist's life and mentioned in passing in a few words at the beginning of a sentence. The Balbec episode numbers 300 pages for a three-month-long time-span; then the lengthy section dealing with life in Paris society (*Côte de Guermantes* and beginning of *Sodome et Gomorrbe*) takes up 750 pages for two and a half years. It should be added that considerable variations occur within this section: 110 pages are devoted to the afternoon party at Mme de Villeparisis's that lasts for about two hours, 150 pages to the dinner of nearly equal length at the Duchesse de Guermantes's, and 100 pages to the evening at the Princesse de Guermantes's. In this vast episode of 750 pages for two and a half years, 360 pages—nearly one half—are taken up by less than ten hours of social life.

The second stay at Balbec (end of *Sodome*) covers approximately six months in 380 pages. Then the Albertine sequence, reporting the hero's involvement with Albertine in Paris (*La Prisonnière* and the beginning of *La Fugitive*), requires 630 pages for an eighteen-month period, of which 300 deal with only two days. The stay in Venice uses 35 pages for a few weeks, followed by a section of 40 pages (astride *La Fugitive* and *Le Temps retrouvé*) for the stay in Tansonville, the return to the country of Marcel's childhood. The first extended ellipsis of the *Recherche* occurs here; the time-span cannot be determined with precision, but it encompasses approximately ten years of the hero's life spent in a rest-home. The subsequent episode, situated during the war, devotes 130 pages to a few weeks, followed by another ellipsis of ten years again spent in a rest-home. Finally, the concluding scene, the party at the Princesse de Guermantes's, devotes 190 pages to a two- or three-hour-long reception.

What conclusions can be derived from this barren and apparently useless enumeration? First of all, we should note the extensive shifts in relative duration, ranging from one line of text for ten years to 190 pages for two or three hours, or from approximately one page per century to one page per minute. The second observation refers to the internal evolution of the *Recherche* as a whole. It could be roughly summarized by stressing, on the one hand, the gradual slowing down of the narrative achieved by the insertion of longer and longer scenes for events of shorter and shorter duration. This is compensated for, on the other hand, by the presence of more and more extensive ellipses. The two trends can be easily united in one formula: increasing discontinuity of the narrative. As the Proustian narrative moves toward its conclusion, it becomes increasingly discontinuous, consisting of gigantic scenes separated from each other by enormous gaps. It deviates more and more from the ideal "norm" of an isochronic narrative.

We should also stress how Proust selects among the traditional literary forms of narrative duration. Among the nearly infinite range of possible combinations of historical and narrative duration, the literary tradition has made a rather limited choice that can be reduced to the following fundamental forms: (1) the *summary*, when the narrative duration is greatly reduced with respect to the historical duration; it is well known that the summary constitutes the main connective tissue in the classical *récit;* (2) the dramatic *scene,* especially the dialogue, when narrative and historical time are supposed to be nearly equal; (3) the narrative *stasis,* when the narrative discourse continues while historical time is at a standstill, usually in order to take care of a description; and (4) *ellipsis,* consisting of a certain amount of historical time covered in a zero amount of narrative. If we consider the *Recherche* from this point of view, we are struck by the total absence of summarizing narrative, which tends to be absorbed in the ellipses, and by the near-total absence of descriptive stasis: the Proustian descriptions always correspond to an actual observation-time on the part of the character; the time-lapse is sometimes mentioned in the text and is obviously longer than the time it takes to read the description (three-quarters of an hour for the contemplation of the Elstir paintings owned by the Duc de Guermantes, when the description takes only four or five pages of the text). The narrative duration is not interrupted—as is so often the case with Balzac—for, rather than *describing,* Proust *narrates* how his hero perceives, contemplates, and experiences a given sight; the description is incorporated within the narrative and constitutes no autonomous narrative form. Except for another effect with which I shall deal at some length in a moment, Proust makes use of only two of the traditional forms of narrative duration: scene and ellipsis. And since ellipsis is a zero point of the text, we have in fact only one single form: the scene. I should add, however, without taking time to develop a rather obvious observation, that the narrative function of this traditional form is rather strongly subverted in Proust. The main number of his major scenes do not have the purely dramatic function usually associated with the classical "scene." The traditional economy of the novel, consisting of summarizing and nondramatic narrative alternating with dramatic scenes, is entirely discarded. Instead, we find another form of alternating movement toward which we must now direct our attention.

FREQUENCY

The third kind of narrative temporality, which has in general received much less critical and theoretical attention than the two previous ones, deals with the relative frequency of the narrated events and of the narrative sections that report them. Speaking once more very schematically, the most obvious form of narration will tell once what happens once, as in a narrative statement such as: "Yesterday, I went to bed early." This type of narrative is so current and presumably normal that it bears no special name. In order to emphasize that it is merely one possibility among many, I propose to give it a name and call it the *singulative* narrative (*récit singulatif*). It is equally possible to tell several times what happened several times, as when I say: "Monday I went to bed early, Tuesday I went to bed early, Wednesday I went to bed early," etc. This type of anaphoric narrative remains singulative and can be equated with the first, since the repetitions of the story correspond one-to-one to the repetitions of the events. A narrative can also tell several times, with or with out variations, an event that happened only once, as in a statement of this kind: "Yesterday I went to bed early, yesterday I went to bed early, yesterday I tried to go to sleep well before dark," etc. This last hypothesis may seem *a priori* to be a gratuitous one, or even to exhibit a slight trace of senility. One should remember, however, that most texts by Alain Robbe-Grillet, among others, are founded on the repetitive potential of the narrative: the recurrent episode of the killing of the centipede, in *La Jalousie,* would be ample proof of this. I shall call *repetitive* narrative this type of narration, in which the story-repetitions exceed in number the repetitions of events. There remains a last possibility. Let us return to our second example: "Monday, Tuesday, Wednesday," etc. When such a pattern of events occurs, the narrative is obviously not reduced to the necessity of reproducing it as if its discourse were incapable of abstraction or synthesis. Unless a deliberate stylistic effect is aimed for, even the simplest narration will choose a formulation such as "every day" or "every day of the week" or "all week long." We all know which of these devices Proust chose for the opening sentence of the *Recherche.* The type of narrative in which a single narrative assertion covers several recurrences of the same event or, to be more precise, of several analogical events considered only with respect to what they have in common, I propose to call by the obvious name of *iterative* narrative (*récit itératif*).

My heavy-handed insistence on this notion may well seem out of place, since it designates a purely grammatical concept without literary relevance. Yet the quantitative amount and the qualitative function of the iterative mode are particularly important in Proust and have seldom, to my knowledge, received the critical attention they deserve. It can be said without exaggeration that the entire Combray episode is essentially an iterative narrative, interspersed here and there with some "singulative" scenes of salient importance such as the motherly good-night kiss, the meeting with the Lady in the pink dress (a retrospective scene), or the profanation of Vinteuil's portrait at Montjouvain. Except for five or six such scenes referring to a single action and told in the historical past (*passé défini*), all the rest, told in the imperfect, deals with what used to happen at Combray regularly, ritualistically, every night or every Sunday, or every Saturday, or whenever the weather was good or the weather was bad, etc. The narrative of Swann's love for Odette will still be conducted, for the most part, in the mode of habit and repetition; the same is true of the story of Marcel's love for Swann's daughter Gilberte. Only when we reach the stay at Balbec in the *Jeunes filles en fleurs* do the singulative episodes begin to predominate, although they remain interspersed with numerous iterative passages: the Balbec outings with Mme de Villeparisis and later with Albertine, the hero's stratagems at the beginning of *Guermantes* when he tries to meet the Duchess every morning, the journeys in the little train of the Raspelière (*Sodome,* II), life with Albertine in Paris (the first eighty pages of *La Prisonnière*) the walks in Venice (*La Fugitive*), not to mention the iterative treatment of certain moments within the singulative scenes, such as the conversations about genealogy during the dinner at the Duchess's, or the description of the aging guests at the last Guermantes party. The narrative synthesizes these moments by reducing several distinct occurrences to their common elements: "the *women* were like this . . . the *men* acted like that; *some* did this, *others* that," etc. I shall call these sections *internal iterations,* in contrast with other, more common passages, in which a descriptive-iterative parenthesis begins in the middle of a singulative scene to convey additional information needed for the reader's understanding and which I shall call *ex-*

ternal iterations. An example would be the long passage devoted, in the middle of the first Guermantes dinner, to the more general and therefore necessarily iterative description of the Guermantes wit.

The use of iterative narrative is by no means Proust's invention; it is one of the most classical devices of fictional narrative. But the frequency of the mode is distinctively Proustian, a fact still underscored by the relatively massive presence of what could be called *pseudo-iterations,* scenes presented (mostly by the use of the imperfect tense) as if they were iterative, but with such a wealth of precise detail that no reader can seriously believe that they could have taken place repeatedly in this way, without variations. One thinks for example of some of the conversations between Aunt Léonie and her maid Françoise that go on for page after page, or of conversations in Mme Verdurin's or Mme Swann's salon in Paris. In each of these cases, a singular scene has arbitrarily, and without any but grammatical change, been converted into an iterative scene, thus clearly revealing the trend of the Proustian narrative toward a kind of inflation of the iterative.

It would be tempting to interpret this tendency as symptomatic of a dominant psychological trait: Proust's highly developed sense of habit and repetition, his feeling for the *analogy* between different moments in life. This is all the more striking since the iterative mode of the narrative is not always, as in the Combray part, based on the repetitive, ritualistic pattern of a bourgeois existence in the provinces. Contrary to general belief, Proust is less aware of the specificity of moments than he is aware of the specificity of places; the latter is one of the governing laws of his sensibility. His moments have a strong tendency to blend into each other, a possibility which is at the root of the experience of spontaneous recollection. The opposition between the "singularity" of his spatial imagination and, if I dare say so, the "iterativity" of his temporal imagination is nicely illustrated in the following sentence from *Swann.* Speaking of the Guermantes landscape, Proust writes: "[Its] specificity would *at times,* in my dreams, seize upon me with almost fantastical power" ("le paysage dont *parfois,* la nuit dans mes rêves, l'individualité m'étreint avec une puissance presque fantastique"). Hence the highly developed sense of *ritual* (see, for example, the scene of the Saturday luncheons at Combray) and, on the other hand, the panic felt in the presence of irregularities of behavior, as when Marcel, at Balbec, wonders about the complex and secret law that may govern the unpredictable absence of the young girls on certain days.

Wayne C. Booth

Wayne Clayson Booth has been the most effective teacher—in the most far-reaching sense—of the Chicago neo-Aristotelians. Booth was born in 1921 in American Fork, Utah, and educated at Brigham Young University and—after serving in the infantry during World War II—at the University of

Chicago. He taught at Haverford and at Earlham College before returning to Chicago as Pullman Professor of English in 1962. He served as president of the Modern Language Association in 1982. Booth's enormous influence on the way we talk about narrative began with the publication of *The Rhetoric of Fiction* (1961; 2nd edition, 1983), which adapted Aristotelian theory to consider the reader and the ways in which literary texts themselves shape the audience they require. His controversial thirteenth chapter questioned the moral impact of certain narrative techniques. Booth promised an "ethics of fiction" to clarify his ideas and delivered it, nearly thirty years later, in *The Company We Keep* (1989). Booth's other books include *A Rhetoric of Irony* (1974), *Modern Dogma and the Rhetoric of Assent* (1974), *Critical Understanding: The Powers and Limits of Pluralism* (1979), *The Vocation of a Teacher* (1990), and *The Art of Growing Older* (1992). Booth has also been the object of study, in *Rhetoric and Pluralism*, edited by Fred Antczak (1995). "Distance and Point of View," an earlier version of chapter 6 of *The Rhetoric of Fiction*, was originally published in 1961.

Distance and Point-of-View:

AN ESSAY IN CLASSIFICATION

> *But he [the narrator] little knows what surprises lie in wait for him, if someone were to set about analysing the mass of truths and falsehoods which he has collected here.*
>
> 'Dr. S.,' in *Confessions of Zeno*

Like other notions used in talking about fiction, point-of-view has proved less useful than was expected by the critics who first brought it to our attention. When Percy Lubbock hailed the triumph of Henry James's dramatic use of the 'central intelligence,' and told us that 'the whole intricate question of method, in the craft of fiction,' is governed by 'the relation in which the narrator stands to the story' he might have predicted that many critics would, like E. M. Forster, disagree with him. But he could hardly have predicted that his converts would produce, in forty years of elaborate investigations of point-of-view, so little help to the author or critic who must decide whether this or that technique in a particular work is appropriate to this or that effect. On the one hand we have been given classifications and descriptions which leave us wondering why we have bothered to classify and describe; the author who counted the number of times the word 'I' appears in each of Jane Austen's novels may be more obviously absurd than the innumerable scholars who have traced in endless detail the 'Ich-Erzählung,' or 'erlebte Rede,' or 'monologue intérieur' from Dickens to Joyce or from James to Robbe-Grillet. But he is no more irrelevant to literary judgment. To describe particulars may be interesting but it is only the preliminary to the kind of knowledge that might help us explain the success or failure of individual works.

On the other hand, our efforts at formulating useful principles have been of little more use because they have been overtly prescriptive. If to count the number of times

'I' occurs tells us nothing about how many times 'I' should occur, to formulate abstract appeals for more 'showing' and less 'telling,' for less authorial commentary and more drama, for more realistic consistency and fewer arbitrary shifts which remind the reader that he is reading a book, gives us the illusion of having discovered criteria when we really have not. While it is certainly true that some effects are best achieved by avoiding some kinds of telling, too often our prescriptions have been for 'the novel' entire, ignoring what James himself knew well: there are '5,000,000 ways to tell a story,' depending on one's overall purposes. Too many Jamesians have tried to establish in advance the precise degree of realistic intensity or irony or objectivity or 'aesthetic distance' his work should display.

It is true that dissenting voices are now heard more and more frequently, perhaps the most important being Kathleen Tillotson's recent inaugural lecture at The University of London, *The Tale and the Teller*. But the clichés about the superiority of dramatic showing over mere telling are still to be found everywhere: in scholarly journals, in the literary quarterlies, in the weekly reviews, in the latest book on how to read a novel, and in dust-jacket blurbs. 'The author does not tell you directly but you find out for yourself from their [the characters] every word, gesture, and act,' a Modern Library jacket tells us about Salinger's *Nine Stories*. That this is praise, that Salinger would be in error if he were found telling us anything directly, is taken for granted.

Since novelist's choices are in fact practically unlimited, in judging their effectiveness we can only fall back on the kind of reasoning used by Aristotle in the *Poetics: if* such-and-such effect is desired, *then* such-and-such points-of-view will be good or bad. We all agree that point-of-view is in some sense a technical matter, a means to larger ends; whether we say that technique is the artist's way of discovering his artistic meaning or that it is his way of working his will upon his audience, we still can judge it only in the light of the larger meanings or effects which it is designed to serve. Though we all at times violate our own convictions, most of us are convinced that we have no right to impose on the artist abstract criteria derived from other kinds of work.

But even when we have decided to put our judgments in the hypothetical 'if-then' form, we are still faced with an overwhelming variety of choices. One of the most striking features of our criticism is the casual way in which we allow ourselves to reduce this variety, thoughtlessly, carelessly, to simple categories, the impoverishment of which is evident whenever we look at any existing novel. On the side of effect critics at one time had a fairly large number of terms to play with—terms like tragedy, comedy, tragicomedy, epic, farce, satire, elegy, and the like. Though the neo-classical kinds were often employed in inflexible form, they did provide a frame of discourse which allowed the critic and artist to communicate with each other: 'if the effect you want is what we have traditionally expected under the concept "tragedy," then your technique here is inadequate.' If what we are working for is a first-rate comedy, Dryden tells us in 'An Essay of Dramatic Poesy,' then here are some rules we can count on; they may be difficult to apply, they may require painstaking discussion, and they will certainly require genius if they are to be made to work, but they can still be of help to artist and critic because they are based on an agreement about a recognised literary effect.

In place of the earlier kinds, we have generally substituted a criticism based on qualities that are supposed to be sought in all works. All novels are said to be aiming for a common degree of realistic intensity; ambiguity and irony are discussed as if they were always beauties, never blemishes. Point-of-view should always be used 'consistently,' because otherwise the realistic illusion will be destroyed.

When technical means are related to such simplified ends, it is hardly surprising that they are themselves simplified. Yet we all know that our experience of particular works is more complex than the simple terminology suggests. The prescriptions against 'telling' cannot satisfy any reader who has experienced *Tom Jones, The Egoist, Light in August,* or *Ulysses* (the claim that the author does not address us directly in the last of these is one of the most astonishingly persistent myths in modern criticism). They explicitly contradict our experience of dozens of good novels of the past fifteen years which, like Joyce Cary's posthumous *The Captive and the Free,* have rediscovered for us how lively 'telling' can be. We all know, of course, that 'too much' of the author's voice is, as Aristotle said, unpoetic. But how much is too much? Is there an abstract rule applicable to 'the novel,' quite aside from the needs of particular works or kinds?

Our experience with the great novels tells us that there is not. Most novels, like most plays, cannot be purely dramatic, entirely shown as taking place in the moment. There are always what Dryden called 'relations,' narrative summaries of action that takes place 'off-stage.' And try as we will to ignore the troublesome fact, 'some parts of the action are more fit to be represented, some to be related.' But related by whom? When? At what length? The dramatist must decide, and his decision will be based in large part on the particular needs of the work in hand. The novelist's case is different mainly in that he has more devices to choose from; he may speak with all of the voices available to the dramatist, and he may also choose—some would say he is also tempted by—some forms of telling not easily adapted to the stage.

Unfortunately our terminology for the author's many voices has been inadequate. If we name over three or four of the great narrators—say Cervantes' Cid Hamete Benengeli, Tristram Shandy, the 'author' of *Middlemarch* and Strether in *The Ambassadors* (with his nearly effaced 'author' using his mind as a reflector of events)—we find again that to describe any of them with conventional terms like 'first-person' and 'omniscient' tells us little how they differ from each other, and consequently it tells us little about why they succeed while others, described in the same terms, fail. Some critics do, indeed, talk about the problem of 'authority,' showing that first-person tales produce difficulties in stories which do not allow any one person to know all that goes on; having made this point, which seems so obvious, they are often then driven to find fault with stories like *Moby Dick,* in which the author allows his narrator to know of events that happen outside his designated sphere of authority.

We can never be sure that enriching our terms will improve our criticism. But we can be quite sure that the terms with which we have long been forced to work cannot help us in discriminating among effects too subtle—as are all actual literary effects—to be caught in such loose-meshed nets. Even at the risk of pedantry, then, it should be worth our while to attempt a richer tabulation of the forms the author's voice can take.

(1) Perhaps the most overworked distinction is that of 'person.' To say that a story is told in the first or the third person, and to group novels into one or the other kind, will tell us nothing of importance unless we become more precise and describe how

the particular qualities of the narrators relate to specific desired effects. It is true that choice of the first person is sometimes unduly limiting; if the 'I' has inadequate access to necessary information, the author may be led into improbabilities. But we can hardly expect to find useful criteria in a distinction that would throw all fiction into two, or at most three, heaps. In *this* pile we see *Henry Esmond,* 'A Cask of Amontillado,' *Gulliver's Travels* and *Tristram Shandy.* In *that* we have *Vanity Fair, Tom Jones, The Ambassadors,* and *Brave New World.* But the commentary in *Vanity Fair* and *Tom Jones* is in the first person, often resembling more the intimate effect of *Tristram Shandy* than that of many third person works. And again, the effect of *The Ambassadors* is much closer to that of the great first-person novels, since Strether in large parts 'narrates' his own story, even though he is always referred to in the third person.

Further evidence that this distinction is ordinarily overemphasised is seen in the fact that all of the following functional distinctions apply to both first and third-person narration alike.

(2) There are *dramatised* narrators and *undramatised* narrators. The former are always and the latter are usually distinct from the implied author who is responsible for their creation.

(a) The Implied Author (the author's 'second self').

Even the novel in which no narrator is dramatised creates an implicit picture of an author who stands behind the scenes, whether as stage-manager, as puppeteer, or as an indifferent God, silently paring his fingernails. This implied author is always distinct from the 'real man'—whatever we may take him to be—who creates a superior version of himself as he creates his work; any successful novel makes us believe in an 'author' who amounts to a kind of 'second self.' This second self is usually a highly refined and selected version, wiser, more sensitive, more perceptive than any real man could be.

In so far as a novel does not refer directly to this author, there will be no distinction between him and the implied, undramatized narrator; for example, in Hemingway's *The Killers* there is no narrator other than the implicit second self that Hemingway creates as he writes.

(b) Undramatised Narrators.

Stories are usually not as rigorously scenic as *The Killers;* most tales are presented as passing through the consciousness of a teller, whether an 'I' or a 'he.' Even in drama much of what we are given is narrated by someone, and we are often as much interested in the effect on the narrator's own mind and heart as we are in learning what *else* the author has to tell us. When Horatio tells of his first encounter with the ghost in *Hamlet,* his own character, though never mentioned explicitly as part of the narrative event, is important to us as we listen. In fiction, as soon as we encounter an 'I' we are conscious of an experiencing mind whose views of the experience will come between us and the event. When there is no such 'I,' as in *The Killers,* the inexperienced reader may make the mistake of thinking that the story comes to him unmediated. But even the most naïve reader must recognise that something mediating and transforming has come into a story from the moment that the author explicitly places a narrator into the tale, even if he is given no personal characteristics whatever.

One of the most frequent reading faults comes from a naïve identification of such narrators with the authors who create them. But in fact there is always a distinction, even though the author himself may not have been aware of it as he wrote. The created author, the 'second self', is built up in our minds from our experience with all of the elements of the presented story. When one of those elements is an explicit reference to an experiencing narrator, our view of the author is derived in part from our notion of how the presented 'I' relates to what he claims to present. Even when the 'I' or 'he' thus created is ostensibly the author himself—Fielding, Jane Austen, Dickens, Meredith—we can always distinguish between the narrator and the created author who presents him. But though the distinction is always present, it is usually important to criticism only when the narrator is explicitly dramatised.

(c) Dramatised Narrators.

In a sense even the most reticent narrator has been 'dramatised' as soon as he refers to himself as 'I,' or, like Flaubert, tells us that 'we' were in the classroom when Charles Bovary entered. But many novels dramatise their narrators with great fullness. In some works the narrator becomes a major person of great physical, mental and moral vividness (*Tristram Shandy, Remembrance of Things Past,* and *Dr. Faustus*); in such works the narrator is often radically different from the implied author who creates him, and whose own character is built up in our minds partly by the way in which the narrator is made to differ from him. The range of human types that have been dramatised as narrators is almost as great as the range of other fictional characters—one must say 'almost' because there are some characters who are unqualified to narrate or reflect a story.

We should remind ourselves that many dramatised narrators are never explicitly labelled as narrators at all. In a sense, every speech, every gesture, narrates; most works contain disguised narrators who, like Molière's *raisonneurs,* are used to tell the audience what it needs to know, while seeming merely to act out their roles. The most important unacknowledged narrators are however, the third-person 'centres of consciousness' through whom authors filter their narrative. Whether such 'reflectors,' as James sometimes called them, are highly-polished, lucid mirrors reflecting complex mental experience, or the rather turbid, sense-bound 'camera eyes' of much fiction since James, they fill precisely the function of avowed narrators.

> Gabriel had not gone to the door with the others. He was in a dark part of the hall gazing up the staircase. A woman was standing near the top of the first flight, in the shadow also. He could not see her face but he could see the terra-cotta and salmon-pink panels of her skirt which the shadow made appear black and white. It was his wife. She was leaning on the banisters, listening to something. Gabriel was surprised at her stillness and strained his ear to listen also. But he could hear little save the noise of laughter and dispute on the front steps, a few chords struck on the piano and a few notes of a man's voice singing. . . He asked himself what is a woman standing on the stairs in the shadow, listening to distant music, a symbol of.[1]

---

[1] The quotation is from *The Dead* (1914), by James Joyce (1882-1941). *Ed.*

The very real advantages of this method, for some purposes, have been a dominant note in modern criticism. Indeed, so long as our attention is on such qualities as naturalness and vividness, the advantages seem overwhelming. It is only as we break out of the fashionable assumption that all good fiction seeks these qualities in the same degree that we are forced to recognise disadvantages. The third-person reflector is only one mode among many, suitable for some effects but cumbersome and even harmful when other effects are desired.

(3) Among dramatised narrators, whether first-person or third-person reflectors, there are mere *observers* (the 'I' of *Tom Jones, The Egoist, Troilus and Criseyde*), and there are *narrator-agents* who produce some measurable effect on the course of events (ranging from the minor involvement of Nick in *The Great Gatsby* to the central role of Tristram Shandy, Moll Flanders, Huckleberry Finn, and—in the third-person—Paul Morel in *Sons and Lovers*). Clearly any rules we might discover about observers may or may not apply to narrator-agents, yet the distinction is seldom made in talk about point-of-view.

(4) All narrators and observers, whether first or third-person, can relay their tales to us primarily as *scene* (*The Killers, The Awkward Age*), primarily as *summary* or what Lubbock called 'picture' (Addison's almost completely non-scenic tales in *The Spectator*) or, most commonly, as a combination of the two.

Like Aristotle's distinction between dramatic and narrative manners, the somewhat different modern distinction between telling and showing does cover the ground. But the trouble is that it pays for broad coverage with gross imprecision. Narrators of all shapes and shades must either report dialogue alone or support it with 'stage directions' and description of setting. But when we think of the radically different effect of a scene reported by Huck Finn and a scene reported by Poe's Montresor, we see that the quality of being 'scenic' suggests very little about literary effect. And compare the delightful summary of twelve years given in two pages of *Tom Jones* (III, i), with the tedious showing of even ten minutes of uncurtailed conversation in the hands of a Sartre when he allows his passion for 'durational realism' to dictate a scene when summary is called for. We can only conclude that the contrast between scene and summary, between showing and telling—indeed, between any two dialectical terms that try to cover so much ground—is not prescriptive or normative but loosely descriptive only. And as description, it is likely to tell us very little until we specify the kind of narrator who is providing the scene or the summary.

(5) Narrators who allow themselves to tell as well as show vary greatly depending on the amount and kind of *commentary* allowed in addition to a direct relating of events in scene and summary. Such commentary can, of course, range over any aspect of human experience, and it can be related to the main business in innumerable ways and degrees. To treat of it as if it were somehow a single device is to ignore important differences between commentary that is merely ornamental, commentary that serves a rhetorical purpose but is not part of the dramatic structure, and commentary that is integral to the dramatic structure, as in *Tristram Shandy*.

(6) Cutting across the distinction between observers and narrator-agents of all these kinds is the distinction between *self-conscious narrators,* aware of themselves as writers (*Tom Jones, Tristram Shandy, Barchester Towers, The Catcher in the Rye,*

Remembrance of Things Past, Dr. Faustus), and narrators or observers who rarely if ever discuss their writing chores (*Huckleberry Finn*) or who seem unaware that they are writing, thinking, speaking, or 'reflecting' a literary work (Camus' *The Stranger,* Lardner's *Haircut,* Bellow's *The Victim*).

(7) Whether or not they are involved in the action as agents, narrators and third-person reflectors differ markedly according to the degree and kind of *distance* that separates them from the author, the reader, and the other characters of the story they relate or reflect. Such distance is often discussed under terms like 'irony,' or 'tone,' but our experience is in fact much more diverse than such terms are likely to suggest. 'Aesthetic distance' has been especially popular in recent years as a catch-all term for any lack of identification between the reader and the various norms in the work. But surely this useful term should be reserved to describe the degree to which the reader or spectator is asked to forget the artificiality of the work and 'lose himself' in it; whatever makes him aware that he is dealing with an aesthetic object and not real life increases 'aesthetic distance,' in this sense. What I am dealing with is more complex and more difficult to describe, and it includes 'aesthetic distance' as one of its elements.

In any reading experience there is an implied dialogue among author, narrator, the other characters, and the reader. Each of the four can range, in relation to each of the others, from identification to complete opposition, on any axis of value or judgment; moral, intellectual, aesthetic, and even physical (does the reader who stammers react to the stammering of H. C. Earwicker[2] as I do? Surely not). The elements usually discussed under 'aesthetic distance' enter in of course; distance in time and space, differences of social class or conventions of speech or dress—these and many others serve to control our sense that we are dealing with an aesthetic object, just as the paper moons and other unrealistic stage effects of some modern drama have had an 'alienation' effect. But we must not confuse these effects with the equally important effects of personal beliefs and qualities, in author, narrator, reader, and all others in the cast of characters. Though we cannot hope to deal with all of the varieties of control over distance that narrative technique can achieve, we can at least remind ourselves that we deal here with something more than the question of whether the author attempts to maintain or destroy the illusion of reality.

(a) The *narrator* may be more or less distant from the *implied author.* The distance may be moral (Jason vs. Faulkner; the barber vs. Lardner, the narrator vs. Fielding in *Jonathan Wild*). It may be intellectual (Twain and Huck Finn, Sterne and Tristram Shandy in the matter of bigotry about the influence of noses, Richardson and Clarissa). It may be physical or temporal: most authors are distant from even the most knowing narrator in that they presumably know how 'everything turns out in the end'; and so on.

(b) The *narrator* also may be more or less distant from the *characters* in the story he tells. He may differ, for example, morally, intellectually and temporally (the mature narrator and his younger self in *Great Expectations* or *Redburn*), morally and intellectually (Fowler the narrator and Pyle the American in Greene's *The Quiet American,* both departing radically from the author's norms but in different directions),

---

[2] The "hero" of James Joyce's *Finnegans Wake* (1939). *Ed.*

morally and emotionally (Maupassant's 'The Necklace,' and Huxley's 'Nuns at Luncheon,' in which the narrators affect less emotional involvement than Maupassant and Huxley clearly expect from the reader).

(c) The *narrator* may be more or less distant from the *reader's* own norms, e.g., physically and emotionally (Kafka's *The Metamorphosis*); morally and emotionally (Pinkie in *Brighton Rock,* the miser in Mauriac's *Knot of Vipers;* the many moral degenerates that modern fiction has managed to make into convincing human beings).

One of the standard sources of plot in modern fiction—often advanced in the name of repudiating plot—is the portrayal of narrators whose characteristics change in the course of the works they narrate. Ever since Shakespeare taught the modern world what the Greeks had overlooked in neglecting character change (compare *Macbeth* and *Lear* with *Oedipus*), stories of character development or degeneration have become more and more popular. But it was not until we had discovered the full uses of the third-person reflector that we found how to show a narrator changing *as he narrates.* The mature Pip, in *Great Expectations,* is presented as a generous man whose heart is where the reader's is supposed to be; he watches his young self move away from the reader, as it were, and then back again. But the third-person reflector can be shown, technically in the past tense but in effect present before our eyes, moving toward or away from values that the reader holds dear. The twentieth-century has proceeded almost as if determined to work out all of the permutations and combinations on this effect: start far and end near; start near and end far; start far, move close, but lose the prize and end far; start near, like Pip, move away but see the light and return close; start far and move farther (many modern 'tragedies' are so little tragic because the hero is too distant from us at the beginning for us to care that he is, like Macbeth, even further at the end); start near and end nearer . . . I can think of no theoretical possibilities that haven't been tried; anyone who has read widely in modern fiction can fill in examples.

(d) The *implied author* may be more or less distant from the *reader.* The distance may be intellectual (the implied author of *Tristram Shandy,* not of course to be identified with Tristram, is more interested in and knows more about recondite classical lore than any of his readers), moral (the works of Sade), and so on. From the author's viewpoint, a successful reading of his book will reduce to zero the distance between the essential norms of his implied author and the norms of the postulated reader. Often enough there is very little distance to begin with; Jane Austen does not have to convince us that pride and prejudice are undesirable. A bad book, on the other hand, is often a book whose implied author clearly asks that we judge according to norms we cannot accept.

(e) The *implied author* (and reader) may be more or less distant from *other characters,* ranging from Jane Austen's complete approval of Jane Fairfax in *Emma* to her contempt for Wickham in *Pride and Prejudice.* The complexity that marks our pleasure in all significant literature can be seen by contrasting the kinds of distance in these two situations. In Emma, the *narrator* is non-committal toward Jane Fairfax, though there is no sign of disapproval. The *author* can be inferred as approving of her almost completely. But the chief *reflector,* Emma who has the largest share of the job of narration, is definitely disapproving of Jane Fairfax for most of the way. In *Pride and Prej-*

udice, on the other hand, the narrator is non-committal toward Wickham for as long as possible, hoping to mystify us; the author is secretly disapproving; and the chief reflector, Elizabeth, is definitely approving for the first half of the book.

It is obvious that on each of these scales my examples do not begin to cover the possibilities. What we call 'involvement' or 'sympathy' or 'identification,' is usually made up of many reactions to author, narrators, observers, and other characters. And narrators may differ from their authors or readers in various kinds of involvement or detachment, ranging from deep personal concern (Nick in *The Great Gatsby,* MacKellar in *The Master of Ballantrae,* Zeitblom in *Dr. Faustus*) to a bland or mildly amused or merely curious detachment (Waugh's *Decline and Fall*).

In talk about point-of-view in fiction, the most seriously neglected of these kinds of distance is that between the fallible or unreliable narrator and the implied author who carries the reader with him as against the narrator. If the reason for discussing point-of-view is to find how it relates to literary effects, then surely the moral and intellectual qualities of the narrator are more important to our judgment than whether he is referred to as 'I' or 'he,' or whether he is privileged or limited, and so on. If he is discovered to be untrustworthy, then the total effect of the work he relays to us is transformed.

Our terminology for this kind of distance in narrators is almost hopelessly inadequate. For lack of better terms, I shall call a narrator *reliable* when he speaks for or acts in accordance with the norms of the work (which is to say, the implied author's norms), *unreliable* when he does not. It is true that most of the great reliable narrators indulge in large amounts of incidental irony, and they are thus 'unreliable' in the sense of being potentially deceptive. But difficult irony is not sufficient to make a narrator unreliable. We should reserve the term unreliable for those narrators who are presented as if they spoke *throughout* for the norms of the book and who do not in fact do so. Unreliability is not ordinarily a matter of lying, although deliberately deceptive narrators have been a major resource of some modern novelists (Camus' *The Fall,* Calder Willingham's *Natural Child,* etc.). It is most often a matter of what James calls *inconscience;* the narrator is mistaken, or he pretends to qualities which the author denies him. Or, as in *Huckleberry Finn,* the narrator claims to be naturally wicked while the author silently praises his virtues, as it were, behind his back.

Unreliable narrators thus differ markedly depending on how far and in what direction they depart from their author's norms; the older term 'tone,' like the currently fashionable 'distance,' covers many effects that we should distinguish. Some narrators, like Barry Lyndon, are placed as far 'away' from author and reader as possible, in respect to every virtue except a kind of interesting vitality. Some, like Fleda Vetch, the reflector in James's *The Spoils of Poynton,* come close to representing the author's ideal of taste, judgment, and moral sense. All of them make stronger demands on the reader's powers of inference than does reliable narration.

(8) Both reliable and unreliable narrators can be *isolated,* unsupported or uncorrected by other narrators (Gully Jimson in *The Horse's Mouth,* Henderson in Bellow's *Henderson the Rain King*) or supported or corrected (*The Sound and the Fury*). Sometimes it is almost impossible to infer whether or to what degree a narrator is fallible; sometimes explicit corroborating or conflicting testimony makes the in-

ference easy. Support or correction differs radically, it should be noted, depending on whether it is provided from within the action, so that the narrator-agent might bene-fit (Faulkner's *Intruder in the Dust*) or is simply provided externally, to help the reader correct or reinforce his own views *as against the narrator's* (Graham Greene's *The Power and the Glory*). Obviously the effects of isolation will be radically different in the two cases.

(9) Observers and narrator-agents, whether self-conscious or not, reliable or not, commenting or silent, isolated or supported, can be either *privileged* to know what could not be learned by strictly natural means or *limited* to realistic vision and infer-ence. Complete privilege is what we usually call omniscience. But there are many kinds of privilege and very few 'omniscient' narrators are allowed to know or show as much as their authors know.

We need a good study of the varieties of limitation and their function. Some lim-itations are only temporary, or even playful, like the ignorance Fielding sometimes im-poses on his 'I' (as when he doubts his own powers of narration and invokes the Muses for aid, e.g. *Tom Jones* XIII, i). Some are more nearly permanent but subject to mo-mentary relaxation, like the generally limited, humanly realistic Ishmael in *Moby Dick,* who can yet break through his human limitations when the story requires (' "He waxes brave, but nevertheless obeys; most careful bravery that!"—murmured Ahab'—with no one present to report to the narrator). And some are confined to what their literal condition would allow them to know (first person, Huck Finn; third person, Miranda and Laura in Katherine Anne Porter's stories).

The most important single privilege is that of obtaining an inside view, because of the rhetorical power that such a privilege conveys upon a narrator. A curious am-biguity in our notions of 'omniscience' is ordinarily hidden by our terminology. Many modern works that we usually classify as narrated dramatically, with everything re-layed to us through the limited views of the characters, postulate fully as much omni-science in the silent author as Fielding claims for himself. Our roving visitation into the minds of sixteen characters in Faulkner's *As I Lay Dying,* seeing nothing but what those minds contain, may seem in one sense not to depend on an omniscient narra-tor. But this method is omniscience with teeth in it: the implied author demands our absolute faith in his powers of divination. We must never for a moment doubt that he knows everything about each of these sixteen minds, or that he has chosen correctly how much to show of each. In short the choice of the most rigorously limited point-of-view is really no escape from omniscience—the true narrator is as 'unnaturally' all-knowing as he ever was. If evident artificiality were a fault—which it is not—modern narration would be as faulty as Trollope's.

Another way of suggesting the same ambiguity is to look closely at the concept of 'dramatic' story-telling. The author can present his characters in a dramatic situa-tion without in the least presenting them in what we normally think of as a dramatic manner. When Joseph Andrews, who has been stripped and beaten by thieves, is over-taken by a stage-coach, Fielding presents the scene in what by some modern standards must seem an inconsistent and undramatic mode. 'The poor wretch, who lay motion-less a long time, just began to recover his senses as a stage-coach came by. The pos-tilion hearing a man's groans, stopped his horses, and told the coachman, he was certain there was a dead man lying in the ditch . . . A lady, who heard what the postilion said, and likewise heard the groan, called eagerly to the coachman to stop and see what was the matter. Upon which he bid the postilion alight, and look into the ditch. He did so, and returned, "That there was a man sitting upright, as naked as ever he was born".' There follows a splendid description, hardly meriting the name of *scene,* in which the selfish reactions of each passenger are recorded. A young lawyer points out that they might be legally liable if they refuse to take Joseph up. 'These words had a sensible effect on the coachman, who was well acquainted with the person who spoke them; and the old gentleman above mentioned, thinking the naked man would afford him frequent opportunities of showing his wit to the lady, offered to join with the company in giving a mug of beer for his fare; till partly alarmed by the threats of the one, and partly by the promises of the other, and being perhaps a little moved with compassion at the poor creature's condition, who stood bleeding and shivering with the cold, he at length agreed'. Once Joseph is in the coach, the same kind of indirect reporting of the 'scene' continues, with frequent excursions, however superficial, into the minds and hearts of the assembly of fools and knaves, and occasional guesses when complete knowledge seems inadvisable. If to be dramatic is to show characters dramatically engaged with each other, motive clashing with motive, the outcome depending upon the resolution of motives, then this scene is dramatic. But if it is to give the impression that the story is taking place by itself, with the characters existing in a dramatic relationship vis-a-vis the spectator, unmediated by a narrator and decipherable only through inferential matching of word to word and word to deed, then this is a relatively undramatic scene.

On the other hand, an author can present a character in this latter kind of dramatic relationship with the reader without involving that character in any internal drama at all. Many lyric poems are dramatic in this sense and totally undramatic in any other. 'That is no country for old men—' Who says? Yeats, or his 'mask', says. To whom? To us. How do we know that it is Yeats and not some character as remote from him as Caliban is remote from Browning in 'Caliban upon Setebos'? We infer it as the dramatised statement unfolds; the need for the inference is what makes the lyric *dramatic* in this sense. Caliban, in short, is dramatic in two senses; he is in a dramatic situation with other characters and he is in a dramatic situation over-against us. Yeats, or if we prefer 'Yeats' mask', is dramatic in only one sense.

The ambiguities of the word dramatic are even more complicated in fiction that attempts to dramatise states of consciousness directly. Is *A Portrait of the Artist as a Young Man* dramatic? In some respects, yes. We are not told about Stephen. He is placed on the stage before us, acting out his destiny with only disguised helps or comments from his author. But it is not his actions that are dramatised directly, not his speech that we hear unmediated. What is dramatised is his mental record of everything that happens. We see his consciousness at work on the world. Sometimes what it records is itself dramatic, as when Stephen observes himself in a scene with other characters. But the report itself, the internal record, is dramatic in the second sense only. The report we are given of what goes on in Stephen's mind is a monologue uninvolved in any modifying dramatic context. And it is an *infallible* report, even less subject to critical doubts than the typical Elizabethan soliloquy. We accept, by convention, the claim that what is reported as going on in Stephen's mind really goes on there, or in other words, that Joyce knows how Stephen's mind works. 'The equation of the page of his scribbler began to spread out a widening tail, eyed and starred like a peacock's; and, when the eyes and stars of its indices had been eliminated, began slowly to fold itself together again. The indices appearing and disappearing were eyes opening and closing; the eyes opening and closing were stars . . .' Who says so? Not Stephen, but the omniscient, infallible author. The report is direct, and it is clearly unmodified by any 'dramatic' context—that is, unlike a speech in a dramatic scene, we do not suspect that the report has here been in any way aimed at an effect on anyone but the reader. We are thus in a dramatic relation with Stephen only in a limited sense—the sense in which a lyrical poem is dramatic.

Indeed if we compare the act of reporting in *Tom Jones* with the act of reporting in *Portrait,* the former is in one sense considerably more dramatic; Fielding dramatises himself and his telling, and even though he is essentially reliable we must be constantly on our toes in comparing word to word and word to deed. 'It is an observation sometimes made, that to indicate our idea of a simple fellow, we say, he is easily to be seen through: nor do I believe it a more improper denotation of simple book. Instead of applying this to any particular performance, we choose rather to remark the contrary in this history, where the scene opens itself by small degrees; and he is a sagacious reader who can see two chapters before him.' Our running battle to keep up with these incidental ironies in Fielding's narration is matched, in *Portrait,* with an act of absolute, unquestioning credulity.

We should note finally that the author who eschews both forms of artificiality, both the traditional omniscience and the modern manipulation of inside views, confining himself to 'objective' surfaces only, is not necessarily identical with the 'undramatised author' under (2) above. In *The Awkward Age,* for example, James allows himself to comment frequently, but only to conjecture about the meaning of surfaces; the author is dramatised, but dramatised as partially ignorant of what is happening.

(10) Finally, narrators who provide inside views differ in the depth and the axis of their plunge. Boccaccio can give inside views, but they are extremely shallow. Jane Austen goes relatively deep morally, but scarcely skims the surface psychologically. All authors of stream-of-consciousness narration attempt to go deep psychologically, but some of them deliberately remain shallow in the moral dimension. We should remind ourselves that any sustained inside view, of whatever depth, temporarily turns the character whose mind is shown into a narrator; inside views are thus subject to variations in all of the qualities we have described above, and most importantly in the degree of unreliability. Generally speaking, the deeper our plunge, the more unreliability we will accept without loss of sympathy. The whole question of how inside views and moral sympathy interrelate has been seriously neglected.

Narration is an art, not a science, but this does not mean that we are necessarily doomed to fail when we attempt to formulate principles about it. There are systematic elements in every art, and criticism of fiction can never avoid the responsibility of trying to explain technical successes and failures by reference to general principles. But the question is that of where the general principles are to be found. Fiction, the novel, point-of-view—these terms are not in fact subject to the kind of definition that alone makes critical generalisations and rules meaningful. A given technique cannot be judged according to its service to 'the novel', or 'fiction', but only according to its success in particular works or kinds of work.

It is not surprising to hear practising novelists report that they have never had help from critics about point-of-view. In dealing with point-of-view the novelist must always deal with the individual work: which particular character shall tell this particular story, or part of a story, with what precise degree of reliability, privilege, freedom to comment, and so on. Shall he be given dramatic vividness? Even if the novelist has decided on a narrator who will fit one of the critic's classifications—'omniscient', 'first-person', 'limited omniscient', 'objective', 'roving', 'effaced', and so on—his troubles have just begun. He simply cannot find answers to his immediate, precise, practical problems by referring to statements that the 'omniscient is the most flexible method', or 'the objective the most rapid or vivid', or whatever. Even the soundest of generalisations at this level will be of little use to him in his page-by-page progress through his novel. As Henry James's detailed records show, the novelist discovers his narrative technique as he tries to achieve for his readers the potentialities of his developing idea. The majority of his choices are consequently choices of degree, not kind. To decide that your narrator shall not be omniscient decides practically nothing. The hard question is, just how *inconscient* shall he be? To decide that you will use first-person narration decides again almost nothing. What kind of first-person? How fully characterised? How much aware of himself as a narrator? How reliable? How much confined to realistic inference, how far privileged to go beyond realism? At what points shall he speak truth and at what points utter no judgment or even utter falsehood?

There are no doubt *kinds* of effect to which the author can refer—e.g., if he wants to make a scene more amusing, poignant, vivid, or ambiguous, or if he wants to make a character more sympathetic or more convincing, such-and-such practices may be indicated. But it is not surprising that in his search for help in his decisions, he should find the practice of his peers more helpful than the abstract rules of the textbooks: the sensitive author who reads the great novels finds in them a storehouse of precise examples, examples of how *this* effect, as distinct from all other possible effects, was heightened by the proper narrative choice. In dealing with the tyes of narration, the critic must always limp behind, referring constantly to the varied practice which alone can correct his temptations to overgeneralise.

Mieke Bal

Mieke Bal was born in 1946 in the Netherlands and received her Ph.D. from the University of Utrecht. She has taught at Utrecht and at the University of Amsterdam in her native Holland, as well as at the University of Rochester, the Harvard Divinity School, and the University of Quebec in Montreal. Her enormously prolific work on literary theory and narratology is combined with an intense interest in the Bible, especially the treatment of women and love in the Old Testament. Bal's books include *Narratology: Introduction to the Theory of Narrative* (1985), from which the following essay is excerpted; *Lethal Love: Feminist Literary Readings of Biblical Love Stories* (1987); *Death and Dissymetry: the Politics of Coherence in the Book of Judges* (1988); *Murder and Difference: Gender, Genre, and Scholarship on Sisera's Death* (1988, 1992); *Reading Rembrandt: Beyond the Word/Image Opposition* (1992): She has also edited *Anti-Covenant: Counter-reading Women's Lives in the Hebrew Bible* (1989) and *The Point of Theory: Practices of Cultural Analysis* (1994). Her most recent book is *On Meaning-Making: Essays in Semiotics* (1994).

Focalization

DIFFICULTIES

Whenever events are presented, they are always presented from within a certain 'vision.' A point of view is chosen, a certain way of seeing things, a certain angle, whether 'real' historical facts are concerned or fictitious events. It is possible to try and give an 'objective' picture of the facts. But what does that involve? An attempt to present only what is seen or is perceived in some other way. All comment is shunned and implicit interpretation is also avoided. Perception, however, is a psychological process, strongly dependent on the position of the perceiving body; a small child sees things in a totally different way from an adult, if only as far as measurements are concerned. The degree to which one is familiar with what one sees also influences perception. When the Central American Indians first saw horsemen, they did not see the same things we do when we see people riding. They *saw* gigantic monsters, with human heads and four legs. These had to be gods. Perception depends on so many factors that striving for objectivity is pointless. To mention only a few factors: one's position with respect to the perceived object, the fall of the light, the distance, previous knowledge, psychological attitude towards the object; all this and more affects the picture one forms and passes on to others. In a story, elements of the fabula are presented in a certain way. We are confronted with a vision of the fabula. What is this vision and where does it come from? These are the questions that will be discussed in these subsections. I shall refer to the relations between the elements presented and the vision through which they are presented with the term *focalization*. Focalization is, then, the relation between the vision and that which is 'seen,' perceived. By using this term I wish to dissociate myself from a number of current terms in this area, for reasons which I shall now explain.

The theory of narration, as it has been developed in the course of this century, offers various labels for the concept here referred to. The most current one is *point of view* or *narrative perspective.* Narrative situation, narrative viewpoint, narrative manner are also employed. More or less elaborate typologies of 'narrative points of view' have been developed, of which I shall include the most well-known in my bibliography. All these typologies have proved more or less useful. They are all, however, unclear on one point. They do not make an explicit distinction between, on the one hand, the vision through which the elements are presented and, on the other, the identity of the voice that is verbalizing that vision. To put it more simply: they do not make a distinction between *those who see* and *those who speak*. Nevertheless, it is possible, both in fiction and in reality, for one person to express the vision of another. This happens all the time. When no distinction is made between these two different agents, it is difficult, if not impossible, to describe adequately the technique of a text in which something is seen—*and* that vision is narrated. The imprecisions of such typologies can sometimes lead to absurd formulations or classifications which are too rough-and-ready. To claim, as has been done, that Strether in Henry James' *The Ambassadors* is 'telling his own story,' whereas the novel is written 'in the third person,' is as nonsensical as to claim that the sentence:

a Elizabeth saw him lie there, pale and lost in thought.

is narrated, from the comma onwards, by the character Elizabeth; that means it is spoken by her. What this sentence does is to present Elizabeth's vision clearly: after all, she does *see* him lying down.

The existing typologies have achieved solid respectability in current literary criticism. There must be an explanation for this: their evident usefulness. All offer interesting possibilities, despite the objection just mentioned. I am of the opinion, however, that their distinctions should be adapted to the insight that the agent that sees must be given a status other than that of the agent that narrates.

If we examine the current terms from this point of view, only the term *perspective* seems clear enough. This label covers both the physical and the psychological points of perception. It does not cover the agent that is performing the action of narration, and it should not do so. Nevertheless, my own preference lies with the term *focalization* for two reasons and despite justly raised objections to the introduction of unnecessary new terminology. The first reason concerns tradition. Although the word 'perspective' reflects precisely what is meant here, it has come to indicate in the tradition of narrative theory both the narrator and the vision. This ambiguity has affected the specific sense of the word, in itself correct. If we were to use it here in a more specific sense, chances are that it would still be associated with the familiar, imprecise meaning.

There is yet another, more practical, objection to this term. No substantive can be derived from 'perspective' that could indicate the subject of the action; the verb 'to perspectivize' is not customary and would, probably, if used, have another meaning than the one meant here. In order to describe the focalization in a story we must have terms such as these at our disposal. These two arguments seemed to me to be weighty enough to justify my choice of a new term for a not completely new concept. *Focalization* offers a number of extra, minor advantages as well. It is a term that looks technical. It is derived from photography and film; its technical nature is thus emphasized. As any 'vision' presented can have a strongly manipulative effect, and is, consequently, very difficult to extract from the emotions, not only from those attributed to the focalizor and the character, but also from those of the reader, a technical term will help us keep our attention on the technical side of such a means of manipulation.

THE FOCALIZOR

In Southern India, at Mahaballipuram, is what is said to be the largest *bas-relief* of the world, the seventh-century *Arjuna's penance*. At the upper left, the wise man Arjuna is depicted in a yoga position. At the bottom right stands a cat. Around the cat are a number of mice. The mice are laughing. It is a strange image. Unless the spectator interprets the signs. The interpretation runs as follows. Arjuna is in a yoga position and is mediating to win Lord Siva's favour. The cat, impressed by the beauty of absolute calm, imitates Arjuna. Now the mice realize they are safe. They laugh. Without this interpretation, there is no relation between the parts of the relief. Within this interpretation the parts form a coherent narrative.

The picture is a comical one, in addition to being a real comic. The comical effect is evoked by the narrativity of the picture. The spectator sees the relief as a whole. Its contents include a succession in time. First, Arjuna assumes the yoga position. Then, the cat imitates him. After that, the mice start laughing. These three successive events are logically related in a causal chain. According to every definition I know, that means this is a fabula.

But there is more. Not only are the events chronologically in succession and logically in a causal relation. They can only occur through the semiotic activity of the actors. And the comical effect can only be explained when this particular mediation is analysed. We laugh because we can identify with the mice. Seeing what they see, we realize with them that a meditating cat is a contradiction; cats hunt, and only wise men meditate. Following the chain of events in reverse, we also arrive at the next one by perceptual identification. The cat has brought about the event for which he is responsible because he has seen Arjuna do something. This chain of perceptions also runs in time. The wise man sees nothing since he is totally absorbed in his meditation; the cat has seen Arjuna and now sees nothing more of this world; the mice see the cat *and* Arjuna. That is why they know they are safe. (Another interpretation is that the cat is simulating; this doesn't weaken my statements but only adds an element of suspense to the fabula.) The mice are laughing because of that very fact, finding the imitation a ridiculous enterprise. The spectator sees more. S/he sees the mice, the cat and the wise man. S/he laughs at the cat, and s/he laughs sympathetically with the mice, whose pleasure is comparable to that felt by a successful scoundrel.

This example, paradoxical because it is not linguistic, illustrates quite clearly the theory of focalizations. We can view the picture of the relief as a (visual) sign. The elements of this sign, the standing Arjuna, the standing cat, the laughing mice, only have spatial relations to one another. The elements of the fabula—Arjuna assumes a yoga position, the cat assumes a yoga position, the mice laugh—do not form a coherent significance as such. The relation between the sign (the relief) and its contents (the fabula), can only be established by mediation of an interjacent layer, the view of the events. The cat sees Arjuna. The mice see the cat. The spectator sees the mice who see the cat who has seen Arjuna. And the spectator sees that the mice are right. Every verb of perception (to *see*) in this report indicates an activity of focalization. Every verb of action indicates an event.

Focalization is the relationship between the 'vision,' the agent that sees, and that which is seen. This relationship is a component of the story part, of the content of the narrative text: A sees that B sees what C is doing. Sometimes that difference is void, e.g. when the reader is presented with a vision as directly as possible. The different agents then cannot be isolated, they coincide. That is a form of 'stream of consciousness.' Consequently, focalization belongs in the story, the layer in between the linguistic text and the fabula. Because the definition of focalization refers to a relationship, each pole of that relationship, the subject and the object of focalization, must be studied separately. The subject of focalization, the *focalizor,* is the point from which the elements are viewed. That point can lie with a character (i.e. an element of the fabula), or outside it. If the focalizor coincides with the character, that character will have a technical advantage over the other characters. The reader watches with the character's eyes and will, in principle, be inclined to accept the vision presented by that character. In Mulisch's *Massuro,* we see with the eyes of the character who later also draws up a report of the events. The first symptoms of Massuro's strange disease are the phenomena which the other perceives. These phenomena communicate Massuro's *condition* to us, they tell us nothing abut the way he feels about it. Such a character-bound focalizor, which we could label, for convenience' sake, CF, brings about *bias* and *limitation.* In Henry James' *What Maisie Knew* the focalization lies almost entirely with Maisie, a little girl who does not understand much about the problematic relations going on around her. Consequently, the reader is shown the events through the limited vision of the girl, and only gradually realizes what is actually going on. But the reader is not a little girl. S/he does more with the information s/he receives than Maisie does, s/he interprets it differently. Where Maisie sees only a strange gesture, the reader knows that s/he is dealing with an erotic one. The difference between the childish vision of the events and the interpretation that the adult reader gives to them determines the novel's special effect.

Character-bound focalization (CF) can vary, can shift from one character to another. In such cases, we may be given a good picture of the origins of a conflict. We are shown how differently the various characters view the same facts. This technique can result in neutrality towards all the characters. Nevertheless, there usually is never a doubt in our minds which character should receive most attention and sympathy. On the grounds of distribution, for instance the fact that a character focalizes the first and/or the last chapter, we label it the hero(ine) of the book.

When focalization lies with one character which participates in the fabula as an actor, we could refer to *internal* focalization. We can then indicate by means of the term *external* focalization that an anonymous agent, situated outside the fabula, is functioning as focalizor. Such an external, non-character-bound focalizor is abbreviated EF. In the following fragment from the opening of Doris Lessing's *The Summer before the Dark* we see the focalization move from EF to CF.

> *b* A woman stood on her back step, arms folded, waiting.
>
> Thinking? She would not have said so. She was trying to catch hold of something or to lay it bare so that she could look and define; for some time now she had been 'trying on' ideas like so many dresses off a rack. She was letting words and phrases as worn as nursery rhymes slide around her tongue: for towards the crucial experiences custom allots certain atti-

tudes, and they are pretty stereotyped. A yes, first love! . . . Growing up is bound to be painful! . . . My first child, you know. . . . But I was in love! . . . Marriage is a compromise. . . . I am not as young as I once was.

From sentence two onwards the contents of what the character experiences are given. A switch thus occurs from an external focalizor (EF) to an internal one (CF). An alternation between external and internal focalizors, between EF and CF, is visible in a good many stories. In *The Evenings*, Frits is the only character that functions as focalizor. Therefore, the two different focalizors are EF and CF-Frits. A number of characters can also alternate as CF focalizor; in that case, it can be useful to indicate the various characters in the analysis by their initials, so that one can retain a clear overview of the division of focalization: in Frits' case, this would mean the notation CF (Fr). An example of a story in which a great many different characters act as focalizor is *Of Old People*. However, the characters do not carry an equal load; some focalize often, others only a little, some do not focalize at all. It is also possible for the entire story to be focalized by EF. The narrative can then appear objective, because the events are not presented from the point of view of the characters. The focalizor's bias is, then, not absent, since there is no such thing as 'objectivity,' but it is unclear.

THE FOCALIZED OBJECT

In *Of Old People* Harold is usually the focalizor when the events in the Indies are being focalized; Lot often focalizes his mother, mama Ottilie, and it is mainly because of this that we receive a fairly likeable image of her despite her unfriendly behaviour. Evidently, it is important to ascertain which character focalizes which object. The combination of a focalizor and a focalized object can be constant to a large degree (Harold-Indies; Lot-mama Ottilie), or it can vary greatly. Research into such fixed or loose combinations is of importance because the image we receive of the object is determined by the focalizor. Conversely, the image a focalizor presents of an object says something about the focalizor itself. Where focalization is concerned, the following questions are relevant.

1. *What* does the character focalize: what is it aimed at?
2. *How* does it do this: with what attitude does it view things?
3. *Who* focalizes it: whose focalized object is it?

What is focalized by a character F? It need not be a character. Objects, landscapes, events, in short all the elements are focalized, either by an EF or by a CF. Because of this fact alone, we are presented with a certain, far from innocent, interpretation of the elements. The degree to which a presentation includes an *opinion* can, of course, vary: the degree to which the focalizor points out its interpretative activities and makes them explicit also varies. Compare, for instance, the following descriptions of place:

c Behind the round and spiny forms around us in the depth endless coconut plantations stretch far into the hazy blue distance where mountain ranges ascended ghostlike. Closer, at my side, a ridged and ribbed violet grey mountainside stretches upward with a sawtooth silhouette combing the white cloudy sky. Dark shadows of the clouds lie at random on the slopes as if capricious dark-grey pieces of cloth have been dropped on them. Close by, in a temple niche, Buddha sits meditating in an arched window of shadow. A dressing-jacket of white exudation of bird-droppings on his shoulders. Sunshine on his hands which lie together perfectly at rest.

(Jan Wolkers, *The Kiss*)

d Then we must first describe heaven, of course. Then the hundreds of rows of angels are clad in glorious shiny white garments. Everyone of them has long, slightly curly fair hair and blue eyes. There are no men here. 'How strange that all angels should be women.' There are no dirty angels with seductive panties, garterbelts and stockings, not to mention bras. I always pictured an angel as a woman who presents her breasts as if on saucers, with heavily made-up eyes, and a bright red mouth, full of desire, eager to please, in short, everything a woman should be. (Formerly, when I was still a student, I wanted to transform Eve into a real whore. I bought her everything necessary, but she did not want to wear the stuff.)

(J. M. A. Biesheuvel, *The Way to the Light*, 'Faust')

In both cases, a CF is clearly involved; both focalizors may be localized in the character 'I.' In *c*, the spatial position of the CF ('I') is especially striking. It is obviously situated on a high elevation, considering the wide prospect it has. The words 'around us,' combined with 'in the depths,' stress that high position. The proximity of the niche with the Buddha statue makes clear that CF ('I') is situated in an eastern temple (the Burubudur in fact), so that 'the round and spiny form' (must) refer to the temple roof. The presentation of the whole, temple roof and landscape, seems fairly impersonal. If the CF ('I') had not identified itself by the use of the first-person personal pronoun in 'at my side' and 'around us,' this would have seemed, on the face of it, an 'objective' description, perhaps taken from a pamphlet or a geography book.

On closer analysis, this proves not to be the case. Whether the CF ('I') is explicitly named or not, the 'internal' position of the focalizor is, in fact, already established by expressions such as 'close by,' 'closer,' and 'at my side,' which underline the vicinity between the place and the perceiver. 'Behind' and 'far into' indicate a specification of the spatial perspective (in the pictorial sense). But more happens here. Without appearing to do so, this presentation *interprets*. This is clear from the use of metaphors, which points to the facts that the CF ('I') attempts to reduce the objects it sees, which impress it a great deal, to human, everyday proportions. In this way, the CF ('I') is undoubtedly trying to fit the object into its own realm of experience. Images like 'sawtooth' and 'combing,' 'capricious dark-grey pieces of cloth,' and clichés like 'mountain ranges' bear this out. The 'dressing-jacket of white exudation of bird-droppings' is the clearest example. Actually, the image is also interesting because of the association mechanism it exhibits. With the word 'dressing-jacket,' the Buddha's statue becomes human, and as soon as it is human, the white layer on its head could easily be dandruff, a possibility suggested by the word 'exudation.' The realistic nature of the presentation—CF ('I') does 'really' *see* the landscape—is restored immediately afterwards by the information about the real nature of the white layer: bird-droppings. Thus, what we see here is the presentation of a landscape which is realistic, reflecting what is actually perceived, and at the same time interpreting the view in a specific way, so that it can be assimilated by the character.

Example *d* exhibits to a certain extent the same characteristics. Here, too, an impressive space is humanized. However, the CF ('I') observes the object less and interprets it more. It concerns a fantasy object with which the CF ('I') is sketchily familiar from religious literature and painting, but which it can adapt as much as it wishes, to its own taste. This is what it does, and its taste is clear. Here, too, an association mechanism is visible. From the traditional image of angels, implied in the second or third sentence, the CF ('I') moves to the assumption that angels are women. In this, the vision already deviates from the traditional vision, in which angels are asexual or male. Against the image thus created of asexual male angels, the CF (`I') sets up, in contrast, its own female image, which by now has moved very far away from the image that we have of angels.

And even before the reader realizes that in doing so a link is made with another tradition, that of the opposition angel-whore, in which 'angel' is used in a figurative sense, the word 'whore' itself appears in the text. In this, the interpretive mode of the description manifests itself clearly. The solemn 'we' of the beginning contrasts sharply with the personal turn which the description takes. The humour is here based on the contrast between the solemn-impersonal and the personal-everyday. The interpretive focalization is emphasized in several ways. The sentence in quotation marks is presented as a reaction to the sentence preceding it. Here, the interpreting focalizor makes an explicit entrance. Later this is stressed again: 'not to mention' is a colloquial expression, and points at a personal subject, expressing an opinion: 'I always pictured an angel as . . .' accentuates even more strongly that a personal opinion is involved.

The way in which a subject is presented gives information about that object itself and about the focalizor. These two descriptions give even more information about the CFS ('I') than about the object; more about the way they experience nature (*c*) or women (*d*), respectively, than about the Burubudur temple and heaven. In principle, it doesn't matter whether the object 'really exists' in actuality, or is art of a fictitious fabula, or whether it is a fantasy created by the character and so a doubly fictitious object. The comparison with the object referred to served in the above analysis only to motivate the interpretation by the CF ('I') in both fragments. The internal structure of the descriptions provides in itself sufficient clues about the degree to which one CF ('I') showed similarity to and differed from the other.

These two examples indicate yet another distinction. In *c* the object of the focalization was perceptible. The CF ('I') 'really' sees something that is outside itself. This is not always the case. An object can also be visible only inside the head of the CF. And only those who have access to it can perceive anything. This cannot be another character, at least not according to the classical rules of the narrative genre, but it might possibly be an EF. Such a 'non-perceptible' object occurs in cases where, for instance, the contents of a character's dream are presented. Concerning the heaven in *d,* we can only decide whether that object is perceptible or not perceptible when we know how the fragment fits into its context. If the 'I,' together with another person—a devil, for instance—is on an excursion to heaven, we will have to accept the first part of the description, until the sentence in quotation marks, as 'perceptible.' Thus, our criterion is that within the fabula there must be another character present that can also perceive the object; if they are the dreams, fantasies, thoughts, or feelings of a character, then these objects can be part of the category 'non-perceptible' objects. This distinction can be indicated by adding to the notation of the focalizor a 'p' or an 'np.' For *b* we end up with CF (woman)-np; for *c*, CF ('I')-p, and for *d*, CF ('I')-np. This distinction too is of importance for an insight into the power-structure between the characters. When in a conflict situation one character is allotted both CF-p and CF-np, and the other exclusively CF-p, then the first character has the advantage as a party in the conflict. It can give the reader insight into its feelings and thoughts, while the other character cannot communicate anything. Moreover, the other character will not have the insight which the reader receives, so that it cannot react to the feelings of the other (which it does not know), cannot adapt itself to them or oppose them. Such an inequality in position between characters is obvious in the so-called 'first-person novels,' but in other kinds this inequality is not always clear to the reader. Yet the latter is manipulated by it in forming an opinion about the various characters. Consequently, the focalization has a strongly manipulative effect. Colette's novel *La Chatte* is a strong case: the reader is manipulated by this device into taking the man's side against his wife.

In this respect, it is important to keep sight of the difference between spoken and unspoken *words* of the characters. Spoken words are audible to others and are thus perceptible when the focalization lies with someone else. Unspoken words— thoughts, internal monologues—no matter how extensive, are not perceptible to other characters. Here, too, lies a possibility for manipulation which is often used. Readers are given elaborate information about the thoughts of a character, which the other characters do not hear. If these thoughts are placed in between the sections of dialogue, readers do not often realize how much less the other character knows than they do. An analysis of the perceptibility of the focalized objects supplies insight into these objects' relationships.

Seymour Chatman

Seymour Chatman was born in Detroit in 1928 and educated at Wayne State University and at the University of Michigan at Ann Arbor, where he earned his doctorate in English in 1956. Chatman has taught at Cornell, at Wayne State, at the University of Pennsylvania, and at the University of California at Berkeley, where he is currently Professor Emeritus of Rhetoric. Chatman has received numerous grants and awards, including NEH, Guggenheim, Rockefeller, and Fulbright Fellowships and has been visiting professor in Zurich and Bologna. Chatman's work has been on the theory of narrative fiction and cinema and on the interconnections and differences between their ways of handling plot and story. His recent books include an edition of the screenplay of Michelangelo Antonioni's *L'Avventura* (1989), *Coming to Terms: The Rhetoric of Narrative in Fiction and Film* (1990), and *Reading Narrative Fiction* (1992). Chatman is currently working on the interrelations between novel and film, on the cinema of Woody Allen, and on literary and cinematic parody. His discussion below of "Voice" is excerpted from his 1980 book, *Story and Discourse.*

Voice

> *Silence is become his mother tongue.*
> Oliver Goldsmith,
> *The Good-Natured Man*

Every narrative—so this theory goes—is a structure with a content plane (called "story") and an expression plane (called "discourse"). Having examined story in Chapters 2 and 3, we turn to the other half of the narrative dichotomy. The expression plane is the set of narrative statements, where "statement" is the basic component of the form of the expression, independent of and more abstract than any particular manifestation—that is, the expression's substance, which varies from art to art. A certain posture in the ballet, a series of film shots, a whole paragraph in a novel, or only a single word—any of these might manifest a single narrative statement. I have proposed that narrative statements are of two kinds—process and stasis—corresponding to whether the deep narrative (not the surface linguistic) predicate is in the mode of existence (IS) or action (DOES).

Crosscutting this dichotomy is another: Is the statement directly presented to the audience or is it mediated by someone—the someone we call the narrator? Direct presentation presumes a kind of overhearing by the audience. Mediated narration, on the other hand, presumes a more or less express communication from narrator to audience. This is essentially Plato's distinction between *mimesis* and *diegesis,*[1] in modern terms between showing and telling. Insofar as there is telling, there must be a teller, a narrating voice.

The teller, the transmitting source, is best accounted for, I think, as a spectrum of possibilities, going from narrators who are least audible to those who are most so. The label affixed to the negative pole of narratorhood is less important than its reality in the spectrum. I say "nonnarrated": the reader may prefer "minimally narrated," but the existence of this kind of transmission is well attested.

The narrator's presence derives from the audience's sense of some demonstrable communication. If it feels it is being told something, it presumes a teller. The alterna-

---

[1] These terms are revived by Gérard Genette in "Frontières du récit," *Communications,* 8 (1966). *Au.*

tive is a "direct witnessing" of the action. Of course, even in the scenic arts like drama and the ballet, pure mimesis is an illusion. But the degree of possible analogy varies. The main question is how the illusion is achieved. By what convention does a spectator or reader accept the idea that it is "as if" he were personally on the scene, though he comes to it by sitting in a chair in a theater or by turning pages and reading words. Authors may make special efforts to preserve the illusion that events "literally unfold before the reader's eyes," mostly by restricting the kinds of statements than can occur.

To understand the concept of narrator's voice (including its "absence") we need to consider three preliminary issues: the interrelation of the several parties to the narrative transaction, the meaning of "point of view" and its relation to voice, and the nature of acts of speech and thought as a subclass of the class of acts in general. These topics form a necessary prolegomena to the analysis of narrator's voice, upon which any discussion of narrative discourse rests.

REAL AUTHOR, IMPLIED AUTHOR, NARRATOR, REAL READER, IMPLIED READER, NARRATEE

That it is essential not to confuse author and narrator has become a commonplace of literary theory. As Monroe Beardsley argues, "the speaker of a literary work cannot be identified with the author—and therefore the character and condition of the speaker can be known by internal evidence alone—unless the author has provided a pragmatic context, or a claim of one, that connects the speaker with himself."[2] But even in such a context, the speaker is not the author, but the "author" (quotation marks of "as if"), or better the "author"-narrator, one of several possible kinds.

In addition, there is a demonstrable third party, conveniently dubbed, by Wayne Booth, the "implied author":

> As he writes, [the real author] creates not simply an ideal, impersonal 'man in general' but an implied version of 'himself' that is different from the implied authors we meet in other men's works. . . . Whether we call this implied author an 'official scribe', or adopt the term recently revived by Kathleen Tillotson—the author's 'second self'—it is clear that the picture the reader gets of this presence is one of the author's most important effects. However impersonal he may try to be, his reader will inevitably construct a picture of the official scribe.[3]

He is "implied," that is, reconstructed by the reader from the narrative. He is not the narrator, but rather the principle that invented the narrator, along with everything else in the narrative, that stacked the cards in this particular way, had these things happen to these characters, in these words or images. Unlike the narrator, the implied author

---

[2] In *Aesthetics* (New York, 1958), p. 240. Cf. Walker Gibson, "Authors, Speakers, Readers, Mock Readers," *College English*, 11 (1950), 265–269; and Kathleen Tillotson, *The Tale and the Teller* (London, 1959). *Au.*

[3] *Rhetoric of Fiction*, pp. 70–71. *Au.* See above, p. 143 *Ed.*

can *tell* us nothing. He, or better, *it* has no voice, no direct means of communicating. It instructs us silently, through the design of the whole, with all the voices, by all the means it has chosen to let us learn. We can grasp the notion of implied author most clearly by comparing different narratives written by the same real author but presupposing different implied authors. Booth's example: the implied author of *Jonathan Wild* "is by implication very much concerned with public affairs and with the effects of unchecked ambition on the 'great men' who attain to power in the world," whereas the implied author "who greets us on page one of *Amelia*" conveys rather an "air of sententious solemnity."[4] The implied author of *Joseph Andrews,* on the contrary, sounds "facetious" and "generally insouciant." Not merely the narrator but the whole design of *Joseph Andrews* functions in a tone quite different from that of *Jonathan Wild* or *Amelia.* Henry Fielding created three clearly different implied authors.

The distinction is particularly evident in the case of the "unreliable narrator" (another of Booth's happy coinages). What makes a narrator unreliable is that his values diverge strikingly from that of the implied author's; that is, the rest of the narrative— "the norm of the work"—conflicts with the narrator's presentation, and we become suspicious of his sincerity or competence to tell the "true version." The unreliable narrator is at virtual odds with the implied author; otherwise his unreliability could not emerge.

The implied author establishes the norms of the narrative, but Booth's insistence that these are moral seems unnecessary. The norms are general cultural codes, whose relevance to story we have already considered. The real author can postulate whatever norms he likes through his implied author. It makes no more sense to accuse the real Céline or Montherlant of what the implied author causes to happen in *Journey to the End of the Night* or *Les Jeunes Filles* than to hold the real Conrad responsible for the reactionary attitudes of the implied author of *The Secret Agent* or *Under Western Eyes* (or, for that matter, Dante for the Catholic ideas of the implied author of the *Divine Comedy*). One's moral fibre cannot really be "seduced" by wily implied authors. Our acceptance of their universe is aesthetic, not ethical. To confound the "implied author," a structural principle, with a certain historical figure whom we may or may not admire morally, politically, or personally would seriously undermine our theoretical enterprise.[5]

There is always an implied author, though there might not be a single real author in the ordinary sense: the narrative may have been composed by committee (Hollywood films), by a disparate group of people over a long period of time (many folk ballads), by random-number generation by a computer, or whatever.[6]

The counterpart of the implied author is the *implied reader*—not the flesh-and-bones you or I sitting in our living rooms reading the book, but the audience presup-

---

[4] Ibid., p. 72. *Au.*
[5] There is an interesting discussion of the question in Susan Suleiman, "Ideological Dissent from Works of Fiction: Toward a Rhetoric of the *Roman à ihèse,*" *Neophilologus* (April 1976), 162–177. Suleiman thinks that the implied author, as well as the narrator, can be unreliable, and thus we can accept imaginatively a narrative that we reject ideologically. *Au.*
[6] Christian Metz, *Film Language*, p. 20. *Au.*

posed by the narrative itself. Like the implied author, the implied reader is always present. And just as there may or may not be a narrator, there may or may not be a *narratee*.[7] He may materialize as a character in the world of the work: for example, the someone listening to Marlow as he unfolds the story of Jim or Kurtz. Or there may be no overt reference to him at all, though his presence is felt. In such cases the author makes explicit the desired audience stance, and we must give him the benefit of the doubt if we are to proceed at all. The narratee-character is only one device by which the implied author informs the real reader how to perform as implied reader, which *Weltanschauung* to adopt. The narratee-character tends to appear in narratives like Conrad's whose moral texture is particularly complex, where good is not easily distinguished from evil. In narratives without explicit narratees, the stance of the implied reader can only be inferred, on ordinary cultural and moral terms. Thus, Hemingway's "The Killers" does not permit us to assume that we too are members of the Mob; the story just will not work if we do. Of course, the real reader may refuse his projected role at some ultimate level—nonbelievers do not become Christians just to read *The Inferno* or *Paradise Lost.* But such refusal does not contradict the imaginative or "as if" acceptance of implied readership necessary to the elementary comprehension of the narrative.

It is as necessary to distinguish among narratees, implied readers (parties immanent to the narrative), and real readers (parties extrinsic and accidental to the narrative) as it is among narrator, implied author, and real author. The "you" or "dear reader" who is addressed by the narrator of *Tom Jones* is no more Seymour Chatman than is the narrator Henry Fielding. When I enter the fictional contract I add another self: I become an implied reader. And just as the narrator may or may not ally himself with the implied author, the implied reader furnished by the real reader may or may not ally himself with a narratee. In *Tom Jones* or *Tristram Shandy* the alliance is reasonably close; in *Les Liaisons dangereuses* or *Heart of Darkness* the distance is great.

The situation of the narratee is parallel to that of the narrator: he ranges from a fully characterized individual to "no one." Again, "absence" or "unmarkedness" is put in quotation marks: in some sense every tale implies a listener or reader, just as it implies a teller. But the author may, for a variety of reasons, leave these components unmentioned, indeed, go out of his way to suggest that they do not exist.

We can now diagram the whole narrative-communication situation as follows:

Narrative text

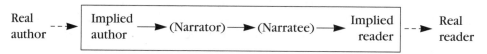

The box indicates that only the implied author and implied reader are immanent to a narrative, the narrator and narratee are optional (parentheses). The real author and

---

[7] The term was first coined, so far as I know, by Gerald Prince, "Notes Toward a Categorization of Fictional 'Narratees,'" *Genre,* 4 (1971), 100–105. Booth's "postulated reader" (157) is what I call the implied reader. *Au.* For Prince on the narratee, see below, pp. 226–241 *Ed.*

real reader are outside the narrative transaction as such, though, of course, indispensable to it in an ultimate practical sense.

. . .

POINT OF VIEW AND ITS RELATION
TO NARRATIVE VOICE

It is the task of narrative theory, like any theory, to deal with the ambiguities and unclarities of terms passed down to it. To understand the concept of narrator's voice—including the case where one is "not" (or minimally) present—we must first distinguish it from "point of view," one of the most troublesome of critical terms. Its plurisignification must give pause to anyone who wishes to use it in precise discussion. At least three senses can be distinguished in ordinary use:

(a) literal: through someone's eyes (perception);
(b) figurative: through someone's world view (ideology, conceptual system, *Weltanschauung*, etc.);
(c) transferred: from someone's interest-vantage (characterizing his general interest, profit, welfare, well-being, etc.).

The following sentences will illustrate these distinctions:

(a) From John's point of view, at the top of Coit Tower, the panorama of the San Francisco Bay was breath-taking.
(b) John said that from his point of view, Nixon's position, though praised by his supporters, was somewhat less than noble.
(c) Though he didn't realize it at the time, the divorce was a disaster from John's point of view.

In the first sentence, "The panorama of the Bay" is reported as actually seen by John; he stands at the center of a half-circle of vision. Let us call that his *perceptual* point of view. In the second, there is no reference to his actual physical situation in the real world but to his attitudes or conceptual apparatus, his way of thinking, and how facts and impressions are strained through it. We can call that his *conceptual* point of view. In the third, there is no reference to John's mind at all, either to perceptual or conceptual powers. Since John is unaware of the mentioned consequences, he is not "seeing," in either the actual or the figurative sense; the term then is a simple synonym for "as far as John is concerned." Let us call this his *interest* point of view. What is confusing is that "point of view" may thus refer to an *action* of some kind—perceiving or conceiving—or to a *passive state*—as in the third sense.

Now texts, any kind of text, even ordinary conversation, may entail one or any combination of these senses. A simple description of an experiment or an explorer's account of a new island may convey only the literal perceptions of the author, but it may also entail his *Weltanschauung,* or his practical interests. A philosophical treatise on abstract issues does not usually entail perceptual point of view, but may express quite eloquently the author's personal interests in the matter, along with his ideology.

When we turn to narrative texts, we find an even more complicated situation, since as we have seen there is no longer a single presence, as in expository essays, sermons, political speeches, and so on, but two—character and narrator—not to speak of the implied author. Each of these may manifest one or more kinds of point of view. A character may literally perceive a certain object or event; and/or it may be presented in terms of his conceptualization; and/or his interest in it may be invoked (even if he is unconscious of that interest).[8]

Thus the crucial difference between "point of view" and narrative voice: point of view is the physical place or ideological situation or practical life-orientation to which narrative events stand in relation. Voice, on the contrary, refers to the speech or other overt means through which events and existents are communicated to the audience. Point of view does *not* mean expression; it only means the perspective in terms of which the expression is made. *The perspective and the expression need not be lodged in the same person.*[9] Many combinations are possible. Consider just literal, that is perceptual, point of view. Events and existents may be perceived by the narrator and recounted by him in his own first person: "I felt myself fall down the hill" or "I saw Jack fall down the hill" (in the first case, the narrator is protagonist, in the second, witness). Or the point of view may be assigned to a character who is not the narrator: then the separate narrating voice may or may not make itself heard—"Mary, *poor dear,* saw Jack fall down the hill" versus "Mary saw Jack fall down the hill." Or the event may be presented so that it is not clear who, if anyone, perceived it (or perception is not an issue): "Jack fell down the hill."

The "camera eye" names a convention (an "illusion of mimesis") which pretends that the events just "happened" in the presence of a neutral recorder. To call such nar-

---

[8] Another ambiguity of "point of view" was recognized by Sister Kristin Morrison in "James's and Lubbock's Differing Points of View," *Nineteenth-Century Fiction,* 16 (1961), 245-256. Lubbock and his followers used the term in the sense of the narrative perspective of the speaker (the narrator), while James usually used it in the sense of the perspective of the knower or reader. Boris Uspensky in *Poetics of Composition,* trans. Valentina Zavarin and Susan Wittig (Berkeley, 1974), ch. 1, distinguishes various kinds of point of view along lines similar to mine. Some alternatives to "point of view" have been proposed: for instance, James's "central consciousness," Allen Tate's "post of observation," and Todorov's *"vision"* (derived from Jean Pouillon). The latter two continue the confusion between cognition and interest. *Au.*

[9] For example a recent article misreads "Eveline" by confusing character's point of view and narrator's voice (Clive Hart, "Eveline," in *James Joyce's Dubliners: Critical Essays,* London, 1969, p. 51). The author argues that Eveline is shallow and incapable of love—which may be true—but supports his argument with questionable evidence: "She over-dramatizes her association with Frank, calls it an 'affair' and him her 'lover'; she thinks of herself in pulp-literature terms as 'unspeakably' weary. But most obvious of all is the strong note of falsity in the language of the passage in which she reasserts her choice to leave: 'As she mused the pitiful vision of her mother's life laid its spell on the very quick of her being . . .' Dublin has so paralysed Eveline's emotions that she is unable to love, can think of herself and her situation only by means of a series of tawdry clichés." Surely the objectionable words are not Eveline's but the narrator's. It is he who is parodying pulp-literature sentimentality in tawdry clichés (as does the narrator of the "Nausicaa" section of *Ulysses*). Eveline may indeed feel maudlin sentiments, but "mused," "pitiful vision," "very quick of her being" are not in her vocabulary. *Au.*

rative transmission "limited third person" is wrong because it specifies only the point of view, not the narrative voice. It is necessary to distinguish between "limited third person point of view voiced by a covert narrator," "limited third person point of view voiced by an overt narrator," and so on.

Perception, conception, and interest points of view are quite independent of the manner in which they are expressed. When we speak of "expression," we pass from point of view, which is only a perspective or stance, to the province of narrative voice, the medium through which perception, conception, and everything else are communicated. Thus point of view is *in* the story (when it is the character's), but voice is always outside, in the discourse. From *A Portrait of the Artist as a Young Man:* "A few moments [later] he found himself on the stage amid the garish gas and the dim scenery." The perceptual point of view is Stephen's, but the voice is the narrator's. Characters' perceptions need not be articulated—Stephen is not saying to himself the *words* "garish gas and dim scenery"; the words are the narrator's. This is a narrator's report. But in "He shivered a little, and I beheld him rise slowly as if a steady hand from above had been pulling him out of the chair by the hair" (*Lord Jim*), not only the voice, but the perceptual point of view is the narrator's, Marlow's, not Jim's. And in "Coffin now. Got here before us, dead as he is. Horse looking round at it with his plume skewways. Dull eye: collar tight on his neck, pressing on a bloodvessel or something. Do they know what they cart out here every day?" ("Hades," *Ulysses*), the perceptual point of view is Leopold Bloom's, and so are the words, but he is no narrator. He is not telling a narratee anything. Indeed, he is not speaking even to himself: the convention argues that he is directly perceiving the coffin and the nag's dull eye, and nothing more. There *is* no narrator.

In all these cases the character perceives: his senses are directed outward upon the story-world. But when that perception is reported, as in the first two examples, there is necessarily presupposed another act of "seeing" with an independent point of view, namely that of the narrator, who has "peered into" the character's mind (metaphors are inevitable) and reports its contents from his *own* point of view. Can this kind of point of view be called "perceptual"? The word sounds strange, and for good reason. It makes sense to say that the character is literally perceiving something within the world of the work ("homodiegetically," as Genette would say). But what the narrator reports from his perspective is almost always outside the story (heterodiegetic), even if only retrospective, that is, temporally distant. Typically, he is looking back at his own earlier perception-as-a-character. But that looking-back is a conception, no longer a perception. The completely external narrator presents an even more purely conceptual view. He never was in the world of the work: discourse-time is not a later extension of story-time. He did not "perceive" in the same direct or diegetic sense that any character did. Literally speaking, he cannot have "seen" anything in that other world.

Thus the use of terms like "view" and "see" may be dangerously metaphorical. We "see" issues in terms of some cultural or psychological predisposition; the mechanism is entirely different from that which enables us to see cats or automobiles. Though it is true that preconceptions of various sorts affect our strictly physiological vision too (people may not see what is literally before their noses because they have compelling personal reasons not to), there remains an essential difference between perceptions and conceptions. Further, the narrator's is second-order or heterodiegetic conceptualizing *about* the story—as opposed to the first-order conceptualizing of a character within the story. These distinctions most clearly emerge where the two conflict, where the narrator is operating under a clearly different set of attitudes than those of the character. Then the narrator's conceptual point of view (except when he is unreliable) tends to override the character's, despite the fact that the latter maintains the center of interest and consciousness. An example is Conrad's *The Secret Agent:* the narrator is clearly unsympathetic to Verloc. Or, more precisely, the character has a conceptual point of view undermined by the narrator's manner of depicting it. Verloc's ideology (such as it is) reeks of indolence; the narrator carefully picks words to so characterize it. For example, Verloc does not simply stay in bed, he "wallows" in it. But the narrator (like all Conrad's narrators) is on the side of vigorous achievement. Similarly, he tells us that Verloc "remained undisturbed by any sort of aesthetic doubt about his appearance." From the narrator's conceptual point of view, implicitly communicated, Verloc's physical messiness is reprehensible and a clear analogue to moral sloth and political dishonesty. Or consider the difference between Verloc's and the narrator's attitudes toward female psychology. Verloc's unpleasant encounter with Mr. Vladimir brings him home in a towering rage. Forgetting that his wife is mourning the death of her brother, for which he is responsible, he is disappointed that she does not soothe him. Yet, immediately, he realizes that she is "a woman of few words." But his notion of his relationship with her, his conceptual point of view, is paraphrased in the narrator's superior diction: "[Winnie's] reserve, expressing in a way their profound confidence in each other, introduced at the same time a certain element of vagueness into their intimacy." Though the "profound confidence in each other" is the narrator's expression, not Verloc's, whose verbal style we know to be less elegant, it can only be Verloc's sentiment. His complacency, of course, turns out suicidal.

Disparity between the character's point of view and the narrator's expression of it need not entail ironic opposition. The narrator may verbalize neutrally or even sympathetically what (for reasons of youth, lack of education or intelligence, and so on), the character cannot articulate. This is the whole structural principle of James's *What Maisie Knew.* Maisie's uncertainty about when next she will visit her mother is expressed thusly: "Mama's roof, however, had its turn, this time, for the child, of appearing but remotely contingent. . . ." Clearly these are not phrases in Maisie's vocabulary. We accept them only because a sensitive little girl might have feelings that somehow matched the narrator's elegant terms. That is, we can "translate" into more childlike verbiage—for instance, "I don't expect to be at Mama's again very soon." The diction is sanctioned only by the convention of the "well-spoken narrator."

"Point of view" expressing someone's interests is even more radically distanced, since there is not even a figurative "seeing." The subject may be completely unconscious that events work for or against his interests (welfare, success, happiness). The identification of interest point of view may follow the clear specification of the character's perceptual and conceptual points of view. Once they are established, we continue identifying with his interests, by a process of inertia, even if he is unaware of something. In *The Ambassadors,* the narrator speaks of Maria Gostrey's powers of "pigeon-holing her fellow mortals": "She was as equipped in this particular as Strether was the reverse, and it made an opposition between them which he might well have shrunk from submitting to if he had fully suspected it." The narrator informs us of aspects of Maria's character that Strether does not know, yet it makes perfect sense to say that the sentence is "from his point of view." The focus of attention remains on him. Maria's traits are significant only in their implications for him—even though he is not aware of them.

Access to a character's consciousness is the standard entree to his point of view, the usual and quickest means by which we come to identify with him. Learning his thoughts insures an intimate connection. The thoughts are truthful, except in cases of willful self-deception. Unlike the narrator, the character can only be "unreliable" to himself.

At the same time, interest point of view can be established quite independently. The point of view may reside in a character who is "followed" in some sense, even if there is no reference at all to his thinking. If Jack and Peter are in the first scene, and Jack and Mary in the second, and Jack and Joseph in the third, we identify with Jack simply because he is the one continually on the scene. This has nothing to do with whether or not we care for him on human or other grounds.

The notion of interest point of view is not very meaningfully applied to an external narrator. His only interest is to get the narrative told. Other sorts of interest arise only if he is or was also a character. Then he may use the narrative itself as vindication, expiation, explanation, rationalization, condemnation, or whatever. There are hundreds of reasons for telling a story, but those reasons are the narrator's, not the implied author's, who is without personality or even presence, hence without motivation other than the purely theoretical one of constructing the narrative itself. The narrator's vested interests may be so marked that we come to think of him as unreliable.

The different points of view usually combine, but in important and interesting cases, they do not. Consider "autobiographical" or first-person narration, as in *Great Expectations.* The protagonist-as-narrator reports things from the perceptual point of view of his younger self. His ideology on the other hand tends to be that of his older self. The narrator is older and wiser for his experiences. In other narratives the ideology may not change; the narrator may exhibit substantially the same traits as characterized his earlier self. Where the narrator is a different person than the hero, he may present his own ideology, against which he judges his hero's actions, either overtly, as in *Tom Jones,* or covertly and inferentially, as in *The Ambassadors.* The narrator may utilize a perceptual point of view possible to no character, for example when he describes a bird's-eye view, or a scene with no one present, or what the character did *not* notice.

Dorrit Cohn

Dorrit Cohn was born in Vienna, Austria, in 1924 and emigrated to the United States in 1939. She was educated at the Lycée Français de New York, at Radcliffe College, and at Stanford, where she did her doctorate in German in 1964. She has taught at Indiana University and at Harvard, where she is Professor of German and Comparative Literature. Cohn has received numerous honors and grants for her work. Her books include *The Sleepwalkers, Elucidations of Hermann Broch's Trilogy* (1966) and *Transparent Minds: Narrative Modes for Presenting Consciousness in Fiction* (1978), from which the selection below is excerpted. Aside from *Transparent Minds,* Cohn has published numerous articles on narrative poetics in such journals as *Poetics Today, New Literary History, Poétique,* and *Comparative Literature.* Her work is closely affiliated with that of Gérard Genette (see p. 132) and Franz Stanzel, and strongly influenced by Käte Hamburger's *Logic of Literature.* She is at present at work on a book examining the borderline between fictional and nonfictional narrative from a narratological vantage point.

Narrated Monologue

INITIAL DESCRIPTION

In a German Naturalist story entitled *Papa Hamlet* (1889), which recounts the mental and physical decay of a Shakespearean actor, one finds the following passage:

> He had of late—but wherefore he knew not—lost all his mirth, forgone all custom of exercises; and indeed it went so heavily with his disposition that this goodly frame, the earth, seemed to him a sterile promontory; this most excellent canopy, the air, this brave o'erhanging firmament, this majestical roof fretted with golden fire, why it appeared no other thing to him than a foul and pestilent congregation of vapours. What a piece of work was a man! how noble in reason! how infinite in faculty! in form and moving how express and admirable! in action how like an angel! in apprehension how like a god! the beauty of the world! the paragon of animals! And yet, to him, what was this quintessence of dust? man delighted him not; no, nor woman neither.

With the assistance of Shakespeare (*Hamlet,* II, 2) the translation is my own; it is no less exact than the "German Shakespeare" (the celebrated Schlegel-Tieck translation) which dictated every detail of this passage in the original. Every detail, that is, except its person and tense. For, as is immediately apparent, this is *Hamlet* with a difference:

third-person pronouns have replaced first-person pronouns, the past tense has replaced the present. The result is not "Shakespeare" (a *quotation* of Hamlet's monologue), but "narrated Shakespeare" (a *narration* of Hamlet's monologue). What is the meaning of this transformation?

The Shakespearean language in this passage cannot be attributed to the narrator of *Papa Hamlet,* who speaks—in the purely narrative portions of the text—the neutrally reportorial language typical for the narrator of a Naturalist story. His protagonist, by contrast, habitually declaims Shakespeare to himself and others, and by this professional deformation feeds his need to dramatize and euphemize his sordid experiences. Even a reader of this story who has never heard of the technique of the "narrated monologue" will recognize that the above passage renders what Papa Hamlet thinks to himself rather than what his narrator reports about him. He will instinctively "redress" this text to mean that Papa Hamlet "thought to himself: 'I have of late—but wherefore I know not—lost all my mirth. . . .'"

A transformation of figural thought-language into the narrative language of third-person fiction is precisely what characterizes the technique for rendering consciousness that will occupy us throughout this chapter, and that I call the narrated monologue. It may be most succinctly defined as the technique for rendering a character's thought in his own idiom while maintaining the third-person reference and the basic tense of narration. This definition implies that a simple transposition of grammatical person and tense will "translate" a narrated into an interior monologue. Such translations can actually be applied as a kind of litmus test to confirm the validity of a reader's apprehension that a narrative sentence belongs to a character's, rather than to a narrator's, mental domain.

But before I discuss this and other critical problems attending the narrated monologue, I will add to the rather farfetched initial illustration others taken from the mainstream of the modern narrative tradition. They will show that, even when fictional characters have less idiosyncratic thinking styles than Papa Hamlet's, their narrated monologues are easy to identify. I provide a minimal context in each case, and italicize the sentences in narrated monologue form.

1. Woolf's Septimus in Regent's Park, after Rezia has removed her wedding ring:

"My hand has grown so thin," she said. "I have put it in my purse," she told him.

He dropped her hand. Their marriage was over, he thought, with agony, with relief. *The rope was cut; he mounted; he was free, as it was decreed that he, Septimus, the lord of men, should be free; alone (since his wife had thrown away her wedding ring; since she had left him), he, Septimus, was alone, called forth in advance of the mass of men to hear the truth, to learn the meaning, which now at last, after all the toils of civilisation—Greeks, Romans, Shakespeare, Darwin, and now himself—was to be given whole to. . . .* "To whom?" He asked aloud. [Woolf's ellipsis]

2. Kafka's K. walking through the night with Barnabas (the messenger from the castle):

At that moment Barnabas stopped. *Where were they? Was this the end of the road? Would Barnabas leave K.? He wouldn't succeed.* K. clutched Barnabas' arm so firmly that he almost hurt himself. *Or had the incredible happened, and were they already in the Castle or at its gates? But they had not done any climbing so far as K. could tell. Or had Barnabas taken him up by an imperceptibly mounting road?* "Where are we?" asked K. in a low voice, more of himself than of Barnabas.

3. Joyce's Stephen Dedalus waiting for confession:

The slide was shot to suddenly. The penitent came out. He was next. He stood up in terror and walked blindly into the box.

At last it had come. He knelt in the silent gloom and raised his eyes to the white crucifix suspended above him. *God could see that he was sorry. He would tell all his sins. His confession would be long, long. Everybody in the chapel would know then what a sinner he had been. Let them know. It was true. But God had promised to forgive him if he was sorry. He was sorry.* He clasped his hands and raised them towards the white form, praying with his darkened eyes, praying with all his trembling body, swaying his head to and fro like a lost creature, praying with whimpering lips.

What the italicized portions of these passages most obviously share is that they cannot be read as standard narration. Narrative language appears in them as a kind of mask, from behind which sounds the voice of a figural mind. Each of its sentences bears the stamp of characteristical limitations and distortions: of Septimus' manic obsessions, K.'s ignorance of present and future circumstance, Stephen's self-serving religiosity. Far more than in ordinary narrative passages, their language teems with questions, exclamations, repetitions, overstatements, colloquialisms. In short, neither the content nor the style of these sentences can be plausibly attributed to their narrators. But both their content and their style become entirely plausible if we understand them as transposed thought-quotations—which is why the "translation" test (as the willing reader can verify) will "work" in each case.

But the point is, of course, that the language a "translation" yields is *not* in the text. Nor are their other indications that someone is thinking. We are told not "Stephen said to himself: 'God can see that I am sorry. I will tell all my sins,'" but simply "God could see that he was sorry. He would tell all his sins." Stephen's personal rapport with the Divinity is treated as *if* he were formulating it in his mind, but the words on the page are not identified as words running through his mind. By leaving the relationship between words and thoughts latent, the narrated monologue casts a peculiarly penumbral light on the figural consciousness, suspending it on the threshold of verbalization in a manner that cannot be achieved by direct quotation. This ambiguity is unquestionably one reason why so many writers prefer the less direct technique.

Another is the seamless junction between narrated monologues and their narrative context. Note how, in the Joyce passage, the text weaves in and out of Stephen's mind without perceptible transitions, fusing outer with inner reality, gestures with thoughts, facts with reflections, as report of posture and gaze—"he knelt . . . and raised his eyes"—gives way to the purely imaginary "God could see . . . God had promised," which in turn gives way to factual report—"He clasped his hands and raised them." By employing the same basic tense for the narrator's reporting language and the character's reflecting language, two normally distinct linguistic currents are made to merge.

The Kafka text alternates more rapidly, but no more perceptibly, between report and reflection: "At that moment Barnabas stopped. *Where were they? . . .* K. clutched Barnabas' arm so firmly that he almost hurt himself. *Or had the incredible happened. . . ?*" By contrast when the very same question that begins the narrated monologue—"*Where were they?*"—is repeated at its end—"Where are we?"—it cuts off the unified current by direct quotation. Such sudden shifts to directly quoted discourse (silent or spoken) underline the potential-actual relationship between narrated monologue and verbal formulation, creating the impression that a mind's vague ruminations have irresistibly led to conceptual expression. We get the same pattern at the end of Septimus' narrated monologue, when an unfinished thought-sentence breaks into a quoted question: "*was to be given whole to . . .* 'To whom?' he asked aloud."

The beginning of the Woolf passage illustrates a different junction between narration and narrated monologue. In another standard pattern, a sentence of psycho-narration—"Their marriage was over, he thought, with agony, with relief"—shapes the transition from the preceding report to the narrated monologue, even as it sets the tone (of agony and relief) that reigns in Septimus' thoughts. As we already noted in the villanelle passage from Joyce's *Portrait* (in Chapter 1), psycho-narration flows readily into a narrated monologue, and the latter clinches the narrator-figure cohesion that the former approximates.

We can now profile the narrated monologue more sharply by examining its linguistic relationship with its closest relatives: first with the two rival techniques for rendering consciousness, second with the narration of fictional reality generally.

The demarcation between the narrated monologue and the two other techniques for rendering consciousness is generally easy to draw. Tense and person separate it from quoted monologue, even when the latter is used in the Joycean manner, without explicit quotation or introduction; the absence of mental verbs (and the resulting grammatical independence) separates it from psycho-narration. The following schema shows how the same thought-phrase would appear in the three techniques:

Quoted Monologue
(He thought:) I am late
(He thought:) I was late
(He thought:) I will be late

Narrated Monologue
He was late
He had been late
He would be late

Psycho-Narration
He knew he was late
He knew he had been late
He knew he would be late

A typical narrated-monologue sentence stands grammatically *between* the two other forms, sharing with quoted monologue the expression in the principle clause, with psycho-narration the tense system and the third-person reference. When the thought is a question, the word-order of direct discourse is maintained in the narrated monologue, increasing its resemblance to quoted monologue and its distinction from psycho-narration:

Quoted Monologue
(He thought:) Am I late?

Narrated Monologue
Was he late?

Psycho-Narration
He wondered if he was late.

Minute as these differences may appear when schematized in this fashion, they reflect in simplest grammatical terms the basic relationship between the three techniques: in its meaning and function, as in its grammar, the narrated monologue holds a mid-position between quoted monologue and psycho-narration, rendering the content of a figural mind more obliquely than the former, more directly than the latter. Imitating the language a character uses when he talks to himself, it casts that language into the grammar a narrator uses in talking about him, thus superimposing two voices that are kept distinct in the other two forms. And this equivocation in turn creates the characteristic indeterminateness of the narrated monologue's relationship to the language of consciousness, suspending it between the immediacy of quotation and the mediacy of narration. Accordingly, its function fluctuates when it is found in the immediate vicinity of the other techniques: when it borders on psycho-narration, it takes on a more monologic quality and creates the impression of rendering thoughts explicitly formulated in the figural mind; when it borders on spoken or silent discourse, it takes on a more narrational quality and creates the impression that the narrator is formulating his character's inarticulate feelings.

The problem of delimiting the narrated monologue from narration generally is far more complex, since purely linguistic criteria no longer provide reliable guidelines. Cloaked in the grammar of narration, a sentence rendering a character's opinion can look every bit like a sentence relating a fictional fact. In purely grammatical terms "He was late" (our sample sentence) could be a narrator's fact, rather than a character's thought. Within a broader context it might become possible to attribute it to a figural mind: for instance, if the next sentence belied the idea that "he was late"; or if the statement were embedded in a recognizable thought sequence. Woolf's "The rope was cut; he mounted; he was free" (in the passage quoted above) could, when taken out of context, be read as a narrator's description of a balloonist taking off for a flight. But in its context—the insane Septimus sitting on the Regent's Park bench, misinterpreting his wife's removal of her wedding ring—we understand these statements as the author means us to understand them, even before the following sentences more clearly signal monologic language. Obviously, an author who wants his reader to recognize a narrated monologue for what it is will have to plant sufficient clues for its recognition. These clues may be contextual, semantic, syntactic, or lexical, or variously combined. A narrated monologue, in other words, reveals itself even as it conceals itself, but not always without making demands on its reader's intelligence. The critic who suggested that the trial against Flaubert for *Madame Bovary* would not have taken place if the prosecutor had recognized that the "immoralities" it contained were Emma's narrated monologues rather than Flaubert's authorial statements may have overstated his case. But there is no doubt that this kind of confusion is responsible for innumerable misreadings—including some in print—of works that employ the technique.

In sum, the narrated monologue is at once a more complex and a more flexible technique for rendering consciousness than the rival techniques. Both its dubious attribution of language to the figural mind, and its fusion of narratorial and figural language charge it with ambiguity, give it a quality of now-you-see-it, now-you-don't that exerts a special fascination. Even dry scholars wax poetical when they describe its effects. Here is an early German theorist's description: "It lights up with vivid hues a realm that the reporting and describing narrator deliberately tones down by keeping it at a distance from himself. And it creates this effect far more readily than a narrative containing occasional monologues, where a more perceptible contrast exists between pure report and quoted thought. Its stirring effect depends on the fact that it is barely discernible to the naked eye: the device is irresistible precisely because it is apprehended almost unconsciously."

Mikhail Bakhtin

Nearly lost to the world because of Soviet totalitarianism in the 1930s, the literary and aesthetic theories of Mikhail Mikhailovich Bakhtin have become ever more influential over the last two decades in America and in Europe. Born in Orel, Russia, in 1909, Bakhtin attended the universities of Odessa and Petersburg. In 1920 he moved to the cultural center of Vitebsk, and in 1924 to Leningrad, where he worked at the Historical Institute. Bakhtin's magisterial *Problems of Dostoevsky's Poetics* appeared in 1929, but its impact was stifled when a Stalinist purge sent its author into exile. During the next six precarious years, Bakhtin wrote the seminal essay *Discourse in the Novel* (from which the following section is excerpted), along with a study of the German *Bildungsroman* that was thought lost when it disappeared from a publishing house during the German invasion. (Fragments of it have been recovered and translated.) On returning from exile in 1936, Bakhtin was offered a position at Saransk Teacher's College (later University), where he taught until his retirement in 1961. In 1963 his suppressed Dostoevsky book was republished and in 1965 appeared his doctoral thesis (written in 1940), entitled *Rabelais and His World.* Bakhtin settled in Moscow in 1969 where he spent his declining years until his death in 1975.

Heteroglossia in the Novel

The compositional forms for appropriating and organizing heteroglossia in the novel, worked out during the long course of the genre's historical development, are extremely heterogeneous in their variety of generic types. Each such compositional form is connected with particular stylistic possibilities, and demands particular forms for the artistic treatment of the heteroglot "languages" introduced into it. We will pause here only on the most basic forms that are typical for the majority of novel types.

The so-called comic novel makes available a form for appropriating and organizing heteroglossia that is both externally very vivid and at the same time historically profound: its classic representatives in England were Fielding, Smollett, Sterne, Dickens, Thackeray and others, and in Germany Hippel and Jean Paul.

In the English comic novel we find a comic-parodic re-processing of almost all the levels of literary language, both conversational and written, that were current at the time. Almost every novel we mentioned above as being a classic representative of this generic type is an encyclopedia of all strata and forms of literary language: depending on the subject being represented, the storyline parodically reproduces first the forms of parliamentary eloquence, then the eloquence of the court, or particular forms of parliamentary protocol, or court protocol, or forms used by reporters in newspaper articles, or the dry business language of the City, or the dealings of speculators, or the pedantic speech of scholars, or the high epic style, or Biblical style, or the style of the hypocritical moral sermon or finally the way one or another concrete and socially determined personality, the subject of the story, happens to speak.

This usually parodic stylization of generic, professional and other strata of language is sometimes interrupted by the direct authorial word (usually as an expression of pathos, of Sentimental or idyllic sensibility), which directly embodies (without any refracting) semantic and axiological intentions of the author. But the primary source of language usage in the comic novel is a highly specific treatment of "common language." This "common language"—usually the average norm of spoken and written language for a given social group—is taken by the author precisely as the *common view,* as the verbal approach to people and things normal for a given sphere of society, as the *going point of view* and the going *value.* To one degree or another, the author distances himself from this common language, he steps back and objectifies it, forcing his own intentions to refract and diffuse themselves through the medium of this common view that has become embodied in language (a view that is always superficial and frequently hypocritical).

The relationship of the author to a language conceived as the common view is not static—it is always found in a state of movement and oscillation that is more or less alive (this sometimes is a rhythmic oscillation): the author exaggerates, now strongly, now weakly, one or another aspect of the "common language," sometimes abruptly exposing its inadequacy to its object and sometimes, on the contrary, becoming one with it, maintaining an almost imperceptible distance, sometimes even directly forcing it to reverberate with his own "truth," which occurs when the author completely merges his own voice with the common view. As a consequence of such a merger, the aspects of common language, which in the given situation had been parodically exaggerated or had been treated as mere things, undergo change. The comic style demands of the author a lively to-and-fro movement in his relation to language, it demands a continual shifting of the distance between author and language, so that first some, then other aspects of language are thrown into relief. If such were not the case, the style would be monotonous or would require a greater individualization of the narrator—would, in any case, require a quite different means for introducing and organizing heteroglossia.

Against this same backdrop of the "common language," of the impersonal, going opinion, one can also isolate in the comic novel those parodic stylizations of generic, professional and other languages we have mentioned, as well as compact masses of direct authorial discourse—pathos-filled, moral-didactic, sentimental-elegiac or idyllic. In the comic novel the direct authorial word is thus realized in direct, unqualified stylizations of poetic genres (idyllic, elegiac, etc.) or stylizations of rhetorical genres (the pathetic, the moral-didactic). Shifts from common language to parodying of generic and other languages and shifts to the direct authorial word may be gradual, or may be on the contrary quite abrupt. Thus does the system of language work in the comic novel.

We will pause for analysis on several examples from Dickens, from his novel *Little Dorrit.*

(1) The conference was held at four or five o'clock in the afternoon, when all the region of Harley Street, Cavendish Square, was resonant of carriage-wheels and double-knocks. It had reached this point when Mr. Merdle came home *from his daily occupation of causing the British name to be more and more respected in all parts of the civilized globe capable of appreciation of wholewide commercial enterprise and gigantic combinations of skill and capital.* For, though nobody knew with the least precision what Mr. Merdle's business was, except that it was to coin money, these were the terms in which everybody defined it on all ceremonious occasions, and which it was the last new polite reading of the parable of the camel and the needle's eye to accept without inquiry. [book 1, ch. 33]

The italicized portion represents a parodic stylization of the language of ceremonial speeches (in parliaments and at banquets). The shift into this style is prepared for by the sentence's construction, which from the very beginning is kept within bounds by a somewhat ceremonious epic tone. Further on—and already in the language of the author (and consequently in a different style)—the parodic meaning of the ceremoniousness of Merdle's labors becomes apparent: such a characterization turns out to be "another's speech," to be taken only in quotation marks ("these were the terms in which everybody defined it on all ceremonious occasions").

Thus the speech of another is introduced into the author's discourse (the story) in *concealed form,* that is, without any of the *formal* markers usually accompanying such speech, whether direct or indirect. But this is not just another's speech in the same "language"—it is another's utterance in a language that is itself "other" to the author as well, in the archaicized language of oratorical genres associated with hypocritical official celebrations.

> (2) In a day or two it was announced to all the town, that Edmund Sparkler, Esquire, son-in-law of the eminent Mr. Merdle of worldwide renown, was made one of the Lords of the Circumlocution Office; and proclamation was issued, to all true believers, that this admirable *appointment was to be hailed as a graceful and gracious mark of homage, rendered by the graceful and gracious Decimus, to that commercial interest which must ever in a great commercial country—and all the rest of it, with blast of trumpet.* So, bolstered by this mark of Government homage, the wonderful Bank and all the other *wonderful* undertakings went on and went up; and gapers came to Harley Street, Cavendish Square, only to look at the house where the golden wonder lived. [book 2, ch. 12]

Here, in the italicized portion, another's speech in another's (official-ceremonial) language is openly introduced as indirect discourse. But it is surrounded by the hidden, diffused speech of another (in the same official-ceremonial language) that clears the way for the introduction of a form more easily perceived as another's speech and that can reverberate more fully as such. The clearing of the way comes with the word "Esquire," characteristic of official speech, added to Sparkler's name; the final confirmation that this is another's speech comes with the epithet "wonderful." This epithet does not of course belong to the author but to that same "general opinion" that had created the commotion around Merdle's inflated enterprises.

> (3) It was a dinner to provoke an appetite, though he had not had one. The rarest dishes, sumptuously cooked and sumptuously served; the choicest fruits, the most exquisite wines; marvels of workmanship in gold and silver, china and glass; innumerable things delicious to the senses of taste, smell, and sight, were insinuated into its composition. *O, what a wonderful man this Merdle, what a great man, what a master man, how blessedly and enviably endowed*—in one word, what a rich man! [book 2, ch. 12]

The beginning is a parodic stylization of high epic style. What follows is an enthusiastic glorification of Merdle, a chorus of his admirers in the form of the concealed speech of another (the italicized portion). The whole point here is to expose the real basis for such glorification, which is to unmask the chorus' hypocrisy: "wonderful," "great," "master," "endowed" can all be replaced by the single word "rich." This act of authorial unmasking, which is openly accomplished within the boundaries of a single simple sentence, merges with the unmasking of another's speech. The ceremonial emphasis on glorification is complicated by a second emphasis that is indignant, ironic, and this is the one that ultimately predominates in the final unmasking words of the sentence.

We have before us a typical double-accented, double-styled *hybrid construction*.

What we are calling a hybrid construction is an utterance that belongs, by its grammatical (syntactic) and compositional markers, to a single speaker, but that actually contains mixed within it two utterances, two speech manners, two styles, two "languages," two semantic and axiological belief systems. We repeat, there is no formal— compositional and syntactic—boundary between these utterances, styles, languages, belief systems; the division of voices and languages takes place within the limits of a single syntactic whole, often within the limits of a simple sentence. It frequently happens that even one and the same word will belong simultaneously to two languages, two belief systems that intersect in a hybrid construction—and, consequently, the word has two contradictory meanings, two accents (examples below). As we shall see, hybrid constructions are of enormous significance in novel style.

(4) But Mr. Tite Barnacle was a buttoned-up man, and *consequently* a weighty one. [book 2, ch. 12]

The above sentence is an example of *pseudo-objective motivation,* one of the forms for concealing another's speech—in this example, the speech of "current opinion." If judged by the formal markers above, the logic motivating the sentence seems to belong to the author, i.e., he is formally at one with it; but in actual fact, the motivation lies within the subjective belief system of his characters, or of general opinion.

Pseudo-objective motivation is generally characteristic of novel style, since it is one of the manifold forms for concealing another's speech in hybrid constructions. Subordinate conjunctions and link words ("thus," "because," "for the reason that," "in spite of" and so forth), as well as words used to maintain a logical sequence ("therefore," "consequently," etc.) lose their direct authorial intention, take on the flavor of someone else's language, become refracted or even completely reified.

Such motivation is especially characteristic of comic style, in which someone else's speech is dominant (the speech of concrete persons, or, more often, a collective voice).

(5) As a vast fire will fill the air to a great distance with its roar, so the sacred flame which the mighty Barnacles had fanned caused the air to resound more and more with the name of Merdle. It was deposited on every lip, and carried into every ear. There never was, there never had been, there never again should be, such a man as Mr. Merdle. Nobody, as aforesaid, knew what he had done; but *everybody knew him to be the greatest that had appeared.* [book 2, ch. 13]

Here we have an epic, "Homeric" introduction (parodic, of course) into whose frame the crowd's glorification of Merdle has been inserted (concealed speech of another in another's language). We then get direct authorial discourse; however, the author gives an objective tone to this "aside" by suggesting that "everybody knew" (the italicized portion). It is as if even the author himself did not doubt the fact.

(6) That illustrious man and great national ornament, Mr. Merdle, continued his shining course. It began to be widely understood that one who had done society the admirable service of *making so much money out of it,* could not be suffered to remain a commoner. A baronetcy was spoken of with confidence; a peerage was frequently mentioned. [book 2, ch. 24]

We have here the same fictive solidarity with the hypocritically ceremonial general opinion of Merdle. All the epithets referring to Merdle in the first sentences derive from general opinion, that is, they are the concealed speech of another. The second sentence—"it began to be widely understood," etc.—is kept within the bounds of an emphatically objective style, representing not subjective opinion but the admission of an objective and completely indisputable fact. The epithet "who had done society the admirable service" is completely at the level of common opinion, repeating its official glorification, but the subordinate clause attached to that glorification ("of making so much money out of it") are the words of the author himself (as if put in parentheses in the quotation). The main sentence then picks up again at the level of common opinion. We have here a typical hybrid construction, where the subordinate clause is in direct authorial speech and the main clause in someone else's speech. The main and subordinate clauses are constructed in different semantic and axiological conceptual systems.

The whole of this portion of the novel's action, which centers around Merdle and the persons associated with him, is depicted in the language (or more accurately, the languages) of hypocritically ceremonial common opinion about Merdle, and at the same time there is a parodic stylization of that everyday language of banal society gossip, or of the ceremonial language of official pronouncements and banquet speeches, or the high epic style or Biblical style. This atmosphere around Merdle, the common opinion about him and his enterprises, infects the positive heroes of the novel as well, in particular the sober Pancks, and forces him to invest his entire estate—his own, and Little Dorrit's—in Merdle's hollow enterprises.

(7) Physician had engaged to break the intelligence in Harley Street. Bar could not at once return to his inveiglements of the most enlightened and remarkable jury he had ever seen in that box, with whom, he could tell his learned friend, no shallow sophistry would go down, and no unhappily abused professional tact and skill prevail (this was the way he meant to begin with them); so he said he would go too, and would loiter to and fro near the house while his friend was inside. [book 2, ch. 25, mistakenly given as ch. 15 in Russian text, tr.]

Here we have a clear example of hybrid construction where within the frame of authorial speech (informative speech)—the beginning of a speech prepared by the lawyer has been inserted, " The Bar could not at once return to his inveiglements . . . of the jury . . . so he said he would go too. . . ." etc.—while this speech is simultaneously a fully developed epithet attached to the subject of the author's speech, that is, "jury." The word "jury" enters into the context of informative authorial speech (in the capacity of a necessary object to the word "inveiglements") as well as into the context of the parodic-stylized speech of the lawyer. The author's word "inveiglement" itself emphasizes the parodic nature of the re-processing of the lawyer's speech, the hypocritical meaning of which consists precisely in the fact that it would be impossible to inveigle such a remarkable jury.

(8) It followed that Mrs. Merdle, as a woman of fashion and good breeding *who had been sacrificed to the wiles of a vulgar barbarian* (for Mr. Merdle was found out from the crown of his head to the sole of his foot, the moment he was found out in his pocket), must be actively championed by her order for her order's sake. [book 2, ch. 33]

This is an analogous hybrid construction, in which the definition provided by the general opinion of society—"a sacrifice to the wiles of a vulgar barbarian"—merges with authorial speech, exposing the hypocrisy and greed of common opinion.

So it is throughout Dickens' whole novel. His entire text is, in fact, everywhere dotted with quotation marks that serve to separate out little islands of scattered direct speech and purely authorial speech, washed by heteroglot waves from all sides. But it would have been impossible actually to insert such marks, since, as we have seen, one and the same word often figures both as the speech of the author and as the speech of another—and at the same time.

Another's speech—whether as storytelling, as mimicking, as the display of a thing in light of a particular point of view, as a speech deployed first in compact masses, then loosely scattered, a speech that is in most cases impersonal ("common opinion," professional and generic languages)—is at none of these points clearly separated from authorial speech: the boundaries are deliberately flexible and ambiguous, often passing through a single syntactic whole, often through a simple sentence, and sometimes even dividing up the main parts of a sentence. This varied *play with the boundaries of speech types,* languages and belief systems is one most fundamental aspects of comic style.

Comic style (of the English sort) is based, therefore, on the stratification of common language and on the possibilities available for isolating from these strata, to one degree or another, one's own intentions, without ever completely merging with them. *It is precisely the diversity of speech, and not the unity of a normative shared language, that is the ground of style.* It is true that such speech diversity does not exceed the boundaries of literary language conceived as a linguistic whole (that is, language defined by abstract linguistic markers), does not pass into an authentic heteroglossia and is based on an abstract notion of language as unitary (that is, it does not require knowledge of various dialects or languages). However a mere concern for language is but the abstract side of the concrete and active (i.e., dialogically engaged) understanding of the living heteroglossia that has been introduced into the novel and artistically organized within it.

In Dickens' predecessors, Fielding, Smollett and Sterne, the men who founded the English comic novel, we find the same parodic stylization of various levels and genres of literary language, but the distance between these levels and genres is greater than it is in Dickens and the exaggeration is stronger (especially in Sterne). The parodic and objectivized incorporation into their work of various types of literary language (especially in Sterne) penetrates the deepest levels of literary and ideological thought itself, resulting in a parody of the logical and expressive structure of any ideological discourse as such (scholarly, moral and rhetorical, poetic) that is almost as radical as the parody we find in Rabelais.

Susan Sniader Lanser

Susan Sniader Lanser was born in 1944 in Buffalo, New York, and grew up in Chicago, where she went to college, majoring in French and English. After having three boys and trying to write the Great American Novel, Lanser went back to the academy and earned a Ph.D. in Comparative Literature from the University of Wisconsin in 1979. Lanser taught English at Georgetown University, then moved on to the University of Maryland, where she is professor of English and Women's Studies and Director of the Comparative Literature Program. Lanser's first book was *The Narrative Act: Point of View in Prose Fiction* (1981). Her second was *Fictions of Authority: Women Writers and Narrative Voice* (1992), from which the following selection is excerpted. As part of the Folger Collective, Lanser is coeditor of *Women Critics 1660-1820: An Anthology* (forthcoming), and she is currently at work once more on her own fiction, as well as on a study of spinsters, sapphists, and female friends in the period between 1660 and 1800.

Toward a Feminist Poetics of Narrative Voice

> *Why this privileged relationship with the voice?*
> —Hélène, "The Laugh of the Medusa"

Few words are as resonant to contemporary feminists as "voice." The term appears in history and philosophy, in sociology, literature, and psychology, spanning disciplinary and theoretical differences. Book titles announce "another voice," a "different voice," or resurrect the "lost voices" of women poets and pioneers; fictional figures ancient and modern, actual women famous and obscure, are honored for speaking up and speaking out.[1] Other silenced communities—peoples of color, peoples struggling against colonial rule, gay men and lesbians—have also written and spoken about the urgency of "coming to voice." Despite compelling interrogations of "voice" as a humanist fiction, for the collectively and personally silenced the term has become a trope of identity and power: as Luce Irigaray suggests, to find a voice (*voix*) is to find a way (*voie*).[2]

In narrative poetics ("narratology"), voice is an equally crucial though more circumscribed term, designating tellers—as distinct from both authors and nonnarrating characters—of narrative. Although many critics acknowledge the bald inaccuracy of "voice" and "teller" to signify something written, these terms persist even among structuralists: according to Gérard Genette, "in the most unobtrusive narrative, someone is speaking to me, is telling me a story, is inviting me to listen to it as he tells it."[3] Narration entails social relationships and thus involves far more than the technical imperatives for getting a story told. The narrative voice and the narrated world are mutually constitutive; if there is no tale without a teller, there is no teller without a tale. This interdependence gives the narrator a liminal position that is at once contingent and privileged: the narrator has no existence "outside" the text yet brings the text into existence; narrative speech acts cannot be said to be mere "imitations," like the acts of characters, because they are the acts that make the "imitations" possible.

Despite their shared recognition of the power of "voice," the two concepts I have been describing—the feminist and the narratological—have entailed separate inquiries of antithetical tendency: the one general, mimetic, and political, the other specific, semiotic, and technical. When feminists talk about voice, we are usually referring to the behavior of actual or fictional persons and groups who assert woman-centered points of view. Thus feminists may speak of a literary character who refuses patriarchal pressures as "finding a voice" whether or not that voice is represented textually. When narrative theorists talk about voice, we are usually concerned with formal structures and not with the causes, ideologies, or social implications of particular narrative practices. With a few exceptions, feminist criticism does not ordinarily consider the technical aspects of narration, and narrative poetics does not ordinarily consider the social

---

[1] A few titles: *In a Different Voice; American Women, American Voices; The Sound of Our Own Voices; The Other Voice: Scottish Women's Writing since 1808; Finding a Voice: Asian Women in Britain; Territories of the Voice: Contemporary Stories by Irish Women Writers; Radical Voices: A Decade of Resistance from "Women's Studies International Forum"; The Indigenous Voice: Visions and Realities. Au.*

[2] Luce Irigaray, *This Sex Which is Not One,* trans. Catherine Porter with Carolyn Burke (Ithaca: Cornell University Press, 1985), 209. As my references to Cixous and Irigaray emphasize, even "poststructuralist" feminists have been unwilling to abandon the word *voice* as a signifier of female power, for women have not *as a body* (in both senses) possessed the logos that deconstruction deconstructs. *Au.*

[3] Gérard Genette, *Narrative Discourse Revisited,* trans. Jane E. Lewin (Ithaca: Cornell University Press, 1988), 101. I consider this distinction not essential but conventional: narratives have narrators because Western literature has continued to construct reading and listening in speakerly terms. The convention may already be disappearing in an age of mechanical reproduction, bureaucratic discourse, and computer-generated texts. For an opposing viewpoint, see Jonathan Culler, "Problems in the Theory of Fiction," *Diacritics* 14 (Spring 1984): 5–11. *Au.*

properties and political implications of narrative voice.[4] Formalist poetics may seem to feminists naively empiricist, masking ideology as objective truth, sacrificing significance for precision, incapable of producing distinctions that are politically meaningful. Feminist criticism may seem to narratologists naively subjectivist, sacrificing precision for ideology, incapable of producing distinctions that are textually meaningful.

These incompatible tendencies, which I have overstated here, can offer fruitful counterpoints. As a narratological term, "voice" attends to the specific forms of textual practice and avoids the essentializing tendencies of its more casual feminist usages. As a political term, "voice" rescues textual study from a formalist isolation that often treats literary events as if they were inconsequential to human history. When these two approaches to "voice" converge in what Mikhail Bakhtin has called a "sociological poetics,"[5] it becomes possible to see narrative technique not simply as a product of ideology but as ideology itself; narrative voice, situated at the juncture of "social position and literary practice,"[6] embodies the social, economic, and literary conditions under which it has been produced.[7] Such a sociological or materialist poetics refuses the idealism to which both narrative poetics and some forms of feminist theory have been prone, an idealism that has led in the first case to a reading of textual properties as universal, inevitable, or random phenomena, and in the second to the assumption of a panhistorical "women's language" or "female form." I maintain that both narrative structures and women's writing are determined not by essential properties or isolated aesthetic imperatives but by complex and changing conventions that are themselves produced in and by the relations of power that implicate writer, reader, and text. In modern Western societies during the centuries of "print culture," with which I am concerned, these constituents of power must include, at the very least, race, gender, class, nationality, education, sexuality and marital status, interacting with and within a given social formation.

So long as it acknowledges its own status as theory rather than claiming to trade in neutral, uninterpreted facts, a historically-situated structuralist poetics may offer a valuable differential framework for examining specific narrative patterns and prac-

---

[4] On the tension between feminism and narrative poetics see Robyn Warhol, *Gendered Interventions: Narrative Discourse in the Victorian Novel* (New Brunswick, N.J.: Rutgers University Press, 1989), 12–20; my essay "Toward a Feminist Narratology," *Style* 20 (1986): 341–63; and my subsequent exchange with Nilli Diengott in *Style* 22 (1988): 40–60. *Au.*

[5] A "sociological poetics" is described in P. N. Medvedev and M. M. Bakhtin, *The Formal Method in Literary Scholarship: A Critical Introduction to Sociological Poetics,* trans. Albert J. Wehrle (Baltimore: Johns Hopkins University Press, 1978), 30. The feminist attention to voice generated by Bakhtinian theory is a welcome new inquiry; see especially Dale M. Bauer, *Feminine Dialogics: A Theory of Failed Community* (Albany: SUNY Press, 1988). On the whole, however, "feminist dialogics" have not focused on the close formal distinctions found, for example, in Bakhtin's "Discourse on the Novel," but have followed Bakhtin's tendency elsewhere to equate "voice" with discourse in the Foucauldian sense. *Au.*

[6] Raymond Williams, *Marxism and Literature* (Oxford: Oxford University Press, 1977), 179. *Au.*

[7] I am using "ideology" throughout to describe the discourses and signifying systems through which a culture constitutes its beliefs about itself, structures the relationships of individuals and groups to one another, to social institutions, and to belief systems, and legitimates and perpetuates its values and practices. This definition does not address the question of whether there is a "real" outside ideology that is not itself ideological. *Au.*

tices. The exploration of narrative structures in women's writings may, in turn, challenge the categories and postulates of narratology, since the canon on which narrative theory is grounded has been relentlessly if not intentionally man-made.[8] As one contribution to such a feminist poetics of narrative, this book explores certain configurations of textual voice in fictions by women of Britain, France, and the United States writing from the mid-eighteenth century to the mid-twentieth—the period that coincides with the hegemony of the novel and its attendant notions of individual(ist) authorship. Recognizing that the "author-function" that grounds Western literary authority is constructed in white, privileged-class male terms,[9] I take as a point of departure the hypothesis that female voice—a term used here simply to designate the narrator's grammatical gender—is a site of ideological tension made visible in textual practices.

In thus linking social identity and narrative form, I am postulating that the authority of a given voice or text is produced from a conjunction of social and rhetorical properties. Discursive authority—by which I mean here the intellectual credibility, ideological validity, and aesthetic value claimed by or conferred upon a work, author, narrator, character, or textual practice—is produced interactively; it must therefore be characterized with respect to specific receiving communities. In Western literary systems for the past two centuries, however, discursive authority has, with varying degrees of intensity, attached itself most readily to white, educated men of hegemonic ideology. One major constituent of narrative authority, therefore, is the extent to which a narrator's status conforms to this dominant social power. At the same time, narrative authority is also constituted through (historically changing) textual strategies that even socially unauthorized writers can appropriate. Since such appropriations may of course backfire, nonhegemonic writers and narrators may need to strike a delicate balance in accommodating and subverting dominant rhetorical practices.

Although I have been speaking about authority as if it were universally desirable, some women writers have of course questioned not only those who hold authority and the mechanisms by which they are authorized, but the value of authority as modern Western cultures have constructed it. I believe, however, that even novelists who challenge this authority are constrained to adopt the authorizing conventions of narrative voice in order, paradoxically, to mount an authoritative critique of the authority that the text therefore also perpetuates. Carrying out such an Archimedean project, which seems to me particularly hazardous for texts seeking canonical status, necessitates standing on the very ground one is attempting to deconstruct. While I will acknowledge ways in which women writers continue to challenge even their own authoritative standing, the emphasis of this book is on the project of self-authorization, which, I argue, is implicit in the very act of authorship. In other words, I assume that

---

[8] Nor is this true only of formalist critics like Genette, Shlomith Rimmon-Kenan, Wolfgang Iser, and (less egregiously) Seymour Chatman. The work of materialists like Fredric Jameson and even Bakhtin, which has been so enthusiastically embraced by critics working with "marginal" discourses, is androcentric in both its textual canon and its assumptions about literature. *Au.*

[9] On the "author-function" see Michel Foucault, "What Is an Author?" in *Language, Counter-Memory, Practice: Selected Essays and Interviews,* ed. Donald F. Bouchard (Ithaca: Cornell University Press, 1977), 113–38. *Au.*

regardless of any woman writer's ambivalence toward authoritative institutions and ideologies, the act of writing a novel and seeking to publish it—like my own act of writing a scholarly book and seeking to publish it—is implicitly a quest for discursive authority: a quest to be heard, respected, and believed, a hope of influence. I assume, that is, that every writer who publishes a novel wants it to be authoritative for her readers, even if authoritatively antiauthoritarian, within the sphere and for the receiving community that the work carves out. In making this assumption I am not denying what Edward Said calls the "molested" or "sham" nature of textual authority in general and of fictional authority in particular, but I am also reading the novel as a cultural enterprise that has historically claimed and received a truth value beyond the fictional.[10]

I have chosen to examine texts that engage questions of authority specifically through their production of narrative voice. In each case, narrative voice is a site of crisis, contradiction, or challenge that is manifested in and sometimes resolved through ideologically charged technical practices. The texts I explore construct narrative voices that seek to write themselves into Literature without leaving Literature the same. These narrators, skeptical of the authoritative aura of the male pen and often critical of male dominance in general, are nonetheless pressed by social and textual convention to reproduce the very structures they would reformulate. Such narrators often call into question the very authority they endorse or, conversely, endorse the authority they seem to be questioning. That is, as they strive to create fictions of *authority,* these narrators expose *fictions* of authority as the Western novel has constructed it—and in exposing the fictions, they may end up re-establishing the authority. Some of these texts work out such dilemmas on their thematic surfaces, constructing fictions *of*—that is, *about*—authority, as well.

When I describe these complexities in some women's writings I am not, however, suggesting any kind of "authentic" female voice or arguing that women necessarily write differently from men. Rather, I believe that disavowed writers of both sexes have engaged in various strategies of adaptation and critique that make their work "dialogical" in ways that Bakhtin's formulation, which posits heteroglossia as a general modern condition, may obscure.[11] It is possible, for example, that women privileged enough to write literature are particularly susceptible to what Margaret Homans describes as "a specific gender-based alienation from language" born of the "simultaneous participation in and exclusion from a hegemonic group."[12] My reading suggests

---

[10] See Edward Said, "Molestation and Authority in Narrative Fiction," in *Aspects of Narrative: Selected Papers from the English Institute,* ed. J. Hillis Miller (New York: Columbia University Press, 1971), 47-68. On the status of fiction see also Peter J. McCormick, *Fictions, Philosophies, and the Problems of Poetics* (Ithaca: Cornell University Press, 1988). *Au.*

[11] Bakhtin's formulation that all novelistic discourse, if not all discourse, is irreducibly double-voiced makes more difficult the differentiating of specific ways in which the words of a disauthorized community are "entangled, shot through with shared thoughts, points of view, alien value judgments and accents," and dwell in "a dialogically agitated and tension-filled environment of alien words" (*The Dialogic Imagination,* trans. Caryl Emerson and Michael Holquist [Austin: University of Texas Press, 1981], 276. *Au.*

[12] Margaret Homans, "'Her Very Own Howl': The Ambiguities of Representation in Recent Women's Fiction," *Signs,* (1983): 205. Homans's suggestion that this ambiguity characterizes all women's discourse seems to me problematic insofar as it presumes that all women are simultaneously inside and outside a hegemony. *Au.*

that different communities of women have had different degrees of access to particular narrative forms. I am especially interested in those female narrators who claim public authority, since within the historical period I am studying it has not been voice in general so much as public voice that women have been denied. As I will suggest further on in this chapter, these concerns lead me less to a new narrative poetics than to a poetics attentive to issues that conventional narratology has devalued or ignored.[13]

. . .

This book begins with the simultaneous "rise" of the novel and emergence of modern gender identity in the mid-eighteenth century, and moves toward what may well be the twilight of both. As I situate narrative practices in relation to literary production and social ideology, I will be asking what forms of voice have been available to women, and to which women, at particular moments. My intention is to explore through specifically formal evidence the intersection of social identity and textual form, reading certain aspects of narrative voice as a critical locus of ideology.

I have organized the book to focus on changing problems and patterns in the articulation of three narrative modes which I call, respectively, authorial, personal, and communal voice. Each mode represents not simply a set of technical distinctions but a particular kind of narrative consciousness and hence a particular nexus of powers, dangers, prohibitions, and possibilities. Across all three modes, however, I will be concerned with two aspects of narration that I consider of greater significance in the construction of textual authority than narrative poetics has traditionally allowed. The first is the distinction between private voice (narration directed toward a narratee who is a fictional character) and public voice (narration directed toward a narratee "outside" the fiction who is analogous to the historical reader). The second is the distinction between narrative situations that do and those that do not permit narrative self-reference, by which I mean explicit attention to the act of narration itself. It is my hypothesis that gendered conventions of public voice and of narrative self-reference serve important roles in regulating women's access to discursive authority.

I use the term *authorial voice* to identify narrative situations that are heterodiegetic, public, and potentially self-referential. (Gérard Genette, observing that every narrator is potentially an enunciating "I," suggests the more precise term *heterodiegetic* for what is traditionally called "third-person" narration in which the narrator is not a participant in the fictional world and exists on a separate ontological plane from the characters.)[14] The mode I am calling authorial is also "extradiegetic" and public, directed to a narratee who is analogous to a reading audience.[15] I have chosen the term "authorial" not to imply an ontological equivalence between narra-

---

[13] In the next section, here omitted, Lanser analyzes a text from the 1832 annual *Atkinson's Casket* titled "Female Ingenuity," a letter from a bride that on the surface seems to express complete happiness; when one reads every other line, however, the bride's story is very different. . . . *Ed.*

[14] Gérard Genette, *Narrative Discourse: An Essay in Method,* trans. Jane E. Lewin (Ithaca: Cornell University Press, 1980), 244–45. *Au.*

[15] On the concept of diegetic levels, see ibid., 227–31. On the distinction between private and public voice, which is not identical to Genette's distinction between primary and inserted narrative, see my book *The Narrative Act: Point of View in Prose Fiction* (Princeton: Princeton University Press, 1981), 133–48, and "Toward a Feminist Narratology," 350–55. *Au.*

tor and author but to suggest that such a voice (re)produces the structural and functional situation of authorship. In other words, where a distinction between the (implied) author and a public, heterodiegetic narrator is not textually marked, readers are invited to equate the narrator with the author and the narratee with themselves (or their historical equivalents). This conventional equation gives authorial voice a privileged status among narrative forms; as Bakhtin states, while the discourse of a character or a stylized narrator is always a contingent "object of authorial understanding," authorial discourse is "directed toward its own straightforward referential meaning."[16] Moreover, since authorial narrators exist outside narrative time (indeed, "outside" fiction) and are not "humanized" by events, they conventionally carry an authority superior to that conferred on characters, even on narrating characters. In using the term "authorial" I mean as well to evoke Franz Stanzel's distinction in *Narrative Situations in the Novel* between "authorial" and "figural" modes: while authorial narrative permits what I am calling narrative self-reference, in the "figural" mode all narration is focalized through the perspectives of characters, and thus no reference to the narrator or the narrative situation is feasible.

I want to suggest as a major element of authorial status a distinction between narrators who engage exclusively in acts of representation—that is, who simply predicate the words and actions of fictional characters—and those who undertake "extrarepresentational" acts: reflections, judgments, generalizations about the world "beyond" the fiction, direct addresses to the narratee, comments on the narrative process, allusions to other writers and texts.[17] I will be using the term *overt authoriality* or simply *authoriality,* to refer to practices by which heterodiegetic, public, self-referential narrators perform these "extrarepresentational" functions not strictly required for telling a tale. I am speculating that acts of representation make a more limited claim to discursive authority than extrarepresentational acts, which expand the sphere of fictional authority to "nonfictional" referents and allow the writer to engage, from "within" the fiction, in a culture's literary, social, and intellectual debates. On the other hand, as Shlomith Rimmon-Kenan has observed, when a narrator "becomes more overt, his chances of being fully reliable are diminished, since his interpretations, judgements, generalizations are not always compatible with the norms of the implied author."[18]

Extrarepresentational acts are especially critical to a polyglossic genre like the novel because they enable the narrator to construct the "maxims" that Genette describes as the foundation of verisimilitude.[19] In other words, the reception of a novel rests on an implicit set of principles by which textual events (for example, characters' behaviors) are rendered plausible. To the degree that a text's values deviate from cul-

---

[16] Mikhail Bakhtin, *Problems of Dostoevsky's Poetics,* ed. and trans. Caryl Emerson (Minneapolis: University of Minnesota Press, 1984), 187. *Au.*

[17] Each of these "extrarepresentational" acts may of course be embedded in sentences of representation; the two activities are sometimes simultaneous. *Au.*

[18] Shlomith Rimmon-Kenan, *Narrative Fiction: Contemporary Poetics* (London: Methuen, 1983), 103. *Au.*

[19] Gérard Genette, *Figures II* (Paris: Seuil, 1968). *Au.*

tural givens (as they will to some degree in all but the most formulaic of fictions), they must be established (or inferred) for each narrative instance so that readers can construct the story as "plausible" and embed it in a "world view."[20] Ideologically oppositional writers might wish, therefore, to "maxim-ize" their narratives in order either to posit alternative textual ideologies or to establish the writer, through her authorial narrator-equivalent, as a significant participant in contemporary debates—all the more during those periods when the novel was one of the few accepted means for women to intervene in public life.

It should not be difficult to understand why, with differences in kind and intensity according to time, place, and circumstance, women writers' adoption of overt authoriality has usually meant transgressing gendered rhetorical codes. In cultures such as the ones I am examining, where women's access to public discourse has been curtailed, it has been one thing for women simply to tell stories and another for their narrators to set themselves forth as authorities. Indeed, authorial voice has been so conventionally masculine that female authorship does not necessarily establish female voice: a startling number of critics have referred in the generic masculine to the narrators of such novels as *La Princesse de Clèves* and *Pride and Prejudice*.[21] Thus, on the one hand, since a heterodiegetic narrator need not be identified by sex, the authorial mode has allowed women access to "male" authority by separating the narrating "I" from the female body; it is of course in the exploitation of this possibility that women writers have used male narrators and pseudonyms (acts that may have profited individual writers or texts, but that have surely also reinforced the androcentrism of narrative authority). On the other hand, when an authorial voice has represented itself as female, it has risked being (dis)qualified. It is possible that women's writing has carried fuller public authority when its voice has not been marked as female.

The narrators I discuss in Part I of this book have sought not simply to tell stories, but through overtly authorial practices to make themselves (and, I presume, their authors) significant literary presences. After examining an eighteenth-century text that proclaims the difficulty of achieving authoriality, Part I focuses on four canonical writers (Jane Austen, George Eliot, Virginia Woolf, and Toni Morrison) in order to explore the means by which each has constructed authorial voice within and against the narrative and social conventions of her time and place. In the work of all four writers I see a reaching for narrative hegemony, for what Wayne Booth has called "direct and authoritative rhetoric,"[22] that is obscured both by the writers' own disclaimers and by

---

[20] On the importance of "maxim" see Nancy Miller, "Emphasis Added: Plots and Plausibilities in Women's Fiction," *PMLA* 96 (1981): 36–48; reprinted in *The New Feminist Criticism*, ed. Elaine Showalter (New York: Pantheon, 1985), 339–60. *Au.*

[21] For example, in *The Dual Voice: Free Indirect Speech and Its Functioning in the Nineteenth-Century European Novel* (Manchester: Manchester University Press, 1977), Roy Pascal insists that Jane Austen's narrator be called by the "generic" masculine; Laurence Gregorio makes a similar insistence "for the sake of clarity" about *La Princesse de Clèves* in *Order in the Court: History and Society in "I a Princesse de Clèves"* (Stanford French and Italian Studies 47, 1986), 1. For the argument that the unmarked narrative voice is neither gendered nor necessarily human, see Culler, "Problems in the Theory of Fiction." *Au.*

[22] Wayne Booth, *The Rhetoric of Fiction* (Chicago: University of Chicago Press, 1961), 6. *Au.*

a tendency in contemporary feminist criticism to valorize "refusals" of authority in ways that seem to me ahistorical.

I use the term *personal voice* to refer to narrators who are self-consciously telling their own histories. I do not intend this term to designate all "homodiegetic" or "first-person" narratives—that is, all those in which the voice that speaks is a participant in the fictional world—but only those Genette calls "autodiegetic," in which the "I" who tells the story is also the story's protagonist (or an older version of the protagonist).[23] In my exploration of personal voice I will exclude forms such as the interior mono-logue, which are not self-consciously narrative and which, like figural narration, can-not construct a situation of narrative self-reference.

The authority of personal voice is contingent in ways that the authority of au-thorial voice is not: while the autodiegetic "I" remains a structurally "superior" voice mediating the voices of other characters, it does not carry the superhuman privileges that attach to authorial voice, and its status is dependent on a reader's response not only to the narrator's acts but to the character's actions, just as the authority of the representation is dependent in turn on the successful construction of a credible voice. These differences make personal voice in some ways less formidable for women than authorial voice, since an authorial narrator claims broad powers of knowledge and judgment, while a personal narrator claims only the validity of one person's right to interpret her experience.

At the same time, personal narration offers no gender-neutral mask or distancing "third person," no refuge in a generic voice that may pass as masculine.[24] A female per-sonal narrator risks the reader's resistance if the act of telling, the story she tells, or the self she constructs through telling it transgresses the limits of the acceptably fem-inine. If women are encouraged to write only of themselves because they are not sup-posed to claim knowledge of men or "the world," when women *have* written only of themselves they have been labeled immodest and narcissistic, and criticized for dis-playing either their virtues or their faults. Moreover, because male writers have cre-ated female voices, the arena of personal narration may also involve a struggle over which representations of female voice are to be authorized.

Although authorial narration, with its omniscient privilege, is usually understood to be fictional, fiction in the personal voice is usually formally indistinguishable from autobiography. Given the precarious position of women in patriarchal societies, woman novelists may have avoided personal voice when they feared their work would be taken for autobiography. The use of personal voice also risks reinforcing the con-venient ideology of women's writing as "self-expression," the product of "intuition" rather than of art;[25] perhaps this is why Maxine Hong Kingston stated recently that

---

[23] See Genette, *Narrative Discourse*, 227–47. *Au.*

[24] Obviously, a woman writer may choose an explicitly male "I"-narrator, as dozens of women writers from Hannah More to the Brontës to Willa Cather and Marguerite Yourcenar have done. When I speak of the teller here, I am speaking of the female *narrator,* not the female writer. *Au.*

[25] See, for example, Jean Larnac's argument that women's literary power resides in their ability to "feel vividly and immediately to release from themselves feelings they have just experienced, without wait-ing for the fruitful germinations that come from slow meditation," in *Histoire de la littérature féminine en France* (Paris: Kra, 1929), 111. *Au.*

she did not believe she would be a "real" novelist until she had written a book in the authorial voice.[26] In view of these constraints, my discussion of personal voice is especially concerned with variations in the accessibility of public and private forms of personal voice to particular communities of women at particular moments in history. Part II attempts to interpret patterns of personal voice respectively in European women's writings from the late eighteenth to the mid-nineteenth century and in African-American women's writings from the nineteenth century to the contemporary period.

Conventional narrative poetics has often viewed authorial and personal voices as formal antitheses, the one constituting the "diegetic" voice of a fictional author, the other constituting the "mimetic" voice of a character. Indeed, the two modes carry different forms of rhetorical authority: paradoxically, authorial narrative is understood as fictive and yet its voice is accorded a superior reliability, while personal narrative may pass for autobiography but the authority of its voice is always qualified. But the opposition is far from definite: the eye-witness narrator used, for example, in Aphra Behn's *Oronooko* (1688) and George Eliot's *Scenes of Clerical Life* transgresses the polarities of "third-person" and "first-person" narration that are usually assumed to be formally unbridgeable.

The tendency to oppose these modes also conceals similarities between them. Both forms bear the potential for public, self-referential narration and thus for enacting a relationship between "writer" and audience and indeed an entire "story" that is the story of the narration itself. Moreover, the narratological tendency to oppose authorial and personal voices conceals the degree to which both forms are invested in singularity—in the presupposition that narration is individual. This narrative individualism that European cultures take for granted explains why authorial and personal voices have been so commonly practiced and so thoroughly analyzed, while so little attention has been given to intermediate forms such as that of Christa Wolf's *Nachdenken über Christa T.* (1967), in which the narrator is reconstructing the life of another woman but is also in some sense a protagonist herself, not simply an eyewitness or biographer.

This individualization of narrative also explains why my third mode, *communal voice,* is likewise a category of underdeveloped possibilities that has not even been named in contemporary narratology. By communal voice I mean a spectrum of practices that articulate either a collective voice or a collective of voices that share narrative authority. Because the dominant culture has not employed communal voice to any perceptible degree, and because distinctions about voice have been based primarily on the features of this dominant literature, there has been no narratological terminology for communal voice or for its various technical possibilities.

By communal narration I do not mean simply the use of an authorial voice that resorts to an inclusive "we" (as George Eliot's narrators sometimes do), nor the multiple narration Faulkner adopts in a novel like *As I Lay Dying,* nor the presentation of

---

[26] Maxine Hong Kingston, in a reading given at Georgetown University, April 1989. Kingston was referring to *Tripmaster Monkey—His Fake Book* (New York: Knopf, 1989), whose authorial voice, she says, is absolutely—and to her, unmistakably—female even though it is never marked as such. *Au.*

divergent and antithetical perspectives on the same events that characterizes episto-lary novels such as *Lady Susan* and *Les Liaisons dangereuses*. I refer, rather, to a prac-tice in which narrative authority is invested in a definable community and textually inscribed either through multiple, mutually authorizing voices or through the voice of a single individual who is manifestly authorized by a community. In Part III, I will distinguish three such possibilities that result from various confluences of social ide-ology with changing conventions of narrative technique: a *singular* form in which one narrator speaks for a collective, a *simultaneous* form in which a plural "we" nar-rates, and a *sequential* form in which individual members of a group narrate in turn. Unlike authorial and personal voices, the communal mode seems to be primarily a phenomenon of marginal or suppressed communities; I have not observed it in fiction by white, ruling-class men perhaps because such an "I" is already in some sense speak-ing with the authority of a hegemonic "we." My survey of communal voice in Part III moves from an exploration of constraints on communal voice in the eighteenth cen-tury, through "singular" manifestations in the nineteenth, to a range of formal possi-bilities available to modern and postmodern narratives.

Because the structures of both narration and plot in the Western novel are indi-vidualist and androcentric, the articulation of a communal female voice is not simply a question of discourse but almost always one of story as well. Although it is possible to represent female community without communal voice, it is difficult to construct communal voice without constructing female community. Communal voice thus shifts the text away from individual protagonists and personal plots, calling into question the heterosocial contract that has defined woman's place in Western fiction. My exami-nation of more and less realized communal forms in the singular, sequential, and si-multaneous modes suggests the political possibilities of constituting a collective fe-male voice through narrative. At the same time, communal voice might be the most insidious fiction of authority, for in Western cultures it is nearly always the creation of a single author appropriating the power of a plurality.

The three modes of narrative voice on which this book concentrates seem to me to represent three distinct kinds of authority that women have needed to constitute in order to make their place in Western literary history: respectively, the authority, to establish alternative "worlds" and the "maxims" by which they will operate, to con-struct and publicly represent female subjectivity and redefine the "feminine," and to constitute as a discursive subject a female body politic. Each form creates its own fic-tions of authority, making certain meanings and not others articulable. Although I be-gin with authorial voice because it is the oldest and most basic mode and end with communal voice because it is the newest and least conventional, I refrain from any ab-solute evaluation of the three modes. I will speculate briefly in my final chapter about the value of each of these narrative "tools" for dismantling, to use Audre Lorde's now-famous metaphor, the "master's house."[27]

A book with a title as general as this one owes its readers some explanation of what it is and is not meant to be. In no way does it embrace the range of techniques

---

[27] Audre Lorde, "The Master's Tools Will Never Dismantle the Master's House," in *Sister/Outsider* (Freedom, CA.: Crossing Press, 1984), 110–13. *Au.*

and questions that are subsumed in the concept of "narrative voice." By choosing certain general categories and distinctions, I hope to demonstrate that even the broadest, most obvious elements of narration are ideologically charged and socially variable, sensitive to gender differences in ways that have not been recognized. Because I have written this book for a general scholarly readership rather than for specialists in narratology, I have tried to keep technical terms to a minimum. Although I have introduced a few new concepts here, my earlier book, *The Narrative Act: Point of View in Prose Fiction,* describes in more detail most of the aspects of narrative voice on which this work relies.

In several ways this is a preliminary and speculative project. Because I focus on moments of crisis or breakthrough at which certain narrative practices become (im)possible, many important writers and literary events do not figure here. Nor do I mean to imply a linear growth in women's narrative authority: the history of voice in women's writings reflects what Mary Poovey affirms are "uneven developments."[28] At the same time, narrative authority—like many other possibilities for women—is currently wider and deeper both for individuals and for previously silenced groups of women than it was two centuries ago, despite historical lapses and contemporary absences that remind us not to see any gains as inevitable, universal, or permanent.

The broad scope of the book makes my work preliminary in still other ways. Although the narrative poetics I envision is fully embedded in material-historical analysis, carrying out such a project would require engaging the conditions of cultural production for each individual text to an impossible degree given the broad historical and geographic arena that this book encompasses. In attempting to illuminate large patterns of voice in Western fiction, I have had to rely more on general developments in literary history than on particular developments in social and material life.

Because literary form has a far more uncertain relation to social history than does representational content, even a fully materialist poetics would be hard-pressed to establish definitive correspondences between social ideology and narrative form. I have nonetheless considered it fruitful to venture speculations about causal relationships that others may be able to establish or refute. Having learned from my biochemist friend Ellen Henderson that "how?" is a scientific question but "why?" is not, I have sought through this project to show how particular writers and texts may have come to use particular narrative strategies.

Finally, this project remains rooted in Western theory and history. I am concerned that my "inclusion" of African-American novels places these texts in a eurocentric framework and thereby imposes the risk of perpetuating the distortions for which I fault literary history. My study does not explore the emerging novelistic traditions by women of Asia, Africa, and Latin America, and I mention only briefly some of the rich new fiction by Asian-American, Latina, Chicana, Arab, and Native American women in the United States. There remains a great deal to learn by studying narrative voice as it has been developing in countries and communities where women are just beginning to write, or where the novel is a relatively new genre produced through complex in-

---

[28] Mary Poovey, *Uneven Developments: The Ideological Work of Gender in Mid-Victorian England* (Chicago: University of Chicago Press, 1988). *Au.*

teractions between native and colonial forms. For this reason, especially, feminist criticism will need many more studies of women's fictions, studies focusing on many different cultures and from many different vantage points, before anyone can speak with authority about women writers and narrative voice.

Ann Banfield

Ann Banfield was born in South Amboy, New Jersey, in 1941 and educated at Avila College and Catholic University before working in the late 1960s at the linguistics department of the Massachusetts Institute of Technology where the renowned Noam Chomsky had revolutionized the theory of syntax. She spent a year in the wake of another revolution, that of 1968, teaching in the American Studies program at the left-of-Mao Vincennes campus of the University of Paris. Banfield took her Ph.D. in English literature at the University of Wisconsin in 1973 with a dissertation on syntax in *Paradise Lost.* Since 1975, she has taught in the department of English at the University of California at Berkeley. Banfield has published numerous articles on Jane Austen, but her main work has been in stylistics, the linguistic analysis of literature, particularly the grammar of fictional discourse. Banfield studies the implications of the way the European languages developed new structures during the eighteenth century, enabling novelists to represent a character's speech and thought within a prose narrative. This intersection between literary history and stylistic analysis appears in sharpest focus in her book *Unspeakable Sentences: Representation and Narration in the Language of Fiction* (1982), from which the following selection is taken. In addition, Banfield has recently translated Jean-Claude Milner's *L'Amour de la langue* (*For the Love of Language,* 1990) and is currently at work on a book about Virginia Woolf and the British philosophers Bertrand Russell and G. E. Moore.

Written Composition and the Emergence of Narrative Style

Writing is thus the extralinguistic factor which allows certain potentials of language, of universal grammar, to be realized in linguistic performance; and the fact that writing develops later than language itself explains why the forms of narrative style arising from these possibilities of language did not always exist. What then is it in the nature of writing which lends itself to the development of the language of narrative fiction?

The term *writing* itself can mean several different things, and we must determine which is relevant to the theory of narrative style. Writing, it is usually assumed, is in essence a method for transcribing speech. We can take this as an historical fact, i.e. that speech preceded writing. But it is not at all obvious what is being transcribed by the written characters. For speech is not language but linguistic performance. Yet in actual linguistic performance there is much that escapes transcription in normal systems of writing, as more modern methods of recording speech, such as the tape recorder, have revealed. And there is much which underlies speech that is only made explicit in writing—for instance, the units called 'words,' which are indicated by a graphic spacing which has no necessary counterpart in the 'speech chain,' as Saussure long ago pointed out. Even though writing can be used simply to record speech, as is done under dictation, this is not all that is meant by writing; this is only 'taking down' or 'writing down.' And even when writing only transcribes speech, it already leaves out much that is actual speech and distils it to something more abstract.

In fact, the normal, current uses of 'writing' do not include this notion of the transcription of an originally oral performance. Rather, writing is seen as itself a kind of linguistic performance. If, then, both writing and speech are independent realizations of language, what is their relation? If language relates sound to meaning, what is the role of sound in writing? In other words, what do the alphabetic symbols stand for?

Some writing systems, of course, are not at all phonetic. Their symbols represent the morphemes or formatives of the language directly.[1] But the phonetic alphabets are commonly thought to represent the units of sound in a language—or if they do not, to fall short of their intended purpose. For, if phonetic transcription might have been their origin, as is well known, the phonetic alphabets used in writing do not result in the kind of exact phonetic transcriptions satisfactory to linguists. To be more precise, the fixed spelling conventions existing in literate cultures only approximate, only partially specify, actual pronunciation.

For, although the alphabets used in western orthography are phonetic, spelling—the conventions for combining the alphabetic symbols into representations of morphemes—is not. At one stage in the history of western orthography, spelling was free and phonetic, i.e. it gave direct representations of pronunciation. This is why, for early written texts, where no speakers of the language or dialects they are written in remain, it is possible to reconstruct their pronunciation. But modern orthography is fixed, and, as we shall see, in this property of spelling, the trace in the text of the writer's own pronunciation normally vanishes.

Modern orthography, as Chomsky and Halle maintain, cannot be considered a directive for pronunciation. From this observation about actual spelling conventions, many—G. B. Shaw among them—have concluded that it *should* do this and therefore that it misrepresents. This is the assumption underlying the various proposals for spelling reform. But spelling misrepresents only if it is assumed that it must represent the phonetic. It is this assumption which has been challenged by generative phonology. Spelling, it insists, is neither obsolete nor misleading, because it represents some other level than the phonetic. At one stage in the development of phonological theory, the idea that, in English at least, this level was eventually that of the 'underlying forms' and that spelling was 'phonological' and not phonetic seemed a plausible hy-

---

[1] For example in Chinese. *Ed.*

pothesis. If this can perhaps no longer be maintained, what is of significance for narrative theory is that orthography represents some level more abstract than pronunciation, one which, rather, must be mapped into a representation of pronunciation. The native speaker reading a written text identifies morphemes or lexical formatives from spelling but already possesses phonological rules in his internalized grammar which enable him to deduce at least one acceptable pronunciation for each morpheme or sequence of morphemes. For the same spelling conventions may be used for any number of widely differing pronunciations—in the case of English, for example, for all the dialects of British and American English.

In other words, a particular combination of written symbols has more than one possible phonetic realization in the language in question. To take a simple illustration, in American English the lexical formative written *-ing* may be pronounced either [*iŋ*]or [*n*], depending on the dialect. In no dialect is [*ing*] the pronunciation. (Interestingly, in the conventional linguistic terminology, the morpheme is given the name of its spelling: 'ing.') When this morpheme is written in conventional spelling, as opposed to when it is spoken, these differences in pronunciation remain unspecified. One could maintain that since a single graphic realization of the morpheme exists, but not a single phonetic one, it is appropriate that its name is its spelling.

Another example is furnished by words like *butter, city, futile, later, latter* and *motto* containing a *t* following a stressed vowel; this *t* is 'voiced' or 'flapped' in American but not in some varieties of British English. In the case of *-ing,* there is a convention for spelling the pronunciation [*ŋ*] *-in',* although this is not a standard dictionary spelling. But for flapped *t* in *butter,* there is no spelling distinct from that with non-flapped *t,* other than the technical notation of linguists.

A phonetic realization is possible for the literate native speaker, given the knowledge of both the language and its orthographical conventions. But it is not at all necessary. This is borne out by the fact that the deaf may read without knowing how to read aloud. Writing makes possible the short-circuiting of the phonetic realization of language. In *The American Heritage Dictionary of the English Language,* Wayne O'Neil suggests one consequence of this short-circuiting:

> Moreover, a spelling system based on phonological, not phonetic, representations removes one of the steps that would otherwise be involved in reading. In receiving speech, or in reading a phonetically based orthography, one has to move from the pronunciation to the abstract phonological representation. But in reading an orthography based on phonological representations, the reader finds, without any intervening steps, the abstract representation. Reading can thus proceed at a rate unlimited by the rate at which speech can be received. (p. xxxvii)

This is the difference we remark between a reading which silently 'mouthes the words' and one which bypasses phonetic realization. O'Neil's point holds, regardless of whether or not conventional orthography can be correctly said to represent the phonological level. Whatever level it represents, it is not the phonetic.

Ultimately, it seems we must allow two possible material realizations of the sequences of lexical formatives which constitute the sentences of linguistic performance, one as sound, represented by phonetic symbols and one as writing, by orthographical symbols. These two possible realizations furnish additional corroboration of the existence of another, more abstract level or levels. But what is the nature of this abstract linguistic level represented by writing, and what contribution does it make toward shaping the form we call 'narrative fiction'?

One consequence of the fact that conventional orthography does not represent pronunciation is that, when it is necessary to do so, some other system must be resorted to. Conventionally, these special markers of pronunciation are enclosed within quotation marks. In literary contexts, these markers never give a complete phonetic representation; instead, only a kind of shorthand, certain minor alterations of spelling, some of which themselves become conventional, are necessary. They rely on the reader's ability to translate them into a particular dialect or pronunciation; but, significantly, he need not know how to imitate this speech correctly or even to have heard it. A dialect or a slip of the tongue is represented in fiction by a minimal number of indicative features in the same way that a character is represented in a way that may leave totally inexplicit or incomplete aspects of his or her appearance or behavior. All that is necessary is that the reader be able to recognize when something is a departure from a standard pronunciation, when this is relevant to point out. Some examples are given in (9).

(9) MACMORRIS: It is no time to discourse, so Chrish save me: the day is hot, and the weather, and the wars, and the king, and the dukes: it is no time to discourse. The town is beseeched, and the trumpet calls us to the breach; and we talk, and be Chrish, do nothing: 'tis shame for us all; so God sa' me, 'tis shame to stand still; it is shame, by my hand; and there is throats to be cut, and works to be done; and there ish nothing done, so Chrish sa' me, la!

JAMY: By the mess, ere theise eyes of mine take themselves to slumber, aile do gud service, or aile lig i' the grund for it; ay, or go to death; an aile pay it as valorously as I may, that I sal suerly do, that is the breff and the long.

(Shakespeare, *Henry V,* III, ii, 116–30)

FLUELLEN: Ay, he was porn at Monmouth, Captain Gower. What call you the town's name where Alexander the Pig was born?

GOWER: Alexander the Great.

FLUELLEN: Why, I pray you, is not pig great?

(*Ibid.,* IV, vii, 12–16)

Mr Graves pronounced his *th* charmingly. Turd and fart, he said, for third and fourth. Watt liked these venerable Saxon words.

(Beckett, *Watt*)

'I say, Jim,' said a young genius of fourteen stretching himself upon the turf, 'I pity them 'ere jarvies a sitting on their boxes all the night and waiting for the nobs what is dancing. They'as no repose.'

(Disraeli, *Sybil*)

'It was the regester—the parish regester,' said Tommy, with his knowing wag of the head, 'that shows as you was born, I allays felt it inside me as I was somebody, and I could see other chaps thought it on me too; and so one day at Littleshaw, where I kep ferrets and a little bit of a public, there comes a fine man looking after me, and walking me up and down wi' questions.'

(Eliot, *Felix Holt the Radical*)

Et dès la veille Françoise avait envoyé cuire dans le four du boulanger, protégé de mie de pain, comme du marbre rose, ce qu'elle appelait du jambon de Nev'York. . . . Aussi, depuis, le mot d'York se faisait précéder dans ses oreilles ou devant ses yeux, si elle lisait une annonce, de: New qu'elle prononçait Nev'.

(Proust, *A l'Ombre des jeunes filles en fleurs*)

[And overnight Françoise had sent to be cooked in the baker's oven, shielded with breadcrumbs, like a block of pink marble packed in sawdust, what she called a Nev'-York ham'. . . . And so, ever since, the word York was preceded in her ears, or before her eyes when she read it in an advertisement, by the affix 'New' which she pronounced 'Nev.']

In narrative fiction, these signs of actual pronunciation are only properly introduced in direct speech or the extended direct quotation which is *skaz*. Otherwise, the language of narrative has no accent; it is written but never spoken. As we noted in Chapter 4, section 3, even in a first person narration, the narrator's telling—a David Copperfield's or a Marcel's—is never a voice with the tones or accents of real speech. Or if it is thought of metaphorically as a voice, it is the disembodied, impersonal voice that, in 'Heart of Darkness,' Marlow's becomes to his listeners separated from him in the darkness: 'For a long time already he, sitting apart, had been no more to us than a voice. There was not a word from anybody. . . . I listened on the watch for the sentence, for the word, that would give me the clue to the faint uneasiness inspired by this narrative that seemed to shape itself without human lips . . .' For, if this narrative has the framework of *skaz,* it becomes in its style a first person narration, and this scene records the moment when the narrator's listeners recede to the distance of readers.

It is this abstractness of the language of written narrative which transforms all the sentences of narration, even those of direct speech. I have referred to direct quotation as an 'imitation' of speech, but that term itself can be qualified. Actually, direct speech is no less a representation of speech than represented speech; it can be said to 'imitate' speech only because it can represent the communicative function in addition to the expressive function. It is the representation of communication which allows but does not require the phonetic to enter writing. Direct speech is not an exact transcription of speech; the speaker's 'exact words' are, in fact, an idealization, although one which must present the features of communication and may include gross indications of pronunciation. The quoted speaker's syntax and lexical choices are given, but, his performance errors may be filtered out, although the conventions of direct speech allow them to be quoted. We have already remarked how the tape recorder has revealed the less than ideal shape of actual oral performance, with all its slips and stops and truncated syntax. Just as Muybridge's photographs of racing horses revealed the mistakes of the eye recorded in earlier paintings, so transcriptions of recorded press conferences often scarcely show a grammatically well-formed sentence. Nonetheless, such sentences are not necessarily perceived as ungrammatical and newspaper quoting of such recorded speech differs from these transcriptions in always presenting complete grammatical units.

Fictionalized conversations in narrative can, then, be fictionalized imitations of idealized speech. 'I say "imitate" and not "copy",' Simone de Beauvoir explains of the novelist's method of creating dialogue, 'for it is not a question of reproducing in a novel this stuttering which a real conversation is'. The novelist chooses direct over represented speech when either the communicative function is to be reproduced or pronunciation indicated. But in either case, what is represented differs from what represents, even when language represents a linguistic reality. And there exists some abstract notion of this linguistic reality that can be independent of the phonetic (and, perhaps, to some extent, even of certain aspects of syntax), so much so that one language can be directly quoted in another. The possibilities for quoting a 'foreign' language range from the completely English sentences from Lawrence and Forster in (10a), qualified by 'in Italian' or 'in French,' to Hemingway's somewhat ridiculous rendering of Spanish by a pidgin English in (10b).

(10) a. 'Look,' said the Contessa, in Italian. 'He is not a man, he is a chameleon, a creature of change.'

> (Lawrence, *Women in Love*)

Then he said in French to his sister, 'Has there been the slightest sign of Frederick?'

> (Forster, *The Longest Journey*)

b. 'Joke. Comes from La Granja. Heard last night comes English dynamiter. Good. Very happy. Get whisky. For you. You like?' . . . .
'Am contented,' Sordo grinned.

> (Hemingway, *For Whom the Bell Tolls*)

'Que' va, it's not true. And I obscenity in the milk of all of you.'

> (*Ibid.*)

'Where the obscenity have you been?'

> (*Ibid.*)

'Put thy hand on my head,' she said, 'and then let me see if I can kiss thee.'

'Was it well?' she asked.

(*Ibid.*)

Underlying this notion of what direct speech represents is, no doubt, an implicit belief in translation, in a kind of universal language which can be represented by particular languages.

Represented speech, on the other hand, can make no attempt to render the phonetic. It represents speech at an even more abstract level, eliminating the communicative relation of *I* and *you* and only retaining the presence of the SELF. Represented thought, in turn, is the attempt to render thought as nonspeech through the medium of language. It is writing which makes language the impersonal tool required for such sophisticated forms of representation by silencing the speaker addressing someone in dialogue.

The abstractness writing acquires in a literate culture has one other consequence for the language of narrative fiction. Naive commentary on language often assumes that there are pronunciations which are transparent, accentless; but this, of course, is only an illusion. All speech is a realization of some particular set of choices; all speech has an accent. It is only in writing that this transparency really exists. Scholars of medieval texts can, in principle, determine whether a writer or scribe spoke Anglo-Norman French, whether his English was Northumbrian or West Midland, precisely because spelling was not fixed and hence, much closer to the phonetic. Modern writing, with its fixed orthography, does not easily betray the accent of the writer, who never speaks in the text.

For this reason, the language of narrative, because it is always written, enjoys a special 'classless' status speech never has. It is separated from the person of its author and the subjective coloration even the most objective statement might have in the mouth of a flesh-and-blood speaker. The study of the genesis of a work might trace back to the author features of vocabulary and style, including dialect words. But within the fictional text, these words lose their markedness; they become as transparent as any other words as far as the creation of the fiction is concerned. What they do not create is the voice and personality of an author/narrator; for them to so function, they must be enclosed within quotation marks. For, as we have seen, the theory of narrative style presented here predicts that the only place for representations of the speaking voice within a narrative text is really in some sense outside it. Its boundaries are set by a graphic notation with no phonetic realization—inverted commas, as noted earlier, can only be read aloud by a gesture or a paraphrase like 'I quote.'

The language of narration, then, is a classless language not achievable in actual speech. Nevertheless, this ability of language to be in some sense universal is often not understood as such, given the naive assumption that there are also transparent pronunciations. For it is not the case that all dialects are treated equally between quotation marks and that the abstract language of pure narration or of the representation of consciousness is equated with no particular dialect. Rather, it is normally the case that standard orthography is taken to represent the 'standard' dialect.

This is readily attested to by the fact that it is always the dialects presumed 'substandard' or 'non-standard' (whichever these may be in a particular context) whose use in direct speech must be signalled by a nonconventional spelling. This is the general practice with novelists. In Faulkner, where the educated southern upper classes presumably speak a dialect which departs from the standard northern dialect, only black and 'poor white' speech is specially marked for pronunciation. In Emily Brontë's *Wuthering Heights,* only the Yorkshire dialect of the servant class is represented in dialogue with an unconventional spelling—the dialect of the others remains unspecified. Similarly, in D. H. Lawrence's stories and novels, the dialect of the Nottinghamshire colliery districts is phonetically spelled in dialogue, whereas the pronunciation of the landed and middle classes in the same direct speech contexts differs in no way from the orthography of the text as a whole. Lawrence's Parkin's or Mellors's speech is marked, but Lady Chatterley's is not:

(11) 'Do you think he's insolent?' said Constance.
'Dunna yer think so yersen, like?' said Clifford, mocking the vernacular
(Lawrence, *The First Lady Chatterley*)

'There's my mother!' he said in a low voice, warning but reckless. 'Ay, come if yer like. But dunna come afore midnight. An' if there's any other bugger i' t' wood afore then I s'll put a bullet in 'im. Come if tha' wilt. I s'll be theer.'
'I shall try to come,' she murmured.
The old woman appeared in the little brick yard.
'Ta'e thy 'bacca then, an' theer's a ha'pny change.'
He took both without a word.
'Well, if I can do anything for you I will: and I'm sure Sir Clifford would,' said Constance, moving through the door.
(*Ibid.*)

'These 'ere bloaters is that salty, they nowt but brine. Pour us another cup o' tea, leass.'
And he would nudge his cup towards her. And she would rise obediently to get the brown teapot from the hob, to pour him his cup-a-tea.
She would never be able to imitate his speech. You couldn't even spell it. He didn't say 'these' but 'thaese', like the Italian *paesano*. And not 'nowt' but 'neôwt', a sound impossible to write.
She gave it up. Culturally, he was another race.
(*Ibid.*)

'The error,' as Raymond Williams has so clearly pointed out, 'consists in supposing that the ordinary spelling indicates how proper people speak'. For instance, we often find the spelling 'wuz' for *was* in what Williams calls 'the orthography of the uneducated' to indicate a nonstandard pronunciation; the fact is, however, that it is also the standard pronunciation. Q. D. Leavis points to the discrepancy that often exists in the indication of dialectal pronunciation in her comments on George Eliot's use of dialect words in *Silas Marner:* 'in the matter of dialect we are forced . . . to note a discrepancy: Nancy's rustic speech stressed here is not what she is reported to speak anywhere else in the book. Elsewhere her speech represents a concession to the literary theory that a heroine must be idealized'. For, as Leavis observes, Nancy's speech is not as common as her sister's in its presentation in the text.

The point is that the abstract language of narration, made possible by writing, which need not distinguish between dialects, privileges some dialects over others by a sleight of hand which, to use Leavis's word, 'idealizes' them. It is, moreover, only within the context of this idealizing literary style that certain dialects can be foregrounded; only a language which is a transparent medium of representation can render some languages opaque.

So if, from the point of view of its structure, the language of the novel is a classless one, it is really certain socially preferred dialects which masquerade in the guise of this classless, abstract and universal language. For the writer who wants to challenge the assumptions about language underlying the practice of representing pronunciation for some dialects only, his linguistic arsenal is defused by the inevitable subversion of writing's classlessness by a class-based interpretation, one which makes one dialect the universal language. Writing is at degree zero, but reading is not. The writer cannot, for instance, create a first person narrator whose dialect is not the standard one and have it understood as such without using other than the conventional orthography. The narration is thereby transformed into *skaz,* making of dialect a kind of screen, which reduces the status of narration, with its truth-creating power, to extended monologue within quotation marks and hence subjects it to falsification, as we will attempt to show in the concluding chapter. The ridiculous barber soliloquizing to a dozing or silenced client or the humorous figure of a Yiddish-speaking milkman naively philosophizing to any passerby he hails does not achieve the status of the idealized language of narration. If the narrator is not to be presented with indulgence, with the taint of condescension, as a humorous character, a 'genre' character, distanced by the frame, then the narration must take the same orthographical form that the standard dialects are presented in. These are the constraints which the form of the written narrative imposes on any writer in our times.

Thus, it is no accident that the literary presentation of dialect is itself tied to those literary forms which are the product of written composition and, most especially, to written narrative. Even *skaz* is posited on writing. The *skaz* narrative is not orally composed; it is a written imitation of an oral narrative, and it is only conceivable if it is written. In a real act of oral composition, the voice and accent of the storyteller is perhaps as equally transparent as the narration of a written text; nevertheless, it is produced concurrently with the story and can be heard as well. It is writing which gives formal shape to the impersonality inherent in the voice of the storyteller, releasing it from its individual qualities, also allowing those individual qualities to become themselves the object of a literary contemplation. In this sense, narration is the pure embodiment of the literary.

The nature of this transparence of narrative language should not be misunderstood. It does not imply that the choice of vocabulary or its arrangement into the characteristic configurations of an individual writer's style is irrelevant to literary criticism. But style approached in this way is not on a par with those aspects of style which create the intentional construct which is a fictional subjectivity. A writer may leave his signature in his writing—it may even contribute a major proportion of what is valued in it—but this is not what his writing creates, but only a byproduct of it. It is writing, by making possible the sentence of narration and the sentence representing consciousness, which allows the literary work to take on an objective life independent of its author.

Roland Barthes

Before his untimely death in a 1980 traffic accident, the French critic and man of letters Roland Barthes was a prolific interpreter, disseminator, and reviser of most of the complex theoretical concepts that wound through his country's centers of learning from the 1950s on. Barthes was born in 1915, grew up in Bayonne, attended secondary school in Paris, and received degrees in classics and grammar and philosophy from the University of Paris. He taught French in Bucharest (1948) and in Alexandria (1949). Although Barthes was director of the social sciences at the Paris École Pratique des Hautes Études from 1960 to 1977, he was more comfortable on the margins of the academy, carrying on a guerrilla conversation with it. *On Racine* (1963) caused a furor because of its nontraditional approach to the canonical playwright. Barthes was elected to the chair of literary semiology at the Collège de France in 1976. Barthes' works, many of which have been translated since his death, include *Writing Degree Zero* (1953), *Mythologies* (1957), *Elements of Semiology* (1964), *S/Z* (1970), *The Pleasure of the Text* (1973), *A Lover's Discourse* (1977), *The Grain of the Voice* (1981), *The Responsibility of Forms* (1982), and *The Rustle of Language* (1984). "Writing and the Novel" is a chapter from *Writing Degree Zero.*

Writing and the Novel

The Novel and History have been closely related in the very century which witnessed their greatest development. Their link in depth, that which should allow us to understand at once Balzac and Michelet, is that in both we find the construction of an autarkic world which elaborates its own dimensions and limits, and organizes within these its own Time, its own Space, its population, its own set of objects and its myths.

This sphericity of the great works of the nineteenth century found its expression in those long recitatives, the Novel and History, which are, as it were, plane projections of a curved and organic world of which the serial story which came into being at that precise moment, presents, through its involved complications, a degraded image. And yet narration is not necessarily a law of the form. A whole period could conceive novels in letters, for instance; and another can evolve a practice of History by means of analyses. Therefore Narration, as a form common to both the Novel and to History, does remain, in general, the choice or the expression of an historical moment.

Obsolete in spoken French, the preterite, which is the cornerstone of Narration, always signifies the presence of Art; it is a part of a ritual of Letters. Its function is no longer that of a tense. The part it plays is to reduce reality to a point of time, and to abstract, from the depth of a multiplicity of experiences, a pure verbal act, freed from the existential roots of knowledge, and directed towards a logical link with other acts, other processes, a general movement of the world: it aims at maintaining a hierarchy in the realm of facts. Through the preterite, the verb implicitly belongs with a causal chain, it partakes of a set of related and orientated actions, it functions as the algebraic sign of an intention. Allowing as it does an ambiguity between temporality and causality, it calls for a sequence of events, that is, for an intelligible Narrative. This is why it is the ideal instrument for every construction of a world; it is the unreal time of cosmogonies, myths, History and Novels. It presupposes a world which is constructed, elaborated, self-sufficient, reduced to significant lines, and not one which has been sent sprawling before us, for us to take or leave. Behind the preterite there always lurks a demiurge, a God or a reciter. The world is not unexplained since it is told like a story; each one of its accidents is but a circumstance, and the preterite is precisely this operative sign whereby the narrator reduces the exploded reality to a slim and pure logos, without density, without volume, without spread, and whose sole function is to unite as rapidly as possible a cause and an end. When the historian states that the duc de Guise died on December 23rd, 1588, or when the novelist relates that the Marchioness went out at five o'clock,[1] such actions emerge from a past without substance; purged of the uncertainty of existence, they have the stability and outline of an algebra, they are a recollection, but a useful recollection, the interest of which far surpasses its duration.

So that finally the preterite is the expression of an order, and consequently of a euphoria. Thanks to it, reality is neither mysterious nor absurd; it is clear, almost familiar, repeatedly gathered up and contained in the hand of a creator; it is subjected to the ingenious pressure of his freedom. For all the great storytellers of the nineteenth century, the world may be full of pathos but it is not derelict, since it is a grouping of coherent relations, since there is no overlapping between the written facts, since he who tells the story has the power to do away with the opacity and the solitude of the existences which made it up, since he can in all sentences bear witness to a communication and a hierarchy of actions and since, to tell the truth, these very actions can be reduced to mere signs.

The narrative past is therefore a part of a security system for Belles-Lettres. Being the image of an order, it is one of those numerous formal pacts made between the writer and society for the justification of the former and the serenity of the latter. The

---

[1] The sentence which for Valéry epitomized the conventions of the novel. *Au.*

preterite *signifies* a creation: that is, it proclaims and imposes it. Even from the depth of the most sombre realism, it has a reassuring effect because, thanks to it, the verb expresses a closed, well-defined, substantival act, the Novel has a name, it escapes the terror of an expression without laws: reality becomes slighter and more familiar, it fits within a style, it does not outrun language. Literature remains the currency in use in a society apprised, by the very form of words, of the meaning of what it consumes. On the contrary, when the Narrative is rejected in favour of other literary genres, or when, within the narration, the preterite is replaced by less ornamental forms, fresher, more full-blooded and nearer to speech (the present tense or the present perfect), Literature becomes the receptacle of existence in all its density and no longer of its meaning alone. The acts it recounts are still separated from History, but no longer from people.

We now understand what is profitable and what is intolerable in the preterite as used in the Novel: it is a lie made manifest, it delineates an area of plausibility which reveals the possible in the very act of unmasking it as false. The teleology common to the Novel and to narrated History is the alienation of the facts: the preterite is the very act by which society affirms its possession of its past and its possibility. It creates a content credible, yet flaunted as an illusion; it is the ultimate term of a formal dialectics which clothes an unreal fact in the garb first of truth then of a lie denounced as such. This has to be related to a certain mythology of the universal typifying the bourgeois society of which the Novel is a characteristic product; it involves giving to the imaginary the formal guarantee of the real, but while preserving in the sign the ambiguity of a double object, at once believable and false. This operation occurs constantly in the whole of Western art, in which the false is equal to the true, not through any agnosticism or poetic duplicity, but because the true is supposed to contain a germ of the universal, or to put it differently, an essence capable of fecundating by mere reproduction, several orders of things among which some differ by their remoteness and some by their fictitious character.

It is thanks to an expedient of the same kind that the triumphant bourgeoisie of the last century was able to look upon its values as universal and to carry over to sections of society which were absolutely heterogeneous to it all the Names which were parts of its ethos. This is strictly how myths function, and the Novel—and within the Novel, the preterite—are mythological objects in which there is, superimposed upon an immediate intention, a second-order appeal to a corpus of dogmas, or better, to a pedagogy, since what is sought is to impart an essence in the guise of an artefact. In order to grasp the significance of the preterite, we have but to compare the Western art of the novel with a certain Chinese tradition, for instance, in which art lies solely in the perfection with which reality is imitated. But in this tradition no sign, absolutely nothing, must allow any distinction to be drawn between the natural and the artificial objects: this wooden walnut must not impart to me, along with the image of a walnut, the intention of conveying to me the art which gave birth to it. Whereas on the contrary this is what writing does in the novel. Its task is to put the mask in place and at the same time to point it out.

This ambiguous function disclosed in the preterite is found in another fact relating to this type of writing: the third person in the Novel. The reader will perhaps recall a novel by Agatha Christie in which all the invention consisted in concealing the murderer beneath the use of the first person of the narrative.[2] The reader looked for him behind every 'he' in the plot: he was all the time hidden under the 'I'. Agatha Christie knew perfectly well that, in the novel, the 'I' is usually a spectator, and that it is the 'he' who is the actor. Why? The 'he' is a typical novelistic convention; like the narrative tense, it signifies and carries through the action of the novel; if the third person is absent, the novel is powerless to come into being, and even wills its own destruction. The 'he' is a formal manifestation of the myth, and we have just seen that, in the West at least, there is no art which does not point to its own mask. The third person, like the preterite, therefore performs this service for the art of the novel, and supplies its consumers with the security born of a credible fabrication which is yet constantly held up as false.

Less ambiguous, the 'I' is thereby less typical of the novel: it is therefore at the same time the most obvious solution, when the narration remains on this side of convention (Proust's work, for instance, purports to be a mere introduction to Literature), and the most sophisticated, when the 'I' takes its place beyond convention and attempts to destroy it, by conferring on the narrative the spurious naturalness of taking the reader into its confidence (such is the guileful air of some stories by Gide). In the same way the use of the 'he' in a novel involves two opposed systems of ethics: since it represents an unquestioned convention, it attracts the most conformist and the least dissatisfied, as well as those others who have decided that, finally, this convention is necessary to the novelty of their work. In any case, it is the sign of an intelligible pact between society and the author; but it is also, for the latter, the most important means he has of building the world in the way that he chooses. It is therefore more than a literary experiment: it is a human act which connects creation to History or to existence.

In Balzac for instance, the multiplicity of 'he's', this vast network of characters, slight in terms of solid flesh, but consistent by the duration of their acts, reveals the existence of a world of which History is the first datum. The Balzacian 'he' is not the end-product of a development starting from some transformed and generalized 'I'; it is the original and crude element of the novel, the material, not the outcome, the creative activity: there is no Balzacian history prior to the history of each third person in the novels of Balzac. His 'he' is analogous to Caesar's 'he':[3] the third person here brings about a kind of algebraic state of the action, in which existence plays the smallest possible part, in favour of elements which connect, clarify, or show the tragedy inherent in human relationships. Conversely—or at any rate previously—the function of 'he' in the novel can be that of expressing an existential experience. In many modern novelists the history of the man is identified with the course of the conjugation: starting from an 'I' which is still the form which expresses anonymity most faithfully, man and author little by little win the right to the third person, in proportion as existence becomes fate, and soliloquy becomes a Novel. Here the appearance of the 'he' is not the

---

[2] The novel is *The Murder of Roger Ackroyd* (1926). *Ed.*
[3] In his *Gallic Wars* Caesar refers to himself in the third person. *Ed.*

starting point of History, it is the end of an effort which has been successful in extracting from a personal world made up of humours and tendencies, a form which is pure, significant, and which therefore vanishes as soon as it is born thanks to the totally conventional and ethereal decor of the third person. This certainly was the course displayed in the first novels of Jean Cayrol whose case can be taken as an exemplar. But whereas in the classics—and we know that where writing is concerned classicism lasts until Flaubert—the withdrawal of the biological person testifies to the establishment of essential man, in novelists such as Cayrol, the invasion of the 'he' is a progressive conquest over the profound darkness of the existential 'I': so true it is that the Novel, identified as it is by its most formal signs, is a gesture of sociability; it establishes Literature as an institution.

Maurice Blanchot has shown, in the case of Kafka, that the elaboration of the impersonal narrative (let us notice, apropos of this term, that the 'third person' is always presented as a negative degree of the person) was an act of fidelity to the essence of language, since the latter naturally tends towards its own destruction. We therefore understand how 'he' is a victory over 'I', inasmuch as it conjures up a state at once more literary and more absent. None the less this victory is ceaselessly threatened: the literary convention of the 'he' is necessary to the belittling of the person, but runs at every moment the risk of encumbering it with an unexpected density. For Literature is like phosphorus: it shines with its maximum brilliance at the moment when it attempts to die. But as, on the other hand, it is an act which necessarily implies a duration—especially in the Novel—there can never be any Novel independently of Belles-Lettres. So that the third person in the Novel is one of the most obsessive signs of this tragic aspect of writing which was born in the last century, when under the weight of History, Literature became dissociated from the society which consumes it. Between the third person as used by Balzac and that used by Flaubert, there is a world of difference (that of 1848): in the former we have a view of History which is harsh, but coherent and certain of its principles, the triumph of an order; in the latter, an art which in order to escape its pangs of conscience either exaggerates conventions or frantically attempts to destroy them. Modernism begins with the search for a Literature which is no longer possible.

Thus we find, in the Novel too, this machinery directed towards both destruction and resurrection, and typical of the whole of modern art. What must be destroyed is duration, that is, the ineffable binding force running through existence: for order, whether it be that of poetic flow or of narrative signs, that of Terror or plausibility, is always a murder in intention. But what reconquers the writer is again duration, for it is impossible to develop a negative within time, without elaborating a positive art, an order which must be destroyed anew. So that the greater modern works linger as long as possible, in a sort of miraculous stasis, on the threshold of Literature, in this anticipatory state in which the breadth of life is given, stretched but not yet destroyed by this crowning phase, an order of signs. For instance, we have the first person in Proust, whose whole work rests on a slow and protracted effort towards Literature. We have Jean Cayrol, whose acquiescence to the Novel comes only as the very last stage of soliloquy, as if the literary act, being supremely ambiguous, could be delivered of a creation consecrated by society, only at the moment when it has at last succeeded in destroying the existential density of a hitherto meaningless duration.

The Novel is a Death; it transforms life into destiny, a memory into a useful act, duration into an orientated and meaningful time. But this transformation can be accomplished only in full view of society. It is society which imposes the Novel, that is, a complex of signs, as a transcendence and as the History of a duration. It is therefore by the obviousness of its intention, grasped in that of the narrative signs, that one can recognize the path which, through all the solemnity of art, binds the writer to society. The preterite and the third person in the Novel are nothing but the fateful gesture with which the writer draws attention to the mask which he is wearing. The whole of Literature can declare *Larvatus prodeo,*[4] As I walk forward, I point out my mask. Whether we deal with the inhuman experience of the poet, who accepts the most momentous of all breaks, that from the language of society, or with the plausible untruth of the novelist, sincerity here feels a need of the signs of falsehood, and of conspicuous falsehood in order to last and to be consumed. Writing is the product, and ultimately the source, of this ambiguity. This specialized language, the use of which gives the writer a glorious but none the less superintended function, evinces a kind of servitude, invisible at first, which characterizes any responsibility. Writing, free in its beginnings, is finally the bond which links the writer to a History which is itself in chains: society stamps upon him the unmistakable signs of art so as to draw him along the more inescapably in its own process of alienation.

---

[4] *Larvatus prodeo* was the motto of Descartes. *Au.*

Peter Rabinowitz

Peter J. Rabinowitz was born and raised in New York City and educated at the University of Chicago where he earned his doctorate in Comparative Literature. Since his undergraduate years, Rabinowitz has negotiated divided loyalties to music and literature, and to educational politics as well. In the summer of 1964 he taught at a Freedom School in Meridian, Mississippi. His next academic appointment was at Kirkland, an experimental women's college, where he and his wife, Nancy, were one of the first couples in the country to share a single tenure-track job. When Kirkland merged with Hamilton College, the Rabinowitzes helped create the comparative literature program at the new institution, where they currently teach. Rabinowitz is the author of *Before Reading: Narrative Conventions and the Politics of Literature* (1987) and academic articles on detective fiction, forgotten novels, theory, and the music of Mahler, Gottschalk, and Scott Joplin. He is coeditor of *Understanding Narrative* (1994) and is at work on a book, with composer Jay Reise, on the act of listening.

Truth in Fiction: A Reexamination of Audiences

1

Some literary arguments, such as those about the fourth book of *Gulliver's Travels*, clarify and enrich the works around which they center. Others—the debate between the New Critics and the Chicago School or the battle over *la nouvelle critique* in France—are valuable because they reveal differences in critical ideologies and suggest alternative ways of looking at texts. But in many ways, the most fascinating are those controversies which force a radical reexamination of our critical vocabulary. These quarrels often deal ostensibly with a specific text, but they unintentionally and unconsciously reveal something more general: a fundamental inadequacy in the way we talk about literature. Not only can't we resolve the differences between the critics, but lacking the terminology to explain the disagreement fully, we are left with the sense that we don't even understand just what it is about or why it has occurred. If pursued, such quarrels can transcend their initial subjects and lead us to substantial critical insights.

One such controversy surrounds Vladimir Nabokov's *Pale Fire*. The novel itself is in the form of a poem by the recently deceased professor-poet John Shade, with an introduction, commentary, and index by Shade's nextdoor neighbor and colleague, Charles Kinbote. Kinbote's elaborate exegesis relates the poem to historical events in a country called Zembla, events which climax in the escape of King Charles at the outbreak of the Zemblan Revolution. The reader soon learns that Kinbote believes himself to be King Charles and that his colleagues consider him to be either a lunatic or a fool.

But perhaps I shouldn't even describe the novel that way, for as soon as it was published, critics disagreed not only about what it meant and how good it was but even about what was "really happening" in the novel. Mary McCarthy argued that Kinbote was really a member of the Russian department named Botkin;[1] Andrew Field claimed that Kinbote had in fact been invented by Shade;[2] and Page Stegner suggested that perhaps, to the contrary, Shade had actually been invented by Kinbote.[3] Kevin Pilon wrote a chronology of *Pale Fire* as if all events—including those in Zembla and those in Shade's poem—had really occurred.[4] John Stark, on the other hand, insisted that actually only "Nabokov and *Pale Fire* (in a sense) are real; any layer inside them (actually *in* the novel) is imagined, and none of those inside layers is more real than any other," although, curiously, he also criticized Shade for the realism of his poetry

---

[1] Mary McCarthy, "A Bolt from the Blue," *The New Republic* 146, no. 23 (4 June 1962): 21. *Au.*
[2] Andrew Field, *Nabokov: His Life in Art* (New York and Toronto, 1967), pp. 316–18. *Au.*
[3] Page Stegner, *Escape into Aesthetics: The Art of Vladimir Nabokov* (New York, 1966), p. 129. *Au.*
[4] Kevin Pilon, "A Chronology of *Pale Fire*," *Russian Literature Triquarterly*, no. 3 (1972): 370–78. *Au.*

("it recreates the past instead of creating and exhausting new possibilities") and praised Kinbote for a commentary that is "purely imaginary."[5]

Who is right? The answer to this question, of course, must come prior to any satisfactory discussion of the overall meaning of the novel: until we know what is going on, we can hardly interpret it, much less evaluate it. But although the flame of controversy has died down as the novel has aged, the question has not been answered. I think that John Stark's contradictory arguments help explain why. Obviously, he is right when he says that only Nabokov and his novel "really" exist—but he is just as obviously wrong. The word "real" has several different meanings here, and we simply do not have, at the present time, a sufficiently precise vocabulary for distinguishing them. It seems, then, that in order to address the question, "What is really happening in *Pale Fire?*" we must first ask ourselves, "How do we even begin to talk about truth in fiction?"

Questions about the status of literary truth are as old as literary criticism, but they have become both more intricate and more compelling as literature has grown progressively more self-conscious and labyrinthian in its dealings with "reality." One might perhaps read *The Iliad* or even *David Copperfield* without raising such issues. But authors like Gide (especially in *The Counterfeiters*), Nabokov, Borges, and Robbe-Grillet seem continually to remind their readers of the complex nature of literary truth. How, for instance, are we to deal with a passage like the following from William Demby's novel *The Catacombs:*

> When I began this novel, I secretly decided that, though I would exercise a strict selection of the facts to write down, be they "fictional" facts or "true" facts taken from newspapers or directly observed events in my own life, once I had written something down I would neither edit nor censor it (myself).[6]

What does this sentence mean? When an apparently fictional narrator (who, to make matters more confusing, has the same name as his author and is also writing a novel entitled *The Catacombs*) distinguishes between "fictional" and "true" facts, what is the status of the word "true"? It clearly does not mean the same as "fictional," for he opposes it to that term. Yet it cannot mean "true" in the sense that historians would use, for he calls what he is writing a novel, and even if he quotes accurately from newspapers, the events of a narrator's life are not "historically" true.

This is but a small version of other more famous literary questions. What precisely do we mean when we ask whether the governess in Henry James' *The Turn of the Screw* is really a trustworthy witness? Or when we ask whether Dostoyevsky's Golyadkin (*The Double*) really has a double, or what really happened last year at Marienbad?

The means of dealing with the problem of truth in the novel have been various, but not, I think, wholly satisfactory. In this essay, therefore, I would like to set forth a model which allows us to talk more clearly about literary truth. The model does not work equally well for all novels, but it works for most, and is particularly useful in clar-

---

[5] John Stark, "Borges' 'Tlön, Uqbar, Orbis Tertius' and Nabokov's *Pale Fire:* Literature of Exhaustion," *Texas Studies in Literature and Language* 14, no. 1 (Spring 1972): 142–43. *Au.*

[6] William Demby, *The Catacombs* (New York, 1970), p. 93. *Au.*

ifying (although not in "solving") the difficulties encountered in texts with involved narrative structures. It gives us a way to talk about *The Double* and *The Turn of the Screw,* and, as I will show at the close of my argument, it explains just what is at issue in the *Pale Fire* dispute.

My model is centered less on the novel's text than on the novel's reader. Such reader-oriented criticism has, of course, become increasingly fashionable of late. Critics like Wayne C. Booth, Stanley E. Fish, Norman Holland, Wolfgang Iser, John Preston, and Walter Slatoff, however diverse their views, have all moved away from the New-Critical emphasis on the "text itself" and have begun to study in detail the ways in which those texts interact with readers.[7] For the purposes of my argument, however, two essays which deal with different *levels* of audience interaction seem particularly relevant: Walker Gibson's classic, "Authors, Speakers, Readers, and Mock Readers,"[8] and Walter J. Ong's more recent development of Gibson's ideas in "The Writer's Audience Is Always a Fiction."[9] Both of these critics have recognized that the act of reading demands a certain pretense. Making an analogy to the familiar distinction between real author and "speaker," Gibson notes:

> I am arguing, then, that there are two readers distinguishable in every literary experience. First, there is the "real" individual upon whose crossed knee rests the open volume, and whose personality is as complex and ultimately inexpressible as any dead poet's. Second, there is the fictitious reader—I shall call him the "mock reader"—whose mask and costume the individual takes on in order to experience the language.[10]

This is a good first step, but unfortunately neither Gibson nor Father Ong is sufficiently concerned with the distinction between fictional and nonfictional modes of address,

---

[7] See, in particular, Wayne C. Booth, *The Rhetoric of Fiction* (Chicago, 1961) and *A Rhetoric of Irony* (Chicago, 1974); Stanley E. Fish, *Self-Consuming Artifacts: The Experience of Seventeenth-Century Literature* (Berkeley, Los Angeles, and London, 1972); Norman Holland, *The Dynamics of Literary Response* (New York, 1968) and *5 Readers Reading* (New Haven and London, 1975); Wolfgang Iser, *Der implizite Leser* (Munich, 1972) appearing in English as *The Implied Reader: Patterns of Communication in Prose Fiction from Bunyan to Beckett* (Baltimore and London, 1974); John Preston, *The Created Self: The Reader's Role in Eighteenth-Century Fiction* (London, 1970); and Walter Slatoff, *With Respect to Readers* (Ithaca and London, 1970). The practitioners of the French *nouvelle critique* and *nouveau roman,* although working in a substantially different tradition, have also paid considerable attention to the active role of the reader and especially the critic. See, for instance, Roland Barthes, *Critique et vérité* (Paris, 1966); Serge Doubrovsky, *Pourquoi la nouvelle critique: Critique et objectivité* (Paris, 1966) appearing in English as *The New Criticism in France,* trans. Derek Coltman (Chicago, 1973); Alain Robbe-Grillet, *Pour un nouveau roman* (Paris, 1963) appearing in English as *For a New Novel,* trans. Richard Howard (New York, 1966), especially the essay, "Temps et description dans le récit d'aujord'-hui" ("Time and Description in Fiction Today"). The interest in reader-oriented criticism can also be seen in the success of the reader seminars and workshops at the 1975 and 1976 MLA Conventions. *Au.*

[8] Walker Gibson, "Authors, Speakers, Readers, and Mock Readers," *College English* 11, no. 5 (February 1950): 265-69. *Au.*

[9] Walter J. Ong, S. J., "The Writer's Audience Is Always a Fiction," *PMLA* 90, no. 1 (January 1975): 9-21. *Au.*

[10] Gibson, pp. 265-66. See also Booth's discussion of this subject in *The Rhetoric of Fiction,* pp. 137-44 and passim. *Au.*

or with the related distinction between speaker (or narrator) and implied author. Both critics treat autobiography and novel in much the same way; Gibson, indeed, moves wittily but carelessly from advertising copy to novel, as if the latter were merely a more elaborate version of the former. But this two-sided model is far too simple to account for the complexity of literary experience; and while they both, toward the ends of their essays, hint of the existence of still further audiences, neither critic develops this idea.

In fact, there are at least four audiences implied in any narrative literary text, and Gibson's "mock audience" and Father Ong's "fictionalized audience" lump several of them together. While the dichotomy proposed by Gibson and Father Ong may be helpful in analyzing criticism, advertising copy, or very simple narratives, it fails with more intricate and ironic works.

2. THE FIRST THREE AUDIENCES DEFINED

My model grows from the simple initial observation that all works of representational art—including novels—are "imitations" in the sense that they appear to be something that they are not. A piece of canvas, for example, appears to be the mayor or the Madonna; a tale about a nonexistent clerk and his overcoat appears to be a "true account."

As a result, the aesthetic experience of such works exists on two levels at once. We can treat the work neither as what it is nor as what it appears to be; we must be aware simultaneously of both aspects. A viewer is hardly responding appropriately to *Othello* if he rushes on the stage to protect Desdemona from the Moor's wrath;[11] nor is the reader of the Sherlock Holmes stories who treats his idol as a historical being, makes pilgrimages to his home on Baker Street, and uses weather reports to determine when certain stories "actually" took place.[12] Neither, however, is it proper to refuse to mourn Desdemona simply because we know that she will soon rise, return to her dressing room, remove her makeup, and go out for a beer with Roderigo. Similarly, anyone who argues that Holmes is simply a fiction, and thus refuses to fear for his safety as he battles Moriarty, is missing the point of the whole experience.

In the proper reading of a novel, then, events which are portrayed must be treated as both "true" and "untrue" at the same time. Although there are many ways to understand this duality, I propose to analyze the four audiences which it generates. More complex works—novels-within-novels, novels with frames, epistolary novels, novels addressed to internal characters, novels with multiple narrators, certain ironic novels—may appear to have more than four, but these are only variations of these basic forms.

(1) First, there is the *actual audience*. This consists of the flesh-and-blood peo-

---

[11] One may recall a scene in Godard's film *Les Carabiniers* in which, while at the movies, one of the characters knocks down the screen trying to join the bathing girl projected on it. *Au.*

[12] For an encyclopedia of this sort of reaction see William S. Baring-Gould, *The Annotated Sherlock Holmes,* 2 vols. (New York, 1967). Much of such research is, of course, tongue-in-cheek; but I wonder, reading through it all, just how much. *Au.*

ple who read the book. While this is the audience in which booksellers have the most interest, it is the only audience which is entirely "real," and the only one over which the author has no guaranteed control.[13]

(2) Second, the author of a novel designs his work rhetorically for a specific hypothetical audience. Like a philosopher, historian, or journalist, he cannot write without making certain assumptions about his readers' beliefs, knowledge, and familiarity with conventions. His artistic choices are based upon these assumptions, conscious or unconscious, and to a certain extent, his artistic success will depend on their accuracy. Demby's *The Catacombs,* for instance, takes place during the early sixties, and the novel achieves its sense of impending doom only if the reader knows that John F. Kennedy will be assassinated when the events of the novel reach 22 November 1963. Had Demby assumed that his audience would be ignorant of this historical event, he would have had to rewrite his book accordingly. Since the structure of a novel is designed for the author's hypothetical audience (which I call the *authorial audience*), we must, as we read, come to share, in some measure, the characteristics of this audience if we are to understand the text.

Just as the implied author is often a person ethically superior to his flesh-and-blood counterpart, so we are often forced to call upon the "best part" of ourselves when we join the authorial audience. But most novelists, even if they do call on our better selves, will only call upon those moral qualities which they believe the actual audience has in reserve, just as they try not to rely on information which we will not in fact possess. For most novelists are concerned with being read and hence try to minimize the distance between the actual and authorial audiences.

There are, of course, exceptions. Some writers, such as the Joyce of *Finnegans Wake,* appear not to care about actual readers at all; others, such as John Barth, have intentions which are so subtle and complex that they can only write for an authorial audience which they know to be, at best, but a tiny portion of their actual audience; and Vladimir Nabokov appears to derive an almost sadistic satisfaction from knowing that his authorial audience is intellectually well above his actual readers—although it is possible that Nabokov in fact writes for an authorial audience quite close to his actual readers but writes in order to make that authorial audience feel intellectually inadequate.

But even if an author makes a serious attempt to write for the "real people out there," the gap between the actual and the authorial audience will always exist. And since all artistic choices, and hence all effects, are calculated in terms of the hypothetical knowledge and beliefs of the authorial audience, this gap must be bridged by readers who wish to appreciate the book. The greater the distance—geographical, cultural, chronological—between the author and his readers, the more of a challenge this is likely to provide.

If historically or culturally distant texts are hard to understand, it is often precisely

---

[13] Few critics have paid much attention to the actual audience, perhaps because it is much harder to gather evidence about real people than it is to discuss the implications of a text. Notable exceptions are Slatoff (*With Respect to Readers*) and Holland (*The Dynamics of Literary Response* and *5 Readers Reading*). Au.

because we do not possess the knowledge required to join the authorial audience. Topical allusions, in particular, lose their clarity through time. (What will our grand-children make of Philip Roth's *Our Gang*?) But even such things as the belief structures of a society must often be "explained" to the reader before he can fully understand the text. Anna Karenina's anguish, for example, might well appear ludicrous to a contemporary student for whom divorce is the social norm. Liberal arts education, to a certain extent, provides the relevant information so that we can join various authorial audiences, and so that the rhetoric of various authors may have its impact; many footnotes do much the same thing.

(3) Since the novel is generally an imitation of some nonfictional form (usually history, including biography and autobiography), the narrator of the novel (implicit or explicit) is generally an imitation of an author. He writes for an imitation audience (which we shall call the *narrative audience*) which also possesses particular knowledge. The narrator of *War and Peace* appears to be an historian. As an historian, he is writing for an audience which not only knows—as does the authorial audience—that Moscow was burned in 1812 but also believes that Natasha, Pierre, and Andrei "really" existed, and that the events in their lives "really" took place. In order to read *War and Peace,* we must therefore do more than join Tolstoy's authorial audience; we must at the same time *pretend* to be a member of the imaginary narrative audience for which his narrator is writing.[14] Whether they think about it or not, this is what all successful readers do when approaching the text.[15]

One way to determine the characteristics of the narrative audience is to ask, "What sort of reader would be implied if this work of fiction were real?" or, even better, "What sort of person would I have to pretend to be—what would I have to know and believe—if I wanted to take this work of fiction as real?" Normally, it is a fairly simple task to pretend to be a member of the narrative audience: we temporarily take on certain minimal beliefs in addition to those we already hold. Thus, for a while we be-

---

[14] Gerald Prince has been working in a similar vein; see his excellent "Introduction à l'étude du narrataire," *Poétique* 14 (1973): 178-96. He develops the idea of *"narrataire"* (narratee), the person to whom the narrator is addressing himself. The *narrataire,* however, is someone perceived by the reader as "out there," a separate person who often serves as a mediator between narrator and reader. The "narrative audience," in contrast, is a role which the text forces the reader to take on. I think that my analysis, centering on an activity on the part of the reader, more successfully explains why certain texts evoke certain responses. *Au.*

[15] The pretense involved in joining the narrative audience is rather different from what Frank Kermode calls "experimental assent" in *The Sense of an Ending* (London, New York, and Oxford, 1967), pp. 38-40. If I understand it correctly, "experimental assent" is an activity on the part of the actual audience through which it relates the novel to reality, accepting the novel if it turns out to be "operationally effective," neglecting it otherwise. The pretense is closer to the "willing suspension of disbelief," except that I would argue not that disbelief is suspended but rather that it is both suspended and not suspended at the same time. In this article, I am not really concerned with the actual psychological processes by which a specific reader performs this act. This subject, however, is treated in a fascinating, if controversial, fashion in Holland's *The Dynamics of Literary Response.* Holland starts out with the same observation as mine: that we both believe and do not believe a literary text. But since he is concerned with the psychological actions of readers (particularly with their unconscious fantasies) rather than with the conscious audience roles implied by a text, his resulting categories (intellecting reader/introjecting reader) differ markedly from mine. *Au.*

lieve that a woman named Anna Karenina really exists, and thinks and acts in a certain way: or, on a broader scale, that Yoknapatawpha County and its inhabitants really exist. Occasionally, a novel's demands are somewhat greater: in *1984,* the narrative audience has knowledge of a series of "facts" about future world history. (To whatever extent the narrative audience possesses "knowledge" of nonexistent facts, these facts must, of course, be provided by the text itself. An author or narrator may allude to actual historical events and expect his audience to understand without explanation; but he cannot, and usually will not, expect the narrative audience to catch unexplained allusions to nonhistory.)

Sometimes, however, we must go even further, and pretend to abandon our real beliefs and accept in their stead "facts" and beliefs which even more fundamentally contradict our perceptions of reality. In much science fiction, for instance, the narrative audience accepts what the authorial audience knows to be false scientific doctrine. And the process can become more complex still. Jules Verne's *From the Earth to the Moon* has obviously lost much of its impact as science fiction now that moon voyages have become a part of our lives. If we wish to read it and get anything like the intended effect, we must first, as authorial audience, pretend *not* to believe in moon travel so that we can then, as narrative audience, pretend to be convinced that it *is* possible.[16]

If we fail to pretend to be members of the narrative audience, or if we misapprehend the beliefs of that audience, we are apt to make invalid, even perverse, interpretations. For instance, the narrative audience of *Cinderella* accepts the existence of fairy godmothers (although the authorial audience does not share this belief). A reader who refuses to pretend to so believe will see Cinderella as a neurotic, perhaps psychotic, young woman subject to hallucinations.

Although there are as many narrative audiences as there are novels, they tend to fall into groups, the members of which are quite similar. We don't have to shift gears very sharply to move from *War and Peace* to *Gone with the Wind,* different as those novels are in quality. Sometimes, however, a novelist is able to create a startling tone or mood by demanding a narrative audience which is unexpected or unfamiliar.[17] Franz Kafka's *Metamorphosis* is a good example. What is striking about this novel is not simply its fantastic premise, which is no more fantastic than the basic premises of *Alice in Wonderland.* Nor can the peculiar quality of Kafka's tale be explained purely in terms of the characters' odd reactions to Gregor's transformation. What strikes me

---

[16] Here I differ significantly with Prince ("Introduction"). He asserts that, unless the text specifies otherwise, it is addressed to a *"degré zero du narrataire"*—a narratee with minimal knowledge (primarily of language and logic) and no ethical or social character. Everything else that he knows must be indicated in the text. The narrative audience, in contrast, is much like ourselves, with our beliefs, our prejudices, our hopes, fears, and expectations, and our knowledge of society and literature—unless there is some evidence (textual or historical) to the contrary. Prince's method would never clarify the *Pale Fire* dispute; such clarification, as we shall see, can only occur if we assume a narrative audience with more knowledge than that explicitly called for by the text. *Au.*

[17] Father Ong, too, argues that much of the character of a literary work stems from the roles it demands of its readers. Once again, however, his analysis is weakened by his failure to distinguish authorial from narrative audience. *Au.*

as most curious about this book is the unusual—and for its time, perhaps unique—nature of the narrative audience. In *Alice* we are asked to pretend that White Rabbits wear watches, that Cheshire Cats fade away, and that numerous other miracles can take place. This is readily done by joining a narrative audience of the sort which is well known from fairy tales. In *Metamorphosis,* however, we are only asked to accept the single fantastic fact that Gregor has been transformed into a gigantic beetle; in all other respects, the narrative audience is a normal, level-headed bourgeois audience. Furthermore, we are asked to accept this without surprise; contrast the matter-of-fact opening of *Metamorphosis* with the equivalent passages in *Alice* or in Gogol's "The Nose," where the narrative audiences are openly warned that the events portrayed will be strange and unusual. There is no doubt that this curiously contradictory role that we are asked to play—half mundane, half fantastic—contributes greatly to the novel's disquieting tone. No other work that I can think of (except for those which imitate Kafka's technique, such as some of Marcel Aymé's short stories) demands that we join a narrative audience which is at once so far from the authorial audience and yet so close to it.

3. THE RELATIONSHIP BETWEEN AUTHORIAL AND NARRATIVE AUDIENCES

When Walker Gibson and Father Ong speak, respectively, of "mock readers" and "fictionalized" audiences, they make no distinction between authorial and narrative audiences.[18] One can agree that both the authorial and the narrative audiences are "fictions" (neither of them exists in the flesh), but they are fictions in radically different senses. When speaking of the authorial audience, we might more accurately use the term "hypothetical" than the term "fictional": for as I have suggested, most authors, in determining the authorial audience they will write for, will try to come as close to the actual audience as possible. For to the extent that an authorial audience is invented, footnotes or other explanations will be required before the text can work as intended. Thus, while some authors such as Barth are forced, because of the subtlety of their intentions, to idealize and write for an audience they know does not exist (or does not

---

[18] In fact, almost all critics who discuss "the reader" are discussing a hybrid form which crosses the lines I have set up. For example, Iser's discussions (*The Implied Reader*) of the reader's discoveries are really studies of the experiences of the narrative and authorial audiences combined. Only toward the end of his book does he suggest a duality in the reader—a duality which stems from the differing personalities of the author and the reader. This intriguing notion is not developed, however: throughout the book, he treats the reader as a unity. So does Stanley E. Fish. In *Self-Consuming Artifacts,* the "reader" seems to be a complex combination of three audiences: at least two actual audiences (the current, informed actual audience, with Fish himself as representative, and the historical audience at the time the work was written), the authorial audience, and—when he is writing about fiction—the narrative audience. Indeed, a primary difference between Fish's model and my own is that his is horizontal (he is concerned with the progress of a unified reader through time) while mine is vertical (I am concerned with distinguishing the different levels on which a reader operates simultaneously). Gerald Prince's distinction ("Introduction," p. 180) between *lecteur réel, lecteur virtuel,* and *narrataire* (even though it does not, as I have pointed out, deal precisely with differing roles played by the reader) seems much more subtle. *Au.*

exist in significant numbers), few authors intentionally strive for such a situation. The distance between authorial and actual audiences, in sum, may be inevitable—but as Tolstoy argues in *What Is Art?*, it is generally undesirable; and authors usually try to keep the gap narrow. The narrative audience, on the other hand, is truly a fiction; the author not only knows that the narrative audience is different from the actual and authorial audiences, but he rejoices in this fact and expects his actual audience to rejoice with him. For it is this difference which makes fiction fiction, and makes the double-leveled aesthetic experience possible. As we shall see, the author plays with this distinction and builds much of his effect on it.

Similarly, the reader's act of joining the authorial audience is not really a pretense in the same way that joining the narrative audience is. As good readers, we usually try to *become* the authorial audience as much as possible. Thus, the authorial audience of Hemingway's *For Whom the Bell Tolls* knows quite a bit about the Spanish Civil War. If, as actual readers, we do not possess this information, we will ideally do our best to acquire it. There are, however, two circumstances under which we may *pretend* to join the authorial audience.

First, we are often lazy; thus, we may decide to forego a research trip to the library and instead simply pretend to understand Hemingway's politics. Underlying this pretense, however, is the knowledge that we could *really* understand the book if we wished; and it is clearly a qualitatively different sort of pretense than the pretense of believing that Robert Jordan, Maria, and Pablo all exist. Second, there are cases where the authorial audience differs from the actual audience not simply because it has additional facts at its disposal (as in Hemingway) but because it operates under assumptions which fundamentally contradict our normal way of thinking. Through research, we may gain a better understanding of the beliefs of another culture. But no matter how much research we do, we are unlikely actually to *believe* what the authorial audiences of the *Iliad* or *From the Earth to the Moon* believe.

To the extent that our joining of the authorial audience is a pretense, we are that much less likely to receive the work's intended effect. But the pretense involved in joining the narrative audience does not interfere with a novel's effect; it is, on the contrary, an essential and desirable element in it. And as we have seen, the reader who does not realize that this is pretense—the reader who looks up Humbert Humbert's murder trial in the newspapers—has clearly missed the point.

Obviously, the narrative and authorial audiences are closer together in some novels than in others. I would argue that the distance between these audiences is a major element in any novel's structure. Indeed, I suspect that one could develop a classification of narrative literature stemming from a theory of "realism" expressed in terms of this distance. Surely, in the most "realistic" novels (*War and Peace* is a paradigm), the narrative audience is asked to accept very little—and usually nothing which in any way contradicts the fundamental beliefs or experiences of the authorial audience. To believe that Natasha exists, for example, in no way contradicts the authorial audience's general experiences—it is not at all improbable that such a person should exist and act as she does. At the extreme end of realism, narrative and authorial audiences are so close as to be almost indistinguishable, as in Henry Miller's *Tropic of Cancer.* When the distinction between the two disappears entirely, we have autobiography or history.

In antirealistic, or fantastic, novels (*Alice in Wonderland*, for example), the narrative audience is asked to take on a great deal more—beliefs which, like belief in the White Rabbit, do moreover contradict the very beliefs and experiences of the authorial audience. Obviously, the wider the gap—the more unusual or outrageous the beliefs that the narrative audience is required to take on—the greater the effort required to bridge it. Thus, we become more conscious that the novel is double-leveled and that we must employ "pretense" to become involved in reading it. This, in turn, increases our awareness of the novel as art, and tends to diminish our direct emotional involvement in it.

The metaphor of distance may suggest the possibility of quantitative measurement; but this is obviously deceptive, for such measurement is difficult, if not impossible, especially since the distances occur along many axes at once. How, for instance, can one compare the distance the novelist causes by asking us to believe that a man can walk through walls (Marcel Aymé's "Le Passe-Muraille") with the distance caused by asking us to believe that a single mad genius named Fu Manchu secretly controls the politics of half the world?

Yet while such a theory of realism would not be able to assign a quantitative "realism factor" to every novel, it would nonetheless have interesting consequences. Most importantly, it would escape from the notion of "verisimilitude," a notion which is misleading because it theoretically measures the novel against the "real" world but in fact only measures the novel against the world as perceived by the current actual audience. Since perceptions of the world change with history, the "verisimilitude" of a novel is less a quality inherent in the novel itself than a fluctuating value dependent upon the beliefs of the particular critics who read it. But by considering the distance between narrative and authorial audience rather than the more traditional distance between narrative and actual audience, realism can become grounded in its proper historical context. The realism of a novel will then depend upon the beliefs (or the author's perception of them) common to the audience at the time when (and in the class of readers for whom) it was written, rather than upon the beliefs common to the audience by which it is now read. The works of Horatio Alger, according to this notion, are extremely realistic, despite their almost comic mimetic inaccuracy, because they conform so well to the beliefs of the audience for which they were written.

Similarly, with this definition of realism, we can view realism outside the confines of "schools" or "traditions." It is thus possible to see realism in a novelist like Alain Robbe-Grillet, even though his works hardly fall into the Tolstoy-James tradition. His novels may require considerable imagination and even creativity from the authorial audience, but at least *The Voyeur* and *Jealousy* do not require much pretense before experienced modern readers can join the narrative audience.

Our notion of audience distance is also suggestive when considering the didactic power of fantastic novels. It would seem that the greater the distance between authorial and narrative audiences (the less realistic the novel in our new definition), the less impact a moral lesson learned by the narrative audience is likely to have on the authorial audience. To use a Tolstoyan metaphor, the greater the distance, the less the possibility of "infection" from one to the other. Thus, for instance, I wonder about the power of the utopian novels of H. G. Wells. As narrative audience, we are asked to accept all kinds of scientific absurdities; once having done this, it is not difficult to accept the necessity of socialism as well. But in our role as authorial audience—where we see the novel *as a novel*—our great distance from the narrative audience takes its toll. Just as we recognize the obvious fictionality of our pretended scientific beliefs, so we are apt to abandon our newly found social beliefs as well. Since the narrative audience's beliefs in the naturalistic novels of Zola are not so far from those of the authorial audience, we are less apt to be conscious of their fictionality. It is thus all the more likely that the lessons learned as narrative audience will stick for the authorial audience too—and, unless the authorial audience is very distant from the actual audience, for the actual audience as well.

The act of joining the narrative audience is not, of course, the ultimate step in literary interpretation—rather, it is the first and most elementary step. It is an essential step, however, and many novels fail to make an impact because they are unable to make their readers join the narrative audience. Such novels are usually deemed "unconvincing." The ability of a novel to convince is related to, but not identical to, its realism as I have defined it above. The realism of a novel depends on the distance between authorial and narrative audiences. The novel is more or less convincing, depending on how skillfully the novelist navigates us across that distance, and on how likely we are to be standing on the dock—in the authorial audience—when the trip begins. Most unconvincing novels are unrealistic, although Horatio Alger's realistic epics no longer persuade. And with skill, a novelist like Kafka can make a highly unrealistic novel entirely convincing: we make the initial leap of imagination and remain with him throughout.

Only after having joined the narrative audience can we begin to study the meanings of a work of art. Thus, we cannot even perceive the moral dimension in Aymé's "Le Passe-Muraille" until we pretend to accept its initial "scientific" premise. A person who merely insists that no one can walk through walls can hardly respond to the hero's situation as the author intended. But the act of accepting this premise does not *in itself* lay bare the story's moral dimension. Decisions as to ultimate meaning or meanings, symbolic significance—in fact, any decision about the work *as art*—are made by the authorial and actual audiences, and not by the narrative audience.

I do not wish to imply that in order to become members of the narrative audience, we must pretend to accept *everything* that the narrator tells us. There *are* unreliable narrators.[19] An unreliable narrator, however, is not simply a narrator who "does not tell the truth"—what fictional narrator ever tells the literal truth? Rather, an unreliable narrator is one who tells lies, conceals information, misjudges with respect to the narrative audience—that is, one whose statements are untrue not by the standards of the real world or of the authorial audience but by the standards of his own narrative audience. It would, for example, be trivial to argue that Dostoyevsky's Underground Man is unreliable because his statements are often false. He is unreliable because even after we have pretended to accept the beliefs of the narrative audience (that he, Liza, and the dinner party actually do exist), we still find that much of what he says—particularly when he analyzes motives—contradicts the other elements of

---

[19] See Booth, *The Rhetoric of Fiction,* pp. 158-59 and passim. *Au.*

his framework. In other words, all fictional narrators are false in that they are imitations; but some are imitations of people who tell the truth, some of people who lie. The narrative audience believes the narrator is a real, existing historian. But it does not automatically assume that he is an accurate historian any more than in reading a work of history we automatically assume the author to be accurate and truthful. It is probably in these terms that we have to understand William Demby's distinction between "real" and "fictional" in the passage quoted above.[20]

4. THE FOURTH AUDIENCE

The idea of unreliable narrators brings us at last to our fourth audience. This is the audience for which the narrator wishes he were writing and relates to the narrative audience in a way roughly analogous to the way that the authorial audience relates to the actual audience. This final audience believes the narrator, accepts his judgments, sympathizes with his plight, laughs at his jokes even when they are bad. I call this the *ideal narrative audience*—ideal, that is, from the narrator's point of view. Thus, in John Barth's *End of the Road,* the authorial audience knows that Jacob Horner has never existed; the narrative audience believes he has existed but does not entirely accept his analyses; and the ideal narrative audience accepts uncritically what he has to say. Similarly, in the Jason section of Faulkner's *The Sound and the Fury* (each section of which has a different ideal narrative audience), the ideal narrative audience believes that Jason has been victimized and sympathizes with his whining misery, although the narrative audience despises him.

As a general rule, the distance between authorial audience and narrative audience tends to be along an axis of "fact," either "historical" or "scientific." That is, the narrative audience believes that certain events could or did take place. The distance between the narrative audience and the ideal narrative audience tends to lie along an axis of ethics or interpretation. The ideal narrative audience agrees with the narrator that certain events are good or that a particular analysis is correct, while the narrative audience is called upon to judge him. Much of the problem—and most of the joy—of reading irony comes from sorting out these three levels, and feeling the tensions among them. But just as there are extremely realistic novels where the narrative and authorial audiences are indistinguishable, so there are non-ironic works where the ideal narrative audience is virtually identical with the narrative audience.

This sort of ironic tension between audiences is found in nonliterary arts as well, even—surprisingly—in certain types of music. Obviously it cannot occur in nonimitative music. In a Bach Prelude and Fugue, for instance, there may be a gap be-

---

[20] Assuming that *The Catacombs* is a novel as it claims to be. The work is deceptive, however, and the implied author (indeed, the "real" author as far as I can tell from the little I know of Demby) and the narrator are all but indistinguishable. As a result, the authorial and narrative audiences of the frame novel (there is also a novel-within-the-novel) are almost indistinguishable, and we have the type of extreme realism found in *Tropic of Cancer,* if not an actual autobiography. It is always possible, therefore, that Demby means "true" in a more literal sense: that is, true on the level of the authorial audience. *Au.*

tween the authorial audience (which knows how to listen to several contrapuntal lines at once) and the actual audience (which often does not). But that gap is clearly undesirable, and when it exists, it diminishes the music's impact. In any case, there is nothing here which is analogous to the narrative audience.

From the point of view of audience dynamics, however, imitative music is considerably more interesting and intricate. What, in fact, happens when an audience listens to the storm music in Liszt's *Les Preludes*? Is there an authorial audience which is listening to these sounds as pure musical sounds and a narrative audience which pretends to believe that it is actually hearing a storm? Or is there a single audience which is hearing music which it relates metaphorically to the sounds of a storm?

I do not know the answer to this question, although I suspect that my model might shed some light on the traditional controversy over program music. There is one subtype of imitative music, however, where our literary model surely holds: music which is imitative of other music.

A good example is Mozart's *A Musical Joke* (K. 522). Why do we react to this as music which is good but comic, rather than as music which is simply bad? For there is no doubt that by normal canons of eighteenth-century style the piece is quite dreadful. What we have here is a musical equivalent of an ironic fictional narrative. Mozart has created a fictional persona, the incompetent composer. The authorial audience knows that this piece is, in fact, by Mozart, and therefore knows that its violations of convention and taste are intentional. The narrative audience, on the other hand, pretends to believe that this piece is in fact written by some hack composer of the time and pretends to believe that the piece is an unintentional failure. Finally, this mock composer has written for an ideal narrative audience, an audience which will listen to his music and, not noticing its crudities, will think it is brilliant. Listening to this sort of music—like reading Jason's narrative or Swift's "A Modest Proposal"—is intellectually demanding since we must play all these parts at once. A similar interplay between audiences is at work when we listen to Charles Ives imitating the sound of a second-rate marching band (as in *The Fourth of July*), or when we listen with ironic pleasure to the absolutely horrendous fanfares which pop up in Offenbach's *La Belle Hélène*.

5. TWO TYPES OF AMBIGUITY AND THE PROBLEMS OF *PALE FIRE*

Since we cannot read a novel properly until we have joined the narrative audience, reading problems can occur when we have difficulties in discovering precisely what are the characteristics of the narrative audience. Usually, this can be determined more or less by common sense and familiarity with literary traditions; occasionally, the author will have to take special steps to avoid confusion. The purpose of "John Ray's" introduction to Nabokov's *Lolita,* for example, is partly to provide the "factual ground work" for the narrative audience. It tells the reader that the narrative audience knows that Humbert Humbert, Lolita, and especially Clare Quilty existed and that the murder and trial actually did take place. As members of the narrative audience, then, we are free not to believe certain details in Humbert's account—but we are *not* free to believe that Quilty is a figment of Humbert's paranoia.

Occasionally, however, there are more difficult problems. It is clear that the evidence in *Frankenstein* informs us that the narrative audience accepts the scientific possibility that a man may create life in a laboratory. But does the narrative audience of Dostoyevsky's *The Double* accept the scientific possibility of a double?

This ambiguity in Dostoyevsky's novel is radically different, both in its structure and in its effects, from the more usual kind of ambiguity found in novels such as *Lord Jim*. In this more familiar form, the ambiguity exists *within* the narrative audience: the narrative audience itself is unaware of where, exactly, the truth lies. This ambiguity may relate to ethics (was Lord Jim a coward?), to motives (why does Quentin Compson commit suicide?), to facts (was Owen Taylor, in *The Big Sleep*, murdered?), or to anything else which may normally be questionable. The effect, however, is "internal." That is, since we are confused on the level of the narrative audience, it is possible to ponder this ambiguity "within the world of the novel." Particularly if the ambiguity relates to ethics or motives, the more we ponder it, the more deeply we get into the characters.

The second kind of ambiguity, found in novels like *The Double*, is far less common and usually accidental. It occurs when we are faced with an ambiguity about which of several narrative audiences we are to accept—although each potential narrative audience may itself face no ambiguity. Thus, for example, we know that the *ideal* narrative audience believes that Golyadkin has a double. But we do not know whether the narrative audience accepts the scientific possibility of a double (in which case Golyadkin is being persecuted—at least in part—by forces external to himself) or denies such a possibility (in which case Golyadkin's double is but a mad projection, a result of his paranoia).

In *The Double*—where the ambiguity is probably accidental—the ambiguity makes it difficult to determine how we are to read the book *on the surface:* but, curiously enough, it makes little difference to its ultimate meaning. Even if, in our role as members of the narrative audience, we assume that the double actually does exist, in our simultaneous roles as members of the authorial and actual audiences, we will interpret it as a symbolic representation of some inner force anyway.

Much of the controversy over *The Turn of the Screw* arises from precisely this same structural source. Once again, the beliefs of the ideal narrative audience are clear; but where does the narrative audience stand? Is James' narrative audience for this novel the narrative audience traditionally implied by gothic novels, one able to believe in ghosts? Or is it closer to the narrative audience of *Portrait of a Lady?* James (unlike Bram Stoker, for instance, in *Dracula*) has made no effort to tell us what are the beliefs of his narrative audience; and since we are used to viewing James as a "realist," we have difficulty accepting the surface meaning of his tale. Perhaps my critical bias is showing here, but I find that in this novel, as in *The Double*, it ultimately makes little difference which reading one chooses. *Dracula* is, in fact, a novel *about* vampires; but even if the narrative audience of *The Turn of the Screw* accepts ghosts, the authorial audience is apt to treat them as in some sense symbolic when called upon to interpret the novel.

The ambiguities of *Pale Fire* are similar but more difficult, and I would like to conclude by showing how my model, by revealing Nabokov's use of this second kind of ambiguity, explains the novel's persistent ability to baffle readers and critics.

Clearly, the novel is largely "about" the relationship between the poem and the commentary, between the poet and his critic. But the subject of a novel is not its substance, and to state a subject is not to explicate it; and while nearly every critic agrees that this is, in fact, one of Nabokov's major concerns, there has been no agreement on just *what* Nabokov is saying about this relationship. For one cannot discuss the relationship between two things until we know what those two things are, and as soon as we try to examine Shade and Kinbote in any detail, we are confronted by those plaguing problems of "fact" which characterize the *Pale Fire* controversy.

For example, does the narrative audience believe that both Shade and Kinbote actually exist—as most critics seem to believe—or does it believe that one has invented the other, or that a man named Botkin has invented them both? Clearly, until we know the answer to this question, we cannot adequately discuss the question of whether Kinbote's commentary is totally "wrong" (as Richard Kostelanetz suggests when he says, "Kinbote's characteristic fault is missing the point"),[21] or whether, to the contrary, Kinbote has actually understood Shade's poem, as Stegner and others have argued. And until this question is answered, no statements about the nature of the relationship between commentary and poem are liable to be worth very much.

And does the narrative audience agree with the ideal narrative audience that the country of Zembla really exists? Is the relation of poem to commentary the relation of "invention" to "history" (even if somewhat distorted history) or the relation of invention to invention? Again, we cannot make any meaningful statements about the nature of the connections between the writings of Shade and Kinbote until we have answers to these questions.

There are other thorny problems as well. Is Shade's poem any good in the eyes of the narrative audience? Does the narrative audience see it as "competent but pedestrian" (as suggested by Claire Rosenfeld)[22] or are we to treat it as Andrew Field does—an important poem in its own right?[23] Who really shoots whom at the end of the book, and why?

I wish that I could answer these questions; but I cannot. I think we are now, however, in a position to understand *why* these kinds of problems have arisen in this novel and why, in fact, they can never be solved. For convenience, let us limit ourselves to two of the questions raised above. (1) Does the narrative audience believe that John Shade is a real poet, or does it believe that he is a figment of Kinbote's imagination? (2) Does the narrative audience believe that the country of Zembla exists?

As we have seen, the novel does not provide answers to these questions. This in itself may not seem remarkable. There are many novels where facts remain unknown

---

[21] Richard Kostelanetz, "Nabokov's Obtuse Fool," in *On Contemporary Literature*, ed. Kostelanetz (New York, 1964), p. 432. *Au.*

[22] Claire Rosenfeld, "The Shadow Within: The Conscious and Unconscious Use of the Double," *Daedalus* 92, no. 2 (Spring 1963): 342. *Au.*

[23] Field, *Nabokov*, p. 106. *Au.*

to the narrative audience. The narrative audience of Camus' *The Fall* never learns whether the events described by the narrator are true or not; the narrative audience of Robbe-Grillet's *Jealousy* never knows whether A. has been unfaithful or not. But the ambiguities of Shade's and Zembla's existence do *not* exist for *Pale Fire*'s narrative audience. They are external to the world of the novel.

We can see this as soon as we start to reconstruct the nature of the narrative audience. It is, first and foremost, an intellectual audience which is interested not only in literature, but also—since the novel is an imitation of a critical treatise—in literary criticism as well. From the broad range of references made by Kinbote, we can further assume it to be well read, familiar not only with Robert Frost but also with some of the more obscure passages in *Timon of Athens.*

It follows from this implicit sophistication that the narrative audience is familiar with the basic facts about contemporary art and politics and, if given the name of a country or a famous American poet, would be able to tell whether it is real or fabricated. The narrative audience, therefore, either knows that John Shade is a great American poet, or else knows that Kinbote has invented him and his poem; it either knows that there is a country named Zembla, or else knows that Kinbote has invented it and its history. The narrative audience cannot be undecided on these questions.[24]

Here then lies an obstacle which prevents us from even the most superficial understanding of the text. Although the narrative audience has facts about Shade and Zembla at its disposal, *we* do not know what they are, and are hence totally unable to join the narrative audience. There is nothing which serves the function performed by John Ray's introduction in *Lolita.* The situation is similar to that faced by readers of *The Turn of the Screw* and *The Double*—but in *Pale Fire,* the ambiguities seem intentional, and there is no simple way for the authorial audience to resolve them.

As I suggested earlier, the moral ambiguities of a novel like *Lord Jim,* which exist on the level of the narrative audience, have the effect of immersing us more deeply in the world of the novel—they get us more involved as narrative audience. The ambiguity of *Pale Fire* has an entirely different—even opposite—effect. Since this ambiguity is perceived only in our capacities as authorial and actual audience, it makes us more aware of the gap between authorial and narrative audience, and hence of the novel as art, as construct. It is thus difficult to get involved in *Pale Fire* as narrative audience, and for many readers, including myself, the book is generally unmoving, witty and brilliant as it may be.

This exaggerated artificiality and remarkable use of our second kind of ambiguity is quite consistent with Nabokov's general aesthetic, but it makes *Pale Fire* a frustrating novel to read, and in some respects an impossible one. It is not simply that the novel raises difficult philosophical questions, as *The Brothers Karamazov* does; it is rather that we can't tell precisely what issues the novel does address. For as I noted above, the central concerns of *Pale Fire* are not whether Shade and/or Zembla exist. Rather, they arise from the relationship of poem and commentary. But the novel's ambiguity prevents us from knowing just what that relationship is. Thus, we may say

---

[24] Although it would be quite impossible, given Prince's methodology (see n. 16), for us to make the same assumptions about a *narrataire.* In a situation like this, his method—while not inherently "wrong"— seems to have little connection with the way we actually read books. *Au.*

vaguely that *Pale Fire* has something to do with the nature of imagination, the nature of criticism, and the relation of truth to illusion. Yet until we know whether or not Shade and Zembla exist, we cannot know, with any more specificity, just what the novel is doing with these subjects—what questions it is asking, what solutions it is proposing. If both Zembla and Shade exist, we have one novel, probing one set of problems: if Zembla does not exist, but Shade does, we have an entirely different novel, with another set of problems: if . . .

How then is one to read the book? The only way, I suppose, is to make an arbitrary choice about which narrative audience one wants to join—or to read the novel several times, making a different choice each time. As in a game, we are free to make several opening moves; what follows will be dependent upon our initial decision. Simply with respect to the questions suggested above, we can generate four novels, all different but all couched, oddly, in the same words. And as we begin to ask further questions—Has Shade invented Kinbote? Is the poem a good one in the eyes of the narrative audience?—the number of possible novels begins to proliferate at a geometric rate.[25]

At present, this model of the four audiences is less a complete theory of fictional structure than a suggestion for an approach which needs further study. The total use of the scheme—just what questions it can answer and what insights it can bring—has yet to be determined. But it does seem a promising way of looking at literature—it does provide a useful critical vocabulary for speaking of fiction, which in turn affords a new perspective on the multifaceted nature of literary experience. It would be useful, no doubt, in examining such works as Robbe-Grillet's *In the Labyrinth* or Doris Lessing's *Briefing for a Descent into Hell,* to mention only two novels where the problem of truth underlies the reader's difficulties in interpretation. And it would certainly help us sort out the complex ironies of novels with multiple narrators, such as Lermontov's *A Hero of Our Times* or Faulkner's *As I Lay Dying.*

Although I have talked primarily about fiction, my method can be adapted to drama as well. It would surely provide a new angle on the problem of aesthetic distance posed by contemporary theater, especially those attempts (for instance, by Pirandello or more recently by the Living Theater) to break down barriers between actors and viewers, and hence, between narrative and actual audiences.

In music, it might help us better understand program music, especially that type in which the musicians, in performing the music, pretend to be other performers performing other music. (This curious technique may not cause particular difficulties when we listen to Don Giovanni's serenade or the interpolated dance music at his parties, but it produces serious analytic problems in its more avant-garde manifestations: Berio's *Recital I [for Cathy],* for instance, or Peter Maxwell Davies' *Missa Super "L'Homme Armé."*)

---

[25] There is at least one novel of infinite regress among the many *Pale Fires.* Suppose the narrative audience knows that the famous poet John Shade has invented a character named "Kinbote." It will then treat the text before it not as a critical commentary but as a "novel." But if it is a novel, it in turn has its own narrative audience—Narrative Audience 2. That narrative audience, in turn, must decide whether Shade and Kinbote both exist—and if it decides that Shade has invented Kinbote, it too will view what it has in front of it as a "novel," with its own narrative audience—Narrative Audience 3. This narrative audience, in turn . . . *Au.*

And, to return to literature, my model would cast some light on the eternal problem of the role of the reader's beliefs. By making distinctions among actual beliefs, authorial beliefs, narrative beliefs, and ideal beliefs we can talk about this issue with considerably more clarity and specificity than has hitherto been possible.

In short, this model is at the very least a new handle by which we can grasp familiar but perplexing problems. How far it enables us to carry them remains to be seen.

Gerald Prince

Gerald Prince was born in 1942 in Alexandria, Egypt, and was educated at Brown University, where he earned his doctorate in 1968. He is currently Lois and Jerry Magnin Term Professor of Romance Languages and co-director of the Center for Cultural Studies at the University of Pennsylvania, where he has taught since 1967. Prince is the author of *Métaphysique et technique dans l'oeuvre romanesque de Sartre* (1968), *A Grammar of Stories* (1973), *Narratology: The Form and Functioning of Narrative* (1982), *A Dictionary of Narratology* (1987), *Narrative as Theme* (1992), and has edited *Alternatives* (1993), and *Autobiography, Historiography, Rhetoric* (1994). He is working on a guide to the twentieth-century novel in French (to appear after the turn of the millenium). Prince's essay, "Introduction to the Study of the Narratee" originally appeared (in French) in *Poétique* in 1973.

Introduction to the Study of the Narratee

All narration, whether it is oral or written, whether it recounts real or mythical events, whether it tells a story or relates a simple sequence of actions in time, presupposes not only (at least) one narrator but also (at least) one narratee, the narratee being someone whom the narrator addresses. In a fiction-narration—a tale, an epic, a novel—the narrator is a fictive creation as is his narratee. Jean-Baptiste Clamence, Holden Caulfield, and the narrator of *Madame Bovary* are novelistic constructs as are the individuals to whom they speak and for whom they write. From Henry James and Norman Friedman to Wayne C. Booth and Tzvetan Todorov, numerous critics have examined the diverse manifestations of the narrator in fictive prose and verse, his multiple roles and his importance.[1] By contrast, few critics have dealt with the narratee

---

[1]   See, for example, Henry James, *The Art of Fiction and Other Essays,* ed. Morris Roberts (New York: Oxford University Press, 1948); Norman Friedman, "Point of View in Fiction: The Development of a Critical Concept," *PMLA* 70 (December 1955): 1160–84; Wayne C. Booth, *The Rhetoric of Fiction* (Chicago: University of Chicago Press, 1961); Tzvetan Todorov, "Poétique" in Oswald Ducrot et al., *Qu'est-ce que le structuralisme?* (Paris: Seuil, 1968), pp. 97–166; and Gérard Genette, *Figures III* (Paris: Seuil, 1972). *Au.*

and none to date has undertaken an in-depth study;[2] this neglect persists despite the lively interest raised by Benveniste's fine articles on discourse (*le discours*), Jakobson's work on linguistic functions, and the evergrowing prestige of poetics and semiology.

Nowadays, any student minimally versed in the narrative genre differentiates the narrator of a novel from its author and from the novelistic *alter ego* of the author and knows the difference between Marcel and Proust, Rieux and Camus, Tristram Shandy, Sterne the novelist, and Sterne the man. Most critics, however, are scarcely concerned with the notion of the narratee and often confuse it with the more or less adjacent notions of receptor (*récepteur*), reader, and arch-reader (*archilecteur*). The fact that the word *narratee* is rarely employed, moreover, is significant.

This lack of critical interest in narratees is not inexplicable. Indeed, their study has been neglected, more than likely, because of a characteristic of the narrative genre itself; if the protagonist or dominant personality of a narration often assumes the role of the narrator and affirms himself as such (Marcel in *A la recherche du temps perdu*, Roquentin in *La Nausée*, Jacques Revel in *L'Emploi du temps*), there is no hero who is above all a narratee—unless one includes narrators who constitute their own narratee,[3] or perhaps a work like *La Modification*. Besides, it should not be forgotten that the narrator, on a superficial if not a profound level, is more responsible than his narratee for the shape and tone of the story as well as for its other characteristics. Finally, many problems of poetic narrative that might have been approached from the angle of the narratee have already been studied from the point of view of the narrator; after all, the individual who relates a story and the person to whom the story is told are more or less interdependent in any narration.

Whatever the case may be, narratees deserve to be studied. Major storytellers and novelists, as well as the less important, bear out this point. The variety of narratees found in fictive narrations is phenomenal. Docile or rebellious, admirable or ridiculous, ignorant of the events related to them or having prior knowledge of them, slightly naive as in *Tom Jones*, vaguely callous as in *The Brothers Karamazov*, narratees rival narrators in their diversity. Moreover, many novelists have in their own way examined the distinctions that should be maintained between the narratee and the receptor or between the narratee and the reader. In a detective novel by Nicholas Blake, for example, and in another by Philip Loraine, the detective succeeds in solving the crime when he realizes that the narratee and the receptor are not the same. In addition, there is no want of narratives that underscore the importance of the narratee, *A Thousand and One Nights* providing an excellent illustration. Scheherazade must exercise her talent as a storyteller or die, for as long as she is able to retain the attention of the caliph with her stories, she will not be executed. It is evident that the heroine's fate and that of the narration depend not only upon her capabilities as a storyteller, but also upon

---

[2] See, among others, Walker Gibson, "Authors, Speakers, Readers, and Mock Readers," *College English* 9 (February 1950): 265-69; Roland Barthes, "Introduction à l'analyse structurale des récits," *Communications* 8 (1966): 18-19; Tzvetan Todorov, "Les Catégories du récit littéraire," *Communications* 8 (1966): 146-47; Gerald Prince, "Notes Towards a Categorization of Fictional 'Narratees,'" *Genre* 4 (March 1971): 100-105; and Genette, *Figures III*, pp. 265-67. *Au.*

[3] In a certain sense, every narrator is his own narratee. But most narrators have other narratees as well. *Au.*

the humor of the narratee. If the caliph should become tired and stop listening, Scheherazade will die and the narrative will end.[4] The same fundamental situation can be found in the encounter of Ulysses with the Sirens,[5] as well as in a more recent work. Like Scheherazade, the hero of *La Chute* has a desperate need for a certain type of narratee. In order to forget his own guilt, Jean-Baptiste Clamence must find someone who will listen to him and whom he will be able to convince of everyone's guilt. He finds this someone at the Mexico City Bar in Amsterdam and it is at that moment that his narrative account begins.

THE ZERO-DEGREE NARRATEE

In the very first pages of *Le Père Goriot,* the narrator exclaims: "That's what you will do, you who hold this book with a white hand, you who settle back in a well-padded armchair saying to yourself: perhaps this is going to be amusing. After reading about old Goriot's secret misfortunes, you'll dine with a good appetite attributing your insensitivity to the author whom you'll accuse of exaggeration and poetic affectation." This "you" with white hands, accused by the narrator of being egotistical and callous, is the narratee. It's obvious that the latter does not resemble most readers of *Le Père Goriot* and that consequently the narratee of a novel cannot be automatically identified with the reader: the reader's hands might be black or red and not white; he might read the novel in bed instead of in an armchair; he might lose his appetite upon learning of the old merchant's unhappiness. The reader of a fiction, be it in prose or in verse, should not be mistaken for the narratee. The one is real, the other fictive. If it should occur that the reader bears an astonishing resemblance to the narratee, this is an exception and not the rule.

Neither should the narratee be confused with the virtual reader. Every author, provided he is writing for someone other than himself, develops his narrative as a function of a certain type of reader whom he bestows with certain qualities, faculties, and inclinations according to his opinion of men in general (or in particular) and according to the obligations he feels should be respected. This virtual reader is different from the real reader: writers frequently have a public they don't deserve. He is also distinct from the narratee. In *La Chute,* Clamence's narratee is not identical to the reader envisioned by Camus: after all, he's a lawyer visiting Amsterdam. It goes without saying that a virtual reader and a narratee can be alike, but once again it would be an exception.

Finally, we should not confuse the narratee with the ideal reader, although a remarkable likeness can exist between the two. For a writer, an ideal reader would be one who would understand perfectly and would approve entirely the least of his words, the most subtle of his intentions. For a critic, an ideal reader would perhaps be one capable of interpreting the infinity of texts that, according to certain critics, can

---

[4] See Tzvetan Todorov, "Les Hommes-récits," *Poétique de la prose* (Paris: Seuil, 1971), pp. 78–91. *Au.*
[5] See Tzvetan Todorov, "Le Récit primitif," in ibid., pp. 66–77. *Au.*

be found in one specific text. On the one hand, the narratees for whom the narrator multiplies his explanations and justifies the particularities of his narrative are numerous and cannot be thought of as constituting the ideal readers dreamed up by a novelist. We need only think of the narratees of *Le Père Goriot* and *Vanity Fair*. On the other hand, these narratees are too inept to be capable of interpreting even a rather restricted group of texts within the text.

If narratees are distinct from real, virtual, or ideal readers,[6] they very often differ from each other as well. Nonetheless, it should be possible to describe each one of them as a function of the same categories and according to the same models. It is necessary to identify at least some of these characteristics as well as some of the ways in which they vary and combine with each other. These characteristics must be situated with reference to a sort of "zero-degree" narratee, a concept which it is now time to define.

In the first place, the zero-degree narratee knows the tongue (*langue*) and the language(s) (*langage[s]*) of the narrator. In his case, to know a tongue is to know the meanings (*dénotations*)—the signifieds as such and, if applicable, the referents—of all the signs that constitute it; this does not include knowledge of the connotations (the subjective values that have been attached to them). It also involves a perfect mastery of grammar but not of the (infinite) paragrammatical possibilities. It is the ability to note semantic and/or syntactic ambiguities and to be able to resolve these difficulties from the context. It is the capacity to recognize the grammatical incorrectness or oddness of any sentence or syntagm—by reference to the linguistic system being used.[7]

Beyond this knowledge of language, the zero-degree narratee has certain faculties of reasoning that are often only the corollaries of this knowledge. Given a sentence or a series of sentences, he is able to grasp the presuppositions and the consequences.[8] The zero-degree narratee knows narrative grammar, the rules by which any story is elaborated.[9] He knows, for example, that a minimal complete narrative sequence consists in the passage from a given situation to the inverse situation. He knows that the narrative possesses a temporal dimension and that it necessitates relations of causality. Finally, the zero-degree narratee possesses a sure memory, at least in regard to the events of the narrative about which he has been informed and the consequences that can be drawn from them.

---

[6] For convenience's sake, we speak (and will speak often) of readers. It is obvious that a narratee should not be mistaken for a listener—real, virtual, or ideal. *Au.*

[7] This description of the linguistic capabilities of the zero-degree narratee nonetheless raises many problems. Thus, it is not always easy to determine the meaning(s) (*dénotation[s]*) of a given term and it becomes necessary to fix in time the language (*langue*) known to the narratee, a task that is sometimes difficult when working from the text itself. In addition, the narrator can manipulate a language in a personal way. Confronted by certain idiosyncrasies that are not easy to situate in relation to the text, do we say that the narratee experiences them as exaggerations, as errors, or on the contrary do they seem perfectly normal to him? Because of these difficulties and many others as well, the description of the narratee and his language cannot always be exact. It is, nevertheless, to a large extent reproducible. *Au.*

[8] We use these terms as they are used in modern logic. *Au.*

[9] See in this regard, Gerald Prince, *A Grammar of Stories: An Introduction* (The Hague: Mouton, 1973). A formal description of the rules followed by all narratives can be found in this work. *Au.*

Thus, he does not lack positive characteristics. But he also does not want negative traits. He can thus only follow a narrative in a well-defined and concrete way and is obliged to acquaint himself with the events by reading from the first page to the last, from the initial word to the final word. In addition, he is without any personality or social characteristics. He is neither good nor bad, pessimistic nor optimistic, revolutionary nor bourgeois, and his character, his position in society, never colors his perception of the events described to him. Moreover, he knows absolutely nothing about the events or characters mentioned and he is not acquainted with the conventions prevailing in that world or in any other world. Just as he doesn't understand the connotations of a certain turn of phrase, he doesn't realize what can be evoked by this or that situation, this or that novelistic action. The consequences of this are very important. Without the assistance of the narrator, without his explanations and the information supplied by him, the narratee is able neither to interpret the value of an action nor to grasp its repercussions. He is incapable of determining the morality or immorality of a character, the realism or extravagance of a description, the merits of a rejoinder, the satirical intention of a tirade. And how would he be able to do so? By virtue of what experience, what knowledge, or what system of values?

More particularly, a notion as fundamental as verisimilitude only counts very slightly for him. Indeed, verisimilitude is always defined in relation to another text, whether this text be public opinion, the rules of a literary genre, or "reality." The zero-degree narratee, however, is acquainted with no texts and in the absence of commentary, the adventures of Don Quixote would seem as ordinary to him as those of Passemurailles (an individual capable of walking through walls) or of the protagonists of *Une Belle Journée.*[10] The same would hold true for relations of implicit causality. If I learn in *La Légende de Saint Julien l'Hospitalier* that "Julien believes he has killed his father and faints," I establish a causal relationship between these two propositions founded upon a certain common sense logic, my experience of the world, and my knowledge of certain novelistic conventions. We are, moreover, aware that one of the mechanisms of the narrative process "is the confusion of consecutiveness and consequence, what comes *after* being read in the narrative as caused by. . . ."[11] But the narratee with no experience and no common sense does not perceive relations of implicit causality and does not fall victim to this confusion. Finally, the zero-degree narratee does not organize the narrative as a function of the major codes of reading studied by Roland Barthes in *S/Z.* He doesn't know how to unscramble the different voices that shape the narration. After all, as Barthes has said: "The code is a convergence of quotations, a structural mirage . . . the resulting units . . . made up of fragments of this something which always has *already* been read, seen, done, lived: the code is the groove of this *already.* Referring back to what has been written, that is, to the Book (of culture, of life, of life as culture), the code makes the text a prospectus of this Book."[12] For the zero-degree narratee, there is no *already,* there is no Book.

---

[10] On verisimilitude, see the excellent issue 11 of *Communications* (1968). *Au.*

[11] Barthes, "Introduction à l'analyse structurale des récits," p. 10. It should be noted that while this confusion has been very much exploited, it is not at all necessary for the development of a narrative. *Au.*

[12] Roland Barthes, *S/Z* (Paris: Seuil, 1970), pp. 27–28. *Au.*

THE SIGNALS OF THE NARRATEE

Every narratee possesses the characteristics that we have enumerated except when an indication to the contrary is supplied in the narration intended for him: he knows, for example, the language employed by the narrator, he is gifted with an excellent memory, he is unfamiliar with everything concerning the characters who are presented to him. It is not rare that a narrative might deny or contradict these characteristics: a certain passage might underline the language-related difficulties of the narratee, another passage might disclose that he suffers from amnesia, yet another passage might emphasize his knowledge of the problems being discussed. It is on the basis of these deviations from the characteristics of the zero-degree narratee that the portrait of a specific narratee is gradually constituted.

Certain indications supplied by the text concerning a narratee are sometimes found in a section of the narrative that is not addressed to him. One has only to think of *L'Immoraliste,* the two *Justine*s, or *Heart of Darkness* to verify that not only the physical appearance, the personality, and civil status of a narratee can be discussed in this fashion, but also his experience and his past. These indications may precede the portion of the narrative intended for the narratee, or may follow, interrupt, or frame it. Most often, they confirm what the rest of the narration has revealed to us. At the beginning of *L'Immoraliste,* for example, we learn that Michel has not seen his narratees for three years and the story he tells them quickly confirms this fact. Nonetheless, sometimes these indications contradict the narrative and emphasize certain differences between the narratee as conceived by the narrator and as revealed by another voice. The few words spoken by Doctor Spielvogel at the end of *Portnoy's Complaint* reveal that he is not what the narrative has led us to believe.[13]

Nevertheless, the portrait of a narratee emerges above all from the narrative addressed to him. If we consider that any narration is composed of a series of signals directed to the narratee, two major categories of signals can be distinguished. On the one hand there are those signals that contain no reference to the narratee or, more precisely, no reference differentiating him from the zero-degree narratee. On the other hand, there are those signals that, on the contrary, define him as a specific narratee and make him deviate from the established norms. In *Un Coeur simple* a sentence such as "She threw herself on the ground" would fall into the first category; this sentence reveals nothing in particular about the narratee while still permitting him to appreciate the sorrow of Félicité. On the contrary, a sentence such as "His entire person produced in her that confusion into which we are all thrown by the spectacle of extraordinary men" not only records the reactions of the heroine in the presence of M. Bourais, but also informs us that the narratee has experienced the same feelings in the presence of extraordinary individuals. By interpreting all signals of the narration as a function of the narratee, we can obtain a partial reading of the text, but a well-defined and reproducible reading. By regrouping and studying the signals of the second cate-

---

[13] We should undoubtedly distinguish the "virtual" narratee from the "real" narratee in a more systematic manner. But this distinction would perhaps not be very helpful. *Au.*

gory, we can reconstruct the portrait of the narratee, a portrait more or less distinct, original, and complete depending upon the text considered.

The signals belonging to the second category are not always easy to recognize or to interpret. In fact, if many of them are quite explicit, others are much less so. The indications supplied on the narratee at the beginning of *Le Père Goriot* are very clear and present no problem: "That's what you will do, you who hold this book with a white hand, you who settle back in a well-padded armchair. . . ." But the first two sentences of *The Sun Also Rises* present more difficulty. Jake does not explicitly state that, according to his narratee, to say that a man has been a boxing champion is to express admiration for him. It is enough for him to imply this: "Robert Cohn was once middleweight boxing champion of Princeton. Do not think that I am very much impressed by that as a boxing title, but it meant a lot to Cohn." A greater number of indications concerning this or that narratee are even more indirect. Obviously, any indication, whether explicit or indirect, should be interpreted on the basis of the text itself, using as a guide the language employed, its presuppositions, the logical consequences that it entails, and the already established knowledge of the narratee.

The signals capable of portraying the narratee are quite varied and one can easily distinguish several types that are worth discussing. In the first place, we should mention all passages of a narrative in which the narrator refers directly to the narratee. We retain in this category statements in which the narrator designates the narratee by such words as "reader" or "listener" and by such expressions as "my dear" or "my friend." In the event that the narration may have identified a specific characteristic of the narratee, for example, his profession or nationality, passages mentioning this characteristic should also be considered in this first category. Thus, if the narratee is a lawyer, all information concerning lawyers in general is pertinent. Finally, we should retain all passages in which the addressee is designated by second-person pronouns and verb forms.

Besides those passages referring quite explicitly to the narratee, there are passages that, although not written in the second person, imply a narratee and describe him. When Marcel in *A la recherche du temps perdu* writes: "Besides, most often, we didn't stay at home, we went for a walk," the "we" excludes the narratee. On the contrary, when he declares: "Undoubtedly, in these coincidences which are so perfect, when reality withdraws and applies itself to what we have dreamt about for so long a time, it hides it from us entirely," the "we" includes the narratee.[14] Often an impersonal expression or an indefinite pronoun can only refer to the narratee: "But, the work completed, perhaps one will have shed a few tears *intra muros* and *extra.*"

Then again, there are often numerous passages in a narrative that, though they contain apparently no reference—even an ambiguous one—to a narratee, describe him in greater or lesser detail. Accordingly, certain parts of a narrative may be presented in the form of questions or pseudo-questions. Sometimes these questions originate neither with a character nor with the narrator who merely repeats them. These questions must then be attributed to the narratee and we should note what excites his curiosity, the kinds of problems he would like to resolve. In *Le Père Goriot,* for ex-

---

[14] Note that even an "I" can designate a "you." *Au.*

ample, it is the narratee who makes inquiries about the career of M. Poiret: "What had he been? But perhaps he had been employed at the Ministry of Justice. . . ." Sometimes, however, the narrator addresses questions to the narratee himself, some of whose knowledge and defenses are thus revealed in the process. Marcel will address a pseudo-question to his narratee asking him to explain the slightly vulgar, and for that reason surprising, behavior of Swann: "But who has not seen unaffected royal princesses . . . spontaneously adopt the language of old bores? . . ."

Other passages are presented in the form of negations. Certain of these passages are no more the extension of a given character's statement than they are the response to a given narrator's question. It is rather the beliefs of the narratee that these passages contradict, his preoccupations that are attacked, and his questions that are silenced. The narrator of *Les Faux-Monnayeurs* vigorously rejects the theory advanced by the narratee to explain Vincent Molinier's nocturnal departures: "No, it was not to his mistress that Vincent Molinier went each evening." Sometimes a partial negation can be revelatory. In *A la recherche du temps perdu*, the narrator, while believing that the narratee's conjectures about the extraordinary suffering of Swann are well-founded, at the same time finds them insufficient: "This suffering which he felt resembled nothing he had ever thought possible. Not only because in his hours of deepest doubt he had rarely imagined anything so painful, but because even when he imagined this thing, it remained vague, uncertain. . . ."

There are also passages that include a term with demonstrative significance that instead of referring to an anterior or ulterior element of the narrative, refers to another text, to extra-textual experience (*hors-texte*) known to the narrator and his narratee. "He looked at the tomb and there buried his final tear as a young man . . . one of those tears which though they fall to the earth flow upward to the heavens." From these few lines, the narratee of *Le Père Goriot* recognizes the kind of tears buried by Rastignac. He has certainly already heard about them, without a doubt he has seen them, perhaps he has shed some himself.

Comparisons or analogies found in a narration also furnish us with information more or less valuable. Indeed, the second term of a comparison is always assumed to be known better than the first. On this basis, we can assume that the narratee of *The Gold Pot*, for example, has already heard the bursting of thunder ("The voice faded like the faraway muffled rumbling of thunder"), and we can accordingly begin the partial reconstruction of the type of universe with which he is familiar.

But perhaps the most revelatory signals and at times the most difficult to grasp and describe in a satisfactory way are those we shall call—for lack of a more appropriate term—*over-justifications (surjustifications)*. Any narrator more or less explains the world inhabited by his characters, motivates their acts, and justifies their thoughts. If it occurs that these explanations and motivations are situated at the level of meta-language, meta-commentary, or meta-narration, they are over-justifications. When the narrator of *La Chartreuse de Parme* advises the narratee that at La Scala "it's customary for visits to the boxes to last only twenty minutes or so," he is only thinking about supplying the narratee with information necessary for the understanding of the events. On the other hand, when he asks to be excused for a poorly phrased sentence, when he excuses himself for having to interrupt his narrative, when he confesses himself incapable of describing well a certain feeling, these are over-justifications that he employs. Over-justifications always provide us with interesting details about the narratee's personality, even though they often do so in an indirect way; in overcoming the narratee's defenses, in prevailing over his prejudices, in allaying his apprehensions, they reveal them.

The narratee's signals—those that describe him as well as those that only provide him with information—can pose many problems for the reader who would wish to classify them in order to arrive at a portrait of the narratee or a certain reading of the text. It's not simply a question of their being sometimes difficult to notice, to grasp, or to explain, but in certain narratives, one can find contradictory signals. Sometimes they originate with a narrator who wishes to amuse himself at the expense of the narratee or underscore the arbitrariness of the text; often the world presented is a world in which the principles of contradiction known to us don't exist or are not applicable; finally, the contradictions—the entirely obvious ones—often result from the different points of view that the narrator strives to reproduce faithfully. Nonetheless it occurs that not all contradictory data can be entirely explained in this fashion. In these cases, they should be attributed to the author's ineptness—or temperament. In many pornographic novels, in the worst as well as in the best, the narrator, like the heroes of *La Cantatrice chauve,* will first describe a character as having blond hair, large breasts, and a bulging stomach and then on the following page will speak with as much conviction of her black hair, her flat stomach, and her small breasts. Coherence is certainly not an imperative for the pornographic genre in which a wild variation is the rule rather than the exception. It nonetheless remains that in these cases, it is difficult—if not impossible—to interpret the semantic material presented to the narratee.

Sometimes it is the signals describing the narratee that form a strangely disparate collection. Indeed, every signal relating to a narratee need not continue or confirm a preceding signal or announce a signal to follow. There are narratees who change much as narrators do or who have a rich enough personality to embrace various tendencies and feelings. But the contradictory nature of certain narratees does not always result from a complex personality or a subtle evolution. The first pages of *Le Père Goriot* indicate that a Parisian narratee would be able to appreciate "the particularities of this scene full of local observations and color." But these opening pages contradict what they have just asserted in accusing the narratee of insensitivity and in judging him guilty of mistaking reality for fiction. This contradiction will never be resolved. On the contrary, other contradictions will be added and it will become more and more difficult to know whom the narrator addresses. A case of ineptitude? Perhaps Balzac does not worry about technical details and sometimes commits errors which in a Flaubert or a Henry James would be shocking. But this is a revelatory instance of ineptitude: Balzac, who is obsessed with problems of identity—these problems are certainly very important in *Le Père Goriot*—does not manage to decide who will be his narratee.

Despite the questions posed, the difficulties raised, the errors committed, it is evident that the kinds of signals used, their respective numbers, and their distribution determine to a certain extent the different types of narrative.[15] Narratives in which

---

[15] See, in this regard, Gérard Genette, "Vraisemblance et motivation," in his *Figures II* (Paris: Seuil, 1969). *Au.*

explanations and motivations abound (*Don Quixote* and *Tristram Shandy, Les Illusions perdues* and *Le Temps retrouvé*) are very different from those in which explanations and motivations play a limited role (*The Killers, The Maltese Falcon, La Jalousie*). The former are often by narrators who find the dimension of discourse (*discours*) more important than that of narrative (*récit*) or who are acutely aware of the gratuitousness—and even the falseness—of any narrative or of a certain type of narrative and consequently try to exorcise it. The latter are produced by narrators who feel perfectly at ease in the narrative (*récit*) or who, for different reasons, wish to be transported from their usual surroundings. Moreover, explanations and motivations can present themselves for what they are or, on the other hand, can dissimulate their nature by disguising themselves more or less completely. A narrator of Balzac or Stendhal does not hesitate to declare the necessity of explaining a thought, an act, or a situation. "We are obliged at this point to interrupt for a moment the story of this bold undertaking in order to supply an indispensable detail which will explain in part the duchess' courage in advising Fabrice upon this quite dangerous flight." But Flaubert's narrators—in particular after *Madame Bovary*—often play upon ambiguity and we no longer know exactly if one sentence explains another or if it merely follows or precedes it: "He assembled an army. It became bigger. He became famous. He was sought after." Explanations can also be presented in the form of universal rules or general laws as in Balzac and Zola or can avoid as much as possible all generality as in the novels of Sartre and Simone de Beauvoir. Explanations can contradict or confirm one another, be repeated or used a single time, appear only at strategic moments or occur anywhere in the narrative. Each time a different type of narration is constructed.

CLASSIFICATION OF NARRATEES

Thanks to the signals describing the narratee, we are able to characterize any narration according to the type of narratee to whom it is addressed. It would be useless, because too long, too complicated, and too imprecise, to distinguish different categories of narratees according to their temperament, their civil status, or their beliefs. On the other hand, it would be comparatively easy to classify narratees according to their narrative situation, to their position in reference to the narrator, the characters, and the narration.

Many narrations appear to be addressed to no one in particular: no character is regarded as playing the role of narratee and no narratee is mentioned by the narrator either directly ("Without a doubt, dear reader, you have never been confined in a glass bottle") or indirectly ("We could hardly do otherwise than pluck one of its flowers and present it to the reader"). Just as a detailed study of a novel such as *L'Education sentimentale* or *Ulysses* reveals the presence of a narrator who tries to be invisible and to intervene as little as possible in the course of the events, so too a thorough examination of a narration that appears to have no narratee—the two works mentioned above as well as *Sanctuary, L'Etranger,* and *Un Coeur simple*—permits his discovery. The narrator of *Un Coeur simple,* for example, does not refer a single time to a narratee in an explicit manner. In his narrative, nonetheless, there are numerous passages indicating more or less clearly that he is addressing someone. It is thus that the narrator identifies the individuals whose proper names he mentions: "Robelin, the farmer from Geoffosses . . . Liébard, the farmer from Touques . . . M. Bourais, a former lawyer." It cannot be for himself that he identifies Robelin, Liébard, or M. Bourais; it must be for his narratee. Moreover, the narrator often resorts to comparisons in order to describe a character or situate an event, and each comparison defines more precisely the type of universe known to the narratee. Finally, the narrator sometimes refers to extratextual experiences ("that confusion into which we are all thrown by the spectacle of extraordinary men"), which provide proof of the narratee's existence and information about his nature. Thus, even though the narratee may be invisible in a narration, he nonetheless exists and is never entirely forgotten.

In many other narrations, if the narratee is not represented by a character, he is at least mentioned explicitly by the narrator. The latter refers to him more or less frequently and his references can be quite direct (*Eugene Onegin, The Gold Pot, Tom Jones*) or quite indirect (*The Scarlet Letter, The Old Curiosity Shop, Les Faux-Monnayeurs*). Like the narratee of *Un Coeur simple,* these narratees are nameless and their role in the narrative is not always very important. Yet because of the passages that designate them in an explicit manner, it is easy to draw their portrait and to know what their narrator thinks of them. Sometimes, in *Tom Jones,* the narrator supplies so much information about his narratee, takes him aside so often, lavishes his advice upon him so frequently, that the latter becomes as clearly defined as any character.

Often instead of addressing—explicitly or implicitly—a narratee who is not a character, the narrator recounts his story to someone who is (*Heart of Darkness, Portnoy's Complaint, Les Infortunes de la vertu*). This character can be described in a more or less detailed manner. We know practically nothing about Doctor Spielvogel in *Portnoy's Complaint,* except that he is not lacking in perspicacity. On the other hand, in *Les Infortunes de la vertu,* we are informed about all of Juliette's life.

The narratee-character might play no other role in the narrative than that of narratee (*Heart of Darkness*). But he might also play other roles. It is not rare, for example, for him to be at the same time a narrator. In *L'Immoraliste,* one of the three individuals listening to Michel writes a long letter to his brother. In this letter, he repeats the story told to him by his friend, entreats his brother to shake Michel from his unhappiness, and records his own reactions to the narrative as well as the circumstances that led to his being present at its telling. Sometimes the narratee of a story can be at the same time its narrator. He doesn't intend the narration to be for anyone other than himself. In *La Nausée,* for example, as in most novels written in the form of a diary, Roquentin counts on being the only reader of his journal.

Then again, the narratee-character can be more or less affected, more or less influenced by the narrative addressed to him. In *Heart of Darkness,* the companions of Marlowe are not transformed by the story that he recounts to them. In *L'Immoraliste,* the three narratees, if they are not really different from what they were before Michel's account, are nonetheless "overcome by a strange feeling of malaise." And in *La Nausée,* as in many other works in which the narrator constitutes his own narratee, the latter is gradually and profoundly changed by the events he recounts for himself.

Finally, the narratee-character can represent for the narration someone more or less essential, more or less irreplaceable as a narratee. In *Heart of Darkness,* it's not necessary for Marlow to have his comrades on the *Nellie* as narratees. He would be able to recount his story to any other group; perhaps he would be able to refrain from telling it at all. On the other hand, in *L'Immoraliste,* Michel wished to address his friends and for that reason gathered them around him. Their presence in Algeria holds out hope: they will certainly not condemn him, they will perhaps understand him, and they will certainly help him get over his current situation. And in *A Thousand and One Nights,* to have the caliph as narratee is the difference between life and death for Scheherazade. If he refuses to listen to her, she will be killed. He is thus the only narratee whom she can have.

Whether or not he assumes the role of character, whether or not he is irreplaceable, whether he plays several roles or just one, the narratee can be a listener (*L'Immoraliste, Les Infortunes de la vertu, A Thousand and One Nights*) or a reader (*Adam Bede, Le Père Goriot, Les Faux-Monnayeurs*). Obviously, a text may not necessarily say whether the narratee is a reader or a listener. In such cases, it could be said that the narratee is a reader when the narration is written (*Hérodias*) and a listener when the narration is oral (*La Chanson de Roland*).

. . . We could probably think of other distinctions or establish other categories, but in any case, we can see how much more precise and more refined the typology of narrative would be if it were based not only upon narrators but also upon narratees. The same type of narrator can address very different types of narratees. Thus, Louis (*Le Noeud de vipères*), Salavin (*Journal de Salavin*), and Roquentin (*La Nausée*) are three characters who all keep a journal and who are very conscious of writing. But Louis changes narratees several times before deciding to write for himself; Slavin does not regard himself as the sole reader of his journal; and Roquentin writes exclusively for himself. Then again, very different narrators can address narratees of the same type. The narrators of *Un Coeur simple* and *La Condition humaine* as well as Meursault in *L'Etranger* all address a narratee who is not a character, who doesn't know them and who is not familiar with the individuals presented in the text nor with the events recounted.

Nonetheless, it is not only for a typology of the narrative genre and for a history of novelistic techniques that the notion of the narratee is important. Indeed, this notion is more interesting, because it permits us to study better the way in which a narration functions. In all narrations, a dialogue is established between the narrator(s), the narratee(s), and the character(s).[16] This dialogue develops—and consequently the narration also—as a function of the distance separating them from each other. In distinguishing the different categories of narratees, we have already used this concept, but without dwelling upon it too much: it is clear that a narratee who has participated in the events recorded is, in one sense, much closer to the characters than a narratee who has never even heard of them. But the notion of distance should be generalized. Whatever the point of view adopted—moral, intellectual, emotional, physical—narrator(s), narratee(s), and character(s) can be more or less close to each other ranging from the most perfect identification to the most complete opposition.

---

[16] We follow here in modifying the perspective, Booth, *The Rhetoric of Fiction,* pp. 155 ff. *Au.*

. . . As there are often several narrators, several narratees, and several characters in a text, the complexity of the rapports and the variety of the distances that are established between them can be quite significant. In any case, these rapports and these distances determine to a great extent the way in which certain values are praised and others are rejected in the course of a narration and the way in which certain events are emphasized and others are nearly passed over in silence. They determine as well the tone and the very nature of the narration. In *Les Cloches de Bâle,* for example, the tone changes completely—and cannot but change—once the narrator decides to proclaim his friendship for the narratee and to speak to him more honestly and more directly than he had previously: abandoning romantic extravagance, he becomes quasi-documentary; leaving behind false detachment, he becomes brotherly. On the other hand, many ironic effects in narration depend upon the differences existing between two images of the narratee or between two (groups of) narratees (*Les Infortunes de la vertu, Werther*), upon the distance existing between narrator and narratee on the one hand and character on the other (*Un Amour de Swann*), or yet again upon the distance existing between narrator and narratee (*Tom Jones*). The complexity of a situation results sometimes from the instability of the distances existing between the narrator, the narratee, and the characters. If Michel's guilt—or innocence—is not clearly established, it is partly because several times he shows himself capable of overcoming the distance separating him from his friends, or, if one prefers, because his friends are unsure of how much distance to put between themselves and him. . . .

THE NARRATEE'S FUNCTIONS

The type of narratee that we find in a given narrative, the relations that tie him to narrators, characters, and other narratees, the distances that separate him from ideal, virtual, or real readers partially determine the nature of this narrative. But the narratee exercises other functions that are more or less numerous and important and are more or less specific to him. It will be worth the effort to enumerate these functions and to study them in some detail.

The most obvious role of the narratee, a role that he always plays in a certain sense, is that of relay between the narrator and the reader(s), or rather between the author and the reader(s). Should certain values have to be defended or certain ambiguities clarified, this can easily be done by means of asides addressed to the narratee. Should the importance of a series of events be emphasized, should one reassure or make uneasy, justify certain actions or underscore their arbitrariness, this can always be done by addressing signals to the narratee. In *Tom Jones,* for example, the narrator explains to the narratee that prudence is necessary for the preservation of virtue, an explanation that allows us to judge better his hero, virtuous but imprudent: "Prudence and circumspection are necessary even to the best men. . . . It is not enough that your designs, nay, that your actions, are intrinsically good, you must take care they shall appear so." Likewise, we know that although Legrandin is a snob, he is not lying when he protests against snobbery because Marcel says quite clearly to his narratee: "And indeed, that doesn't mean that Legrandin was not sincere when he inveighed against snobs." Indeed, the mediation doesn't always operate that directly: thus, narrator-narratee relations are sometimes developed in the ironic mode and the reader cannot always interpret literally the statements of the former to the latter. There exist other conceivable relays than direct and explicit asides addressed to the narratee, other possibilities of mediation between authors and readers. Dialogues, metaphors, symbolic situations, allusions to a particular system of thought or to a certain work of art are some of the ways of manipulating the reader, guiding his judgments, and controlling his reactions. Moreover, those are the methods preferred by many modern novelists, if not the majority of them; perhaps because they accord or seem to accord more freedom to the reader, perhaps because they oblige him to participate more actively in the development of the narrative, or perhaps simply because they satisfy a certain concern for realism. The role of the narratee as mediator is rather reduced in these cases. Everything must still pass via the narratee since everything—metaphors, allusions, dialogues—is still addressed to him; but nothing is modified, nothing is clarified for the reader by this passage. Whatever the advantages may be of this type of mediator it should nonetheless be recognized that from a certain point of view, direct and explicit statements by the narrator to the narratee are the most economical and the most effective sort of mediation. A few sentences suffice to establish the true significance of an unexpected act or the true nature of a character; a few words suffice to facilitate the interpretation of a complex situation. Although we can question indefinitely Stephen's esthetic maturity in *Portrait of the Artist as a Young Man* or the significance of a particular act in *A Farewell to Arms,* we always know exactly—or almost always—according to the text, what to think of Fabrice and la Sanseverina or of the intrigues of Mlle. Michonneau.[17]

Besides the function of mediation, the narratee exercises in any narration a function of characterization. . . . In the case of narrator-characters, the function of characterization is important although it can be reduced to a minimum even here: because he is at a distance from everything and from himself, because his strangeness and solitude depend upon this distance, Meursault would not know how to engage in a true dialogue with his narratee and, thus, cannot be described by this dialogue. Nonetheless, the relations that a narrator-character establishes with his narratee reveal as much—if not more—about his character than any other element in the narrative. In *La Religieuse,* Sister Suzanne, because of her conception of the narratee and her asides addressed to him, emerges as much less naïve and much more calculating and coquettish than she would like to appear.

. . . Moreover, the relations between the narrator and the narratee in a text may underscore one theme, illustrate another, or contradict yet another. Often the theme refers directly to the narrative situation and it is the narration as theme that these relations reveal. In *A Thousand and One Nights,* for instance, the theme of narration as life is emphasized by the attitude of Scheherazade toward the caliph and vice-versa: the heroine will die if her narratee decides not to listen to her any more, just as other characters in the narrative die because he will not listen to them: ultimately, any narrative is impossible without a narratee. But often, themes that do not concern the nar-

---

[17] See, in this regard, the book by Wayne C. Booth already mentioned. *Au.*

rative situation—or perhaps concern it only indirectly—reveal the positions of the narrator and the narratee in relation to each other. In *Le Père Goriot,* the narrator maintains relations of power with his narratee. From the very beginning, the narrator tries to anticipate his narratee's objections, to dominate him, and to convince him. All means are used: the narrator coaxes, entreats, threatens, derides, and in the final analysis we suspect that he succeeds in getting the better of his narratee. In the last part of the novel, when Vautrin has been put in prison and Goriot is advancing more and more quickly toward death, the narrator rarely addresses his narratee. This is because the narrator has won the battle. He is now sure of his effects, of his domination, and he need no longer do anything but recount the story. This sort of war, this desire for power, can be found at the level of the characters. On the level of the events as well as on the level of narration, the same struggle takes place.

If the narratee contributes to the thematic of a narrative, he is also always part of the narrative framework, often of a particularly concrete framework in which the narrator(s) and narratee(s) are all characters (*Heart of Darkness, L'Immoraliste, The Decameron*). The effect is to make the narrative seem more natural. The narratee like the narrator plays an undeniable *verisimilating (vraisemblabilisant)* role. Sometimes this concrete framework provides the model by which a work or narration develops. In *The Decameron* or in *L'Heptameron,* it is expected that each of the narratees will in turn become a narrator. More than a mere sign of realism or an index of verisimilitude, the narratee represents in these circumstances an indispensable element for the development of the narrative.

. . . Finally it sometimes happens that we must study the narratee in order to discover a narrative's fundamental thrust. In *La Chute,* for example, it is only by studying the reactions of Clamence's narratee that we can know whether the protagonist's arguments are so powerful that they cannot be resisted, or whether, on the contrary, they constitute a skillful but unconvincing appeal. To be sure, the narratee doesn't say a single word throughout the entire novel and we don't even know if Clamence addresses himself or someone else: we only understand, from the narrator's remarks, that his narratee, like himself, is a bourgeois, in his forties, a Parisian, familiar with Dante and the Bible, a lawyer. . . . Nevertheless, this ambiguity emphasizing the essential duplicity of the protagonist's world does not represent a problem for the reader who would wish to discover the way in which Clamence is judged in the novel: whatever the identity of the narratee may be, the only thing that counts is the extent of his agreement with the theses of the hero. The latter's discourse shows evidence of a more and more intense resistance on the part of his interlocutor. Clamence's tone becomes more insistent and his sentences more embarrassed as his narrative progresses and his narratee escapes him. Several times in the last part of the novel he even appears seriously shaken. If at the end of *La Chute* Clamence is not defeated, he certainly has not been triumphant. If his values and his vision of the world and men are not entirely false, neither are they incontestably true. There are perhaps other professions than that of judge-penitent and there are perhaps other acceptable ways to live than Clamence's.

The narratee can, thus, exercise an entire series of functions in a narrative: he constitutes a relay between the narrator and the reader, he helps establish the narrative framework, he serves to characterize the narrator, he emphasizes certain themes, he contributes to the development of the plot, he becomes the spokesman for the moral of the work. Obviously, depending upon whether the narrator is skillful or inept, depending upon whether or not problems of narrative technique interest him, and depending upon whether or not his narrative requires it, the narratee will be more or less important, will play a greater or lesser number of roles, will be used in a way more or less subtle and original. Just as we study the narrator to evaluate the economy, the intentions, and the success of a narrative, so too we should examine the narratee in order to understand further and/or differently its mechanisms and significance.

The narratee is one of the fundamental elements of all narration. The thorough examination of what he represents, the study of a narrative work as constituted by a series of signals addressed to him, can lead to a more sharply delineated reading and a deeper characterization of the work. This study can lead also to a more precise typology of the narrative genre and a greater understanding of its evolution. It can provide a better appreciation of the way a narrative functions and a more accurate assessment of its success from a technical point of view. In the final analysis, the study of the narratee can lead us to a better understanding not only of the narrative genre but of all acts of communication.

part III

Ideologies

$\mathbf{A}$ generation ago the approaches to narrative that appear in this section would not have formed any part of what we all needed to know to read literary texts; indeed many of the thoughts expressed here would have been considered heretical. The formalisms that were then in the saddle operated from premises that stressed what was universal in literature. It was presumed that literary meaning was more complicated than the meaning of "everyday" language, that literary texts were ambiguous or indeed bore multiple levels of meaning, each of which needed to be explored. Nevertheless, it was taken as given that this complex of meaning was not a private meaning subjectively produced by the operations of a specific reader, but a public meaning objectively available to any seeker. So reading was supposed to be universal in two senses, as a participle and as a verbal noun. Reading as an action was universal in that, from our own perspectives as readers, we were expected to leave behind us in our engagement with the text whatever personal baggage we had brought along—including our race and ethnicity, our gender and sexual orientation—and to read the text as universal human beings. But our reading was universal in a second sense as well. For the canon of the works we studied, our reading, was thought of as selected and sifted by the impersonal forces of Time operating through the collective taste and judgment of humanity: what had survived was only the greatest—the most powerful and the most universal. Reading those texts connected us with a common culture that they collectively expressed: a common American culture, perhaps, or that of Western civilization. That was then; today things are very different.

First and most obviously, the canon of the narrative we study has drastically shifted. Today it seems almost embarrassing to think how seriously we once took the debate over F. R. Leavis's vision of the "great tradition" of the novel—a pantheon running from Jane Austen and Emily Brontë through Dickens, George Eliot and Henry James to the modernists Joseph Conrad and D. H. Lawrence. These were the greats: life was too short to bother with secondary masters such as Fielding or

Woolf. Today Leavis's reading list looks both obvious and parochial. Lawrence's realism now looks a lot like that of the other high modernists, and modernism itself no longer seems the goal of history it once did. Since Lawrence and Hemingway, we have played the postmodern games of Nabokov and Calvino, and slid on to the dirty realism of Carver and the magical realism of García Marquez. Nor does contemporary anglophone culture any longer seem to contain the world: my students are often more excited by the recent novels of Naguib Mahfouz, Salman Rushdie, and Milan Kundera, or by exotic antiques like *The Tale of Genji* or *The Story of the Stone.* They are as likely to do their masters theses on Nella Larsen or Kazuo Ishiguro or Amy Tan as on Dickens or Hawthorne or Joyce.

However, it is not only that our interests have broadened to include those who were Others, racially or culturally. We can no longer view the canonized "great tradition" as an unquestionable fact of life, as something given. The canon of literature is not constructed by any single magisterial critic, even one as magisterial as F. R. Leavis. It is constructed by thousands of relatively privileged individuals: literary agents, editors, publishers, teachers, even writers of textbooks like the one you have in your hand. Their decisions to reprint this work rather than that one shape the reading of the present and the future.

And those constructions are unlikely to be ideologically neutral: As Nina Baym suggests in her well-known essay, "Melodramas of Beset Manhood," one construction, the Great American Novel, seems to have been designed purposely to exclude everyone but white males. By defining the key American issue as the Frontier (as Frederick Jackson Turner had proposed), by presuming that the key American novels must deal with the key American issues, the important texts must be the ones which deal with that edge-phenomenon, the intersection of wild nature and civilized culture: Cooper's Leatherstocking novels, Hawthorne's *Scarlet Letter,* Melville's *Moby-Dick,* Twain's *Huckleberry Finn.* . . . With the issue so defined, no women need apply. But the logic is of course less than impeccable: why must there be one key American issue? And why must great fiction deal with major world-historical events? Surely Austen wrote great novels about getting married; Eliot about the struggle to be true to oneself in a leveling society. There seems to be something wrong about the way the question has been laid out about the American novel.

It may have become obvious that the canon cannot remain a closed club for white heterosexual males, but it is not so obvious how it can be corrected in practice. Currently trends seem to be favoring the creation of "countercanons": separate groupings of texts by women, by African Americans, by Latinos and Latinas, by Asian-Americans and Native Americans. These courses have the benefit of giving the reader a bit of depth on each of these subjects. But there may be a down side. Robert Hemenway—author of a prize-winning biography of Zora Neale Hurston— suggests that the current trends toward multiculturalism have only succeeded in ghettoizing African American writers into specific Black Literature courses while leaving the (required) American literature surveys as lily-white as ever.[1]

---

[1] Collections such as the *Heath Anthology of American Literature,* edited by Paul Lauter, seem to be motivated by a desire to radically reshape the American Literature survey course, by providing extensive ma-

Cultural fragmentation also motivates Hortense Spillers's critique in "Who Cuts the Border?" which interrogates the meaning of "America" and the way its definition has been used to exclude from our consideration writers and thinkers from border lands that the United States dominates in all but name. Spillers presents her own notion of a canon and has her own candidate for the key American issue that would control its new borders. For her the crucial moment precedes the establishment of any Frontier: it is that of the colonization of America, the invasion and appropriation of the already populated Americas by Europeans and the forced transplantation of Africans to work there as slaves. Caliban, slave of Prospero, is in effect the antihero of this national epic, the native who contests control of the island with the European colonizer. This conflict between possessors by right and possessors by force recurs wherever the border between Europeans and natives or between Africans and Europeans is cut. Spillers weaves her themes into a reading of William Faulkner's *Absalom, Absalom!*—a text whose structure unravels any notion of a "common American culture."

Whatever the canonical status of their writings, disadvantaged minority groups perforce write what French critics Gilles Deleuze and Félix Guattari call "minor literature." In "What Is Minor Literature?" Deleuze and Guattari take time from their study of novelist Franz Kafka to theorize about the special character his writing derived from his being a Jew in Prague, writing not in Yiddish or Hebrew (the languages of his ethnic group) nor in Czech (the language of a majority of the natives of Prague) but in German, the language of the Austro-Hungarian imperial elite who ruled the province of Bohemia ("an oppressive minority that speaks a language cut off from the masses"). This German language is "deterritorialized" in the sense that it speaks not for a country or province but rather for a diaspora of dispersed people living as Others in a land not their own. Because of this, within such minor literatures "everything . . . is political" and "everything takes on a collective value" as every observation speaks about the hegemonic society from the perspective of the silenced members of the minority. Deleuze and Guattari conclude paradoxically that there can be no major literature except minor literature, arguing that poetic value resides precisely in the tensions inherent in using the language of the oppressors to speak for the oppressed.

Deleuze and Guattari do not hint that narrative by women is "minor literature" in this sense, but that is almost precisely what Rachel Blau DuPlessis argues in "Breaking the Sentence, Breaking the Sequence." Blau DuPlessis takes off from Virginia Woolf's problem of finding a "female sentence" given the fact that the dominant linguistic patterns are set by men. Women perforce write in men's language: to write their own requires that they use male language against itself, in "a dissent from, a self-conscious marking of, dominant statement." Though the novelists about which she writes often resist being labeled as feminists, Blau DuPlessis suggests that "these authors are 'feminist' because they construct a variety of

---

terials by previously ignored individuals and groups. But the *Heath* is 6000 pages of small print, only a small fraction of which can be visited during even a year's course of study. Instructors who are in fullest sympathy with the anthology's motives are (as I hear in private) still trying to figure out how to use it.

oppositional strategies to the depiction of gender institutions in narrative . . . by attacking elements of narrative that repeat, sustain or embody the values in question." Women "break the sentence" in order to "break the sequence": the ideological ordering of patriarchy. One of the terms Blau DuPlessis finds to express the way women can learn to write their own narratives of oppression in the language of the oppressor is "doubled consciousness"—W.E.B. DuBois's phrase for the psychological mode in which African Americans must negotiate with white society.

Although Deleuze and Guattari ignore women, they suggest the strong parallels between Kafka's creation of "minor literature" and the literary creativity of African Americans in the United States. From his own perspective, Henry Louis Gates argues almost the reverse view. In *The Signifying Monkey* and elsewhere, Gates has contended that the key to African American literature is the "speakerly text," written literature that finds its roots in spontaneous black oral performance: sermonizing, testifying, signifying, doing the dozens. It may be typified in Zora Neale Hurston's *Their Eyes Were Watching God,* whose power depends so intensely on its "representation of the speaking black voice in writing." Gates's vision defines a certain canon for African American literature for which Hurston is central and where Jean Toomer, Ralph Ellison, Ishmael Reed, Alice Walker, Toni Morrison fare very well—but it is a canon that marginalizes other sorts of African American writers such as James Baldwin and Paule Marshall. The paradox of producing countercanons is that often they fall afoul of precisely the same issues that troubled Nina Baym about the canon of American fiction: arbitrary criteria that favor one particular group within the countercanon over another.

These canonical questions have a very different relevance to another disadvantaged group: gays and lesbians. Whereas there are various historical and social reasons why women, African Americans, Latinos/as, and Native Americans are poorly represented in the British and American literary canon, there is little doubt that many canonized authors (including Shakespeare, Marlowe, Walt Whitman, Henry James, E. M. Forster, Virginia Woolf) were either gay or bisexual. As Eve Sedgwick suggests in *The Epistemology of the Closet,* the problem is not that gays are inadequately represented in the canon, but that their sexual orientation is often treated as a guilty secret to be hidden from students. When teaching Shakespeare's sonnets addressed to the "noble youth," teachers sometimes tell students to imagine the sonnet as addressed to a woman if they can't cope with the sexual orientation of the poet's passion. But as Sedgwick reminds us, this is ethically questionable: it collaborates with the homophobia in today's society to let readers who are antigay (or even merely squeamish) off the hook in this facile way. It is also intellectually dishonest: we misconstrue the force and quality of feeling in a text, and grossly or subtly misread it, when we "translate" all desire into socially acceptable heterosexual desire.

Sexual desire is also the key issue in Peter Brooks's notion of narrative processing as a "textual erotics" in *Reading for the Plot.* As with an erotic situation, our first introduction to a narrative, its opening paragraph, begins to arouse in us not only a desire but a prospective sense of what might fulfill that desire: a possible ending. The ending is a fulfillment but also a death: the end of the course of the desire. We want to get to that ending eventually, and we would be disturbed if the ending were to be withheld, but at the same time the pleasure would be lost if we got there too soon. The "play" of plot has to do with the circuitous shapings and reshapings of narrative desire. Brooks's essay demonstrates the way in which Freudian ideas about narrative, once crudely attached to the psychic "content" brought by the author to the text, now view psychological forces as intimately engaged in the aesthetic realizations of narrative.

Like Freudian criticism, Marxist analysis of narrative too was once engaged almost exclusively with the "content" of the text, particularly the social content of class attitudes which authors brought as baggage to the artistic process. Fredric Jameson, like Peter Brooks, has revolutionized his own mode of literary analysis by demonstrating that such "content" has a form, just as the formal elements in a text have an ideological content. In "The Realist Floor-Plan," Jameson demonstrates the content of the form down to the level of the sentence. Jameson's analysis of a single short paragraph of Flaubert's *Un Coeur simple* reveals an elaborate network of social symbolism that connects up Flaubert's "realism" with the particular moment in the development of capitalism at which it appears. Typically, the essay concludes with what Jameson calls "metacommentary": a critique of the commentary's "own intellectual instruments" operating "as part of its own working structure." Jameson insists that he must not only situate and historicize Flaubert, but situate his own reading of Flaubert as one that could have been written only in the postmodern world of late capitalism.

The essays by Brooks and Jameson suggest the essential lack of conflict, indeed the interdependence, between formal and structural narratology and the various extra-formal modes of criticism that have arisen in the last two decades. They depend on analogies and connections between formal and social patterns, or formal and psychological ones. Whether the feminist and multicultural concerns can be incorporated within a formal narratology—as Susan Sniader Lanser has been attempting to do—or whether they operate as parallel, mutually supportive modes of analysis, we can expect this convergence to continue, and to continue to enrich our understanding of stories and the ways stories get told.

Robert Hemenway

Robert E. Hemenway was born in 1941 in Sioux City, Iowa, and educated at the University of Omaha and at Kent State University, where he earned his Ph.D. in English in 1966. Hemenway taught at the University of Kentucky and the University of Wyoming, then returned in 1980 to the University of Kentucky where he successively became professor of English, president, and chancellor of the university. Hemenway's books include *The Black Novelist* (1971), the award-winning *Zora Neale Hurston: A Literary Biography* (1977), and *Uncle Remus* (1982). Hemenway has also edited the autobiography of Zora Neale Hurston, *Dust Tracks on a Road,* and has written articles on William Faulkner, Zora Neale Hurston, and V. S. Naipaul. The following essay appeared in *Redefining American Literary History* (1989).

In the American Canon

Once upon a time I was asked to speak at a summer meeting of English department chairpersons. I accepted the invitation with solemn allopathic purpose, sure that I could offer restorative therapy to this honorable group of ex-idealists, these staff officers regularly battered by occupational hazards. I planned to energize those slipping toward ennui and levitate those seeking higher ground amidst that alligator-infested swamp known as "The Department."

Then a funny thing happened on the way to therapy. In what was viewed by some as co-option, by others as the university's death wish, I was ambushed into a chairmanship before I could begin ministrations.

Today, after five years as a department chair, three years as a dean, and one year as a chancellor, I find that although my own idealism may have begun a long, slow slide toward that dismal slough known as "administrative responsibility," the perspective of administration has helped me understand better than ever before the importance of a literary canon. I find that I have lost none of my idealism about what should constitute that canon, and I have become even more convinced that a rethinking of the canon is essential for the health of our discipline.

Instead of retreating from the gains of the 1960s and 1970s, we must continue to evaluate our canon; and we must work even harder to include minority writers in it. In what follows, I wish to bring into question, as the theorists say, some of our ideas about that canon and challenge some of the reactionary self-congratulation (a kind of collective sigh of relief) that has greeted the move toward a return to the traditional library of English and American texts.

Because African American literature is my specialty, my thesis will concentrate on black authors, but much of what I say can apply equally to other ethnic literatures. Chicano, Puerto Rican, Asian American, Native American, and African American writers have been excluded from our classrooms, often by English professors standing in the doorway, waving copies of a mystical writ called the standard canon.

Although it sounds immodest to say so, English professors largely define the literary canon by choosing to teach certain works. The individual professor may respond, consciously or unconsciously, to subtle pressures from other domains of the literary world—the *New York Times Book Review,* the economics of hardcover publishing, the snob appeal of the Great Tradition—but no writer, no book, is likely to be accepted into the canon without the sanction of the university curriculum.

The modern idea of a literary canon originates in ancient ecclesiastical scholarship, where the sacred canon consisted of the books accepted as genuine and inspired holy scriptures. Eventually, any collection of sacred books was called a canon. The word carries a strong sense of authority and has the effect of validating certain works as the most respected and profound writing in the language. Just as the church canonizes saints, scholars and teachers elevate texts to the canon. Having a canon means that you divide the best from the rest. We have always considered canon central to our authority. Murray Krieger has, playfully but seriously, called our respect for the canon a form of "fetishization." He says that "the ground for our primal reading experience" as scholars and teachers "is the elite body of works made sacred by the special attention we grant them."

My very practical purpose is to urge that we press forward in our efforts to expand the canon, that we open the door even wider than before by including black writers in our standard English curriculum at every level and in every way—not just in the obligatory black literature class created during the late 1960s to purchase peace and keep the students from occupying the faculty club, but in all our American literature classes, all our genre courses, all our composition courses.

Even more practically, I want to urge chairpersons to support and encourage scholars engaged in research on African American literary issues, indeed to urge them to protect such scholars—who are almost always young—from hoary mugwumps who advise them to work with "a major author," or who call their areas of specialization "peripheral" to the grand march of Western civilization.

I want to argue for the restructuring of the graduate curriculum so that our departments do not train students ignorant of black literature. Training in black literature will soon become as useful to graduates seeking jobs as training in rhetoric is now. Finally, I advocate a program of faculty development that will help remedy the ignorance of the current professoriate about black literature. There is a body of African American texts, authenticated by scholarly research, that should be a part of every literature teacher's repertoire. In sum, I want the intellectual borders of the English department to expand so that it is not, as it is now, simply the North Atlantic division of the ethnic studies curriculum.

I firmly believe that these actions are essential to the English department of the future, not only because they have distinct pedagogical benefits for a rapidly changing student population but also because an enlarged canon signals health and intellectual vigor for the profession of English studies, just as the promulgation of that canon in the literature classroom contributes directly to health and humanism in the society at large. Although it is now fashionable to congratulate the profession for returning from the streets, for adopting an attitude of aloofness from social issues, such a retreat may also be dangerous to our professional well-being.

We have a president who played on racial fears in his election campaign, suggesting that black rapists were being sponsored by his opponent. Our former president told a national television audience that there was "no racial problem" in his youth. Sociologists see what they call a new "meanness" characterizing our racial interactions. Black students are beaten on campus, and black youths are killed for eating at the wrong pizza joint or for trying to buy a used car in the wrong neighborhood. Crosses burn in the Ivy League. High school seniors in Concord, Massachusetts—the hometown of Ralph Waldo Emerson and Henry David Thoreau, a town whose citizens harbored fugitive slaves on their flight to Canada—list membership in the Ku Klux Klan as one of their yearbook activities, just after the glee club, just before the lacrosse team: "KKK, 3, 4."

Yet at this time our profession seems to be withdrawing from the tentative steps toward democratizing literary study that were taken in the 1960s and 1970s. During those decades, did we really alter our ideas of what constitutes the departmental canon? Many fear that we did. I wish I had more confidence in their anxiety.

As the politics of the country become more conservative, as we begin to feel the effects of a federal judiciary that has passed a litmus test of neoconservative ideology, as the average age of the professoriate approaches fifty, as departments at major universities (all of which are not just predominantly white but white beyond the racial demographics of the society) become gridlocked with tenure, as a secretary of education, in the late 1980s, asked us to compare the value of the literary experience we offer with the pleasure of owning a small business—as these events occur, there will be less and less room for the black author in the modern classroom.

In a speech given in the late 1970s, J. Hillis Miller frankly admitted what he called his "preservative and conservative instincts." Using a linguistic structure whose paradigm is the Apostles' Creed, Miller said, "I believe in the established canon of English and American literature and in the validity of the concept of privileged texts." [I believe in God the Father Almighty, Maker of heaven and earth: and in Jesus Christ his only Son our Lord. . . .] "I think it is more important to read Spenser, Shakespeare, or Milton than to read Borges in translation or even, to say the truth, to read Virginia Woolf."

As we all know, the concept of "privileged" texts is central to modern critical theory. Although my argument is not new, it is, I believe, still valid: the political and class assumptions in the metaphor of privilege all too often reflect the political and class assumptions of the academic study of literature. In fact, by collapsing the idea of the privileged nature of literature in Western culture into the idea of privilege for a class of superior texts (and, incidentally, for those who teach them), Miller provides an unintentional gloss on one of Dennis Brutus's remarks about South Africa. The problem of South Africa, Brutus says, may be less the question of who has the power than a question of the surrender of privilege.[1] The protection for privilege has, of course,

---

[1] Dennis Brutus, "English and the Dynamics of South African Creative Writing," in Fiedler, Leslie, and Houston F. Baker, Jr., Eds., *English Literature: Opening Up the Canon* (Baltimore: Johns Hopkins UP, 1981): 12. *Au.*

been carried to Olympian heights by Allan Bloom in *The Closing of the American Mind.*

Miller's essay appears in an ADE special issue published in 1979 and entitled *The State of the Discipline: 1970s–1980s.* The issue accurately reports on what has crossed the borders into this state named "discipline." It clearly indicates that curricular innovation characterized the 1970s and will continue to be a dominant influence in the future. Paul Hunter sees one of the "healthiest" curricular developments of the 1970s to be the "addition of new literary and quasi-literary areas, such as film, to the canons of our domain." Jonathan Culler urges English department graduate programs to teach psychoanalytic and philosophical texts as literature. Carolyn Heilbrun argues that new courses in feminist criticism will invigorate the department. Nowhere does this special ADE issue mention a black writer or a black critic. In fact, Murray Krieger, one of the contributors, ties the tin can of ethnic studies courses to the anthropological tail of structuralist and poststructuralist poetics, which he sees as an

> enemy to the assumptions on which the definition of the functions of a department of English literature is based. Chief among these assumptions . . . is the claim to the elite nature of literary works, or at least of those works that constitute the canon out of which our department curriculum and the syllabi of the individual courses within it are constructed.[2]

The "political arm of structuralism," Krieger goes on to say, "in its attack on literary privilege, is also—in the name of the third world—attacking the exclusivistic concern with the Western literary tradition, as characterized by the production of its high (as opposed to its popular) culture."

I am not suggesting that the contributors to *The State of the Discipline* are guilty of serious omissions. They accurately surveyed the field of literature in colleges and universities, and black writers were not part of the topography.

What is interesting is that black writers should continue to be absent—what we used to call invisible—from the curriculum even though most major university English departments offer black literature courses and even though standard anthologies include black writers. Obviously, there is nothing wrong with African American literature courses. Many of us have earned a reasonable living teaching them, a living much better, in fact, than most of the authors taught in them ever earned by their writing. But having one or two black literature courses, taught by the department's black lit man or woman, is a form of ghettoization. The response elicited is, black writing does not have to be taught in other courses because that is Hemenway's thing, his area of expertise. Time after time, when Frederick Douglass and W.E.B. Du Bois are suggested for the nineteenth-century course, the reply is, "But don't you teach them in the black lit course? I don't know anything about them. That's why we have you here." Perversely, one effect of opening up the curriculum to black authors has been to preserve the traditional canon. We are now in the peculiar position where the "Americanists"

---

[2] Murray Krieger, "The Recent Revolution in Theory and the Survival of the Literary Disciplines." *ADE Bulletin* 62 (1979): 27–34. *Au.*

know virtually nothing about African American literature, while the "African Americanists" know nearly everything about the so-called American literature. In effect, our "Americanists" are incompletely trained in their area of specialization, and their students emerge culturally deprived.

Nor does the appearance of black writers in the standard anthologies translate into a meaningful appearance by black writers in the classroom or the canon. True, the anthologies have improved. The one-volume Norton anthology of American literature in wide use throughout the 1970s—edited by Bradley, Beatty, and Long—included one black writer, LeRoi Jones, who occupied the last 2 of the book's 1,906 pages. The reader was told that "race is not often an issue in Jones's poetry and does not restrict its appeal." Yet a new Norton anthology, published in 1979 under the general editorship of Ronald Gottesman, includes seven black writers among its eighty-seven authors and gives 70 of its 1,925 pages over to black writings. The quality of editorial comment has improved somewhat, but not overwhelmingly. The last sentence of the commentary on Langston Hughes, for example, raises the non sequitur to the level of cultural politics: "While Hughes never militantly repudiated cooperation with the white community, the poems which protest against white racism are bold and direct." The remark leaves me at a loss about how to interpret such poets as Robert Frost, who "militantly repudiated cooperation with the white community."[3]

With Nina Baym's editing of the most recent Norton anthology, the situation is further improved. Baym's two-volume edition of 1989 devotes 310 of its 5,242 pages to the works of twenty-one black writers.

Superficially, the numbers are encouraging. You might conclude from the 1979 edition that the black part of the American literature canon had increased thirty-five-fold, and from the 1989 edition that it had more than quadrupled in a decade—even though the pages devoted to black writings constitute only 3.6% of Gottesman's anthology and 5.9% of Baym's. But the more relevant questions are: Do the black selections get taught? Do they get taught sensitively and well? And does their inclusion in the anthology, given our notions of a sacred canon, mean that they have now been accepted? I rather suspect not. What may happen in the anthologies of the 1990s is that black writers will slowly begin to fade from the tables of contents, just as black writers began to disappear from publishers' lists in the 1980s and just as works by black authors now go rapidly out of print. It is an instructive sign of the times that when Toni Morrison appeared on the cover of *Newsweek,* two of her four books were out of print and unavailable for classroom use.

But if departments have survived the decades since the 1960s without really incorporating black writing into the canon, why should they do so now, when the heat's off? (Of course, the heat is not entirely off. Advocates of cultural and gender studies are keeping the heat on.) One answer is that the acceptance of black works is morally right; another is that it would reflect our commitment to egalitarian principles, democratic education, and academic humanism. But I would like to suggest two quite practical reasons. First, black literature can release the literary classroom from its aura

---

[3] See Harold H. Kolb, Jr., "Defining the Canon," in *Redefining American Literary History,* ed. A. Lavonne Ruoff and Jerry W. Ward (New York: Modern Language Association of America, 1990): 35–51. *Au.*

of privilege—no small benefit for a student population that from now to the end of the century will be increasingly from the working class and increasingly black. Second, black literature, as predominantly a literature based on folklore, can help to liberate our theories of narrative, trope, and aesthetic performance, concerns that frequently are a part of the latest critical theory.

The Carnegie Commission Report on the next twenty years for higher education, *Three Thousand Futures,* published in 1981, was cautious in many of its projections, but about one prediction it was dead certain: many more black students would be entering colleges and universities in the next twenty to thirty years. By the year 2000, the report stated, minority students will constitute 25% of the total student body.

Although the Carnegie projections have proved incorrect in the short run—black undergraduate enrollments, for example, have actually declined since the mid-1980s, the result of cutbacks in student aid and attacks on affirmative action—the long-range projections will, I believe, be on target. Particularly at state universities, where tuition is lower, black enrollments will be substantially higher by the end of the century.

I see no reason why the many additional black students entering college will not appear in our literature classes. In an era of declining English majors and poor economic opportunities for humanities graduates, these students may not specialize in English, but they are certainly going to be a presence, particularly in lower-division courses.

These black students will not necessarily demand black literature—as students did in the 1960s—but *we* should demand it in order to promulgate the values of serious art to a student population increasingly suspicious of our product. This does not mean that we should teach what we think the students want or what they read last week. Curricular populism was one of the worst mistakes of the 1960s, reflecting the idea that we could win converts by offering courses in the dormitory's latest, drug-inspired library list. (Remember *Steppenwolf?*) Black students will not enter the classroom panting to read Ralph Ellison. They must be taught why his writing is important to their lives.

Let no one misunderstand. It is racism to suggest that without African American literature English teachers cannot reach black students. Almost four hundred years of evidence proves that Spenser, Shakespeare, and Milton—to accept Miller's triune god—have been important to young black readers. But black students will be more receptive to such a profound trinity if they do not feel that men and women of color have been excluded, a priori, from the literature classroom.

We must be more honest about what that classroom represents to many students. One of the dangers in the concept of canonization, the theory of texts with privilege, is that the literary classroom can become, literally, what Victor Doyno of the State University of New York, Buffalo, has called a CLASS-ROOM—in other words, an arena for reinforcing the professor's class prejudices (and for hiding his or her insecurities) by putting down the students' proletarian instincts. Too often the traditional classroom and the traditional canon become a bludgeon in the cause of high culture. We must admit that in the classroom, literature becomes an institution primarily maintained by its teachers; limiting the canon becomes a political act in the politics of culture. As Leslie Fiedler remarks in his preface to the 1979 English Institute essays, *Opening Up the Canon,* "The contributors to this volume raise critical questions about the study of literature in the university, limited as it is by unconscious assumptions of the teachers, rooted in race, class and gender. Merely to recognize the problem is to begin solving it."[4]

But is Fiedler correct, that recognition leads to remedy? The assumptions he refers to did not notably diminish during the 1970s, despite all the decade's upheavals. One reason may be the kind of fundamental threat that black literature poses for professional preconceptions.

As the pop psychologists say, the problem is one of value clarification. How do we determine what we value as a culture? If we value literature, how do we determine what literature we value most? As professional academics, we presume to be able to answer such questions, and we have traditionally prided ourselves on being able to make such determinations, usually on aesthetic grounds, under the label of "universality."

As the criteria for determining value has begun to deconstruct (universality is largely a discredited critical concept) and as the assault on the canon has continued, many sensitive and decent scholars have responded by arguing for a more inclusive but merit-structured canon.

Possibly drawing a parallel with the academic rank structure, where the work of full professors is assumed by definition to be of greater value than that of assistant professors, these scholars have suggested a ranked canon in which some authors are more important than others. All qualified applicants, regardless of race, enter the canon, but most minorities cluster at the lowest levels, while the upper ranks remain predominantly white, male, and relatively free of the coming and going of literary reputations. In the lower ranks, meanwhile, because they are more inclusive, a good deal of substitution occurs—a situation analogous to the coming and going of assistant professors in the search for tenure. Under the merit-system canon, Melville's place is secure, Hemingway is good but not of the first rank (an associate professor, presumably), and Langston Hughes has a precarious hold. (This ranking system ignores, of course, the fact that Melville's canonization is a historically recent phenomenon reflecting the changing values that accompanied the rise of modernism.)

While such efforts may be well-meaning, and while they do have an effect on the classroom—since black writers are more likely to be taught under an inclusionary rule than not—the ranked canon seems an attempt to preserve the power of traditional value determination without confronting the fundamental interrelationship between social class and aesthetic value. Although no one has ever accused him of understatement, Bruce Franklin focused on this issue when he said:

> The fundamental definition of American literature remains what it was before 1964, with Afro-American literature safely ghettoized within the curriculum and represented by tokens in the anthologies. Certainly since 1964, those professors who edit the anthologies, survey the literary history, and decide the curriculum, have been actively searching for black authors who

---

[4] Fiedler in Fiedler and Baker, 1981, viii. *Au.*

fit their notion of excellence. That is precisely the point, for the criteria they apply are determined by their own people and social class, and most Afro-American literature conforms to criteria determined by a different people and a different social class. And, thus, any large-scale inclusion of Afro-American literature within what we call American literature forces a fundamental redefinition and a complex process of revaluation.[5]

No one has yet redefined or revalued American literature in Franklin's sense, but the process has begun and will gain strength in the next twenty years. All the elements are in place. There is now an established body of African American literary scholarship, and more is added each day. The dross of the 1960s, the rhetoric without substance, has dropped away, leaving a core of profound explorations of African American texts. The work of Robert Stepto, Houston Baker, Henry Louis Gates, Arnold Rampersad, Sherley Williams, George Kent, Stephen Henderson, Werner Sollors, Mary Helen Washington, and many others has helped to sharpen the theoretical tools for understanding black writers. There is a renewed effort to liberate African American texts from the sociological straitjacket that meant that each black poem had to serve as an anecdote about school busing. The racist texts in the field have been largely discredited. White critics who could not separate African American writing from their own pathological fantasies of what it must mean to be black are no longer taken seriously.

Moreover, changes that have occurred in the discipline of history suggest that many more breakthroughs will be forthcoming. Indeed, as Robert Stepto has suggested, the way our historians have truly made African American history a part of United States history might well serve as a model for American literary scholarship. An impressive group of white and black scholars—led by John Blassingame, Nell Painter, Nathan Huggins, and Lawrence Levine, among others—has revolutionized American historical study by accepting radically new kinds of testimony into the canon of historical evidence.

Black texts challenge traditional literary ideas. That the slave narrative is unquestionably the first indigenous written literary genre America offered the world places a whole literary tradition in a new perspective and helps us understand both generic properties and the European influence on American literature. Gates has suggested that black texts predict their opposites, that slave narratives provide a kind of perverse literary foregrounding, virtually ensuring the creation of the plantation novel as a reversed image of the slave narrative's indictment. Such a theory begins to assess the dialectic between white aesthetics and black aesthetics.

Earlier I mentioned that black literature can have positive effects on the literature classroom and on our notions of a literary canon because of black literature's folkloric content. As a body of works that has developed out of an oral narrative tradition, black literature is much like Native American literature. (At one of the first conferences in the United States on ethnic contributions to American literature, at the University of Oklahoma in the 1930s, the Native American representative rose and announced that the Indians' contribution to American literature was nothing—Indians never put it on paper. Then he sat down.)

---

[5] H. Bruce Franklin, *The Victim and Criminal and Artist* (New York: Oxford UP, 1978). *Au.*

There is a long history of written African American narrative, but the chief form of art making during slavery and reconstruction was folklore. Black people created a special narrative tradition that provided unique forms and unique subjects for the act and art of storytelling. Embodied in the spirituals, heroic legends, proverbs, and traditional jokes, but especially in folktales, this tradition eventually became a reservoir of stylized expression that helped black people survive and affirm themselves as a culturally unique group. When black people began to publish in fairly significant numbers during the last half of the nineteenth century, the tradition crossed over into written literature, where its positive, heuristic, group-affirming function has continued to be displayed.

A literature assumes patterns and replicates forms, because these patterns and forms communicate a shared understanding of the world. The most viable aesthetic forms of African American writing arise from the traditional poetic performances of black people, those acts of creative communication within small groups called folklore. Ralph Ellison has said, "Negro folklore, evolving within a larger culture which regarded it as inferior, was an especially courageous expression. It announced the Negro's willingness to trust his own experience, his own sensibilities as to the definition of reality, rather than allow his masters to define these crucial matters for him." The understanding of African American art, whether in the classroom or in written discourse, must be founded on folk expression. Folklore was what "black people had before they knew there was such a thing as art." (*Shadow and Act* 173; NAL, 1964).

The role of folklore in black literature is so widespread, and so integral to formal properties such as genre and trope, that the literature itself challenges our preconceptions—many of which derive from our faith in the canon—about the function and nature of art.

An instructive folktale told by black people during reconstruction illustrates my point. An illiterate young black man, reared in the North, came South to seek employment. He was filled with stories about the ways of white Southerners, and he expected hostility. But surprisingly, the first man he encountered, a rich farmer, was extremely polite. The planter explained that he had no work now, but maybe Colonel Jones, down the lane, did. The farmer gave the man a note of introduction, and the worker took it to Colonel Jones. No, Jones didn't have work, but why not take the note to Cap'n Smith, a mile across the pasture? Cap'n Smith didn't have work either; why not try widow Breckinridge, on the river road? After a long day of this kind of traveling, the tired young man found himself a considerable distance from his starting point. Trudging along, he met a brother passing the other way and told him of his troubles. The man looked at the note and read: "The bearer of this paper is a trouble maker. Do not give him work. Keep him moving."

Anyone who has read Ralph Ellison's *Invisible Man* identifies the story immediately as the source for a major structuring device in that novel. Ellison's book is organized around a series of incidents, each introduced by the narrator's receiving a piece of paper. Once he receives a letter of recommendation he is not to open; another time a scholarship to a Tuskegee-like institution; a third time a slip of paper giving him a new identity. In each of their forms, the papers say essentially the same thing: in Ellison's words, "Keep this nigger boy running."

The American literary canon must not be interpreted as pieces of paper containing messages coded to say, keep this boy moving. Yet I fear that the idea of a privileged canon may very well make some of our students feel that way. Our celebration of the properties of art must be less supremacist, less didactic, less dependent on the class assumptions built into the idea of a canon. In fact, we would do well to consider the teaching strategy of the folktale just cited.

On a superficial level, the tale's meaning is political. Passed from one generation to another around a campfire, after Sunday school, in a barbershop, on a street corner, the tale teaches that whites cannot be trusted, that The Man will do you wrong. Beware of white folks bearing gifts. One can laugh at the young man's naiveté and resolve not to commit the same mistake. In this sense the story is a protest tale and could be dismissed as such—just as other black writings have been categorized as protest literature and denied access to the established canon.

But at a deeper cultural level, the tale serves as a heuristic instrument demonstrating the importance of education. The young man is duped because he cannot read. The tale teaches that illiteracy enslaves. If you cannot read, you are vulnerable, as the youth was vulnerable, to manipulation by forces that control the word.

The "words" of black narrative tradition have often originated in speech, not on paper. And, unfortunately, they gained stature as literature only after they were put into children's books. Priests of the written canon have often considered black folklore the primitive art of a limited race, childlike tales with obvious meanings. To a great extent, the person responsible for this view is Joel Chandler Harris, the creator of Uncle Remus.

Harris's career becomes a parable for my subject. His literary genius was to know that Br'er Rabbit—the revolutionary trickster, created by black storytellers to transmit a culture of resistance and self-affirmation amid the darkest despair of slavery—would never be accepted by whites unless his outlaw antics, his demonstrations of the weak triumphing over the strong, were defused, juvenilized, by being put into the mouth of an old-time darky named "Uncle" Remus. Uncle Remus tells Br'er Rabbit's stories to a young white boy, who thinks of the animal in the same way he thinks of his teddy bear. Yet these tales, every one of which was created by black storytellers long before Harris ever heard of them, were accepted by black people as adult entertainments, art forms of enormous subtlety and profound purpose. Br'er Rabbit's stories became part of the canon of American literature because a white voice came forth to authenticate their right to a literary audience. And because the source was folklore, the stories entered that canon through the back door of children's literature.

We, as a profession, must reject paternal primitivism—the idea that a few, but only a few, talented black writers have evolved beyond the crude forms of oral expression, have mastered our written traditions, and can now receive club privileges. Much more viable is a communal sense of creation—the individual storyteller merely being the latest manifestation of the narrative art that has enabled the group to survive, the individual story a culmination of linguistic possibilities, both written and oral, perpetuated by the community.

It is this sense of literary creation that black literature offers to our semiological, structuralist, and deconstructionist theoreticians, as well as to our traditionalists. Krieger and others are worried that if all discourse is brought to the same level of significance, there will be no way to distinguish between privileged literary texts and scientific reports, between James Joyce and your neighborhood barber's conversation. But this fear seems to me to ignore the lessons of Brazzle's mule.

Brazzle's mule is a cantankerous yellow animal owned by Matthew Brazzle, a man so cheap he buys side meat by the slice. The mule serves as the constant source of inspiration for a group of storytellers who inhabit the front porch of the general store in the all-black village of Eatonville, Florida, in Zora Neale Hurston's novel *Their Eyes Were Watching God* and in a play entitled "Mule Bone" coauthored by Hurston and Langston Hughes.

The mule is "so skinny that the women use his rib bones for a rub board and hang clothes on his hock bones to dry." He's so mean he refuses to get fat, staying poor and rawbony just for spite. He is the kind of mule who sticks his head in the Pearsons' window while the family is at the dinner table, and Mrs. Pearson mistakes him for the Reverend and hands him a plate. He is the kind of mule who sleeps in the kitchen one night and fights until he gets a cup of coffee for his breakfast the next morning.

When Brazzle's mule eventually dies, he is buried in a town ceremony that "mocked everything human in death." Six months later, two men near the grave begin arguing over a girl. During the dispute, one man gropes for a weapon and comes up with the hock bone of Brazzle's mule, which just happens to be lying nearby. He knocks out his opponent with a well-placed blow.

In a subsequent trial for assault and battery, the assailant admits to hitting his adversary but argues that a common brawl does not constitute a criminal act. His ingenious defense is shattered by a shrewd villager, a keeper of the sacred canon perhaps, who points out, with impeccable logic, that anyone who has ever been kicked by a mule knows that the closer one gets to the mule's rear, the more dangerous the animal becomes. Thus if Samson could slay a thousand Philistines with the jawbone of an ass, just think what a hock bone could do.

Clearly, the storytelling canon of Eatonville recognized no special privileges. The most sacred text of all, the Bible, can easily cross borders between written and oral art. The town's storytellers did not worry about whether they were in the schoolroom or the barbershop. Creative inspiration comes in both divine and secular forms, to saints and sinners alike. The classroom was one with the literature itself, not set apart as a special cultural institution.

I think Eatonville has much to teach us about what constitutes literature and the art-making intelligence, just as Hurston has much to offer us as we step into the classroom of the future.

Hortense Spillers

Hortense J. Spillers was born in 1942 in Memphis, Tennessee, and was raised, as she has said, "in the church" so as to know at first hand the African American sermon on which she has eloquently written. Spillers was educated at Bennett College and Memphis State University, where she took a B.A. in English Literature and American History, then went to Brandeis University, where she earned her Ph.D. in 1974. Spillers has received numerous awards, including fellowships from the National Endowment for the Humanities and the Rockefeller and Ford Foundations. She has taught at Wellesley College, the University of Nebraska, Cornell, and Emory University, where she is currently professor of English. Spillers's books include *Conjuring: Black Women, Fiction, and Literary Tradition* (1985, with Marjorie Pryse), and *American Identities: Race, Sex, and Nationality in the Modern Text* (1990), from which the following essay is taken. Spillers is currently working on *In the Flesh: A Situation for Feminist Inquiry,* of which she told Lucius Outlaw: "I am trying to work out a theoretical position from which African-American women might speak to a number of discursive postures that surround them, including feminist inquiry. I am arguing that gender, at least as far as the sociopolitical instance of the United States goes, defines nothing more than an instrument of racial solidarity in the Anglo-American rise to power. For that reason, some women in America 'have' gender, others don't; so that gender itself becomes as problematic a category as 'race' and 'class.'"

Who Cuts the Border?

SOME READINGS ON "AMERICA"

The January 10, 1891 edition of *La Revista Illustrada* carried the initial publication of José Martí's celebrated essay, "Our America." Later, almost exactly a year to the day, "El Partido Revolucionario Cubano"—the Cuban Revolutionary Party—was created, with Martí acknowledged as "its leading spirit, inspirer, and organizer." The compressed background of historical events that Philip Foner provides in the Introduction to the second of four English-language volumes of Martí's writings reacquaints readers in the United States with a larger-than-life romantic instance, whose initiating moments date back to one's childhood and its ephemeral encounters with symptoms of the heroic: Simón Bolívar, Father Hidalgo and "the cry of Dolores," alongside Martí, are entailed with the same fabric of cultural memory and a curiously elided time-space continuum that threads the name of A. Philip Randolph with the successes of the Brotherhood of Sleeping Car Porters and the heady political maneuvers of Adam Clayton Powell, Jr. It remains, then, a matter of surprise that, even as one eventually grasps the reasons why, Martí's "our" and "America" do not usually embrace us at all—except by the logic of a clearly defined dualism of antagonists, who, in the febrile

260

imagination of his writings, must contend, in effect, for the right to name and claim "America." As Foner observes, that vast stretch of formidably organized political power (at which site all nine of the essayists writing here live and work, if not originate), ninety miles north of the island and nation of Cuba, demarcates, for Martí, that "other America," neither "*his* America," nor "Mother America" of Martí's dream of wholeness. About seventy years following the writing of the lectures that comprise *The Philosophy of History,* G.W.F. Hegel himself might have been offered occasion for surprise at the exemplary boldness of one José Martí:

> The European university must bow to the American university. The history of America, from the Incas to the present, must be taught in clear detail and to the letter, even if the archons of Greece are overlooked. Our Greece must take priority over the Greece which is not ours. We need it more. Nationalist statesmen must replace foreign statesmen. Let the world be grafted onto our republics, but the trunk must be our own. And let the vanquished pedant hold his tongue, for there are no lands in which a man may take greater pride than in our long-suffering American republics. (p. 88)

Interestingly enough, Martí and Hegel, inhabiting either end of the nineteenth century, posited, for radically different reasons and toward radically different and reversed ends, two contrastive "Americas." For Martí, as the excerpted passage suggests, "Our America," of indigenous historical currents, fires, on the one hand, the profoundly figurative polemic of his revolutionary moment and impulse, those "long suffering American republics, raised up from among the silent Indian masses by the bleeding arms of a hundred apostles, to the sounds of battle between the book and the processional candle" (p. 86). On the other hand, the "other America," the United States, "this avaricious neighbor who admittedly has designs on us," arouses Martí to the visionary urgencies of an Armageddon. Perhaps the longest syntactic chain in "Our America" throws forth immitigable linkage between "since/then," *post hoc, ergo propter hoc,* embedded in oppositional ground:

> And since strong nations, self-made by law and shotgun, love strong nations, and them alone; since the time of madness and ambition—from which North America may be freed by the predominance of the purest elements in its blood, or on which it may be launched by its vindictive and sordid masses, its tradition of expansion, or the ambitions of some powerful leader . . . since its good name as a republic in the eyes of the world's perceptive nations puts upon North America a restraint that cannot be taken away by childish provocations or pompous arrogance or parricidal discords among our American nations—the pressing need of Our America is to show itself as it is, one in spirit and intent . . . (p. 93)

Though far too schematic, one learns, to exhaust, or even adequately account for, the range of Martí's thought, his rhetorical binary, nonetheless, subtends one of the chief critical functions of his solidary political and intellectual engagement.

Martí's expressly dramatic protocol of pronouns is neither more nor less presumptuous than Hegel's implied one, which also distinguishes "America," New World, from the "United States of North America, but an emanation from Europe" (p. 82). Hegel's "other America" "has always shown itself physically and psychically powerless, and still shows itself so" (p. 81). These aboriginal societies "gradually vanished at the breath of European activity" (p. 81); we needn't add that such "breath" ferociously animated the winds of multiple violence—epistemic, linguistic, iconographic, genocidal. Hegel's European-emanated United States, with its "republican constitution," its Christian sects of Protestant enthusiasm, its "Universal protection for property" belongs, finally and dismissively, for Hegel, to an American "future," "where, in the ages that lie before us, the burden of the World's History shall reveal itself—perhaps in a contest between North and South America" (p. 86).

That Hegelian "perhaps" is borne out, amazingly so, in hemispheric wars of national liberation, so far, including Cuba (in its First and Second Wars of Independence) and Cuba again, under the successful insurgency of Fidel Castro, shortly past the midpoint of the twentieth century. No one can fail to read current affairs in Ibero-Hispanic America and the Caribbean—from Sandinista Nicaragua, to post-Noriega Panama—outside an ironized perspective on this "future" and the culture texts inscribed and unfolding about it.

Ensnared, then, between Old World and New, past and future, the contrary ideas of "America" instantiate the text and the materiality on a historico-cultural ground long fabled and discursive in acts of European invention and intervention. It is as if the Word, for Europe, engenders Flesh. Peter Hulme argues, for example, that the discourse of English colonialism arises fundamentally on the career of two key terms—"hurricanes" and "Caribbees"—that mark relatively new lexemes in the English language. "Not found before the middle of the sixteenth century," these terms do not settle into "their present forms before the latter half of the seventeenth." Both originate in Native American languages, and "both were quickly adopted into all the major European languages" (p. 58). Raymond Williams's *Keywords* does not carry entries on either term, but it is rather startling that as innocuous as they might appear in the lexicon, "hurricanes" and "Caribbees/Caribbean," especially the latter, have achieved keyword status over a significant spate of modern intellectual history. Any subsequent addenda that we might devise on Williams's project concerning the evolution of terministic cruxes "in the West" might well inaugurate around "Caribbean" and its own emanations.

Contemporary Cuban intellectual, Roberto Fernández Retamar—poet, essayist, and distinguished editor of *Casa de las Americas*—offers, in his classic essay, a highly informative synthesis of the history of related terms—"Caribbean/Caribbees/Caliban." As background and framework that situate Retamar's reading of culture in "Our America," this rich congruence of terms is biographically reinscribed in the exemplary instance of Martí's public life and career. Retamar tracks "Caribbean" from its eponymous Carib community of Native Americans, who, we are told, valiantly resisted European incursion in the sixteenth century, to its philosophical and terministic transformations, by way of "Caliban," in the contemporary period, with specific reference to the works of Aimé Césaire, Frantz Fanon, and O. Mannoni. As if a moment of phantasmogoria that perfectly mirrors the Freudian formula of media cross-dressing—the dream as *visual* transliteration of the day's *grammar* events—"Carib" is translated as a "deformation" and "defamation" into "cannibal." The latter generates an anagram in "Caliban," as Shakespeare had already made use of "cannibal" to mean anthropophagus "in the third part of *Henry IV* and *Othello*" (p. 11).

This nested semiotic filiation, inaugurated by a reputed "look," retailed as truth to Christopher Columbus, will stage a paradigm of discursive, scopophilic behavior for colonizing and enslaving powers toward "peoples of color," and most dramatically in its duration, for Hegel's "Negro" of Subsaharan "Africa," which demonstrates "no historical part of the world," it was said; ". . . has no movement or development to exhibit," it was concluded (p. 99). For Columbus's reporters (and Hegel), anthropophagi reside on that border between nature and culture, inhabited by "'men with one eye and others with dog's muzzles, who ate human beings.'"

Would we dare, then, risk a simplistic and essentialist reduction? "Someone," perhaps, saw "something" or "someone" in a stage of cultural production long before Columbus came, and even now with pure revisionary heart-work and devotion to the politics of the plural, we cannot decipher exactly what it was. Having few corrective narratives to counterpoise, the future-laden actor reenacts an analogy on a child's game: a sentence is passed along a spatial sequence, person to person, and at the end of it the garbled "message" makes only comic sense. Just so (or almost), we will not "know" now, since the "first speakers," either way, are not "available." By the time Shakespeare sifts "cannibal" through the sieve of his imagination, it is an already inspissated narrative of plenitude, crystallized in the sixteenth century by, among other sources, Thomas Moore's *Utopia* (1580) and Michel de Montaigne's "De los Caníbales" (1580); the translation of Montaigne's work by way of Giovanni Floro's *Essays* was available to Shakespeare, Retamar observes (p. 14).

The construction and invention of "America," then—a dizzying concoction of writing and reportage, lying and "signifying," jokes, "tall tales," and transgenerational nightmare, all conflated under the banner of Our Lord—exemplify, for all intents and purposes, the oldest game of *trompe de l'oeil,* the perhaps-mistaken-glance-of-the-eye, that certain European "powers" carried out regarding indigenous Americans. *Misprision,* therefore, constitutes law and rule of "Our America" in its "beginnings" for Europe. "Made up" in the gaze of Europe, "America" was as much a "discovery" on the retinal surface as it was the appropriation of land and historical subjects.

From what angle does one insert the "United States but-an-emanation from Europe" into this picture, or perhaps, more ambitiously, a series of perpendicular pronouns—the "I's"/"eyes" of this collection of writings on the New World?

At least one thing is doubtless: At whatever point one cuts into this early modern discourse on what will become, quite by accident, by arbitrary design, by the most complicated means of economic (and otherwise) exchange, and the entire repertoire of genetic play and chance, her space, his space, of central habitation in the unimagined "future" of World History, the initial news is hardly good for anyone. "Physically and psychically powerless" and overcome by men who *eat* (the) other(s), this orientalized, Europe-fabled "America" could not be salvaged by even the hippest stunts of the televisual media, except that a Martí, for one, will reclaim it as a necessary project of historical demolition and reconstruction. But the United States, carved out of this

New World ground, must be read, just as it is intimately connected, with this unfolding historical text of unpromise. The seams will show now, but that is also part of the picture. This ground is broken—by culture and "race," language and ethnicity, weather and land formation, in generative and historical time, as more or less gendered "situation-specificities," in various postures of loves and hungers, cohabit it—even though, given any point at which the multiple "I"/"We" are positioned on its axes, it appears to be monolithic ground. Retamar, pursuing the implications of Martí's "mestizo America," identifies as *the* "distinctive sign of our culture," those ". . . descendants both ethnically and culturally speaking, of aborigines, Africans, and Europeans" (p. 9). He goes on to interrogate, in rhetorical accents sometime reminiscent of Martí's own writings: "From Túpac Amaru . . . to Nicolás Guillén, to Aimé Césaire, to Violeta Parra, to Frantz Fanon—what is our history, what is our culture, if not the history and culture of Caliban?" (p. 24).

It seems clear that at great expense to the national "pursuit of happiness," a United States culture text/praxis, in the dreamful flattening out of textures of the historical, would repress its calibanesque potential, just as we would amend Retamar's strategy of evocation to account for at least one other strand of the "sixties without apology." If, for instance, Bartolomeo Las Casas and José Martí touch my life-line at some distant point of reverberation, then certainly Isabella Baumfree, become "Sojourner Truth," and Rosa Parks, Malcolm El-Hajj Malik, and Martin Luther King, Jr., among others, must sound through Retamar's at no greater distance. The problem of the pronouns—and *we* mustn't mistake this, as the late sixties taught—cannot, will not resolve itself in a too-easy "hands around the world" embrace among hemispheric cross-cultural communities. But if one concedes "Caliban" as a joining figure, then by virtue of what set of moves is the notion applicable along a range of culture practices in light of the hegemonic entailment of operations out of which certain US communities express relations to "Our America"? In other words, in order to disrupt the homogeneous narrative that the United States, as an idea-form, or that "other America" provokes in Martí's, or Retamar's view, or even George Bush's view, the contradictions of proximity must be brought further out: Some of US render unto Caesar, more or less, is not simply locutional.

Apparently everywhere one might look on this massive scene of heterogeneous historical attitudes, it seems that "Caliban" designates a copulative potential by way of the Atlantic system of slavery—the ownership of man by man (Virginia's "chattels personal," say), man's ownership of "private property" (Cuba's seigneurial ownership of the sugar product, say), and the captive communities' occasional revolt in the teeth of it (Canada's Caribbean marronage, for example). In the sociopolitical arrangements here stipulated, "man," wherever he appears in the bargain, articulates with juridical, axiomatic, historical, ontological, and local *specificity*. "America," with its US, locates a prime time of "the fruits of merchant capital" as a stunning chapter in the modern history of patriarchal law and will. In other words, America/US shows itself as a "scene of instruction" in the objectifying human possibility across an incredibly various real estate and human being. This vulgar oxymoron of purposes and motivations insists on the combo—human-as-property—and there, in all the astonishing foreclosures of certainty, "English," among other Indo-European languages, enters its currency in the "execrable trade."

It would seem highhanded, then, to read this Real as *a discourse,* but certainly the conceptual narratives around "cannibal"/"Caliban"—a colonial topos, common to the seventeenth century, Hulme argues, projects slavery "as the necessary stage between savagery and civilization" (p. 62). "Caliban" designates itself a moment of convergence between Old World and New, inasmuch as the idea-formation demonstrates "features of both the Mediterranean wild man, or classical monster . . . with an African mother, whose pedigree leads back to Book X of *The Odyssey*" (p. 70). Further, Caliban, as the issue of Sycorax, entertains "particular connection with the moon . . . whose signs the Caribs could read . . ." (p. 70). Need we be reminded here of the "intersections of blood and the moon, the mother and home: towards that terrain which traditionally has been given and denied the name of 'woman'"?

When Martí invokes "Mother America," one imagines that he means the formulation of "mother" in relation to nurture and security, but the term might also mark, under the precise historical circumstance upon which his vision of "America" is raised, the *silence* bred by defeat. If Columbus's *Diaries,* compounded of report, offered the explorer a useful fiction for entering New World communities, then that available discourse evinces a remarkable instance of "rhetorical enargeia," which Patricia Parker describes as "convincing description or vivid report, [containing] within it the same visual root as the name of 'Argus,' sent with his many eyes to spy." The Columbian reporters, for example, were not only providing "promotional narratives," but "a 'blazing,' or publishing of the glories of this *feminized* New World, of the possibilities of commercial abundance and 'return'" (emphasis mine; p. 141). Perceiving a link here between language and spectacle, Parker speaks of discursive inventiveness as a "transgressive uncovering, or opening up of a secret place, of exposing what was hidden in the womb of a feminized Nature . . ." (p. 142). These "ocular proofs," giving rise to discursive elaboration, as we have observed in the Caliban/Caribbean/cannibal semiosis, yoke the gaze and the profit in a rhetoric of property (p. 147).

The inventory of both the American land and the figure of Caliban—"ugly, hostile, ignorant, devilish"—inscribes a "rhetorical and an economic instrument, one way of controlling the territory in question . . ." (p. 150). Even though Sycorax is given no script in *The Tempest,* as we recall, her "absence," except in comminatory provocation, confirms the "unrepresentability" of Caliban, the mothered-womaned, to a spectator-audience. A not-sayable offers a strategy for describing the "future," which is always a pregnant possibility in the now.

Hulme describes the locus of *The Tempest* as an "extraordinary topographical dualism" because of its "double series of connotations"—the Mediterranean and the Caribbean. This scene of double inscription is borne out further in "tempest" itself, from the Mediterranean repertoire, and Gonzalo's "plantation," from the Atlantic repertoire (p. 71). But practically speaking, beyond the "rarefied latitudes" of Shakespeare's art, the "discovery of America" may be read as "a magnetic pole compelling a reorientation of traditional axes." Superimposing two planes—a palimpsest, "on which there are two texts" (p. 72), "America" juxtaposes "two referential systems" that inhabit "different spaces except for that area which is the island [neither here nor there] and its first native Caliban" (p. 72). As a "geometrical metaphor," Caliban intermediates a "central axis about which both planes swivel free of one another." As a "textual metaphor," Caliban inscribes an "overdetermination," "peculiarly at odds with his place of habitation which is described as an 'uninhabitable island'" (p. 72). Caliban translates the "monstrous" in his mediating posture "between two sets of connotations" and a "compromise formation . . . achieved . . . only at the expense of distortion elsewhere" (p. 72). Precisely metaphorical in the collapse of distinctive features of contrast, Caliban can "exist only within discourse . . . fundamentally and essentially beyond the bounds of representation" (p. 72).

Or is it the *bonds,* the *bonds* of representation? William Faulkner's Luster, the grandson of his "enduring" Dilsey, tries to recall to young Quentin Compson, his proximate age-mate, the name of the wild male child now installed in the shadows of "Sutpen's Hundred" and decides that his not-so-ready-to-hand last name exemplifies a "lawyer's word": "what they puts you under when the Law catches you" (p. 215). Inflected from "Bon," by way of his paternity in Charles Etienne de Saint Valery Bon and a maternity situated by Faulkner's narrator as a "gorilla" of a woman, "Jim Bond" stands free, if not emancipated, in his US/African/European/Americanity as an embodied instance of the "ferocious play of alphabets," but not unlike Caliban, "he" also marks a would-be place, or a "geometrical metaphor" on the verge of being in an American wilderness—fictitious Jefferson, Mississippi (trapped in a once dark pastoral frame) after the "fall" of the South. Verging on past and future, Jim Bond, a live-wire instance of the law's most persistent social invention, assumes the status of deictic, or nonverbal marker, *here* and *there, this* and *that,* as the conventions of discourse out of which he arises proffer him no claim to a "present/presence," except as the unkinned "monster," feared and despised, from Caliban, to Bigger Thomas. Though I am suggesting here a narrative of filiations across a broad swatch of Western discourse, there are, admittedly, considerable differences between these "impression-points": If we accept the argument of Hulme and others that Caliban describes sheer and fateful discursivity that evades the trammels of representation, then what must we make of a figure like Jim Bond whose representability prescribes and provokes *all* that he is?

Both cultural vestibularity and an after-word, "America/US," from Caliban's perspective and that of his diverse relations, must come upon Language and the Law (and in a sense, they overlap the same item from the store of Europe's hardy "beneficence") as the inimical "property" of "civilized man." ("You taught me language, and my profit on't/Is, I know how to curse. The red plague rid you/For learning me your language.") This place, this text, as Jim Bond embodies it, as the European interventionist/invader might have imagined, orchestrates representation as the already-coded "future." Some of US know this process—in discourse and discourse/politics—as history as *mugging.*

This overdetermined representability, or texts overwritten, locates authority on an exterior, as the seizing of discursive initiative seems to define a first order of insurgency wherever it appears in the New World. Colonial North America as the final port-of-call on a trajectory that starts up the triangular trade all over again would mute its involvement in the narratives of Caliban, as we have observed before, by the fateful creation of "minority" communities in the United States, but it is the ascribed task of such communities to keep the story of difference under wraps through the enactments and reenactments of difference in the flesh. The single basis for a myth of national unity is raised, therefore, on negation and denial that would bring a Jim Bond to stand in the first place. In that space—like the return to the scene of a crime—we can recite the triangulation of a particular mapping that might demonstrate new ground for the workings of Hulme's "geometrical metaphor."

The historic triangular trade interlarded a third of the known world in a fabric of commercial intimacy so tightly interwoven that the politics of the New World cannot always be so easily disentangled as locally discrete moments. Nowhere is this narrative of involvement more pointedly essayed than in Faulkner's *Absalom, Absalom!* that choreographs Canada, the Caribbean, Africa, Europe, and the United States as geographical and/or figurative points of contact in this fictive discourse. If Caliban as a narrative paradigm links American communities in a repertoire of sporadic historico-cultural reference, then we might traverse its play in *Absalom, Absalom!*.

In this layer upon layer of "graphireading," Faulkner never quite comes to the point, but puts it off again and again in the successful evasion of closure. The tales that converge on "Thomas Sutpen," both the narrated and the sign-vehicle that starts up the narrative and sustains it, are related by speakers who recall the character from some vantage of time long past (as Rosa Coldfield), or, at even greater narrative remove, the recollections of others' *inherited* recollection of Sutpen (as Quentin Compson). At the intersection of a plurality of texts, Sutpen aptly demonstrates the notion of character as a structure of assumptions that reading embodies and, not altogether unlike the orientalized Carib/cannibal formation, is concocted in the imaginings of each speaker from a repertory of rancor, grudging admiration, gossip, rumor, hearsay, and more or less stabilized impression. The work plunders and reworks itself as narrators not only elaborate what they cannot have known, but also correct passed-down information, fill in gaps, piece together disparities, disprove or improve inherited conclusions, assume identities, even invent new ones, that the novel has not embedded. For instance, Quentin Compson's Canadian roommate Shreve McCannon/McKenzie (also "transported" from *The Sound and the Fury* to *Absalom, Absalom!*) posits a quite likely character of a lawyer to the mother of Charles Bon and offers an intercessory "gift" that the "author," we're led to imagine, had not thought of. We also learn from McKenzie that Thomas Sutpen could not have been born in *West* Virginia, if he were 25 years old in Mississippi in 1833, which would establish his birth year as 1808 (p. 220). Having acquired his "American history" in a western Canadian classroom, Shreve, after all, a Harvard man, knows very well that West Virginia was not admitted to the Union until 1863. But the traditional reading on Sutpen, as Quentin receives it down the paternal line, requires him to have been born "in West Virginia, in the mountains." Reading in the interstices, we surmise that Sutpen "comes from" nowhere that an early US map would have articulated.

Essentially originless, if the continuities of kinship and place of birth, relatedly, mean anything, Thomas Sutpen, reminiscent of the colonized European subject before him, "arises" in "Old Bailey" and a criminality inscribed in notary's ink. But achieving the means to efface these corrupt "beginnings" founds both the desire of Sutpen's own fictional biotext and "Sutpen's Hundred," the 10 square miles of virgin land carved out of north Mississippi. The shadow of Sutpen's imputed desire falls between two poignant moments, collapsed into a single, dreaded economy of recall and forgetfulness. The homeless prepubescent boy, wandering the surrounding country with an unspecified number of siblings and a drunken father, learns very slowly (in the tempo of the Faulknerian sentence) what hierarchy and difference are and how they work: "He had learned the difference between white men and black ones, but he was learning that there was a difference between white men and white men, not to be measured by lifting anvils, gouging eyes or how much whiskey you could drink then get up and walk out of the room" (p. 226).

As the story is interpreted by Quentin and Shreve, somewhere in Harvard Yard, Sutpen's memory so freezes on these scenes that it would be plausible to think of them as analogous to birth trauma. But if one's "second birth" marks the coming to "consciousness," then the second time around for Sutpen is doubly painful, engendered by the outraged shame of *being-looked-at*. The drunken father has somehow landed work on a plantation whose owner lives in the "biggest house [Sutpen] had even seen" (p. 227). This man who owns things—"all the land and the niggers"—spends "most of the afternoon . . . in a barrel stave hammock between two trees, with his shoes ["that he didn't even need to wear"] off . . ." (pp. 227–28). When young Sutpen, bearing an unread message from his father to the man in the Big House, arrives at the front door, something quite astonishing takes place: ". . . the monkey-dressed nigger butler kept the door barred with his body while he spoke . . ." (p. 231), and "even before [Sutpen] had had time to say what he came for," the butler tells him "never to come to that front door again but to go around to the back" (p. 232).

Sutpen's "birth" in the moment strikes with such force that the narrator insinuates it as *rupture:* Even before the butler completes the message, Sutpen "seemed to kind of dissolve and a part of him turn and rush back through the two years they had lived there" (pp. 229–30). The rip in the fabric of memory occurs, so to speak, over the bar of the black body, standing in the doorway so that the enormous privation in young Sutpen is abruptly named, materialized, and objectified in the butler's own impeding presence. Suddenly, the boy gets an inkling of what he looks like to a momentarily superior other, denied by the statistical recurrence of the lexemes "nigger," "monkey-nigger," "niggers," that overtakes the passage, but be that as it may, Sutpen gets the point and it sticks: This *face,* and "he was unable to close the *eyes* of it—was looking out from *within* . . . just as the man who did not even have to wear the shoes he owned . . . looked out from whatever *invisible place* he (the man) happened to be at the moment, at the boy *outside* the barred door in his patched garments and *splayed bare feet* . . ." (emphasis mine; pp. 234–35).

"Outside" the bar defines precisely that moment of negation from which meaning can work, since, in the positing of a not-"inside" and a not-"within," Sutpen brutally discovers who is/not. Not only is he "born" to himself then, but commences to read his "history" as it is rendered through the borrowed gaze of his profoundest beholders: ". . . he himself seeing his own father and sisters and brothers as the owner . . . must have been seeing them all the time"—

> as cattle, creatures heavy and without grace, brutely evacuated into a world without hope or purpose for them, who would in turn spawn with brutish and vicious prolixity, populate, double treble compound, fill space and earth with a *race* whose future would be a succession of cut-down and patched

and made-over garments bought on exorbitant credit because they were white people. . . . (emphasis mine; p. 235)

It is fair to say that the young Thomas Sutpen "gets" his culture's sociotext violently and all at once through the ventriloquized medium of others' seeing, as "race"—now objectified *for* him by way of a barred doorway—and the threat of castration—in the hint of male bonding and hierarchy—become the power drive of his fundamental hunger. "Splayed bare feet" and "shoes," projecting a theory here from off the ground, let's say, not only address the downcast, "cut-down" detail, but also flirt with the missing phallus. "Niggers" will take on a certain usefulness of social economy for Sutpen, as it is surprising to him and the reader that "they" are not "inside" the bar so much as its moment of substantiation to be transcended. Sutpen is marked, then, by the "discovery" of "race," or more pointedly, by the striking news that he "has" "race," as the message is hammered home by the crucial marker of difference in a US Real—the vital sign of "Africanity" itself. In a very real sense, this coming to manhood, in all the brutality of ungentle revelation, fixes Thomas Sutpen in the inescapable madness of his own veritably now-felt difference. Mattering even less in the relay of gazes than that "monkey-dressed nigger," who is "given . . . garments free" (p. 235), Sutpen instantiates the barefoot, bareass white boy who will spend his fictional career overcoming.

Since human valuation is posited in this narrative as the distance between privation and gratification, we observe that the young Sutpen also comes upon the efficacies of "class" in this episode, but features of the sociotext are so carefully intertwined here that "race," "class," and masculine (hetero) "sexuality" are represented as a single bundle of nerves. For sure, the character, as imputed to him, grasps a human psychology and sociometry under the auspices of *lack,* as the latter offers its unsaid name to a far more sophisticated, covering notion—*desire* writ large and, in this particular instance, inscribed in the balloon face of the Negro butler. To say that Sutpen imposes, in time, the weight of his rage on "peoples of color" will not surprise; indeed, we can anticipate it with a good degree of certainty, but *how* it is so (inasmuch as the African-American person has very little to do with him in the historical situations that we come to accept as "true") focuses the puzzle of US "race" magic itself: We might suggest now that the ideology of "race" in the New World text is founded on the fundamental suspicion that one is *not* a "man," if, as in Sutpen's case, castration fear and the mark and knowledge of "race" can be said to belong to the same stuff of cognition/recognition. The utter ruthlessness of "class," then, with its relegation of women, period, though for radically different reasons, to the circuit of exchange, not only describes the violence that is interrupted by nothing at all, but does not bear distinction as a discrete feature of the socionom from "race" and "sexuality." Thomas Sutpen, in the course of things, will efface his "race" (as the myth of the "land of opportunity" requires the ascendant "race" to do) and take on a new "class" (the displacement of "race" onto "property"), but in order to do so, he must not only run away from those viciously spawned siblings, but must "split" the unmapped countryside and the unfinished cartographies of the new nation.

To make an interminable story quite a bit shorter (Faulkner, after all, was trying to capture the whole world between "a cap and a period"): Sutpen, and *how* he does so is about as clear as the involuted syntax of the narrative can be, lands on a "little island set in a smiling and fury-lurked and incredible indigo sea, which was the halfway point between what we call the jungle and what we call civilization, halfway between the dark inscrutable continent . . . and the cold known land to which it was doomed . . ." (p. 250). The narrative remains ignorant of the proper name of this "little island," but plants symptoms of it, as if the name itself were a postponed expectation, just as that mountainous region of Virginia, where Sutpen was born, will come to be called *West* Virginia. In effect, this generalized nominative order—"in a latitude which would require ten thousand years of equatorial heritage to bear its climate" (p. 251)—cannot be named in its global dispersion insofar as it revolves in a "heart of darkness" that cannot read itself. (This conjecture is aided by our knowledge that Sutpen is semi-literate at best.) To that extent, Conrad's Marlowe/Kurtz and Faulkner's Sutpen/ Quentin/Shreve—variously positioned in the scale of literate-being—encounter the same massive display of a self-generated phantasm that bites back. Sutpen nonetheless falls in the binary between that "dark inscrutable continent" on the one hand and that "cold known land . . . the civilized land and people which had expelled some of its own blood and thinking and desires that had become too crass to be faced and borne longer . . ." on the other hand (pp. 250–51). In this romance of the "bloods," the narrator does not actually approach a geopolitical order that could be thought of as a mimesis of some "real" place, but Sutpen's role in the scheme as an overseer and "the incredible paradox of peaceful greenery and crimson flowers and sugar cane sapling size and three times the height of a man" gesture symptomatically toward the notion of the colonial/plantation system of the Hispanic and Francophone Caribbean; that "cold known land" seems to look toward Europe, as ambiguity of reference delineates the entire passage in paroxysms of modification.

In this fret and fever of telling, layers of other narratives "migrate" to the different context and signify on Faulkner's semantic surface, but at least one of the convergent texts (or shades of it) is rewritten here to establish Sutpen as an apprentice-factotum of Law and Order: The revolt of the little island's by-now indigenous black population is put down, *singlehandedly,* in John Wayne style, by Sutpen, who "[walks] out into the darkness and [subdues] them, maybe by yelling louder, maybe by standing, bearing more than they believed any bones and flesh could or should . . ." (p. 254). The most celebrated revolution in the colonial African Diaspora, or, perhaps, within this complex at *any* time, records quite a different outcome: "The slaves defeated . . . the local whites and the soldiers of the French monarchy, a Spanish invasion, a British expedition of some 60,000 men, and a French expedition of similar size under Bonaparte's brother-in-law." Historian C.L.R. James is referring here, of course, to the San Domingo struggle (1791–1803), which established Haiti as the modern world's first black nation-state. Sutpen's "creators," however, are not only constructing/reconstructing Sutpen's biotext through willful and wishful distortions that posit the deeds of an "identity," but even at the risk of parody, insinuating an exalted and aggrandized figure. This economy of narrative means dwarfs the background and its particularities, as the "hero" is dramatically foregrounded at all costs.

But there is still something on Thomas Sutpen's mind. That face with eyes that "he was unable to close" acquires obsessive force, *is* the all-over memory that repeats like a rhetorical tic. Here, in an ambiguous space, Sutpen, searching for one of the missing house servants, "the half breeds," "hunts" for two days, "without even knowing that what he was meeting was a blank wall of black secret faces, a wall behind which almost anything could be preparing to happen and, as he later learned, almost anything was . . ." (p. 252). This "text," which Sutpen can neither read nor erase, overlaps the tale of the butler, as both episodes share their common source in a weave of related textures—from some secret and invisible posture, a putative subject of an interior generates unspecified, unspecifiable power that Sutpen can only guess. In both instances, he, we might say, intimates his own production *as* knowledge-for-another, so that in his own eyes, he has taken on objectness, "double-consciousness," or the seeing himself as an interiorized other (to his "outsiderliness") might see him. The founding of "Sutpen's Hundred," with its handcrafted, baronial mimicries, is vexed by a habit and poetics of pathos that now seem clearer to the grasp—"Home" breaches the blank wall; the barred doorway. Gaining "Home" offers him the key and extraordinary imperative.

One final piece: Sutpen's first-born son, Charles Bon, who is the father, in turn, of Charles Etienne de St. Valery Bon, is given birth to in the ambiguously fictionalized space—the son of Eulalia Bon, the daughter of the Haitian sugar plantation's owner. When Sutpen, discovering his new wife's suspect racial origins, descends, finally, on Mississippi, Eulalia and child have been installed in New Orleans, perhaps, and in a more or less morganatic arrangement—at least this is the plausible text that Quentin and Shreve co-hatch. The meeting of Henry Sutpen, the "true" son and legitimate heir of Thomas by Ellen Coldfield, and Charles Bon (whom—like Sutpen—we never actually "see," except as the splendidly regressive, sartorial, and eroticized narrative object of desire in others) provides the vertiginous motions that take the reader toward the storm center of the US culture text—"race" as that awful moment of incestuous possibility *and* praxis, yearning *and* denial, refusal *and* accomplishment, wild desire *and* repression, that cannot be uttered and that cannot *but* be uttered: Jim Bond, the grandson of Charles, outside the burning ruins of an impossible and impassable history, with "Africa," "Europe," and "African-America" coursing his veins, abrupts the "return" that Sutpen wished to repress altogether. At the embodied intersection of heteronomies— and they are just about all there in the play of demography, geography, history, ethnicity, sexuality, the declensions of "class," and the signs of repression and difference in "race"—Jim Bond, in the flesh, installs a reading on the paralogisms of US in "Our America."

It seems that Sutpen has been perfectly poised for this tale of contingency by way of a great-grandson whom he could not/would not have *recognized*, starting in the son. Going back to keywords in his early fictive biotext, we would try to tease out a meaning as to the *how* in recourse to three scattered resonances: 1) ambiguity; 2) evacuate/evacuation; 3) blank wall/barred entry. It will not be surprising that "blankness" does not describe a not-written upon so much as it locates a site for new, or overinscriptions—Lillian Hellman's "pentimento," Hulme's "palimpsest." The screen, or canvas, or framed circumstance carries traces of preceding moments that alter the contemporaneous rendition, making the latter both an "originality" and an "affiliated," or the initiation of a new chain of signifying as well as an instance of significations already in intervened motion. The descriptive discourse attributed to Sutpen's dream of the "nigger" (which arises *persistently* after the fact of his coming into knowledge of self-division and "race") is laden with notions of surface and masking. It could be said that Sutpen's first and most significant hodological instruments are "flashed" by the "monkey-dressed nigger," who sends him spinning in negative self-reflection. But I think that in this particular instance, it would be too easy to dismiss the occurrence of the butler as simple mirroring, or the surface upon which young Sutpen is played back to himself. (The latter case would identify more precisely the cultural production of minstrelsy, wherein the "blank wall" of faces is "made up" in hideous, even pornotrophic, caricature. The segregation of lips, teeth, eyes, and hair, for instance, in the facial contour would fit any number of artistic programs, but wed to a scheme of [over] representation—both "over and over again," and "written" on top of, designed to reenforce instances of sociopolitical dominance—the surreal strategies of minstrelsy exact a fatal mockery of art and entertainment.) In Sutpen's case, contrastingly, the commotions stirred up on the interior *posit* an "inward." I actually mean to say that the commotions *are* the coming about of, the markings of, an interior space. (A wedge that is driven between a Real and an Imaginary, even though the verb here is perhaps too volitional?) Sutpen's "blank" describes, then, the moment of tension between a "self-created" and a "self-alienated," or the moment when he "realizes" that he is not who he thought he was; *as* he thought he was. This enablement occurs under the auspices of ignorance (a conundrum that he cannot read) and impedance (his stalled movement forward). *Blocking* and *puzzlement* compel him—literally—to *flight* and the alienated "inwardness."

This thematics might be positioned to gather up "ambiguity" and "evacuate/evacuation" as contrastive movements of a local narrative etiology. Since "evacuate" is itself a figure of ambiguity in juxtaposing double meaning, it works well to describe Sutpen's new "moment of being" (an emptying out of contents) and the "his-story" that he wears on his feet (those "cattle, creatures heavy . . . without grace . . . brutely *evacuated* . . ."). Trapped always between pre- and co-eval texts, Sutpen himself is nowhere to be found, "in person," in Faulkner's work, but those symptoms of "him," dreadfully, densely read through the various narrative devices of *Absalom, Absalom!*, suggest that such as "he" still haunts the memory of a nation that commits the Sutpen error: Bearing the weight of knowledge, one cannot act *otherwise*, or *simply*. (Can he?) Sometimes, one's cultural project mandates the tracking down his own contingent "ambiguous" that was "written" long before.

So, who cuts the border? This question is not as mysterious as it might sound. It arose from a real circumstance around my house last summer when we wondered out loud who was responsible for cutting the border of grass on the edge of our property, simultaneous with the church's, south of the house. For several days the grass grew there, making neat quarantine in the midst of mowed lawn all around it. Small, local "wars" must start that way and massive, international ones, too, concerning the touchy question of borderlines. An instanteous household narrative lays hold here of a broader purpose: We might ask not only where the Sutpens belong in an American/US order of things, but by what finalities of various historico-cultural situations are we frozen forever in precisely defined portions of culture content?

Gilles Deleuze
and Félix Guattari

Gilles Deleuze was born in Paris in 1925 and was educated at the Sorbonne under Jean-Paul Sartre before undertaking an academic career in philosophy and literature. Félix Guattari was born in 1930 in the Parisian suburb of Villeneuve-les-Sablons and trained to become a psychoanalyst in the neo-Freudian style of Jacques Lacan. They met in 1968—the year Paris teetered on the edge of a revolution led by its radical intelligentsia. The result of the meeting was a series of collaborations in which (as Deleuze recalled) "everything became possible, even if we failed." Together they wrote *Anti-Oedipus* (1972), the first volume of *Capitalism and Schizophrenia,* a political critique of Freudian psychology. Their sequel was *A Thousand Plateaux* (1980), which used the eternal conflict between civilization and nomadism as a metaphor for the unstable relations between the various arts and sciences. In 1975 they published *Kafka: Toward a Minor Literature,* from which the selection below is excerpted, and in 1991 their final collaboration: *Qu'est-ce que la philosophie?* (What is philosophy?). Gilles Deleuze is professor of philosophy at Université de Paris VIII at Saint-Denis. Félix Guattari, for nearly forty years a psychoanalyst practicing at the Clinique de la Borde at Cour-Cheverny, died in 1992.

What Is a Minor Literature?

So far we have dealt with little more than contents and their forms: bent head–straightened head, triangles–lines of escape. And it is true that in the realm of expression, the bent head connects to the photo, and the erect head to sound. But as long as the form and the deformation or expression are not considered for themselves, there can be no real way out, even at the level of contents. Only expression gives us the *method.* The problem of expression is staked out by Kafka not in an abstract and universal fashion but in relation to those literatures that are considered minor, for example, the Jewish literature of Warsaw and Prague.[1] A minor literature doesn't come from a minor lan-

---

[1] Franz Kafka (1883–1924) was a Jewish native of Prague, capital of what is now the Czech Republic, but before 1918 was the capital of the province of Bohemia in the Austro-Hungarian Empire. Kafka was a lawyer and civil servant who wrote his surrealistic narratives in his spare time. His works defy literal interpretation, inspiring critics to read them as allegories of the author's psychological conflicts or philosophical fables about man's relationship to a distant and obscure God. During his lifetime, Kafka published two novellas, *The Metamorphosis* (1915) and *In the Penal Colony* (1919), and two collections of stories, *A Country Doctor* (1919) and *The Hunger Artist* (1924). His novels were edited and published after his death: *The Trial* in 1925, *The Castle* in 1926, and *Amerika* in 1927. As a Prague Jew, Kafka spoke Czech (the native tongue of the Bohemian population), German (the language of the Austro-Hungarian administration), and Yiddish (a creole of Middle High German, Polish, Russian and Hebrew spoken by Eastern European Jews), and at the time of his death was learning Hebrew. He wrote exclusively in German. *Ed.*

guage; it is rather that which a minority constructs within a major language. But the first characteristic of minor literature in any case is that in it language is affected with a high coefficient of deterritorialization. In this sense, Kafka marks the impasse that bars access to writing for the Jews of Prague and turns their literature into something impossible—the impossibility of not writing, the impossibility of writing in German, the impossibility of writing otherwise.[2] The impossibility of not writing because national consciousness, uncertain or oppressed, necessarily exists by means of literature ("The literary struggle has its real justification at the highest possible levels"). The impossibility of writing other than in German is for the Prague Jews the feeling of an irreducible distance from their primitive Czech territoriality. And the impossibility of writing in German is the deterritoralization of the German population itself, an oppressive minority that speaks a language cut off from the masses, like a "paper language" or an artificial language; this is all the more true for the Jews who are simultaneously a part of this minority and excluded from it, like "gypsies who have stolen a German child from its crib." In short, Prague German is a deterritorialized language, appropriate for strange and minor uses. (This can be compared in another context to what blacks in America today are able to do with the English language.)

The second characteristic of minor literatures is that everything in them is political. In major literatures, in contrast, the individual concern (familial, marital, and so on) joins with other no less individual concerns, the social milieu serving as a mere environment or a background; this is so much the case that none of these Oedipal intrigues are specifically indispensable or absolutely necessary but all become as one in a large space. Minor literature is completely different; its cramped space forces each individual intrigue to connect immediately to politics. The individual concern thus becomes all the more necessary, indispensable, magnified, because a whole other story is vibrating within it. In this way, the family triangle connects to other triangles—commercial, economic, bureaucratic, juridical—that determine its values. When Kafka indicates that one of the goals of a minor literature is the "purification of the conflict that opposes father and son and the possibility of discussing that conflict," it isn't a question of an Oedipal phantasm but of a political program. "Even though something is often thought through calmly, one still does not reach the boundary where it connects up with similar things, one reaches the boundary soonest in politics, indeed, one even strives to see it before it is there, and often sees this limiting boundary everywhere. . . . What in great literature goes on down below, constituting a not indispensable cellar of the structure, here takes place in the full light of day, what is there a matter of passing interest for a few, here absorbs everyone no less than as a matter of life and death."[3]

The third characteristic of minor literature is that in it everything takes on a collective value. Indeed, precisely because talent isn't abundant in a minor literature, there are no possibilities for an individuated enunciation that would belong to this or that "master" and that could be separated from a collective enunciation. Indeed, scarcity of talent is in fact beneficial and allows the conception of something other

[2] See letter to Brod, Kafka, *Letters,* June 1921, 289, and commentaries in Wagenbach, *Franz Kafka,* 84. *Au.*
[3] Kafka, *Diaries,* 25 December 1911, 194. *Au.*

than a literature of masters; what each author says individually already constitutes a common action, and what he or she says or does is necessarily political, even if others aren't in agreement. The political domain has contaminated every statement (*énoncé*). But above all else, because collective or national consciousness is "often inactive in external life and always in the process of break-down," literature finds itself positively charged with the role and function of collective, and even revolutionary, enunciation. It is literature that produces an active solidarity in spite of skepticism; and if the writer is in the margins or completely outside his or her fragile community, this situation allows the writer all the more the possibility to express another possible community and to forge the means for another consciousness and another sensibility; just as the dog of "Investigations" calls out in his solitude to *another science*. The literary machine thus becomes the relay for a revolutionary machine-to-come, not at all for ideological reasons but because the literary machine alone is determined to fill the conditions of a collective enunciation that is lacking elsewhere in this milieu: *literature is the people's concern.*[4] It is certainly in these terms that Kafka sees the problem. The message doesn't refer back to an enunciating subject who would be its cause, no more than to a subject of the statement (*sujet d'énoncé*) who would be its effect. Undoubtedly, for a while, Kafka thought according to these traditional categories of the two subjects, the author and the hero, the narrator and the character, the dreamer and the one dreamed of.[5] But he will quickly reject the role of the narrator, just as he will refuse an author's or master's literature, despite his admiration for Goethe. Josephine the mouse renounces the individual act of singing in order to melt into the collective enunciation of "the immense crowd of the heros of [her] people." A movement from the individuated animal to the pack or to a collective multiplicity—seven canine musicians. In "The Investigations of a Dog," the expressions of the solitary researcher tend toward the assemblage (*agencement*) of a collective enunciation of the canine species even if this collectivity is no longer or not yet given. There isn't a subject; *there are only collective assemblages of enunciation,* and literature expresses these acts insofar as they're not imposed from without and insofar as they exist only as diabolical powers to come or revolutionary forces to be constructed. Kafka's solitude opens him up to everything going on in history today. The letter K no longer designates a narrator or a character but an assemblage that becomes all the more machine-like, an agent that becomes all the more collective because an individual is locked into it in his or her solitude (it is only in connection to a subject that something individual would be separable from the collective and would lead its own life).

The three characteristics of minor literature are the deterritorialization of language, the connection of the individual to a political immediacy, and the collective as-

---

[4] Ibid., 193: "[L]iterature is less a concern of literary history, than of the people." *Au.*
[5] See "Wedding Preparations in the Country," in Kafka, *Complete Stories:* "And so long as you say 'one' instead of 'I,' there's nothing in it" (p. 53). And the two subjects appear several pages later: "I don't even need to go to the country myself, it isn't necessary. I'll send my clothed body," while the narrator stays in bed like a bug or a beetle (p. 55). No doubt, this is one of the origins of Gregor's becoming-beetle in "The Metamorphosis" (in the same way, Kafka will give up going to meet Felice and will prefer to stay in bed). But in "The Metamorphosis," the animal takes on all the value of a true becoming and no longer has any of the stagnancy of a subject of enunciation. *Au.*

semblage of enunciation. We might as well say that minor no longer designates specific literatures but the revolutionary conditions for every literature within the heart of what is called great (or established) literature. Even he who has the misfortune of being born in the country of a great literature must write in its language, just as a Czech Jew writes in German, or an Ouzbekian writes in Russian. Writing like a dog digging a hole, a rat digging its burrow.[6] And to do that, finding his own point of underdevelopment, his own *patois,* his own third world, his own desert. There has been much discussion of the questions "What is a marginal literature?" and "What is a popular literature, a proletarian literature?" The criteria are obviously difficult to establish if one doesn't start with a more objective concept—that of minor literature. Only the possibility of setting up a minor practice of major language from within allows one to define popular literature, marginal literature, and so on.[7] Only in this way can literature really become a collective machine of expression and really be able to treat and develop its contents. Kafka emphatically declares that a minor literature is much more able to work over its material.[8] Why this machine of expression, and what is it? We know that it is in a relation of multiple deterritorializations with language; it is the situation of the Jews who have dropped the Czech language at the same time as the rural environment, but it is also the situation of the German language as a "paper language." Well, one can go even farther; one can push this movement of deterritorialization of expression even farther. But there are only two ways to do this. One way is to artificially enrich this German, to swell it up through all the resources of symbolism, of oneirism,[9] of esoteric sense, of a hidden signifier. This is the approach of the Prague school, Gustav Meyrink and many others, including Max Brod.[10] But this attempt implies a desperate attempt at symbolic reterritorialization, based in archetypes, Kabbala,[11] and alchemy, that accentuates its break from the people and will find its political result only in Zionism and such things as the "dream of Zion." Kafka will quickly choose the other way, or, rather, he will invent another way. He will opt for the German language of Prague as it is and in its very poverty. Go always farther in the direction of deterritorialization, to the point of sobriety. Since the language is arid, make it vibrate with a new intensity. Oppose a purely intensive usage of language to all symbolic or even significant or simply signifying usages of it. Arrive at a perfect and unformed expression, a materially intense expression. (For these two possible paths, couldn't we find the same alternatives, under other conditions, in Joyce and Beckett? As Irishmen, both of them live within the genial conditions of a minor literature. That is the glory of this sort of minor literature—to be the revolutionary force for all liter-

---

[6] Deleuze and Guattari allude to Kafka's story, "Investigations of a Dog" (1922). *Ed.*

[7] See Michel Ragon, *Histoire de la littérature prolétarienne en France* (Paris: Albin Michel, 1974) on the difficulty of criteria and on the need to use a concept of a "secondary zone literature." *Au.*

[8] Kafka, *Diaries,* 25 December 1911, 193: "A small nation's memory is not smaller than the memory of a large one and so can digest the existing material more thoroughly." *Au.*

[9] Writing that conveys the feeling of the dream-state. *Ed.*

[10] See the excellent chapter "Prague at the turn of the century," in Wagenbach, *Franz Kafka,* on the situation of the German language in Czechoslovakia and on the Prague school. *Au.* Brod was Kafka's friend and literary executor; he assembled Kafka's novels for publication. *Ed.*

[11] Collective term for medieval Jewish mystical writings. *Ed.*

ature. The utilization of English and of every language in Joyce. The utilization of English and French in Beckett.[12] But the former never stops operating by exhilaration and overdetermination and brings about all sorts of worldwide reterritorializations. The other proceeds by dryness and sobriety, a willed poverty, pushing deterritorialization to such an extreme that nothing remains but intensities.)

How many people today live in a language that is not their own? Or no longer, or not yet, even know their own and know poorly the major language that they are forced to serve? This is the problem of immigrants, and especially of their children, the problem of minorities, the problem of a minor literature, but also a problem for all of us: how to tear a minor literature away from its own language, allowing it to challenge the language and making it follow a sober revolutionary path? How to become a nomad and an immigrant and a gypsy in relation to one's own language? Kafka answers: steal the baby from its crib, walk the tightrope.[13]

. . .

Let's return to the situation in the Hapsburg empire. The breakdown and fall of the empire increases the crisis, accentuates everywhere movements of deterritorialization, and invites all sorts of complex reterritorializations—archaic, mythic, or symbolist. At random, we can cite the following among Kafka's contemporaries: Einstein and his deterritorialization of the representation of the universe (Einstein teaches in Prague, and the physicist Philipp Frank gives conferences there with Kafka in attendance); the Austrian dodecaphonists and their deterritorialization of musical representation (the cry that is Marie's death in *Wozzeck,* or Lulu's, or the echoed *si* that seems to us to follow a musical path similar in certain ways to what Kafka is doing);[14] the expressionist cinema and its double movement of deterritorialization and reterritorialization of the image (Robert Wiene, who has Czech background; Fritz Lang, born in Vienna; Paul Wegener and his utilization of Prague themes). Of course, we should mention Viennese psychoanalysis and Prague school linguistics.[15] What is the specific situation of the Prague Jews in relation to the "four languages?" The vernacular language for these Jews who have come from a rural milieu is Czech, but the Czech language tends to be forgotten and repressed; as for Yiddish, it is often disdained or viewed with suspicion—it *frightens,* as Kafka tells us. German is the vehicular lan-

---

[12] James Joyce (1882-1941) and Samuel Beckett (1906-1989) were born in or near Dublin but lived and worked in Paris. *Ed.*

[13] In a section of the essay omitted here, Deleuze and Guattari discuss technical psycholinguistic aspects of minor literature. *Ed.*

[14] Here Deleuze and Guattari refer to the Viennese composer Arnold Schönberg and his disciples Alban Berg and Anton von Webern, who wrote "dodecaphonic" or twelve-tone music, avoiding a home key by using equally all the notes of the chromatic scale. They particularly center on Berg's operas in this style: *Lulu* (in which the heroine is killed by Jack the Ripper) and *Wozzeck* (based on a play by George Büchner) in which Marie is murdered while the single tone B (*si* in the French nomenclature) is repeatedly and obsessively played. *Ed.*

[15] On the Prague Circle and its role in linguistics, see *Change,* No. 3 (1969) and 10 (1972). (It is true that the Prague circle was only formed in 1925. But in 1920, Jakobson came to Prague where there was already a Czech movement directed by Mathesius and connected with Anton Marty who had taught in the German university system. From 1902 to 1905, Kafka followed the courses given by Marty, a disciple of Brentano, and participated in Brentanoist meetings.) *Au.*

guage of the towns, a bureaucratic language of the state, a commercial language of exchange (but English has already started to become indispensable for this purpose). The German language—but this time, Goethe's German—has a cultural and referential function (as does French to a lesser degree). As a mythic language, Hebrew is connected with the start of Zionism and still possesses the quality of an active dream. For each of these languages, we need to evaluate the degrees of territoriality, deterritorialization, and reterritorialization. Kafka's own situation: he is one of the few Jewish writers in Prague to understand and speak Czech (and this language will have a great importance in his relationship with Milena).[16] German plays precisely the double role of vehicular and cultural language, with Goethe always on the horizon (Kafka also knows French, Italian, and probably a bit of English). He will not learn Hebrew until later. What is complicated is Kafka's relation to Yiddish; he sees it less as a sort of linguistic territoriality for the Jews than as a nomadic movement of deterritorialization that reworks German language. What fascinates him in Yiddish is less a language of a religious community than that of a popular theater (he will become patron and impresario for the travelling theater of Isak Lowy).[17] The manner in which Kafka, in a public meeting, presented Yiddish to a rather hostile Jewish bourgeois audience is completely remarkable: Yiddish is a language that frightens more than it invites disdain, "dread mingled with a certain fundamental distaste"; it is a language that is lacking a grammar and that is filled with vocables that are fleeting, mobilized, emigrating, and turned into nomads that interiorize "relations of force." It is a language that is grafted onto Middle-High German and that so reworks the German language from within that one cannot translate it into German without destroying it; one can understand Yiddish only by "feeling it" in the heart. In short, it is a language where minor utilizations will carry you away: "Then you will come to feel the true unity of Yiddish and so strongly that it will frighten you, yet it will no longer be fear of Yiddish but of yourselves. Enjoy this self-confidence as much as you can!"[18]

Kafka does not opt for a reterritorialization through the Czech language. Nor toward a hypercultural usage of German with all sorts of oneiric or symbolic or mythic flights (even Hebrew-ifying ones), as was the case with the Prague school. Nor toward an oral, popular Yiddish. Instead, using the path that Yiddish opens up to him, he takes it in such a way as to convert it into a unique and solitary form of writing. Since Prague German is deterritorialized to several degrees, he will always take it farther, to a greater degree of intensity, but in the direction of a new sobriety, a new and unexpected modification, a pitiless rectification, a straightening of the head. Schizo politeness, a drunkenness caused by water.[19] He will make the German language take flight on a line of

---

[16] Milena Jesenska was a Czech journalist and translator with whom Kafka had a stormy, passionate love affair. *Ed.*

[17] On Kafka's connections to Lowy and Yiddish theater, see Brod, *Franz Kafka,* 110–16, and Wagenbach, *Franz Kafka,* 163–67. In this mime theater, there must have been many bent heads and straightened heads. *Au.*

[18] "An Introductory Talk on the Yiddish Language," trans. Ernst Kaiser and Eithne Wilkins, in Franz Kafka, *Dearest Father* (New York: Schocken Books, 1954), 381–86. *Au.*

[19] A magazine editor will declare that Kafka's prose has "the air of the cleanliness of a child who takes care of himself" (see Wagenbach, *Franz Kafka,* 82). *Au.*

escape. He will feed himself on abstinence; he will tear out of Prague German all the qualities of underdevelopment that it has tried to hide; he will make it cry with an extremely sober and rigorous cry. He will pull from it the barking of the dog, the cough of the ape, and the bustling of the beetle. He will turn syntax into a cry that will embrace the rigid syntax of this dried-up German. He will push it toward a deterritorialization that will no longer be saved by culture or by myth, that will be an absolute deterritorialization, even if it is slow, sticky, coagulated. To bring language slowly and progressively to the desert. To use syntax in order to cry, to give a syntax to the cry.

There is nothing that is major or revolutionary except the minor. To hate all languages of masters. Kafka's fascination for servants and employees (the same thing in Proust in relation to servants, to their language). What interests him even more is the possibility of making of his own language—assuming that it is unique, that it is a major language or has been—a minor utilization. To be a sort of stranger *within* his own language; this is the situation of Kafka's Great Swimmer.[20] Even when it is unique, a language remains a mixture, a schizophrenic mélange, a Harlequin costume in which very different functions of language and distinct centers of power are played out, blurring what can be said and what can't be said; one function will be played off against the other, all the degrees of territoriality and relative deterritorialization will be played out. Even when major, a language is open to an intensive utilization that makes it take flight along creative lines of escape which, no matter how slowly, no matter how cautiously, can now form an absolute deterritorialization. All this inventiveness, not only lexically, since the lexical matters little, but sober syntactical invention, simply to write like a dog (but a dog can't write—exactly, exactly). It's what Artaud did with French—cries, gasps; what Celine did with French, following another line, one that was exclamatory to the highest degree. Celine's syntactic evolution went from *Voyage* to *Death on the Credit Plan,* then from *Death on the Credit Plan* to *Guignol's Band.* (After that, Celine had nothing more to talk about except his own misfortunes; in other words, he had no longer any desire to write, only the need to make money. And it always ends like that, language's lines of escape: silence, the interrupted, the interminable, or even worse. But until that point, what a crazy creation, what a writing machine! Celine was so applauded for *Voyage* that he went even further in *Death on the Credit Plan* and then in the prodigious *Guignol's Band* where language is nothing more than intensities. He spoke with a kind of "minor music." Kafka, too, is a minor music, a different one, but always made up of deterritorialized sounds, a language that moves head over heels and away.) These are the true minor authors. An escape for language, for music, for writing. What we call pop—pop music, pop philosophy, pop writing—Worterflucht.[21] To make use of the polylingualism of one's own language, to make a minor or intensive use of it, to oppose the oppressed quality of this language to its oppressive quality, to find points of nonculture or underdevelopment, linguistic Third World zones by which a language can escape, an animal enters into things, an

---

[20] "The Great Swimmer" is undoubtedly one of the most Beckett-like of Kafka's texts: "I have to well admit that I am in my own country and that, in spite of all my efforts, I don't understand a word of the language that you are speaking." *Au.*
[21] The word is German for "language's lines of escape"—as in the previous paragraph. *Ed.*

assemblage comes into play. How many styles or genres or literary movements, even very small ones, have only one single dream: to assume a major function in language, to offer themselves as a sort of state language, an official language (for example, psychoanalysis today, which would like to be a master of the signifier, of metaphor, of wordplay). Create the opposite dream: know how to create a becoming-minor. (Is there a hope for philosophy, which for a long time has been an official, referential genre? Let us profit from this moment in which antiphilosophy is trying to be a language of power.)

Rachel Blau DuPlessis

Rachel Blau DuPlessis is professor of English at Temple University. Her first book was *Writing Beyond the Ending: Narrative Strategies of Twentieth-Century Women Writers* (1985), from which the following selection was taken. Her later works of literary criticism include *H.D.: The Career of that Struggle* (1986) and *The Pink Guitar: Writing as Feminist Practice* (1990). Blau DuPlessis also writes poetry for which she has received numerous grants and awards; her work is published in *Tabula Rosa* (1987) and *Drafts 3-14* (1991). Blau DuPlessis has also edited *The Selected Letters of George Oppen* (1990) and *Signets: Reading H.D.* (with Susan Friedman). She is currently writing a book on modern poetries and co-editing *The Objectivist Nexus* and *The Feminist Memoir Project.*

Breaking the Sentence; Breaking the Sequence

> *I am almost sure, I said to myself, that Mary Carmichael is playing a trick on us. For I feel as one feels on a switchback railway when the car, instead of sinking, as one has been led to expect, swerves up again. Mary is tampering with the expected sequence. First she broke the sentence: now she has broken the sequence.... Perhaps she had done this unconsciously, merely giving things their natural order, as a woman would, if she wrote like a woman. But the effect was somehow baffling; one could not see a wave heaping itself, a crisis coming round the next corner.... For whenever I was about to feel the usual things in the usual places, about love, about death, the annoying creature twitched me away, as if the important point were just a little further on.*
>
> Virginia Woolf
> *A Room of One's Own* (1929)

... Charlotte was gazing up into the dark eyes of Redmond. "My darling," he breathed hoarsely. Strong arms lifted her, his warm lips pressed her own. ...

That was the way it was supposed to go, that was the way it had always gone before, but somehow it no longer felt right. I'd taken a wrong turn somewhere; there was something, some fact or clue, that I had overlooked.

Margaret Atwood

Lady Oracle (1976)

One approach to the feminist criticism of these modern writers is suggested in an analysis of "Mary Carmichael's first novel, *Life's Adventure*," a work and author invented by Virginia Woolf and explicated in *A Room of One's Own*.[1] This is a novel by the last of the series of ancestral mothers alluded to in the Elizabethan ballad of the Four Marys, which forms a frame for the essay. The first two are Mary Beton, with her legacy of money, and Mary Seton, who provides "room"—institutional and psychological space. Both are necessary for Mary Carmichael, the modern author, and all of them express the baffled and unmentioned Mary Hamilton, from the ages when women had no way to dissent, except through infanticide and anonymous song. Woolf scrutinizes this novel's style, plot, and purpose with a diffident casualness, finding "some fact or clue" of great importance: "Mary is tampering with the expected sequence. First she broke the sentence; now she has broken the sequence" (*AROO*, 85). In these matching statements are telescoped a poetics of rupture and critique.

The sentence broken is one that expresses "the ridicule, the censure, the assurance of inferiority" about women's cultural ineptitude and deficiencies.[2] To break the sentence rejects not grammar especially, but rhythm, pace, flow, expression: the structuring of the female voice by the male voice, female tone and manner by male expectations, female writing by male emphasis, female writing by existing conventions of gender—in short, any way in which dominant structures shape muted ones. For a woman to write, she must experiment with "altering and adapting the current sentence until she writes one that takes the natural shape of her thought without crushing or distorting it" (*G&R*, 81).[3]

---

[1] Virginia Woolf, *A Room of One's Own* (New York: Harcourt, Brace and World, Inc., 1957); abbreviated in the text as *AROO*. The epigraphs come from pp. 85 and 95. *Au.*

[2] Virginia Woolf, "Women and Fiction" (1929), in *Granite and Rainbow* (New York: Harcourt, Brace and Company, 1958), p. 80; abbreviated as *G&R*. *Au.*

[3] The sentence is further qualified as being "too loose, too heavy, too pompous for a woman's use" (*G&R*, 81). A parallel, but slightly softened, statement about the sentence is found in *AROO*, 79, and an elaboration in the 1923 review of Dorothy Richardson, "Romance and the Heart," reprinted in *Contemporary Writers: Essays on Twentieth Century Books and Authors* (New York: Harcourt Brace Jovanovich, 1965), pp. 123-25. Working with these passages, Josephine Donovan also notes that the differences between "male" and "female" sentences exist in the tone of authority, the declaration of the insider in one, the under-the-surface life in the other, which rejects the authoritarian. Donovan also links Woolf's achievements in subjective realism to her critique of gender ideologies in narrative. "Feminist Style Criticism," in *Images of Women in Fiction: Feminist Perspectives*, ed. Susan Koppelman Cornillon (Bowling Green: Bowling Green University Popular Press, 1972), pp. 339-52. A further note on the analysis of Woolf's "sentence." In this study as a whole, I am carefully (too?) agnostic on the subject of those actual disruptions

At first it appeared as if Mary Carmichael would not be able to break this sentence and create her own. Her style was jerky, short, and terse, which "might mean that she was afraid of something; afraid of being called 'sentimental' perhaps; or she remembers that women's writing has been called flowery and so provides a superfluity of thorns . . ." (*AROO*, 85). Here she overcompensated for femaleness in deference to existing conventions.

But eventually, facing gender in an authentic way, the writer produces "a woman's sentence," "the psychological sentence of the feminine gender," which "is used to describe a woman's mind by a writer [Dorothy Richardson] who is neither proud nor afraid of anything that she may discover in the psychology of her sex."[4] The sentence is "psychological" not only because it deepens external realism with a picture of consciousness at work but also because it involves a critique of her own consciousness, saturated as it is with discourses of dominance.

There is nothing exclusively or essentially female about "the psychological sentence of the feminine gender," because writers of both sexes have used that "elastic" and "enveloping" form. But it is a "woman's sentence" because of its cultural and situational function, a dissension stating that women's minds and concerns have been neither completely nor accurately produced in literature as we know it. Breaking the sentence is a way of rupturing language and tradition sufficiently to invite a female slant, emphasis, or approach. Similarly there is nothing innately gendered about the signifier "I," yet in *A Room of One's Own* the speaker's "I" is both female and plural—"a woman's voice in a patriarchal literary tradition"—and another "I," shadowing the page, is "polished, learned, well-fed," an explicitly male subject speaking of and from dominance.[5]

Woolf's "woman's sentence," then, has its basis not in biology, but rather in cultural fearlessness, in the attitude of critique—a dissent from, a self-conscious marking of, dominant statement. It can be a stress shifting, the kind of realignment of emphasis noted by Nancy Miller, following Luce Irigaray: "an italicized version of what passes for the neutral or standard face . . . a way of marking what has already been said. . . ."[6]

A "woman's sentence" is Woolf's shorthand term for a writing unafraid of gender as an issue, undeferential to male judgment while not unaware of the complex relations between male and female. A "woman's sentence" will thus be constructed in considered indifference to the fact that the writer's vision is seen as peculiar, incompetent, marginal. So Woolf summarizes "the first great lesson" mastered by Mary Carmichael: "she wrote as a woman, but as a woman who has forgotten that she is a woman . . ." (*AROO*, 96). The doubled emphasis on woman, yet on forgetting woman, is a significant maneuver, claiming freedom from a "tyranny of sex" that is nonetheless palpable and dominant, both negated and affirmed.[7]

---

of syntax, grammar, and words more characteristic of, say, Gertrude Stein; however, what Julia Kristeva calls the semiotic and symbolic registers may be another oscillation of dominant discourse in dialogue with marginality. *Au.*

[4] "Romance and the Heart," *Contemporary Writers*, pp. 124–25. *Au.*

[5] This is Nelly Furman's argument. "Textual Feminism," in *Women and Language in Literature and Society*, ed. Sally McConnell-Ginet, Ruth Borker, and Nelly Furman (New York: Praeger, 1980), pp. 50–51. *Au.*

[6] Nancy Miller, "Emphasis Added: Plots and Plausibilities in Women's Fiction," *PMLA* 96,1 (January 1981): 38. *Au.*

[7] "Women Novelists," reprinted in *Contemporary Writers*, p. 25. *Au.*

In both *A Room of One's Own* and the related "Women and Fiction," Woolf criticizes women for "resenting the treatment of [their] sex and pleading for its rights," because, in her view, this threatens the poise a writer achieves by the transcending of "indignation" on the one hand and "resignation" on the other, the "too masculine" here and the "too feminine" there.[8] This movement between complicity and critique expresses Woolf's version of a doubled dynamic that is, as we shall see momentarily, characteristic of other women writers.[9]

What binds these writers is their oppositional stance to the social and cultural construction of gender.[10] This opposition has a number of origins. Perhaps the most suggestive is that of marginality in two arenas.[11] When a female writer is black (Alice Walker, Zora Neale Hurston, Gwendolyn Brooks, Toni Morrison), colonial (Olive Schreiner, Doris Lessing, Jean Rhys), Canadian (Margaret Atwood) of working-class origin (Tillie Olsen, Marge Piercy), of lesbian or bisexual orientation (H.D., Virginia Woolf, Adrienne Rich, Joanna Russ), or displaced and déclassé (Dorothy Richardson), double marginalization can be produced. Either it compels the person to negate any possibility for a critical stance, seeking instead "conformity and inclusion" because the idea of an authoritative center is defensively affirmed, or it enlivens the potential for critique by the production of an (ambiguously) nonhegemonic person, one in marginalized dialogue with the orders she may also affirm.[12]

---

[8] *Granite and Rainbow,* p. 80. *Au.*

[9] Here in the twenties, Woolf holds in conflictive tension her materialist and idealist views of writing. She argues that through art one may—indeed one must—transcend the cultural conditions of one's own formation. So in *A Room of One's Own,* Woolf combines a materialist analysis of the conditions that determine a woman's identity and capacity for work and an idealist vision of androgyny, a unity of the warring and unequal genders in luminous serenity. This point is made by Michèle Barrett in her introduction to a collection of essays by Virginia Woolf, *Women and Writing* (New York: Harcourt Brace Jovanovich, 1979), pp. 20, 22. *Au.*

[10] For example, Woolf compared living with the institutions of gender as they are to living in "half-civilized barbarism," a slap at the meliorism of liberal ideology. Reply to "Affable Hawk" from the *New Statesman* of 1920, in *The Diary of Virginia Woolf, Volume Two: 1920-1924,* ed. Anne Olivier Bell and Andrew McNeillie (New York: Harcourt Brace Jovanovich, 1978), p. 342. *Au.*

[11] Carolyn G. Heilbrun points toward the role of double determining when she suggests that "to be a feminist one had to have an experience of being an outsider more extreme than merely being a woman." *Reinventing Womanhood* (New York: W. W. Norton and Company, 1979), pp. 20-24. Adrienne Rich describes that tension leading to a doubled vision: "Born a white woman, Jewish or of curious mind / —twice an outsider, still believing in inclusion—" *A Wild Patience Has Taken Me This Far* (New York: W. W. Norton and Company, 1981), p. 39. *Au.*

[12] Myra Jehlen, "Archimedes and the Paradox of Feminist Criticism." *Signs* 6, 4 (Summer 1981): 594. Jehlen makes this point about nineteenth-century American women, attempting to explain the literature of sentiment and limited challenge that they produced. ". . . in this society, women stand outside any of the definitions of complete being; hence perhaps the appeal to them of a literature of conformity and inclusion." "(Ambiguously) nonhegemonic" from my essay "For the Etruscans: Sexual Difference and Artistic Production—the Debate over a Female Aesthetic," in *The Future of Difference,* ed. Hester Eisenstein and Alice Jardine (Boston: G. K. Hall & Co., 1980). A further development of the phrase "(ambiguously) nonhegamonic" is found in Margaret Homans, "'Her Very Own Howl': The Ambiguities of Representation in Recent Women's Fiction," *Signs* 9, 2 (Winter 1983): 186-205. Homans suggests that "there is a specifically gender-based alienation from language" visible in thematic treatments of language in women's fiction, which derives from "the special ambiguity of women's simultaneous participation in and exclusion from a hegemonic group. . . ," p. 205. *Au.*

The woman writers studied here are further unified by their interested dissent from androcentric culture in nonfictional texts: essay memoir, polemic, and social study. The texts will be seen, case by case, to contribute to their fictional elaborations and narrative stances.[13] Hence while hardly all of the writers would describe themselves as feminists, and some, indeed, resist that term, one may assert that any female cultural practice that makes the "meaning production process" itself "the site of struggle" may be considered feminist.[14] These authors are "feminist" because they construct a variety of oppositional strategies to the depiction of gender institutions in narrative. A writer expresses dissent from an ideological formation by attacking elements of narrative that repeat, sustain, or embody the values and attitudes in question. So after breaking the sentence, a rupture with the internalization of the authorities and voices of dominance, the woman writer will create that further rupture which is a center for this book: breaking "the sequence—the expected order" (*AROO*, 95).

Breaking the sequence is a rupture in habits of narrative order, that expected story told when "love was the only possible interpreter" of women's textual lives (*AROO*, 87). In her study of *Life's Adventure,* Woolf notes that the novelist Mary Carmichael alludes to "the relationship that there may be between Chloe and Roger," but this is set aside in favor of another bond, depicted "perhaps for the first time in literature" (*AROO*, 84, 86). "Chloe liked Olivia. They shared a laboratory together," begins Woolf (*AROO*, 87). The romance names with the allusions to Shakespearean transvestite characters are very suggestive, especially as opposed to the firmly heterosexual "Roger," with a whole history of slang behind him. One of these women is married, with children; the other is not. Their work—finding a cure for pernicious anemia—may suggestively beef up women's weakness of nerve with a good dose of female bonding.

The ties between Chloe and Olivia may be homosocial or, given the subsequent sexual-cultural metaphor of exploring the "serpentine cave" of women, they may be lesbian.[15] In either case, Woolf clearly presents a nonheterosexual relation nourished by the healthy vocation of women. She is also eloquent about the meaning of these changes. The women's friendship, based on their work life, will be "more varied and lasting because it will be less personal" (*AROO*, 88). "Personal" is Woolf's word (in essays throughout the twenties) for the privatization and exclusiveness that is part of the

---

[13] For example: Olive Schreiner, *Women and Labour;* Charlotte Perkins Gilman, *The Man-Made World; or, Our Androcentric Culture* and *Women and Economics;* Virginia Woolf, *Three Guineas, A Room of One's Own,* and various essays; H.D., *Tribute to Freud, End to Torment* and *The Gift;* Dorothy Richardson, essays on women; Adrienne Rich, *Of Woman Born* and *On Lies, Secrets and Silence;* Tillie Olsen, *Silences;* Doris Lessing, *A Small Personal Voice;* Alice Walker, *In Search of Our Mother's Gardens. Au.*

[14] Annette Kuhn, *Women's Pictures: Feminism and Cinema* (London: Routledge and Kegan Paul, 1982), p. 17. The first chapter is a sterling exposition of feminist analysis of culture. *Au.*

[15] In the course of her research on the draft of *A Room of One's Own,* Alice Fox communicated to Jane Marcus that Woolf originally, wittily left a blank unfilled by the word *laboratory.* "Then she wrote that she was afraid to turn the page to see what they shared, and she thought of the obscenity trial for a novel." The allusion made and excised is to the contemporary trial of *The Well of Loneliness;* the implication that Woolf handled differently in her published text is that homophobic censorship and self-censorship alike conspire to mute discussion of relational ties between women. Jane Marcus, "Liberty, Sorority, Misogyny," in *The Representation of Women in Fiction,* ed. Carolyn G. Heilbrun and Margaret R. Higonnet (Baltimore: Johns Hopkins University Press, 1983), p. 82. *Au.*

script of heterosexual romance. So the tie between Chloe and Olivia, a model for modern women writers, makes a critique of heterosexuality and the love plot, and offers (Woolf implies) a stronger and more positive sense of female quest. One is no longer allowed to "feel the usual things in the usual places, about love, about death" (*AROO*, 95). So breaking the sequence can mean delegitimating the specific narrative and cultural orders of nineteenth-century fiction—the emphasis on successful or failed romance, the subordination of quest to love, the death of the questing female, the insertion into family life. "The important point . . . just a little further on" that Mary Carmichael pushes her reader to see might be such narrative strategies as reparenting, female bonding, including lesbian ties, mother-child dyads, brother-sister pairs, familial transpositions, the multiple individual, and the transpersonal protagonist.

This study is also designed to suggest what elements of female identity would be drawn on to make plausible the analytic assumption that there is a women's writing with a certain stance toward narrative.[16] The narrative strategies of twentieth-century writing by women are the expression of two systemic elements of female identity—a psychosexual script and a sociocultural situation, both structured by major oscillations. The oscillations occur in the gendering process and in the hegemonic process. Oscillation is a swinging between two positions, a touching two limits, or, alternately, a fluctuation between two purposes, states, centers, or principles. The narrative strategies I will present here all take basic elements of female identity, such as the gendering sequence, and realign their components.

The possibilities for heterosexual love and romance take shape in the object relations within the family, that is, in the ties of kinship forged between child and parent, and in the processes of gendering, all given very complete cultural and social support. As we know, there is a sequence that assists these arrangements—a psychosexual script that is one of our first dramas. The occasion of our "learning the rules of gendering and kinship" and the apparatus for the production of sexual personality is, of course, the oedipal crisis.[17]

Freudian theory, postulating the telos of "normal femininity" as the proper resolution of the oedipal crisis, bears an uncanny resemblance to the nineteenth-century endings of narrative, in which the female hero becomes a heroine and in which the conclusion of a valid love plot is the loss of any momentum of quest. The pitfalls to be avoided by a woman seeking normal femininity are very consistent with the traits of the female hero in narrative: defiance, activity, selfishness, heroic action, and identification with other women. For Freudian theory puts a high premium on female passivity and narcissism and on the "end" of husband, home, and male child. As for quest or individual aspiration, Freud poignantly realizes that the achievement of femininity has left "no paths open to [a woman] for further development; . . . [it is] as though, in fact, the difficult development which leads to femininity had exhausted all the possi-

---

[16] Elaine Showalter proposes "that the specificity of women's writing [is] not . . . a transient by-product of sexism but [is] a fundamentally and continually determining reality." "Feminist Criticism in the Wilderness," *Critical Inquiry* 8, 2 (Winter, 1981): 205. *Au.*

[17] Gayle Rubin. "The Traffic in Women: Notes on the 'Political Economy' of Sex," in *Toward an Anthropology of Women*, ed. Rayna [Rapp] Reiter (New York: Monthly Review Press, 1975): pp. 157–210. *Au.*

bilities of the individual."[18] By the repressions and sacrifices involved in becoming feminine, quest is at a dead end—a sentiment that we have seen replicated in narrative endings.

The "original bisexuality" or "bisexual disposition" of every individual is the major starting point for this account.[19] The oedipal crisis is a social process of gendering that takes "bisexual, androgynous," libidinally active, and ungendered infants and produces girls and boys, giving to the male future social and sexual domination, and to the female future domesticated status within the rules of the sex-gender system of its society.[20] Thus gender is a product. That there must be some kind of passage of an infant "into a social human being" is not at issue. It will involve the "[dialectical] process of struggle with and ultimate supersession (including integration) of symbolic figures of love, desire, and authority." As this citation from Ortner proposes, the theoretical possibility that the oedipal crisis is historically mutable must not be overlooked.[21] The drama might unfold with some alternate figures and some alternate products or emphases.

Another major element of the oedipal crisis for girls is the requisite shift of object choice from "phallic" or preoedipal mother—the mother of power—to a heterosexual object, the father. Little boys must shift generations, but not genders, in their object choice. The reason for the female shift has been contested. Freud postulated that a girl will turn from her mother, sometimes with hatred and hostility, when the mother is discovered to be bereft of the genital marker of male power. In feminist revisions of Freud, this revelation, called "penis envy" by Freud, has been viewed as the delivery of knowledge well beyond the perception of sheer genital difference, the shock of learning a whole array of psychosocial rules and orders valorizing maleness.

To Freud, the girl's tasks in the oedipal drama involve the repression of what he calls the "little man" inside her, that active, striving, clitoral self, and the repression of love for her mother, a person of her own sex. Yet even the Freudian account somewhat reluctantly presents a recurring tension between the oedipal and preoedipal phases for the female, whereas in most males (as far as the theory tells) the oedipus complex has a linear and cumulative movement. Freud has found that "Regressions to fixations at these pre-oedipal phases occur very often; in many women we actually find a repeated alternation of periods in which either masculinity or femininity has obtained the upper hand."[22] So the oedipal crisis can extend over years and follow an in-

[18] Sigmund Freud: "The Psychology of Women" (1933), in *New Introductory Lectures on Psycho-Analysis,* trans. W.J.H. Sprott (New York: W. W. Norton and Company, Inc., 1933), p. 184. The same essay is called "Femininity" in *The Standard Edition of the Complete Psychological Works of Sigmund Freud,* vol. xxii, trans. James Strachey (London: The Hogarth Press and The Institute of Psychoanalysis, 1964). *Au.*

[19] Freud, "The Psychology of Women," p. 158. *Au.*

[20] Gayle Rubin, "The Traffic in Women," p. 185. *Au.*

[21] Sherry B. Ortner, "Oedipal Father, Mother's Brother, and The Penis: A Review of Juliet Mitchell's *Psychoanalysis and Feminism," Feminist Studies* II, 2/3 (1975): 179. As Michèle Barrett has remarked, "no substantial work has yet been produced that historicizes the [gendering] processes outlined in psychoanalytic theory." *Women's Oppression Today: Problems in Marxist Feminist Analysis* (London: Verso and New Left Books, 1980), p. 197. *Au.*

[22] Freud, "The Psychology of Women," p. 179. By female masculinity is meant the pre-oedipal object choice of a female; by femininity is meant the oedipal object choice of a male. *Au.*

dividual woman right into adulthood. Or, to say it another way, the "feminine" or "correct" resolution of women's gender identity comes easily unstuck and cannot be counted on.

A further elaboration of the oedipal crisis in women is available in Nancy Chodorow's analysis of mothering as a key institution in the social and psychic reproduction of gender. In her view, in the development of a girl, the preoedipal attachment to the mother is never entirely given up; it persists in coloring oedipalization, in shaping problems and issues of the female ego (boundlessness and boundary problems, "lack of separation or differentiation"), and in its influence on both the fact and the way that women mother. So while the gendering process is the "arena" where the goal of heterosexuality is "negotiated," it is also where the mother-daughter dyad and female bonding are affirmed.[23]

The narrative and cultural implications of this neo-Freudian picture of gendering are staggering. With no easy or one-directional passage to "normal femininity," women as social products are characterized by unresolved and continuous alternations between allegiance to males and to females, between heterosexuality and female-identified, lesbian, or bisexual ties. The "original bisexuality" of the individual female is not easily put to rest or resolved by one early tactical episode; rather the oscillation persists and is reconstituted in her adult identity. Further, the emotional rhythms of female identity involve repeated (and possibly even simultaneous) articulations of these two principles or states, which are taken (ideologically) as opposing poles.[24]

Twentieth-century women writers undertake a reassessment of the processes of gendering by inventing narrative strategies, especially involving sequence, character, and relationship, that neutralize, minimize, or transcend any oversimplified oedipal drama. This occurs by a recognition in various elements of narrative of the "bisexual oscillation" in the psychic makeup of characters, in the resolutions of texts, in the relationships portrayed. In twentieth-century narratives, effort is devoted to depicting masculine and feminine sides in one character—in Woolf's androgyny and in similar procedures in Richardson. Original bisexuality is extended the length of a character's life in H.D. and in Woolf. Women writers readjust the maternal and paternal in ways that unbalance the univocal sequence of object choices. This is why some female quest plots, like *To the Lighthouse* and *The Four-Gated City,* loop backward to mother-child attachments. Narratives of twentieth-century women, notably their *Künstlerromane,* may invent an interplay between the mother, the father, and the hero, in a "relational triangle."[25] These changes are often accompanied by pointed remarks about the plots, characters, and situations once expected in narrative: gender polarization, patrisexual

---

[23] Nancy Chodorow, *The Reproduction of Mothering: Psychoanalysis and the Sociology of Gender* (Berkeley: University of California Press, 1978), p. 112. *Au.*

[24] Chodorow summarizes the female's "emotional, if not erotic bisexual oscillation between mother and father—between preoccupation with 'mother-child' issues and 'male-female' issues." *The Reproduction of Mothering,* p. 168. I am indebted to Chodorow for the concept of oscillation. *Au.*

[25] "The asymmetrical structure of parenting generates a female oedipus complex . . . characterized by the continuation of preoedipal attachments and preoccupations, sexual oscillation in an oedipal triangle, and the lack of either absolute change of love object or absolute oedipal resolution." Chodorow, *The Reproduction of Mothering,* pp. 133–34. *Au. Künstlerroman*: a novel about the development of an artist. *Ed.*

romantic love, the arrest of female quest, the "happy ending"—remarks that, as we shall see, underline the self-consciousness of this critique of narrative scripts and the psychosexual drama that forms them.[26]

These representations of gendering could be achieved irrespective of whether any of the authors were aware of the exact terms of Freudian theory, although no doubt a number were, or whether they explicitly connected their narratives to any aspect of Freud's position (something that does occur in Woolf's *Orlando,* in H.D.'s *Helen in Egypt* and *Tribute to Freud,* and in Doris Lessing's *The Golden Notebook*).[27] For women artists, this sense of "remaining in the Oedipus situation for an indefinite period" would not have to be consciously understood.[28] One may simply postulate that the habit of living with an "unresolved" oedipus complex would lead the bearer to a greater identification of the unstable elements, greater intuitive knowledge of these components of one's interior life.

Indeed, Freud suggests a massive slippage of effectiveness, so that the learning of the rules of gender may need a good deal of extrafamilial reinforcement, especially where the girl is concerned. The formation of the superego—the acceptance of social rules, including those governing gender—is the result of "educative influences, of external intimidation threatening loss of love."[29] That is, education as an institution of gender, and culture as a whole, including literary products like narrative, channel the girl into dominant structures of the sex-gender system. The romance plot in narrative thus may be seen as a necessary extension of the processes of gendering, and the critique of romance that we find in twentieth-century female authors, as part of the oppositional protest lodged against both literary culture and a psychosexual norm.

The psychosexual oscillation of the gendering process, so distinctly theorized, interacts with another systemic aspect of female identity, which shows the same wavering, dialogic structure: a sociocultural oscillation of hegemonic processes. In the social and cultural arena, there is a constant repositioning between dominant and muted, hegemonic and oppositional, central and colonial, so that a woman may be described as (ambiguously) nonhegemonic or, with equal justice but less drama, as (ambiguously) hegemonic if her race, class, and sexuality are dominant. Virginia Woolf envisions this oscillating consciousness in *A Room of One's Own.*

---

[26] In an analysis related to my point here, Elizabeth Abel sees the theme and presence of same-sex friendship in literary works by women as an expression of female identity and the particularities of female oedipalization. As well, Abel offers striking remarks on the theory of literary influence that can be derived from Chodorow. "(E) Merging Identities: The Dynamics of Female Friendship in Contemporary Fiction by Women," *Signs* 6, 3 (Spring 1981): 413–35. *Au.*

[27] For example, H.D. was psychoanalyzed by Freud, and engaged, according to Susan Friedman, in a constant interior debate with Freud on several issues, including gender. *Psyche Reborn: The Emergence of H.D.* (Bloomington: Indiana University Press, 1981). Virginia Woolf noted her "very amateurish knowledge of Freud and the psychoanalysts" and admitted that "my knowledge is merely from superficial talk." In her circle, however, the talkers might have included James Strachey, the translator of Freud's *Complete Psychological Works,* cited in note 18. *The Letters of Virginia Woolf Volume Five, 1932–1935,* ed. Nigel Nicolson and Joanne Trautmann (New York: Harcourt Brace Jovanovich, 1979), 36 and 91. *Au.*

[28] Freud, "The Psychology of Women," p. 177. *Au.*

[29] Freud, "The Passing of the Oedipus-Complex," in *Collected Papers, Volume II* (London: The Hogarth Press, 1957), p. 275. The paper dates from 1924. *Au.*

It [the mind] can think back through its fathers or through its mothers, as I have said that a woman writing thinks back through her mothers. Again if one is a woman one is often surprised by a sudden splitting off of consciousness, say in walking down Whitehall, when from being the natural inheritor of that civilization, she becomes, on the contrary, outside of it, alien and critical.

(AROO, 101)

Note how Woolf passes from the oedipal-preoedipal division in object relations to the social oscillation, suggesting the relation of both processes to female identity. The debate between inheritor and critic is a movement between deep identification with dominant values and deep alienation from them. Whitehall, a street in London, is a synecdoche for British civil service and administrative agreements that endure beyond changes in specific governments, and thus is a metaphor for broad sociocultural agreement.

The shifting into alternative perspectives is taken by Woolf as a phenomenon peculiarly resonant for a woman. Her use of the word *natural* as opposed to the word *critical* sums the process up. *Natural* is what every ideology happily claims it is; the beliefs, social practices, sense of the self are second nature, assumed. The word *critical*, however, has the force of a severe and transgressive dissent from cherished mental structures and social practices. This contradictory quiver, this social vibrato creates a critical sensibility: dissent from the culture by which women are partially nourished, to which they are connected.

A major originating moment of Woolf's "outsider's feeling" came, significantly enough, in her confrontation at the turn of the century with the banal but forceful social and romantic expectations represented by George Duckworth, her half-brother and self-appointed substitute parent. At issue was her green dress, unconventionally made of upholstery fabric. From the moment of his anger at her appearance, from her as yet muted defiance, Woolf crystallizes that hegemonic set: proper dress, patterned feminine behavior, "tea table training," the absolute necessity for romance, the "patriarchal machinery" creating rigid, polarized male and female personalities. What astonished Woolf most was the female role of passive, appreciative spectator and the acrobatic—almost Swiftean—jumping through hoops demanded of males; the whole "circus" or "required act" was accomplished with no irony or critical questioning.[30]

Many commentators on women as a group and on female identity have isolated as systemic some kind of dual relationship to the definitions offered by various dominant forces. Simone de Beauvoir sees the female child "hesitating between the role of *object, Other,* which is offered to her, and the assertion of her liberty" as subject.[31] John Berger argues that the "social presence" of women and their ingenuity in living in "the keeping of men" have created "two constituent yet always distinct elements of

---

[30] Virginia Woolf, *Moments of Being,* ed. Jeanne Schulkind (New York: Harcourt Brace Jovanovich, 1978), pp. 132, 129, 132. *Au.*

[31] Simone de Beauvoir, *The Second Sex,* trans. H. M. Parshley (New York: Bantam Books, 1972), p. 47. *Au.*

her identity as a woman": the "surveyor and the surveyed."[32] The "duality of women's position in society" is Gerda Lerner's explanation for the fact that women as a group can be both victims and upholders of the status quo: "Women live a duality—as members of the general culture and as partakers of women's culture."[33] Nancy Cott similarly views "women's group consciousness as a subculture uniquely divided against itself by ties to the dominant culture."[34] Sheila Rowbotham describes the war of parts of the self, given the attitudes of the dominant group on the Left. "One part of ourselves mocked another, we joined in the ridicule of our own aspirations. . . . Part of us leapt over into their world, part of us stayed at home. . . . We were never all together in one place, we were always in transit, immigrants into alien territory."[35] And Alice Walker, in "In Search of Our Mothers' Gardens" cites Woolf's *A Room of One's Own* to come to terms with the "contrary instincts" in certain work by black women from Phillis Wheatley to Zora Neale Hurston.[36] In sum, women writers as women negotiate with divided loyalties and doubled consciousnesses, both within and without a social and cultural agreement. This, in conjunction with the psychosexual oscillation, has implications for "sentence" and "sequence"—for language, ideology, and narrative.

Later in her career, Woolf continued her analysis of the source of women's sociocultural oscillation. In *Three Guineas,* Woolf finds that women's structural position enables them to take an adversarial stance to institutions of dominance. Women, she argues, are basically outsiders, formed by their nondominant ("unpaid for") education, as they observe the privileges of maleness and the sacrifices exacted from women themselves for those privileges. The lived experience of women and men even from the same social class differs so greatly that their world views and values are irreconcilably distinct: "though we look at the same things, we see them differently."[37]

Constituting a separate group within their social class, women should capitalize on this built-in zone of difference to think of themselves as an interested, coherent political bloc: an actual Society of Outsiders. They can and should refuse male society and its values (militarism, hierarchy, authoritarianism) even as they enter formerly all-male professions. And women have, Woolf is certain, less chance than men for being apologists for political, economic, and social oppression so intense that—her central point—the patriarchal politics of bourgeois liberalism is on a continuum with fascism and the authoritarian state. Being already outsiders, women should turn its negative markers ("poverty, chastity, derision, freedom from unreal loyalties") into positive markers of difference, and turn their marginal status to political advantage and analytic power (*TG,* 78).

---

[32] John Berger, *Ways of Seeing* (New York: Viking Press, 1972), p. 46. *Au.*

[33] Gerda Lerner, *The Majority Finds its Past: Placing Women in History* (Oxford: Oxford University Press, 1979), pp. xxi, 52. *Au.*

[34] Nancy Cott, "Introduction," *Root of Bitterness: Documents of the Social History of American Women* (New York: E. P. Dutton and Co., 1972), p. 3. *Au.*

[35] Sheila Rowbotham, *Women's Consciousness, Man's World* (London: Penguin, 1973), pp. 30–31. *Au.*

[36] Alice Walker, "In Search of Our Mothers' Gardens," in *In Search of Our Mothers' Gardens* (San Diego: Harcourt Brace Jovanovich, 1983), p. 235. *Au.*

[37] Virginia Woolf, *Three Guineas* (New York: Harcourt, Brace and World, Inc., 1938), p. 5. Abbreviated in the text as *TG. Au.*

The function of *Three Guineas* is to drive a politically motivated wedge of analysis and polemic between dominant and muted, inheritor and critic, class and gender allegiances, to try to convince educated women no longer to cooperate with the politics of their class. Indeed, in 1940 Woolf argued that women are in a position to make cross-class alliances with working-class men and women because their identification as "commoners, outsiders" will override apparent class distinctions.[38]

Yet the shift to the imperative mode and the call for a vow in *Three Guineas* betray the fact that women are not purely and simply Outsiders; otherwise one would not have to exhort them to remain so. They are, however, less integrated into the dominant orders than are men of their class. Women are a muted or subordinate part of a hegemonic process. Raymond Williams suggests that seeing hegemonic processes would be a way of visualizing culture to credit the internal debate between affirmation and critique. Hegemony includes a relationship in conflictual motion between the ideologies and practices of a dominant class or social group and the alternative practices, which may be either residual or emergent, of the muted classes or groups. Any set of hegemonic assumptions—notions orthodox in a given society and historical era—are "deeply saturating" and pervasive, "organized and lived," woven into the most private areas of our lives.[39] Still the hegemonic is always in motion, being "renewed, recreated, defended and modified."[40] These hegemonic processes are a site for both sociocultural reproduction and sociocultural dissent. The debate that women experience between the critic and the inheritor, the outsider and the privileged, the oppositional and the dominant is a major example of a hegemonic process, one whose results are evident in both social and narrative texts. Constantly reaffirmed as outsiders by others and sometimes by themselves, women's loyalties to dominance remain ambiguous, for they are not themselves in control of the processes by which they are defined.

Issues of control of voice and definition, then, allow Edwin Ardener's otherwise more static model to offer a complementary set of terms to define gender relations: the articulate or dominant men and then the nondominant or muted women. The latter term recalls the muted sonority of a musical instrument—the sound different, tamped down, repressed, but still speaking, with the speech bearing the marks of partial silencing. Interestingly, giving voice to the voiceless and making visible the invisible are two prime maneuvers in feminist poetics. As Ardener would gloss this, "The muted structures are 'there' but cannot be 'realized' in the language of the dominant structure."[41] To depict these relationships, Ardener posits two almost overlapping circles, one standing for dominant vision, the other for muted. The larger uncontested space where the circles overlap is shared by men and women in a given society as par-

---

[38] Virginia Woolf, "The Leaning Tower," in *The Moment and Other Essays* (New York: Harcourt Brace Jovanovich, 1948), p. 154. *Au.*

[39] Raymond Williams, "Base and Superstructure in Marxist Cultural Theory," *New Left Review* 82 (Nov.–Dec. 1973): 7. *Au.*

[40] Raymond Williams, *Marxism and Literature* (Oxford: Oxford University Press, 1977), p. 112. *Au.*

[41] Edwin Ardener, "The 'Problem' Revisited," a coda to "Belief and the Problem of Women," in *Perceiving Women*, ed. Shirley Ardener (New York: John Wiley and Sons, 1975), p. 22. Elaine Showalter made Ardener's analysis available to feminist criticism in "Feminist Criticism in the Wilderness," *Critical Inquiry* 8, 2 (Winter 1981), especially 199–201. *Au.*

allel inhabitants of main culture. The tiny crescent-shaped band left over for women is their zone of difference. Visualizing the relationship between dominant and muted in this fashion suggests that women can oscillate between the two parts of the circle that represents them, between difference and dominance.

The concept of a "double-consciousness" that comes from one's oscillation between a main and a muted position is not, nor could it ever be, a way of describing women exclusively, but it offers a way of seeing the identity of any group that is at least partially excluded from or marginal to the historically current system of meaning, value, and power.[42] Feminist criticism, then, may be said to begin with W.E.B. DuBois, postulating for blacks this double consciousness, born in negotiation with hegemonic processes.

Ellen Moers analyzed distinctive female stances based not on innate or essential femininity but on the shared cultural experiences of secondary status—constraints on travel, education, social mediations of childhood and motherhood—and reflected in particular uses of certain cultural tropes, such as the Gothic, the monster, the landscape.[43] This postulate was given forceful statement by Elaine Showalter: that women are parallel to other minority groups in their subcultural position "relative to a dominant society" and that this position leads to a unity of "values, conventions, experiences and behaviors" from which women draw and to which they respond with various fictional and biographical strategies.[44] Following Showalter's emphasis on formal and biographical strategies of response, Sandra Gilbert and Susan Gubar pose a repeated and reinvoked struggle as the master plot for women of the nineteenth century: in a dynamic generational confrontation in which dominant culture is the father and women are either sage daughters or mad wives in relation to patriarchal power. A nineteenth-century woman writer is the site of an internalized cultural debate: her own rage that she cannot speak and her culture's rage that she can. This contradiction is resolved in a powerful fictional motif: the madwoman, in whom expression struggles with repression.[45]

Where a reading of twentieth-century materials necessarily differs from the nine-

---

[42] "Double-consciousness" is, in fact, the influential formulation of black identity made in 1903 by W.E.B. DuBois in *The Souls of Black Folk* (in *Three Negro Classics,* ed. John Hope Franklin [New York: Avon Books, 1965], p. 215). "It is a peculiar sensation, the double-consciousness, this sense of always looking at one's self through the eyes of others, of measuring one's soul by the tape of a world that looks on in amused contempt and pity. One ever feels his twoness—an American, a Negro; two souls, two thoughts, two unreconciled strivings; two warring ideals in one dark body, whose dogged strength alone keeps it from being torn asunder." Richard Wright made a similar point in 1956: "First of all, my position is a split one. I'm black. I'm a man of the West. These hard facts condition, to some degree, my outlook . . ." (*Présence Africaine* [November 1956], cited in *The Black Writer in Africa and the Americas,* ed. Lloyd W. Brown [Los Angeles: Hennessey & Ingalls, Inc., 1973], p. 27). *Au.*

[43] Ellen Moers, *Literary Women: The Great Writers* (Garden City, N.Y.: Doubleday and Company, Inc., 1976). *Au.*

[44] Elaine Showalter, *A Literature of Their Own: British Women Novelists from Brontë to Lessing* (Princeton, N.J.: Princeton University Press, 1977), p. 11. The postulation of "unity" is also generally assumed in this study. However, other perspectives on women's writing might make other assumptions, now that "women's writing" is an accepted critical category. *Au.*

[45] Sandra M. Gilbert and Susan Gubar, *The Madwoman in the Attic: The Woman Writer and the Nineteenth-Century Literary Imagination* (New Haven: Yale University Press, 1979), p. 49. *Au.*

teenth-century texts most profoundly analyzed by Showalter and Gilbert and Gubar is that, by the twentieth century, middle-class women are technically—on paper—rather more part of the economic world, rather less legally and politically circumscribed than they were in the nineteenth. This changed position does not alter the negotiation process, but it does mean that women have an interior identification with dominant values (traditionally expressed as a rejection of female specialness) as well as an understanding of muted alternatives. Dominant and muted may be more equally balanced opponents in the twentieth century than in the nineteenth.

Mary Jacobus has also noted, and made central to her analysis of women's writing, the split between alien critic and inheritor that I have taken as a key text for this book. Jacobus further argues that, given this situation, "at once within culture and outside it," a woman writer must simultaneously "challenge the terms and work within them."[46] This precisely parallels my argument—that woman is neither wholly "subcultural" nor, certainly, wholly main-cultural, but negotiates difference and sameness, marginality and inclusion in a constant dialogue, which takes shape variously in the various authors, but with one end—a rewriting of gender in dominant fiction. The two processes in concert—the gendering and the hegemonic process—create mutual reinforcement for the double consciousness of women writers. This is the social and sexual basis of the poetics of critique.[47]

All forms of dominant narrative, but especially romance, are tropes for the sex-gender system as a whole.[48] Given the ideological and affirmative functions of narrative, it is no surprise that the critique of story is a major aspect of the stories told by twentieth-century women writers. Having begun this discussion, in chapter 2, with a text from the 1880s, let me end with a survey of several contemporary works, to show how the critique of story is not only a thematic fact but an indication of the moral, ideological, and political desire to rescript the novel.

---

[46] Mary Jacobus, "The Difference of View," in *Women Writing and Writing about Women,* ed. Mary Jacobus (London: Croom Helm, 1979), pp. 19–20. *Au.*

[47] Myra Jehlen's summary of the relationship of women to culture is exemplary.

> Women (and perhaps some men not of the universal kind) must deal with their situation as a *pre*condition for writing about it. They have to confront the assumptions that render them a kind of fiction in themselves in that they are defined by others, as components of the language and thought of others. It hardly matters at this prior stage what a women wants to write; its political nature is implicit in the fact that it is she (a "she") who will do it. All women's writing would thus be congenitally defiant and universally characterized by the blasphemous argument it makes in coming into being. And this would mean that the autonomous individuality of a woman's story or poem is framed by engagement, the engagement of its denial of dependence. We might think of the form this necessary denial takes (however it is individually interpreted, whether conciliatory or assertive) as analogous to genre, in being an issue, not of content, but of the structural formulation of the work's relationship to the inherently formally patriarchal language which is the only language we have.

"Archimedes," p. 582. The proposal this book makes for the "structural formulation" analogous to genre is the act of critique, drawing on the oscillations of female identity. *Au.*

[48] The sex-gender system involves a linked chain of institutions such as the sexual division of labor in production and in the socialization of children, valorized heterosexuality and the constraint on female sexuality, marriage and kinship, sexual object choice and desire, gender asymmetry and polarization. *Au.*

Toni Morrison makes plain that *The Bluest Eye* concerns desperate material conditions that create and perpetuate racism and race self-hatred. Circumstances destroy the family that cannot "breed love" without also breeding pain and destruction. And stories—with their ideologies—are one of the circumstances. *The Bluest Eye* opens with three repeated paragraphs taken from one influential text promulgating vision and values: the "Dick and Jane" readers. This banal account of suburban family bliss is a primer for denatured language and a picture book of bourgeois values (contrasting with the choral complexity of the black world).[49] This memorable American series, with its reductive repetitions ("See the dog. See the dog run") and its uncanny commands ("Laugh, Mother, laugh") is the broad ideological backdrop that Morrison evokes. She gives it first in its own graceless prose, second, with the punctuation out, lacking priority or emphasis, and finally as one gigantic run-on block of gibberish and pain: the contents of the mind of someone who sees the whole story run over her like a freight train. As epigraphs to a number of the chapters, stony blocks of the run-on Dick and Jane material make ironic introductory remarks about prime childhood categories like family, house, mother, father, and play, which contrast with the Gordian knot of Pecola's life. Blue eyes—"story book eyes"—are, she intuits, the answer to every problem (*TBE*, 40). She is hardly wrong. These blue eyes, the white world's norm, are the image of all niceness and rightness, all superiority and advantage whose damage Morrison measures. Pecola wants the blue eyes of whiteness so she will no longer cause disgust, revulsion, and distaste in others, but will be able to "get somebody to love her"—an announced goal from the moment she reaches menarche at the beginning of the book (*TBE*, 29).

If that primer offers one set of stories about beauty and advantage, the movies offer another set to Pecola's mother. After poverty, hard work, and an uneasy marriage undermine Pauline's sense of self, movies complete her "education," and she gives way to her own ugliness, that is, to the rejection of any positive vision of blackness.

> Along with the idea of romantic love, she was introduced to another—physical beauty. . . . In equating physical beauty with virtue, she stripped her mind, bound it, and collected self-contempt by the heap. . . . She was never able, after her education in the movies, to look at a face and not assign it some category in the scale of absolute beauty, and the scale was one she absorbed in full from the silver screen.
>
> (*TBE*, 97)

The black and silver-white glamour of packaged romance displaces Pauline's own aesthetic and sexual experiences of "the rainbow"—all the sensuous colors she remembers from the past, the June bugs, the lemonade, the purple berry stains. Morrison shows the process by which a personality becomes socially fixed within the framework of these stories, as Pauline turns from the rich colors of blackness to the superficial pastels of the white child for whom she cares.

---

[49] Toni Morrison, *The Bluest Eye* (1970) (New York: Pocket Books, 1972). Abbreviated in the text as *TBE*. *Au.*

The story is framed in the voice of Claudia, a friend of Pecola's. When given a doll that should have represented her "fondest wish"—that is, a blond, blue-eyed, pink-skinned doll—Claudia will resist and destroy it (*TBE,* 19–22). Claudia is then one site of the critique of ideology, a break with the story of white niceness and appropriate girl behavior, exhibiting the same resistance to dominant stories that characterizes female writers and their fictional spokespeople. Claudia hates Shirley Temple, hates "white baby dolls." But she is also torn in a way we recognize—she oscillates between critique and the temptation of lightness and "good hair," the internal color line of the black community.

Among the narratives of romance and the romance of narrative, the Gothic remains to this day a major organizing grid for female consciousness. It is a form of sexual feudalism: the masochistic powerlessness of the generic female confronted with the no-frills, cruel-but-tender male. The proposition that Gothic paradigms are a major narrative ideology imbedded in female consciousness is treated comically and critically, yet seductively, in Margaret Atwood's *Lady Oracle.* The female hero is a doubled self: Joan Foster the person and Louisa Delacourt the writer. She is a woman self-conscious enough to write these Gothic fictions, great suety slabs of which are cited throughout the novel, and to manipulate these highly stylized conventions and their banal language. On the other hand, she is still seduced by these fictions, finding that, no matter how hard she tries—or perhaps because she tries—her life invariably falls into Gothic patterns. She doesn't know if she is a hero or a heroine, a quester or a victim, a woman with a career of romance writing or a career of romance. Her double names indicate the bifurcation of possibility, and the book oscillates between schemes that reveal her as a plotter and as the object of others' plots. By making Joan/Louisa a writer of, and a believer in, Gothic fictions, Atwood indicates how this narrative is an ideology sustained in consciousness and behavior.[50]

The doubled men of Gothic fiction (bland nice man who is unmasked as the villain, cruel moody man who is revealed as the hero), the murder, the senses of warning, menace, and premonition occur constantly and are comically deflated, yet recur, toy dolls that pop up, even when punched down. The "escape fiction" that Joan analyzes coolly is still warmly desired, despite the fact that her invention of mysterious disappearance, fantastic disguise, and intricate "plot" is easily pierced, both by herself and by others. Her self-parody is so thick that the parodic element is neutralized.

---

[50] Margaret Atwood, *Lady Oracle* (New York: Avon Books, 1976). Atwood has herself noted, in discussions of her poetry, the tensions between examination by lens and presentation by mirrors, which give a "backward reflection." This split is analogous to critical analysis and scrutiny on one hand, and remystification, the backward reflection, on the other. Karla Hammond, "An Interview with Margaret Atwood," *The American Poetry Review* (Sept.–Oct. 1979): 27. Atwood has also considered the woman question over the years from 1960 to the present, always in a demystifying tone. Her position can be exactly characterized by the oscillation between membership in the group *woman,* with all that means in terms of cultural stereotypes and limitations (for she uses a Woolfean trope of herself as a "graduate studentess" at Harvard, attempting to enter Widener Library in the early 1960s), and, on the other hand, membership in the group *human,* with a bluff impatience with any writer's version of reality, whether masculinist or liberationist, that puts the "capital W" on "Woman." *Second Words: Selected Critical Prose* (Toronto: House of Anansi Press, 1982), pp. 329, 227. *Au.*

Atwood leaves quite ambiguous the question of the main character's complicity in the creation of Gothic from the unpromising material of life: does her life "really" fall into these shapes? Is the female hero nudging it along? Or is her interpretive grid—narrative ideology—so powerful that it produces a Gothic script from plain old middle-class life in twentieth-century Toronto? Even the title, *Lady Oracle,* can be split between the compliant heroine and the myth-piercing seer, between complicity and critique. Like a Gail Godwin hero, a cover-illustrator for mass-market Gothics, Louisa/Joan keeps "one foot in the door of the Unknown, the other still holding open its place in the book of Old Plots."[51]

Jean Rhys's concerns for the social place of women and for a critique of narrative as ideology are given dramatic shape in her final novel, *Wide Sargasso Sea.*[52] Here Rhys revises Charlotte Brontë's *Jane Eyre,* taking the first Mrs. Rochester, Antoinette ("Bertha") Mason, as a representative of the muted side of Brontë's story. By turning a classic nineteenth-century novel inside out and giving its voiceless character an explanatory story, Rhys has constructed a critical examination of romantic thralldom and marital power—internalized and external institutions that support gender inequality.

Rhys's own social background, a white woman in a black society, may have drawn her to consider the history of the heiress from the West Indies, whom we assume and accept as a figure of horror at the center of *Jane Eyre.* An interpretation from a non-dominant perspective, from the eye of the other, the object, the outcast, breaks narrative *doxa* and opens a firmly closed text to heterodox questions. By the levels of passivity and fear developed in her as a child, Antoinette was readied for a savior and for a thralldom both financial and emotional. Rochester, a bourgeois male formed in a nexus of money and calculation, is making a future profit directly from the capital she provides. Antoinette's childhood history of isolation and rejection has contributed to a blank vulnerability (typical of other Rhys heroines), which brings her, devoid of a center, to a marriage without marriage contract, settlement, or legal protection. Deprived of her money, then rejected for her richly emerging sensuality, which Rochester associates with the lushness of the island and with blacks, Antoinette is driven, and then declared, mad, taken to England, and imprisoned by Rochester in an attic room, whence to haunt Brontë's novel. As Antoinette—a white and privileged but vulnerable child—she is traumatized by fire and a black uprising; as Bertha—a dark and enraged woman—she revolts by an act of destruction that mimics the arson of colonial uprisings.[53]

By a maneuver of encirclement (entering the story before) and leverage (prying the story open), Rhys ruptures *Jane Eyre.* She returns us to a framework far from the triumphant individualism of the character Jane Eyre by concentrating on the colonial situation. Through the realistic melodrama of black-white relations, Rhys allows us to

---

[51] Gail Godwin, *Violet Clay* (New York: Alfred A. Knopf, 1978), p. 45. *Au.*

[52] Jean Rhys, *Wide Sargasso Sea* (1966) (London: Penguin Books, 1968). *Au.*

[53] Elizabeth Baer makes this point. "The Sisterhood of Jane Eyre and Antoinette Cosway," in *The Voyage In: Fictions of Female Development,* ed. Elizabeth Abel, Marianne Hirsch, and Elizabeth Langland (Hanover: University Press of New England, 1983). *Au.*

see that the "personalities" of colonizer and colonized are transformed and fixed by their complementary functions.[54] So it is with the relations between the sexes in a nineteenth-century arranged marriage; a woman from a colony is a trope for the woman as a colony. *Wide Sargasso Sea* states that the closures and precisions of any tale are purchased at the expense of the muted, even unspoken narrative, which writing beyond the ending will release. ("Remember," Doris Lessing reminds us, "that for all the books we have in print, there are as many that have never reached print, have never been written down.")[55]

---

[54] Analyses such as Albert Memmi, *The Colonizer and the Colonized* (Boston: Beacon Press, 1967). *Au.*

[55] Doris Lessing, "The Preface to *The Golden Notebook*," in *A Small Personal Voice* (New York: Alfred A. Knopf, 1974), p. 39. *Au.*

Henry Louis Gates, Jr.

Henry Louis Gates, Jr., was born in Keyser, West Virginia, in 1950 and received his bachelor's degree in history from Yale. At 20, he hitchhiked through Africa on a Carnegie Foundation fellowship. In 1973, Gates studied at Clare College, Cambridge, where his tutor, the African writer Wole Soyinka, shifted Gates's interests to the ways in which African mythology and folktales underlay the literature of Africa and the African diaspora. Gates completed his Ph.D. in English literature at Cambridge in 1979 and was appointed to a professorship at Yale, where he had been teaching since 1976. Gates's first ground-breaking publication was the rediscovery and reprinting in 1983 of the first novel by a black woman anywhere, Harriet Wilson's *Our Nig* (1859). Gates has continued his recovery of "lost" texts by black Americans in the forty-volume *Schomberg Library of Nineteenth Century Black Women's Writings,* of which he is series editor. Gates's work has involved more than the canon of African American literature. In 1988 he published two books, *Figures in Black: Words Signs, and the Racial Self,* and *The Signifying Monkey: Towards a Theory of Afro-American Literature,* from which the following selection is reprinted. These books established him as one of the premier black theorists at work in the world today. Drawing on his work with Soyinka in African mythology, Gates presented a poststructuralist approach to African American literature that defined its particular way of "signifying" in the written word based on an inherited oral tradition. His work is equally concerned with the continuities between African and African American modes of reader-response and interpretation. Since the publication of these works, Gates has taught at Cornell, Duke, and Harvard, where he is W.E.B. Du Bois Professor of the Humanities. His most recent book is *Loose Canons: Notes on the Culture Wars* (1992).

Introduction from *The Signifing Monkey*

The black tradition is double-voiced. The trope of the Talking Book, of double-voiced texts that talk to other texts, is the unifying metaphor within this book. Signifyin(g) is the figure of the double-voiced, epitomized by Esu's depictions in sculpture as possessing two mouths.[1] There are four sorts of double-voiced textual relations that I wish to define.

TROPOLOGICAL REVISION

By tropological revision I mean the manner in which a specific trope is repeated, with differences, between two or more texts. The revision of specific tropes recurs with surprising frequency in the Afro-American literary tradition. The descent underground, the vertical "ascent" from South to North, myriad figures of the double, and especially double consciousness all come readily to mind. But there are other tropes that would seem to preoccupy the texts of the black tradition. The first trope shared in the black narrative tradition is what I shall call the Talking Book. This compelling trope appears in James Gronniosaw's 1770 slave narrative, and then is revised in at least four other texts published between 1785 and 1815. We might think of this as the ur-trope of the tradition. The form that repetition and difference take among these texts is the first example of Signifyin(g) as repetition and difference in the Anglo-African narrative tradition.

THE SPEAKERLY TEXT

The second mode of Signifyin(g) that I have chosen to represent in this text is exemplified in the peculiar play of "voices" at work in the use of "free indirect discourse" in Zora Neale Hurston's *Their Eyes Were Watching God*. Above all else, Hurston's narrative strategy seems to concern itself with the possibilities of representation of the speaking black voice in writing. Hurston's text, I shall claim, seems to aspire to the status of what she and, later, Ishmael Reed call the Talking Book. It is striking that this figure echoes the first figure repeated and revised in the tradition. Hurston's use is remarkably complex, and accomplished. Free indirect discourse is represented in this canonical text as if it were a dynamic character, with shifts in its level of diction drawn upon to reflect a certain development of self-consciousness in a hybrid character, a character who is neither the novel's protagonist nor the text's disembodied narrator, but a blend of both, an emergent and merging moment of consciousness. The direct discourse of the novel's black speech community and the initial standard English of the narrator come together to form a third term, a truly double-voiced narrative mode. That element of narration that the Russian Formalists called *skaz*—when a text seems

---

[1] Esu-Elegbara is the divine Trickster/Messenger of the Gods in Yoruba mythology found in various forms today in Nigeria, Benin, Brazil, Cuba, and the United States. *Ed.*

to be aspiring to the status of oral narration—is most clearly the closest analogue of Hurston's rhetorical strategy. The attendant ramifications of this device upon received modes of mimesis and diegesis occupy my attention in this chapter. Finally, I shall use Hurston's own theory of Signifyin(g) to analyze her narrative strategy, including the identification of Signifyin(g) rituals in the body of her text.

TALKING TEXTS

Chapter 5 explores one instance of a black form of intertextuality. Within the limits of the metaphor of the double-voiced that I am tracing from Esu-Elegbara to Alice Walker's novel *The Color Purple*, I have chosen to explicate Reed's novel *Mumbo Jumbo* to show how black texts "talk" to other black texts. Since *Mumbo Jumbo* would seem to be a signal text of revision and critique, cast in a so-called postmodern narrative, the implicit relation among modernism, realism, and postmodernism comes to bear here in the texts of *Invisible Man, Native Son, Black Boy,* and *Mumbo Jumbo.* Again, the relation of mimesis to diegesis shall occupy my attention in *Mumbo Jumbo's* foregrounded double voices.

REWRITING THE SPEAKERLY

If Hurston's novel seems to have been designed to declare that, indeed, a text could be written in black dialect, then it seems to me that Walker's *The Color Purple* aims to do just that, as a direct revision of Hurston's explicit and implicit strategies of narration. Walker, whose preoccupation with Hurston as a deeply admired antecedent has been the subject of several of her critical comments, revises and echoes Hurston in a number of ways. Her use of the epistolary form to write a novel in the language seemingly spoken by Hurston's protagonist is perhaps the most stunning instance of revision in the tradition of the black novel. Here, let me introduce a distinction: Reed's use of parody would seem to be fittingly described as motivated Signifyin(g), in which the text Signifies upon other black tests, in the manner of the vernacular ritual of "close reading." Walker's use of pastiche, on the other hand, corresponds to unmotivated Signifyin(g), by which I mean to suggest not the absence of a profound intention but the absence of a negative critique. The relation between parody and pastiche is that between motivated and unmotivated Signifyin(g).

Whereas Reed seems to be about the clearing of a space of narration, Walker seems to be intent on underscoring the relation of her text to Hurston's, in a joyous proclamation of antecedent and descendant texts. The most salient analogue for this unmotivated mode of revision in the broader black cultural tradition might be that between black jazz musicians who perform each other's standards on a joint album, not to critique these but to engage in refiguration as an act of homage. Such an instance, one of hundreds, is the relationship between two jazz greats on the album they made together, *Duke Ellington and John Coltrane.* This form of the double-voiced implies unity and resemblance rather than critique and difference.

The premise of this book is that the literary discourse that is most consistently "black," as read against our tradition's own theory of itself, is the most figurative, and that the modes of interpretation most in accord with the vernacular tradition's theory of criticism are those that direct attention to the manner in which language is used. Black texts Signify upon other black texts in the tradition by engaging in what Ellison has defined as implicit formal critiques of language use, of rhetorical strategy. Literary Signification, then, is similar to parody and pastiche, wherein parody corresponds to what I am calling motivated Signification while pastiche would correspond roughly to unmotivated Signification. By motivation I do not mean to suggest the lack of intention, for parody and pastiche imply intention, ranging from severe critique to acknowledgment and placement within a literary tradition. Pastiche can imply either homage to an antecedent text or futility in the face of a seemingly indomitable mode of representation. Black writers Signify on each other's texts for all of these reasons, and the relations of Signification that obtain between and among black texts serve as a basis for a theory of formal revision in the Afro-American tradition. Literary echoes, or pastiche, as found in Ellison's *Invisible Man,* of signal tropes found in Emerson, Eliot, Joyce, Crane, or Melville (among others) constitute one mode of Signifyin(g).

But so does Ellison's implicit rhetorical critique of the conventions of realism found in Richard Wright's *Native Son, The Man Who Lived Underground,* and *Black Boy.* Reed's parodies of Wright and Ellison constitute a Signification of a profoundly motivated order, especially as found in the text of *Mumbo Jumbo.* Hurston's multi-leveled use of voice in *Their Eyes Were Watching God* represents a Signification upon the entire tradition of dialect poetry as well as a brilliant and subtle critique of received notions of voice in the realistic novel, amounting to a remarkably novel critique and extension of Henry James's use of point-of-view as point-of-consciousness. Hurston's novel, like Sterling A. Brown's *Southern Road,* amounts to a refutation of critics such as James Welson Johnson who argued just six years before the publication of *Their Eyes* that the passing of dialect as a literary device among black authors was complete. Moreover, by representing her protagonist as a mulatto, who eschews the bourgeois life and marries a dark-complexioned migrant worker, Hurston Signifies upon the female novel of passing, an ironic form of fantasy that she inherited from Nella Larsen and Jessie Fauset. Finally, Walker's decision to place *The Color Purple* in a line of descent that runs directly from *Their Eyes* by engaging in a narrative strategy that tropes Hurston's concept of voice (by shifting it into the form of the epistolary novel and a written rather than a spoken vernacular) both extends dramatically the modes of revision available to writers in the tradition and reveals that acts of formal revision can be loving acts of bonding rather than ritual slayings at Esu's crossroads.

Eve Kosofsky Sedgwick

$\mathbf{F}$ew would have guessed from Eve Kosofsky Sedgwick's 1975 Yale doctoral dissertation, published as *The Coherence of Gothic Conventions* in 1980, that she was to be one of the founders of gay and lesbian studies in America, or that her 1989 MLA talk titled "Jane Austen and the Masturbating Girl" (published 1991 in *Critical Inquiry*) would be singled out for attack by right-wing columnist Roger Kimball as a prime example of "tenured radicalism." Sedgwick was born in Dayton, Ohio, and educated at Cornell before going on to Yale. Her strikingly original work on homosocial desire began from lectures she gave while teaching Women's Studies at Boston University. Sedgwick has written: "When I began work on *Between Men: English Literature and Male Homosocial Desire* (1986), I saw myself as working mainly in the context of feminist literary criticism and theory. By the time I published *The Epistemology of the Closet* in 1990, it was unmistakeably clear that lesbian/gay criticism was a going concern in its own right. I see my work as being strongly marked by a queer politics that is at once anti-separatist and anti-assimilationist; by a methodology that draws on deconstruction among other techniques; and by writerly experimentation." A poet as well as critic, Sedgwick has taught writing and literature at Hamilton College, Boston University, and Amherst College. She is currently Newman Ivey White Professor of English at Duke University. Her most recent book is *Tendencies* (1993). The following is excerpted from *The Epistemology of the Closet.*

Epistemology of the Closet

AXIOM 6: THE RELATION OF GAY STUDIES TO DEBATES ON THE LITERARY CANON IS, AND HAD BEST BE, TORTUOUS.

Early on in the work on *Epistemology of the Closet,* in trying to settle on a literary text that would provide a first example for the kind of argument I meant the book to enable, I found myself circling around a text of 1891, a narrative that in spite of its relative brevity has proved a durable and potent centerpiece of gay male intertextuality and indeed has provided a durable and potent physical icon for gay male desire. It tells the story of a young Englishman famous for an extreme beauty of face and figure that seems to betray his aristocratic origin—an origin marked, however, also by mystery and class misalliance. If the gorgeous youth gives his name to the book and stamps his bodily image on it, the narrative is nonetheless more properly the story of a male triangle: a second, older man is tortured by a desire for the youth for which he can find no direct mode of expression, and a third man, emblem of suavity and the world, presides over the dispensation of discursive authority as the beautiful youth murders the tortured lover and is himself, in turn, by the novel's end ritually killed.

But maybe, I thought, one such text would offer an insufficient basis for cultural hypothesis. Might I pick two? It isn't yet commonplace to read *Dorian Gray* and *Billy Budd* by one another's light, but that can only be a testimony to the power of accepted English and American literary canons to insulate and deform the reading of politically important texts. In any gay male canon the two contemporaneous experimental works must be yoked together as overarching gateway texts of our modern period, and the conventionally obvious differences between them of style, literary positioning, national origin, class ethos, structure, and thematics must cease to be taken for granted and must instead become newly salient in the context of their startling erotic congruence. The book of the beautiful male English body foregrounded on an international canvas; the book of its inscription and evocation through a trio of male figures—the lovely boy, the tormented desirer, the deft master of the rules of their discourse; the story in which the lover is murdered by the boy and the boy is himself sacrificed; the deftly magisterial recounting that finally frames, preserves, exploits, and desublimates the male bodily image: *Dorian Gray* and *Billy Budd* are both that book.

The year 1891 is a good moment to which to look for a cross-section of the inaugural discourses of modern homo/heterosexuality—in medicine and psychiatry, in language and law, in the crisis of female status, in the career of imperialism. *Billy Budd* and *Dorian Gray* are among the texts that have set the terms for a modern homosexual identity. And in the Euro-American culture of this past century it has been notable that foundational texts of modern gay culture—*A la recherche du temps perdu* and *Death in Venice,* for instance, along with *Dorian Gray* and *Billy Budd*—have often been the identical texts that mobilized and promulgated the most potent images and categories for (what is now visible as) the canon of homophobic mastery.

Neither *Dorian Gray* nor *Billy Budd* is in the least an obscure text. Both are available in numerous paperback editions, for instance; and, both conveniently short, each differently canonical within a different national narrative, both are taught regularly in academic curricula. As what they are taught, however, and as what canonized, comes so close to disciplining the reading permitted of each that even the contemporaneity of the two texts (*Dorian Gray* was published as a book the year *Billy Budd* was written) may startle. That every major character in the archetypal American "allegory of good and evil" is English; that the archetypal English fin-de-siècle "allegory of art and life" was a sufficiently American event to appear in a Philadelphia publisher's magazine nine months before it became a London book—the canonic regimentation that effaces these international bonds has how much the more scope to efface the intertext and the intersexed. How may the strategy of a new canon operate in this space?

Contemporary discussions of the question of the literary canon tend to be structured either around the possibility of change, of rearrangement and reassignment of texts, within one overarching master-canon of literature—the strategy of adding Mary Shelley to the Norton Anthology—or, more theoretically defensible at the moment, around a vision of an exploding master-canon whose fracture would produce, or at least leave room for, a potentially infinite plurality of mini-canons, each specified as to its thematic or structural or authorial coverage: francophone Canadian or Inuit canons, for instance; clusters of magical realism or national allegory; the blues tradition; working-class narrative; canons of the sublime or the self-reflexive; Afro-Caribbean canons; canons of Anglo-American women's writing.

In fact, though, the most productive canon effects that have been taking place in recent literary studies have occurred, not from within the mechanism either of the master-canon or of a postfractural plurality of canons, but through an interaction between these two models of the canon. In this interaction the new pluralized mini-canons have largely failed to dislodge the master-canon from its empirical centrality in such institutional practices as publishing and teaching, although they have made certain specific works and authors newly available for inclusion in the master-canon. Their more important effect, however, has been to challenge, if not the empirical centrality, then the conceptual anonymity of the master-canon. The most notorious instance of this has occurred with feminist studies in literature, which by on the one hand confronting the master-canon with alternative canons of women's literature, and on the other hand reading rebelliously within the master-canon, has not only somewhat rearranged the table of contents for the master-canon but, more important, given it a title. If it is still in important respects *the* master-canon it nevertheless cannot now escape naming itself with every syllable also *a* particular canon, a canon of mastery, in this case of men's mastery over, and over against, women. Perhaps never again need women—need, one hopes, anybody—feel greeted by the Norton Anthology of mostly white men's Literature with the implied insolent salutation, "I'm nobody. Who are you?"

This is an encouraging story of female canon-formation, working in a sort of pincers movement with a process of feminist canon-*naming,* that has been in various forms a good deal told by now. How much the cheering clarity of this story is indebted, however, to the scarifying coarseness and visibility with which women and men are, in most if not all societies, distinguished publicly and once and for all from one another emerges only when attempts are made to apply the same model to that very differently structured though closely related form of oppression, modern homophobia. It is, as we have seen, only recently—and, I am arguing, only very incompletely and raggedly, although to that extent violently and brutally—that a combination of discursive forces have carved out, for women and for men, a possible though intensively proscribed homosexual identity in Euro-American culture. To the extent that such an identity is traceable, there is clearly the possibility, now being realized within literary criticism, for assembling alternative canons of lesbian and gay male writing *as* minority canons, as a literature of oppression and resistance and survival and heroic making. This modern view of lesbians and gay men as a distinctive minority population is of course importantly anachronistic in relation to earlier writing, however; and even in relation to modern writing it seems to falter in important ways in the implicit analysis it offers of the mechanisms of homophobia and of same-sex desire. It is with these complications that the relation between lesbian and gay literature as a minority canon, and the process of making salient the homosocial, homosexual, and homophobic strains and torsions in the already existing master-canon, becomes especially revealing.

It's revealing only, however, for those of us for whom relations within and among canons are active relations of thought. From the keepers of a dead canon we hear a rhetorical question—that is to say, a question posed with the arrogant intent of maintaining ignorance. Is there, as Saul Bellow put it, a Tolstoi of the Zulus? Has there been, ask the defenders of a monocultural curriculum, not intending to stay for an answer, has there ever yet been a Socrates of the Orient, an African-American Proust, a female Shakespeare? However assaultive or fatuous, in the context of the current debate the question has not been unproductive. To answer it in good faith has been to broach inquiries across a variety of critical fronts: into the canonical or indeed world-historic texts of non-Euro-American cultures, to begin with, but also into the nonuniversal functions of literacy and the literary, into the contingent and uneven secularization and sacralization of an aesthetic realm, into the relations of public to private in the ranking of genres, into the cult of the individual author and the organization of liberal arts education as an expensive form of masterpiece theatre.

Moreover, the flat insolent question teases by the very difference of its resonance with different projects of inquiry: it stimulates or irritates or reveals differently in the context of oral or written cultures; of the colonized or the colonizing, or cultures that have had both experiences; of peoples concentrated or in diaspora; of traditions partially internal or largely external to a dominant culture of the latter twentieth century.

From the point of view of this relatively new and inchoate academic presence, then, the gay studies movement, what distinctive soundings are to be reached by posing the question our way—and staying for an answer? Let's see how it sounds.

> Has there ever been a gay Socrates?
>
> Has there ever been a gay Shakespeare?
>
> Has there ever been a gay Proust?

Does the Pope wear a dress? If these questions startle, it is not least as tautologies. A short answer, though a very incomplete one, might be that not only have there been a gay Socrates, Shakespeare, and Proust but that their names are Socrates, Shakespeare, Proust; and, beyond that, legion—dozens or hundreds of the most centrally canonic figures in what the monoculturalists are pleased to consider "our" culture, as indeed, always in different forms and senses, in every other.

What's now in place, in contrast, in most scholarship and most curricula is an even briefer response to questions like these: Don't ask. Or, less laconically: You shouldn't know. The vast preponderance of scholarship and teaching, accordingly, even among liberal academics, does simply neither ask nor know. At the most expansive, there is a series of dismissals of such questions on the grounds that:

1. Passionate language of same-sex attraction was extremely common during whatever period is under discussion—and therefore must have been completely meaningless. Or

2. Same-sex genital relations may have been perfectly common during the period under discussion—but since there was no language about them, *they* must have been completely meaningless. Or

3. Attitudes about homosexuality were intolerant back then, unlike now—so people probably didn't do anything. Or

4. Prohibitions against homosexuality didn't exist back then, unlike now—so if people did anything, it was completely meaningless. Or

5. The word "homosexuality" wasn't coined until 1869—so everyone before then was heterosexual. (Of course, heterosexuality has always existed.) Or

6. The author under discussion is certified or rumored to have had an attachment to someone of the other sex—so their feelings about people of their own sex must have been completely meaningless. Or (under a perhaps somewhat different rule of admissible evidence)

7. There is no actual proof of homosexuality, such as sperm taken from the body of another man or a nude photograph with another woman—so the author may be assumed to have been ardently and exclusively heterosexual. Or (as a last resort)

8. The author or the author's important attachments may very well have been homosexual—but it would be provincial to let so insignificant a fact make any difference at all to our understanding of any serious project of life, writing, or thought.

These responses reflect, as we have already seen, some real questions of sexual definition and historicity. But they only reflect them and don't reflect *on* them: the family resemblance among this group of extremely common responses comes from their closeness to the core grammar of *Don't ask; You shouldn't know.* It didn't happen; it doesn't make any difference; it didn't mean anything; it doesn't have interpretive consequences. Stop asking just here; stop asking just now; we know in advance the kind of difference that could be made by the invocation of *this* difference; it makes no difference; it doesn't mean. The most openly repressive projects of censorship, such as William Bennett's literally murderous opposition to serious AIDS education in schools on the grounds that it would communicate a tolerance for the lives of homosexuals, are, through this mobilization of the powerful mechanism of the open secret, made perfectly congruent with the smooth, dismissive knowingness of the urbane and the pseudo-urbane.

And yet the absolute canonical centrality of the list of authors about whom one might think to ask these questions—What was the structure, function, historical surround of same-sex love in and for Homer or Plato or Sappho? What, then, about Euripides or Virgil? If a gay Marlowe, what about Spenser or Milton? Shakespeare? Byron? But what about Shelley? Montaigne, Leopardi . . . ? Leonardo, Michelangelo, but . . . ? Beethoven? Whitman, Thoreau, Dickinson (Dickinson?), Tennyson, Wilde, Woolf, Hopkins, but Brontë? Wittgenstein, but . . . Nietzsche? Proust, Musil, Kafka, Cather, but . . . Mann? James, but . . . Lawrence? Eliot? but . . . Joyce? The very centrality of this list and its seemingly almost infinite elasticity suggest that no one *can* know *in advance* where the limits of a gay-centered inquiry are to be drawn, or where a gay theorizing of and through even the hegemonic high culture of the Euro-American tradition may need or be able to lead. The emergence, even within the last year or two, of nascent but ambitious programs and courses in gay and lesbian studies, at schools including those of the Ivy League, may now make it possible for the first time to ask these difficult questions from within the very heart of the empowered cultural institutions to which they pertain, as well as from the marginal and endangered institutional positions from which, for so long, the most courageous work in this area has emanated.

Furthermore, as I have been suggesting, the violently contradictory and volatile energies that every morning's newspaper proves to us are circulating even at this moment, in our society, around the issues of homo/heterosexual definition show over and over again how preposterous is anybody's urbane pretense at having a clear, simple story to tell about the outlines and meanings of what and who are homosexual and heterosexual. To be gay, or to be potentially classifiable as gay—that is to say, *to be sexed or gendered*—in this system is to come under the radically overlapping aegises of a universalizing discourse of acts or bonds and at the same time of a minoritizing discourse of kinds of persons. Because of the double binds implicit in the space overlapped by universalizing and minoritizing models, the stakes in matters of definitional control are extremely high.

Obviously, this analysis suggests as one indispensable approach to the traditional Euro-American canon a pedagogy that could treat it neither as something quite exploded nor as something quite stable. A canon seen to be genuinely unified by the maintenance of a particular tension of homo/heterosexual definition can scarcely be dismantled; but neither can it ever be treated as the repository of reassuring "traditional" truths that could be made matter for any settled consolidation or congratulation. Insofar as the problematics of homo/heterosexual definition, in an intensely homophobic culture, are seen to be precisely internal to the central nexuses of that culture, this canon must always be treated as a loaded one. Considerations of the canon, it becomes clear, while vital in themselves cannot take the place of questions of pedagogic relations within and around the canon. Canonicity itself then seems the necessary wadding of pious obliviousness that allows for the transmission from one generation to another of texts that have the potential to dismantle the impacted foundations upon which a given culture rests.

· · ·

Peter Brooks

Peter Preston Brooks was born in New York City and educated at Harvard University, where he received his Ph.D. in French in 1965. Since 1965 he has been professor of French and comparative literature at Yale. Brooks was a Guggenheim Fellow in 1973 and became Tripp Professor of Humanities at Yale in 1980. His publications include *The Novel of Worldliness* (1969), *The Child's Part* (1972), and *The Melodramatic Imagination* (1975). Recent essays have analyzed works by Balzac, Flaubert, Maupassant, Zola, and Henry James. His most influential book, a classic manifesto of the relationship between literature and modern French psychoanalysis, is *Reading for the Plot: Design and Intention in Narrative* (1984; second edition 1990), from which the following selection is excerpted. His most recent books are *Body Work* (1993) and *Psychoanalysis and Storytelling* (1994).

Narrative Desire

I

Plot as we have defined it is the organizing line and intention of narrative, thus perhaps best conceived as an activity, a structuring operation elicited in the reader trying to make sense of those meanings that develop only through textual and temporal succession. Plot in this view belongs to the reader's "competence," and in his "performance"—the reading of narrative—it animates the sense-making process: it is a key component of that "passion of (for) meaning" that, Barthes says, lights us afire when we read. We can, then, conceive of the reading of plot as a form of desire that carries us forward, onward, through the text. Narratives both tell of desire—typically present some story of desire—and arouse and make use of desire as dynamic of signification. Desire is in this view like Freud's notion of Eros, a force including sexual desire but larger and more polymorphous, which (he writes in *Beyond the Pleasure Principle*) seeks "to combine organic substances into ever greater unities."[1] Desire as Eros, desire in its plastic and totalizing function, appears to me central to our experience of reading narrative, and if in what follows I evoke Freud—and, as a gloss on Freud, Jacques Lacan—it is because I find in Freud's work the best model for a "textual erotics." I am aware that "desire" is a concept too broad, too fundamental, almost too banal to be defined. Yet perhaps it can be described: we can say something about the forms that it takes in narrative, how it represents itself, the dynamic it generates.

Desire is always there at the start of a narrative, often in a state of initial arousal, often having reached a state of intensity such that movement must be created, action undertaken, change begun. The *Iliad* opens with Agamemnon and Achilles locked in passionate quarrel over the girl Briseis, and the *Odyssey* with Odysseus, detained on Calypso's island, expressing the longing of his *nostos,* the drive to return home. To cite an explicitly erotic instance, Jean Genet's *Notre-Dame des fleurs* opens on an act of masturbation, and the narrative and its persons are called forth as what is needed for the phantasies of desire. One could no doubt analyze the opening paragraph of most novels and emerge in each case with the image of a desire taking on shape, beginning to seek its objects, beginning to develop a textual energetics. A rock-bottom paradigm of the dynamic of desire can be found in one of the very earliest novels in the Western tradition, *Lazarillo de Tormes* (1554), where all of the hero's tricks and dodges are directed initially at staying alive: Lazaro, the ragged, homeless *pícaro,*[2] must use his wits, his human ingenuity, to avoid the ever-present threat of starvation. Each chapter develops as a set of tricks and stratagems devised to overcome a specific form of the threat, and thus literally to enable life, and narrative, to go forward: the most telling

---

[1] Sigmund Freud, *Beyond the Pleasure Principle [Jenseits des Lustprinzips]* (1920), in *The Standard Edition of the Complete Psychological Works of Sigmund Freud,* ed. James Strachey (London: Hogarth Press, 1953-1974), vol 18, p. 50. Subsequent references to Freud are to this edition and simple page citations will be given in the text. *Au.*

[2] *Pícaro:* "rogue hero." *Ed.*

illustration may be the second chapter, where Lazaro must simulate the actions of a mouse and a snake to work his way into his master the priest's locked bread chest. The resistance to desire in this novel is simply, and brutally, total deprivation of what sustains life; while the traditional comic structure—in theater and then in novel—presents the resistance of an older generation of "blocking figures" to the plotting of the younger generation, seeking erotic union. As in a great many folktales—the example of "Jack the Giant Killer" and its permutations comes to mind—the specifically human faculty of ingenuity and trickery, the capacity to use the mind to devise schemes to overcome superior force, becomes a basic dynamic of plot. If the giants of folktale are always stupid, it is because they stand opposed to human wit, which is seen as a capacity for leverage on the world, precisely that which overcomes inert obstacles, sets change in motion, reformulates the real.

By the nineteenth century, the *pícaro*'s scheming to stay alive has typically taken a more elaborated and socially defined form: it has become ambition. It may in fact be a defining characteristic of the modern novel (as of bourgeois society) that it takes aspiration, getting ahead, seriously, rather than simply as the object of satire (which was the case in much earlier, more aristocratically determined literature), and thus it makes ambition the vehicle and emblem of Eros, that which totalizes the world as possession and progress. Ambition provides not only a typical novelistic theme, but also a dominant dynamic of plot: a force that drives the protagonist forward, assuring that no incident or action is final or closed in itself until such a moment as the ends of ambition have been clarified, through success or else renunciation. Somewhat in the manner of the traditional sequence of functions in the folktale analyzed by Propp, ambition provides an armature of plot which the reader recognizes, and which constitutes the very "readability" of the narrative text, what enables the reader to go about the construction of the text's specific meanings. Ambition is inherently totalizing, figuring the self's tendency to appropriation and aggrandizement, moving forward through the encompassment of more, striving to have, to do, and to be more. The ambitious hero thus stands as a figure of the reader's efforts to construct meanings in ever-larger wholes, to totalize his experience of human existence in time, to grasp past, present, and future in a significant shape. This description, of course, most obviously concerns male plots of ambition. The female plot is not unrelated, but it takes a more complex stance toward ambition, the formation of an inner drive toward the assertion of selfhood in resistance to the overt and violating male plots of ambition, a counter-dynamic which, from the prototype *Clarissa* on to *Jane Eyre* and *To the Lighthouse,* is only superficially passive, and in fact a reinterpretation of the vectors of plot.[3]

The ambitious heroes of the nineteenth-century novel—those of Balzac, for in-

---

[3] On the bourgeoisie and the novel, see Harry Levin, *The Gates of Horn* (New York: Oxford University Press, 1963), especially chap. 2; and Ian Watt, *The Rise of the Novel*, 3rd ed. (Berkeley and Los Angeles: University of California Press, 1962), which also discusses the protestant and dissenting role represented by the female consciousness, as in *Clarissa*. On women's plots, see Nancy K. Miller, *The Heroine's Text* (New York: Columbia University Press, 1980). One might recall here that the folktale "All-Kinds-of-Fur" in some measure represents the female plot, a resistance and what we might call an "endurance": a waiting (and suffering) until the woman's desire can be a permitted response to the expression of male desire. *Au.*

stance—may regularly be conceived as "desiring machines" whose presence in the text creates and sustains narrative movement through the forward march of desire, projecting the self onto the world through scenarios of desire imagined and then acted upon. Etymology may suggest that the self creates a circle—an *ambitus*—or aureola around itself, mainly in front of itself, attempting ever to move forward to the circumference of that circle and to widen it, to cast the nets of the self ever further. A most obvious example would be Eugène de Rastignac, hero of Balzac's *Le Père Goriot,* who, as the action of that novel begins, has just returned from his first soirée in Parisian high society and has discovered the uses of ambition:

> To be young, to have a thirst for society, to be hungry for a woman, and to see two houses open to oneself! to place one's foot in the Faubourg Saint-Germain with the Vicomtesse de Beauséant, and one's knee in the Chaussée d'Antin, with the Comtesse de Restaud! to plunge with one's glance into the salons of Paris all in a line, and to believe oneself a handsome enough young man to find there aid and protection in the heart of a woman! to feel oneself ambitious enough to give a proud stamp of the foot to the tightrope on which one must walk with the assurance that the acrobat won't fall, and to have found the best of balancing poles in a charming woman!

The disarming directness, even crudity, of the quotation suggests how Rastignac is conceived as a bundle of desires which need only be given a field for their exercise—the topography of which is suggested in the quotation—for the narrative to move forward.

The novel will indeed unfold as an anatomy of human desire, where the introduction of the professional master-plotter, Vautrin, will serve explicitly to theorize desire and the logical consequences of its full enactment. In a world so charged with desire, the central drama becomes—as in the Christian arch-drama—one of temptation. If Rastignac is able to resist the specific terms of Vautrin's plot, which offers the dowered maiden as the direct consequence of murder—a temptation that makes *too* clear a certain logic of desire—it is because he has found a more nuanced system for the realization of ambition in the conjunction of erotic and financial power represented by another woman, Delphine de Nucingen. Rastignac negotiates a path between the absolutes of plot expounded by his two would-be fathers, Vautrin and Goriot. It is sign and condition of his success that he gives absolute allegiance to neither and goes beyond both, escaping the constraints of paternity, moving forward with the hyperbolic rapidity typical of Balzacian narratives of ambition, accelerating toward a goal that here is represented in the famous final scene in which the hero, from his vantage point on the rise of Père-Lachaise cemetery, can view the *beaux quartiers*[4] of Paris as ready for his possession: a world charged with meaning and possibility because it is charged, like the glance that takes visionary possession of it, with desire. In other cases (for instance, in the career of Lucien de Rubempré, across the two novels *Illusions perdues* and *Splendeurs et misères des courtisanes*) the narrative of ambition accelerates to

---

[4] *Beaux quartiers:* wealthy neighborhoods. *Ed.*

the overheating and loss of energy of the desiring machine, indeed sometimes to its explosion.[5]

. . .

My interest in these emblematic motors and engines invented by novelists, as by Freud, derives from my dissatisfaction with the various formalisms that have dominated critical thinking about narrative, and from my search for models that would be more adequate to our experience of reading narrative as a dynamic operation—what makes plot move us forward to the end, to put it in simplest terms. As Jacques Derrida once wrote in criticism of Jean Rousset's *Forme et signification,* a book he found typical of a certain structuralist thought, in such work "the geometric or the morphologic is corrected only by a mechanics, never by an energetics." Derrida writes further: "*Form* fascinates when one no longer has the force to understand force from within itself." Like Derrida, I can make no claim to understanding force in itself. But I think we do well to recognize the existence of textual force, and that we can use such a concept to move beyond the static models of much formalism, toward a dynamics of reading and writing. In the motors and engines I have glanced at, including Eros as motor and motor as erotic, we find representations of the dynamics of the narrative text, connecting beginning and end across the middle and making of that middle—what we read *through*—a field of force.[6]

. . .

Desire as narrative thematic, desire as narrative motor, and desire as the very intention of narrative language and the act of telling all seem to stand in close interrelation. This interrelation demands further thought, and we might start by returning for a moment to Freud, to a passage in *Beyond the Pleasure Principle* where he encounters Goethe's *Faust,* pre-eminently the representation of man's unquenchable striving. In his study of instinctual drives, Freud sets aside the wishful belief that there might be an "instinct toward perfection at work in human beings," and goes on to suggest how the dynamic that appears to produce forward and upward movement really works:

> What appears in a minority of human individuals as an untiring impulsion towards further perfection can easily be understood as a result of the instinctual repression upon which is based all that is most precious in human civilization. The repressed instinct never ceases to strive for complete satisfaction, which would consist in the repetition of a primary experience of satisfaction. No substitutive or reactive formations and no sublimations will suffice to remove the repressed instinct's persisting tension; and it is the difference in amount between the pleasure of satisfaction which is *demanded* and that which is actually *achieved* that provides the driving factor

---

[5] In the section omitted here, Brooks explores the nineteenth-century fascination with thermodynamics, the physics of engines, motors, forces, heat and energy flow, and how it underlies both Freud's psychoanalytical theories and the social explorations of novelists like Balzac and Zola. *Ed.*

[6] In the section omitted here, Brooks analyzes the plot of Balzac's novel *Le Peau de chagrin. Ed.*

which will permit of no halting at any position attained, but, in the poet's words, *"ungebändigt immer vorwärts dringt"* ["presses ever forward unsubdued"]. (p. 42)

Freud's version of Faustian man is inhabited by a motor whose "driving factor" is the result of tension caused by difference which powers his life's story forward, striving upward to its end.

Here we can introduce another return to Freud, Lacan's interpretation of the concept of desire, desire as born of the difference or split between need and demand: for instance, the infant's need for the breast (for nourishment) and his demand, which is in essence a demand for love from the other (for instance, from the mother). To cite Jean Laplanche and J.-B. Pontalis: "Desire is born from the gap [*l'écart*] between need and demand; it is irreducible to need, for it is not in its principle relation to a real object, independent of the subject, but rather to a phantasy; it is irreducible to demand, in that it seeks to impose itself without taking account of language and the unconscious of the other, and insists upon being absolutely recognized by the other." In this gap, desire comes into being as a perpetual want for (of) a satisfaction that cannot be offered in reality. Desire is inherently unsatisfied and unsatisfiable since it is linked to memory traces and seeks its realization in the hallucinatory reproduction of indestructible signs of infantile satisfaction: it reposes on phantasmatic scenarios of satisfaction. Such unconscious desire becomes, in the later life of the subject, a motor of actions whose significance is blocked from consciousness, since interpretation of its scenarios of fulfillment is not directly accessible to consciousness.

One can now begin to grasp the manner in which desire comes to inhabit the language of narration. In Lacan's interpretation of the Saussurian analysis of the sign, the bar separating signifier from signified (S/s) becomes the bar of repression, indicating the inaccessibility of the true signified (the object of unconscious desire). Discourse hence becomes the interconnection of signifiers one with another in a "signifying chain" where meaning (in the sense of access to the meaning of unconscious desire) does not consist in any single link of the chain, yet through which meaning nonetheless *insists.* The analyst, for instance, hears in the analysand's language the pressure *toward* meaning, which is never pinned down or captured since there is a perpetual sliding or slippage of the signified from under the signifier. Thus it is that language can "mean" something other than what it "says," can suggest intentions of which the subject is not consciously aware. This slippage is particularly characteristic of the metonymic pole of language—the particular tropology of narrative, according to Roman Jakobson. If narrative desire keeps moving us forward, it is because narrative metonymy can never quite speak its name. As Lacan writes, "The enigmas that desire poses to any 'natural philosophy,' its frenzy miming the abyss of the infinite, the intimate collusion in which it envelops the pleasure of knowing and that of dominating with pleasure, belongs to no other derangement of instinct than its being caught on the rails—eternally extended toward the *desire of something else*—of metonymy." Narrative is hence condemned to *saying* other than what it *would mean,* spinning out its movement toward a meaning that would be the end of its movement.[7]

. . .

"If only you knew my life," Raphaël has said to Emile, in a phrase that could stand for most tellings of the life's story, where the claim that intelligibility, meaning, understanding depend on a fully predicated narrative sentence, on a narrative totality, never is and never can be realized. Yet the performance of the narrative act is in itself transformatory, predicating the material of the life story in a changed context—subordinating all its verbs to the verb "I tell"—and thus most importantly soliciting the entry of a listener into relation with the story. The narrative act discovers, and makes use of, the intersubjective nature of language itself, medium for the exchange of narrative understandings. Here in the dialogic dynamic of the narrative transference—a topic for later elaboration—we may make our nearest approach to the antique dealer's notion of *savoir,* the knowledge wrested from the doomed dialectic of *vouloir* and *pouvoir,* in the transformatory function of narrating itself.

The paradigm of what I have in mind would be the *Thousand and One Nights,* Balzac's inspiration as he sought to make the magic of an "oriental tale" unfold within the frame of contemporary Paris. In the *Thousand and One Nights,* Shahrazad's storytelling takes a desire that has gone off the rails—the Sultan's desire, derailed by his wife's infidelity, become sadistic and discontinuous, so that the mistress of the night must have her head chopped off in the morning—and cures it by prolonging it, precisely by narrativizing it. Desire becomes reinvested in tellings of and listenings to stories, it is reconstituted as metonymy—over a thousand and one nights—until the Sultan can resume a normal erotic state, marrying Shahrazad, who thus fulfills her name as "savior of the city." Narration, in this allegory, is seen to be life-giving in that it arouses and sustains desire, ensuring that the terminus it both delays and beckons toward will offer what we might call a lucid repose, desire both come to rest and set in perspective.

Narratives portray the motors of desire that drive and consume their plots, and they also lay bare the nature of narration as a form of human desire: the need to tell as a primary human drive that seeks to seduce and to subjugate the listener, to implicate him in the thrust of a desire that never can quite speak its name—never can quite come to the point—but that insists on speaking over and over again its movement toward that name. For the analyst of narrative, these different yet convergent vectors of desire suggest the need to explore more fully the shaping function of desire, its modeling of the plot, and also the dynamics of exchange and transmission, the roles of tellers and listeners. But prior to pursuing the theoretical questions thus implied, I shall turn to consider in some detail a single novel, attempting to disengage the models of plot and plotting that it appears to propose, and to understand what these have to do with individual biography and collective history.

---

[7] In the section omitted here, Brooks discusses *Le Peau de chagrin* as exemplary of the way the novel's narrative converts one unrealizable desire (the desire to possess fully the beloved object) into another desire (the desire to tell one's story, to fully capture a listener) and how both desires are ultimately "beyond the pleasure principle," deathly desires for the end. *Ed.*

Fredric Jameson

Without challenge the foremost Marxist literary critic in America today, Fredric R. Jameson was born in Cleveland, Ohio, in 1934, raised in New Jersey, and educated at Haverford College and Yale University, where he received his Ph.D. in 1960. He has taught at Harvard University (1959-67), the University of California at San Diego (1967-76), Yale University (1976-83), the University of California at Santa Cruz (1983-85), and since 1986 has been Lane Professor of Comparative Literature at Duke University. His books include studies of Jean-Paul Sartre (1961) and Wyndham Lewis (1979). His major works include *Marxism and Form: Twentieth Century Dialectical Theories of Literature* (1971), *The Prison-House of Language: A Critical Account of Russian Formalism and Structuralism* (1972), *The Political Unconscious: Narrative as a Socially Symbolic Act* (1979), two volumes of collected essays entitled *The Ideologies of Theory* (1988), *Modernism and Imperialism* (1988), a book of film criticism titled *Signatures of the Visible* (1990), *Postmodernism: The Cultural Logic of Late Capitalism* (1991), and *The Geo-Political Aesthetic: Cinema and Space in the World System* (1992).

The Realist Floor-Plan

The hypothesis to be tested in the following essay is a conception of the moment of novelistic "realism" as the literary equivalent (both on the level of discourse and on that of "realistic" narrative) of what Deleuze and Guattari (in the *Anti-Oedipus*) call "decoding": the secularization of the older sacred codes, the systematic dissolution of the remaining traces of the hierarchical structures which very unequally and over many centuries characterized the organization of life and practices under the *ancien régime* and even more distantly under feudalism itself. The process is evidently at one with the whole philosophical programme of secularization and modernization projected by the Enlightenment *philosophes,* who thematize it essentially in terms of the defence of nascent science and the elimination of superstition or error, as well as the subversion of the older forms of theological power in the church and the monarchy.

I call this enormous process of decoding on all levels the *bourgeois cultural revolution:* a formulation which suggests that we cannot be content with a merely negative account of the whole Enlightenment demolition programme, but must also attempt to convey what "positively" was set in place in the moment of desacralization. Even on a first approach, one would assume the emergence of a new space and a new temporality, a whole new realm of measurability and Cartesian extension, as well as of measurable clock time, a realm of the infinite geometrical grid, of homogeneity and equivalence.

All this can be said in a somewhat different way if we pause to interrogate the function of the writers and the artists of this transitional period, and the culture they produce, in that immense "great transformation", in which the production of legitimizing ideologies by the philosophers, journalists and scientists is only one component. The artists also are to be seen as *ideologues* but not in the narrow and debunking sense of the producers of false consciousness: their service to ideology in the vastest sense of daily practices is a virtually demiurgic one, the production of a whole new world—on the level of the symbolic and imaginary[1]—which will henceforth constitute the objective lived appearance of that equally objective production of the infrastructure of the emergent market system of industrial capitalism. What is at stake in their cultural production is therefore the retraining, the collective re-education, of a whole population whose mentalities and habits were formed in the previous mode of production, feudalism or the *ancien régime.* This is of course, no punctual event, and in the case of this particular "transition" extends from the sixteenth century (Weber's Protestant ethic is one of the early key mechanisms in such a cultural revolution) all the way to the late nineteenth century in France, in which a landed aristocracy and an old agriculture still largely survive. (Indeed, under the direction of what is euphemistically called "modernization", this particular cultural revolution is still going on in the Third World today, although sometimes combined, in the sense of Trotsky's permanent revolution and "uneven development", with a more properly socialist cultural revolution.)

In general, only the negative or destructive features of the bourgeois cultural revolution have been insisted on: most particularly the vast demolition efforts of the Enlightenment *philosophes,* as they seek to clear a space for what will become contemporary science. But the positive features of such a revolution are no less significant, and essentially include the whole new life world to which people are to be retrained: a new form of space, whose homogeneity abolishes the old heterogeneities of various forms of sacred space—transforming a whole world of qualities and libidinal intensities into the merely psychological experience of what Descartes called "secondary sensations", and setting in their place the grey world of quantity and extension, of the purely measurable—together with the substitution of the older forms of ritual, sacred or cyclical time by the new physical and measurable temporality of the clock and the routine, of the working day. In this sense, we may go even further in our account of the ideological mission of the nineteenth century realistic novelists, and assert that their function is not merely to produce new mental and existential habits, but in a virtual or symbolic way to produce this whole new spatial and temporal configuration itself: what will come to be called "daily life", the *Alltag,* or, in a different terminology, the "referent"—so many diverse characterizations of the new configuration of public and private spheres or space in classical or market capitalism. When we think of the genealogy of the Renaissance city itself, which derived from the painters' invention of perspective, itself derived from late medieval theatrical space, this productive function of the novelists may seem less paradoxical: at least it usefully underscores the active role of Flaubert's linguistic revolution, and

---

[1] The "Imaginary" and the "Symbolic" are two of the three "fields" in the psychoanalytic theories of Jacques Lacan, referring to desires and the way those desires are rechanneled from one object to another; the third field is "the Real." *Ed.*

offers a characterization of "realism" less passive than the conventional notions of "reflexion", "representation" and the like.

But something else follows from our initial hypothesis, namely, that we must not be content to model this process as two distinct and discontinuous moments, related to each other only by the rubble of some incomprehensible restructuration. Rather, recoding, realism, desacralization (what I shall call in a moment the production of the referent and of daily life) is all to be seen as a production process in which the older forms and structures now serve as the *raw materials* to be worked over and transformed into the new system. The two moments of the *ancien régime* and the bourgeois market system are therefore here to be described as a synchronic coexistence, as a dialectical surcharge, in which old and new find themselves locked at every instant in a grisly cannibalization: the new drawing its vitality from the old and draining it off, as has often been pointed out by those who have perceived the degree to which the culture of capital—the most sterile of all human cultures—is constantly obliged to renew itself by drawing on more vital precapitalist forms.

I have found it useful to describe this process as the virtual production of the referent or of daily life in order to underscore the radical difference between the secular life of modern times and the industrial city, in this immense new world which has become one gigantic factory, and the older kinds of communal experience which organized the life of the village or the peasant or aristocratic *Gemeinschaft*[2] (and still minimally do so, as John Berger's account of peasant life in *Pig Earth* vividly conveys). As for the referent itself, the sense of raw data existing objectively out there, the object so radically sundered from the subject that our language and symbolic systems can do no more than designate it from afar, it is for modern linguistics and post-structuralism a myth, a mirage, or an ideology. Indeed, the text we are about to examine, from Flaubert's tale *Un Coeur simple,* is particularly strategic at this point, since it was the occasion for Roland Barthes' most powerful attack on precisely the concept of reference and realism, in his article *"L'effet de réel"* (in *Communications,* vol. 11, 1968). From my own point of view, however, which is that of a radical historicism, we can bracket the truth-claims of both positions, of the nineteenth-century "belief" in science and the referent, as well as of late-twentieth-century scepticism in this respect. What is significant for us, even if reference is taken to be a mirage, lies in the "reality of the appearance" and the way in which belief in reference governs the practices of nineteenth-century daily life and of the nineteenth-century "realistic" aesthetic. But historicism will also want to bracket or to estrange the "beliefs" of the late-twentieth-century linguistics and post-structuralism as well: and indeed, in our subsequent exhibits, one of the key stories we shall have to tell will be very precisely the curious and complex, dialectical ways in which the referent has slowly been effaced again.

This is, however, the moment to turn to the text itself, which is a description of the provincial house in which the maid Félicité will pass the rest of her earthly existence:

> Cette maison, revêtue d'ardoises, se trouvait entre un passage et une ruelle
> aboutissant à la rivière. Elle avait intérieurement des différences de niveau

---

[2] *Gemeinschaft:* community. *Ed.*

qui faisaient trébucher. Un vestibule étroit séparait la cuisine de la *salle* où Madame Aubain se tenait tout le long du jour, assise près de la croisée dans un fauteuil de paille. Contre le lambris, peint en blanc, s'alignaient huit chaises d'acajou. Un vieux piano supportait, sous un baromètre, un tas pyramidal de boîtes et de cartons. Deux bergères de tapisserie flanquaient la cheminée en marbre jaune et de style Louis XV. La pendule, au milieu, représentait un temple de Vesta, —et tout l'appartement sentait un peu le moisi, car le plancher était plus bas que le jardin.

[This house had a slate roof and stood between an alley-way and a lane leading down to the river. Inside there were differences in level which were the cause of many a stumble. A narrow entrance-hall separated the kitchen from the parlour, where Madame Aubain sat all day long in a wicker easy-chair by the window. Eight mahogany chairs were lined up against the white-painted wainscoting, and under the barometer stood an old piano loaded with a pyramid of boxes and cartons. On either side of the chimney piece, which was carved out of yellow marble in the Louis Quinze style, there was a tapestry-covered armchair, and in the middle was a clock designed to look like a temple of Vesta. The whole room smelt a little musty, as the floor was on a lower level than the garden.]

We must look at a description of this kind in a new way, as a form of programming. The house itself is a pretext, and in that sense Barthes was not wrong to isolate a detail from this paragraph as his central illustration for what he calls *"l'effet de réel"*[3], a purely connotative function in which a wealth of *contingent* details—without any symbolic meaning—emit the signal, "this is reality", or better still, "this is realism". Balzac's houses are indeed so many signs: materiality in Balzac, the quantities of objects and descriptions which freight the lengthy preparatory work of a Balzacian narrative, are in this sense quite unmaterial, and when examined closely have all the transparency of the sign or symbol—designating meanings, serving as shorthand for the social condition of the inhabitants or for their moral qualities. This is not noticeably the case with the Flaubert description in question here: on the other hand, it is difficult to accept Barthes' conception of an empty sign—a passage which would function as pure connotation without any denotative content (inasmuch as for him this content is contingent, or meaningless, anything would do, any house would do).

Our characterization of the work of Flaubert's *écriture*[4] as a form of programmation—as unlovely as this terminology may be—will allow us to isolate some of these mechanisms in a way which is usefully distinct either from stylistic analysis (which presupposes the modernist aesthetic of a unique personal style) or from current forms of structural analysis which essentially foreground the systemic content of such texts.

The active remoulding of the reader's "mentality" begins at once, with a sentence in which the central object—the house—is immediately decentred by its twin bound-

---

[3] The reality-effect. *Ed.*
[4] *Ecriture:* mode of writing. *Ed.*

aries, the alley-way and the lane. The only thing we are told about the ostensible object of description in this initial sentence concerns its roofing; and roofs obviously also at once empty down into the adjacent spaces, spilling the reader with them. This "dominant" is clearly an abstract form: it does not yield qualities or adjectives of any kind, but rather sensitizes us to the empty fact of a dual system of proximate levels, levels which are neither liminal nor forms of closure, which have no particular content in their own right but function simply as the parallel lines of a grid. What is imposed on the reading mind here is a training in uneven surfaces, in the abstract, empty feeling for the inequality of adjacent co-ordinates.

This characterization may well seem an excessive deduction from the relatively impoverished data of the initial sentence: it is, however, largely confirmed by the second, which rematerializes the abstract form of this experience in terms of *"différences de niveau"*—virtually the first information we are given about the interior of the house, and surely a peculiar feature by which to introduce it. Yet the "stumbling" over this uneven surface subliminally inscribes this empty form on the reading body itself: the sentence is no longer inert or denotative, but has gestural content and energy: this tripping over the levels within the house is thus what Bakhtin calls a chronotope—a spatio-temporal unity—albeit a deliberately anonymous one, belonging to no particular individual or character of the tale, an experience of the Heideggerian "man" or nobody, which is thus fully as abstract as the empty form which it undertakes to dramatize for us.

A dual system of parallel lines, an abstract experience of sheer unevenness extending in all directions: let us relate all this to Cosimo Tura's painting *Flight into Egypt* and grasp these two parallel lines as analogous to the stripes of Joseph's switch on the donkey's flanks, an alteration meant to drive the donkey forward in a straight line, just as it here programmes the reader to drive forward head-on into the infinite space of Cartesian extension. All this now combines in the third sentence to model the interior of the house as a dual and uneven world: the kitchen on the one side (uncharacterized, yet already marked by our knowledge of the central character of the tale to come, whose privileged space this is) and the parlour on the other, in which the mistress passes her days looking out of the window, much like Proust's Tante Léonie. This comparison reinforces a significant distinction that must be stressed between the empty form or spatial grid in question here and the conventional "structural" conception of a binary opposition. The latter is a form of closure, in which the twin terms are fatally asymmetrical to each other, and enforce a generally repressive system of essential and inessential terms, of self and other, or centre and margin: the binary opposition thereby becomes the generator or marginality and marginalization in general. But we have already noted that the "boundaries" of the house are not closed limits of this kind: the space of extension stretches far beyond "alley-way" and "lane" to include the village and ultimately France and Europe itself. "Alley-way" and "lane" are thus not marked terms of the binary type, and what is generated by their juxtaposition is a system of dual inequality, a most unstable dualism in which "two" is not a meaningful unit in itself, but rather a deconstructive weapon against "one", against the conception of the house as a central substance in its own right.

This is why it would be a mistake to assume that the third sentence of our paragraph, in which the inhabitants of the house finally seem to make their appearance, has as its primary function the expression of some hierarchical relationship of domination between mistress and servant. Domination and hierarchy are certainly present, but of a peculiarly decentred kind, as I now want to show. Félicité is, of course, so far present only as the "implied subject" of the kitchen space; but this shadowy absence is emblematic enough of her marginalization throughout the tale, which insistently stages her life by proxy through the children and destinies of the family she serves, and later on, through the metonymic-metaphoric displacement of her libido onto the wellnigh Benjaminian allegorical relics of that family history.

I think that it is important for interpretive purposes, however, to understand the peculiar class position of servants as such in this world, who are neither working-class people (with at least a potentiality for a genuine, centred class culture of their own) nor peasants—a class position explicitly abandoned by Félicité in the opening pages of our story. An adequate social and historical interpretation of Félicité's peculiar vacancy is possible only if we keep in mind the uniquely parasitical situation of the *servidumbre*[5] of these periods, who can attain no class consciousness of their own, but must necessarily in one way or another reflect the class consciousness of their masters.

On the other hand—and this is equally crucial—it would be a great mistake to read Madame Aubain as a simple representation of the place of the master, whether the latter is understood as a decaying feudal aristocracy or an emergent business or bourgeois caste. The master, in that sense, is dead; his place is vacant: it is not Madame Aubain's class affiliation but her status as a woman which assigns her a position not less marginalized than that of her own servant. She also lives by proxy, her affairs managed by a male surrogate, whose very defection is itself another demonstration of her marginality.[6] Indeed, a more ambitious study of the social investments of Flaubert's libido—the privileged relationship between woman's experience, as in *Madame Bovary* itself, and the construction of narrative—would probably explain this affinity less in terms of sexuality than in terms of social marginalization. At any rate, the twin and parallel spaces of kitchen and parlour—however binary and hierarchical with respect to one another—are in their symbiosis both uniquely marginalized and decentred by this new space of infinite divisibility, a space which knows no sacred centres any longer, and which might, following Sartre, be described as the space of seriality, of serial flight, in which the centre is always *elsewhere*.

But then this makes for an unusual compositional problem: Flaubert will have to describe the contents of this ec-centric room, and convey the latter's structural displacement in what must remain essentially positive terms, terms of existing things, terms of a present of visible contents. It is the solution to this dilemma which we observe in the next four sentences, beginning with the chairs, which, counted up and indifferently substitutable for one another, become detached from their blank support, as though the room were nothing but a wall on which they were hung when not in use: an additive space is here clearly replacing an organic or qualitative one.

---

[5] Personal servant. *Ed.*

[6] Madame Aubain is a wealthy widow; her fortune vanishes when her lawyer runs away with the funds she has entrusted to him. *Ed.*

Yet this cultural revolution—this infinite process of quantification, before which the older primary perceptual qualities dry up and evaporate, this universal process of what Max Weber called *"Entzauberung"*, the disenchantment or the desacralization of the older pre-capitalist life world—such a cultural revolution does not make its way without certain resistances, which are slyly registered in Flaubert's text. Thus, in our next three sentences, it is *culture* which stages a holding operation, a desperate pitched battle of resistance. This resistance can essentially be described as the attempt to recentre space, to stem the serial flight of infinite divisibility, to pull back the contents of the room into a genuine centred hierarchy. So in the second of these two moments, the mantelpiece draws the two armchairs around itself in an elaborated version of that "pyramidal structure" already emerging in the first sentence, that "crowns" the piano. But such an operation demands the power of a specified agency; it is scarcely an automatic momentum that can resist the momentum of quantification under its own steam—it needs the rallying point of some ideological slogan, in short, it needs content.

The agency of our first sentence here is, of course, the barometer, well known from Roland Barthes' remarks on the subject in his essay "L'effet de réel". I find that my own reading is perturbed by a very peculiar slippage from barometer to metronome; and it would be interesting to see whether other people find the sentence rewriting itself in those terms against its and their own will. None the less, the barometer itself proves to be a most ambiguous symbol of resistance indeed, marking if anything the triumph of science and measurement over the older cyclical and qualitative time of the seasons. In the next two sentences, therefore, a more symbolic and ideological slogan or pretext will be devised: a most classical bourgeois solution indeed, which always finds it convenient to identify the opposite of science as *culture,* in the most limited and pejorative senses of that term. Now the realignment of space, the two armchairs flanking the mantelpiece, will be staged under the sign of bourgeois taste—the temple of Vesta—kitsch culture, the cultural bric-à-brac and decorative allusion to which, in the new middle-class world, the great collective styles of the past are reduced. It is not inappropriate here, I feel, to juxtapose this dramatic moment of Flaubert's paragraph with Heidegger's account, in *The Origins of the Work of Art,* of the sacred temple as the recentring of the world and deconcealment of being itself. To that august collective and social function of the temple in the ancient *polis,* Flaubert's art-object makes a trivializing and desolately ironic allusion.

But the problem with the little temple of Vesta can be underscored in another way, by remaining within the text itself—for this decorative emblem houses that very different thing, the clock: which, like the barometer or metronome, is as E. P. Thompson and others have shown, one of the prime agencies for the rationalization of time and the organization of the modern labour process. The counter-offensive, the attempt to recentre, organized around the vacuous ideology of culture, is thus contradictory in its own terms, and, as the final Flaubertian cadence confirms, it is doomed in advance to failure: *"car le plancher était plus bas que le jardin"* ("as the floor was on a lower level than the garden"). Here, in the so characteristic afterthought, the process of infinite fission and metonymization returns with a vengeance—once again the two levels, in their inequality, floor and ground level outside: and the return of the process, sealed by the great Flaubertian mannerism, the seemingly aimless rationalizing and logical connective *"car"* ("as" or "since") which offers the very symptom of a cause-and-effect logic running wild and consuming the universe.

One final textual event must, however, be noted, and it is a significant one, significant in its very triviality: "The whole room smelt a little musty." A further contingent or meaningless detail, documenting the Barthesian reality-effect and giving further, quite unnecessary evidence as to the "concreteness" and solidity of this textbook piece of realistic representation? I think not; and our reading of Cosimo will have alerted us to something very different at work here. For this is the only perceptual sentence in the entire description—the only one which flexes what survives of the older bodily sensorium, the only concrete practice of perception still feebly surviving in a new odourless and qualityless universe. This musty hold of a forgotten past—this faint trace of some olfactory historicism, last survival of what Adorno called the most archaic of all the senses—this event (for it is just that, the only genuine *event* in this lengthy paragraph) marks an indispensable stage of the process, but one which has seemingly been omitted until now. However abstract and impersonal the world which has here slowly been set in place, it will necessarily be accompanied by forms of subjectivity specific to it, of which we can expect that—in the historically original situation of a radical split between subject and object—they will necessarily be historically original as well. The musty smell, in my opinion, is to be seen as the place of the emergence of the new bourgeois subject, a process which has most strikingly been described by Deleuze and Guattari in the following terms:

> Something on the order of a subject can be discerned on the recording surface: a strange subject, with no fixed identity, wandering about over the body without organs, yet always remaining peripheral to the desiring-machines, being defined by the share of the product it takes for itself, garnering here, there and everywhere a reward, in the form of a becoming or an avatar, being born of the states that it consumes and being reborn with each new state: *"C'est donc moi, c'est donc à moi!"* . . . .[7] The subject is produced as a mere residue alongside the desiring-machines: a conjunctive synthesis of consumption in the form of a wonderstruck: *"C'était donc ça!!"* ["Wow"]
>
> (Gilles Deleuze and Félix Guattari, "The Desiring-Machine," *Anti-Oedipus,* New York, 1977, p. 3)

On my reading, therefore, this sudden and unexpected burst of "affect" announces the fitful emergence of the subject in Flaubert's text: the "musty smell" inscribing, with a triumphant, desolate flourish, the place of subjectivity in a henceforth reified universe.

I want to conclude this reading with two very suggestive objections that have been made to it, or rather with two interesting alternative readings which my critics have proposed, and which will allow us to return to our initial model of "cultural revolution" and to dramatize it in an unexpected way. These are, briefly, "symbolic" readings of Flaubert's passage, interpretations which to my mind return us to the earlier

---

[7] "This is me, and this is mine!" *Ed.*

critical moment of high modernism and propose the kinds of image-unification prac-tised by such canonical but now rather archaic myth-critical studies as those of Wilson Knight on Shakespeare's imagery, for instance.

My own reading of the text as a kind of programmation is admittedly a purely formal one, if by that you understand the description of an abstract process whose contents are relatively indifferent. What my critics pointed out was that there existed a functional content in this passage which retained an essentially symbolic value: thus, the temple of Vesta is to be grasped, not only as the mere abstract place of culture, not as a mere empty gratuitous decoration, but as staging a very immediate symbolic reference to the destinies of the two women protagonists—themselves virtual vestal virgins in the isolation of the bourgeois household. Meanwhile, the "musty smell" at the conclusion of the fragment is not "innocent" either—not some mere abstract marker which signifies "perception" and "subjectivity"—but stages a far more meaningful reference to the increasingly dominant role of odour in this tale, and can already stand as a symbolic prefiguration of the ultimate destiny of Félicité, and her olfactory ecstasy in death as she inhales the incense of the religious procession outside her open window.

Now these are very interesting proposals indeed and I am very far from thinking that the interpretations they propose are in any conceivable sense *wrong;* I shall also only too readily agree that such interpretations or readings are radically incompatible with the one I proposed above. Our business, however, is less to choose between them and to make some ultimate *decision* about the meaning of the text one way or the other (after all, was it not the very author of our textual exhibit who once told us: *"La bêtise consiste à vouloir conclure"?*).[8] The existence of two distinct type of reading now transforms our text into the place of what Ricoeur called the "conflict of inter-pretations", and on the methodological level presents a historical overlap between two moments of theory and critical practice, two moments which you will not be surprised to find me identifying as those of high modernism and postmodernism respectively.

In order to situate this conflict more sharply, it may not be inappropriate to re-turn one last time to the essay of Roland Barthes we have had several occasions to mention here; and to quote briefly from his own suggestive account of the emergence of contemporary sensibility:

> The pure and simple "representation" of the "real," the naked account of "what is" (or what has been), thus proves to resist the meaning; such resis-tance confirms the great mythic opposition between the *vécu* [the experi-ential, or "lived experience"] (or the living) and the intelligible; we have only to recall how, in the ideology of our time, the obsessional evocation of the "concrete" (in what we rhetorically demand of the human sciences, of liter-ature, of social practices) is always staged as an aggressive arm against mean-ing, as though, by some *de jure* exclusion, what lives is structurally incapable of carrying a meaning—and vice versa.
>
> (Barthes, "L'effet de réel")

---

8 "Stupidity consists in wanting to come to a conclusion." *Ed.*

I believe that the symbolic and iconographic readings which have been proposed of the temple and the "musty smell" correspond to a nostalgia for meaning in the sense of Barthes' diagnosis; a high modernist longing for symbolic unification which seeks to convert the work of art into an immense organic totality, most frequently under the sign of "myth". I happen to believe that at the present time we feel a certain historical resistance to such symbolic interpretations as well as to the practice of symbolism in the literary texts themselves (wherever such a relatively archaic practice persists in contemporary writing). Yet this overlap between two moments of theory and criticism cannot be said to be a false one: it is an objective feature of the discontinuous world in which we still live, and such ideologies of the symbolic are no doubt among the traces, survivals and anachronisms which our own cultural revolution—that of late or multinational capitalism—has as its mission to transform and to eradicate.

Yet we will not fully understand the consequences of all this unless we return to Flaubert's text itself, where I am equally willing to believe that such interpretative *temptations*—the persistence of the iconographic meaning and of the symbol—also retain an objective existence, albeit of a ghostly and fantastical type. But the opposition, the coexistence, the overlap, in Flaubert is of a different kind historically: not, as for us, on the level of theory, between the moment of high modernism and that of postmodernism, but rather between the older still feebly sacred iconology of the *ancien régime* and the new abstract decoding apparatus of a middle-class realism. But at this point we return to the model of cultural revolution as the synchronic work of the new forms on the persistent and inherited raw material of the older content. The symbolism of the temple and of incense is really present in Flaubert, but on the point of extinction: it hovers above the textual apparatus as a ghostly remanence, as the faint after-image of what the text was called upon to transform and to suppress, of what is, in the very process of this paragraph, in the course of dissolution. Far from constituting a damaging alternative to the interpretive model I have proposed here, therefore, the symbolic readings I have alluded to end up as a dramatic reconfirmation of an ideological and formal production process which works the raw materials of the older mode of production over in the very moment in which the forms, practices and daily life of the new mode of production are being for the first time produced, and as the bourgeois floor-plan of the new society is being set in place.

I had already completed the preceding essay when, returning after an absence of some thirty years to Pound's *Cantos,* I happened with some astonishment on the following, once cryptic allusion:

> Un peu moisi, plancher plus bas que le jardin.
> "Contre le lambris, fauteuil de paille,
> "Un vieux piano, et sous le baromètre . . ."
>
> Ezra Pound, *The Cantos* (New York:
> New Directions, 1970) p. 24

I was now in a better position to admire a translation process whereby a classic Flaubertian sentence is transformed into an all-too-characteristic Poundian idiolect, into the fragmentary notation of the *Cantos'* archaic potsherds.[9] But the unidentified reference projects, I think, a more substantive comment on the passage that interests us here, a comment developed by Pound's juxtaposition of the French stylist with his English-language opposite, Henry James. Both are, more generally in Pound, the objects of a professional admiration limited and qualified by their own restriction to the medium prose, but also by their historical situation, as this Canto makes clear.

For Canto VII is the place of the great transitional moment, in which for the first time the epic swings away from that archaic immediacy in which the gods existed in the early *Cantos* toward the junk-filled contemporary space of a *belle époque* on its way to the First World War. The James alluded to here ("the great domed head . . . weaving an endless sentence") is one whose work is evaluated by means of the spatial co-ordinates which govern all the early *Cantos,* a James who is defined principally, not by the late novels, with their intricate psychology, but rather by the ghost stories, most notably "The Jolly Corner":

We also made ghostly visits, and the stair
That knew us, found us again on the turn of it . . .

Both Flaubert and Henry James, in other words, are in Canto VII presented to us as committed, self-punishing artists whose fundamental historical raw material is the empty room, the room in which life once was lived (Flaubert) or in which it might have been lived (James), but in which it is present no longer, a vacant interior space overlaid with unnecessary ornament and decoration and inhabited by the husks and shells of former human beings. Unlike Mallarmé's empty rooms, however, virtual mausoleums through whose casements a distant constellation shines, the Poundian drawing room is haunted by the surcharged energy of older dwellings ("house expulsed by this house") in a way that makes historical commemoration possible, and epic, dialectical, retrieval of the past. The spatial implications of Pound's montage, in Canto VII, can at the least be taken as confirmation of the privileged, historically exemplary nature of the descriptive text of Flaubert with which we have been concerned.

---

[9] Pound's "idiolect"—individual mode of utterance—involved juxtaposed fragments of discourse like fragments of pottery discovered in an archeological dig. *Ed.*

Glossary

BY LAURA WADENPFUHL.

Analepsis. A segment of the narrative future intruded into the narrative present, giving a sense of what is to come. A "flashforward" or anticipation.

Authorial Audience. The audience implicit in a text responding to the desires and expectations aroused by that text, which they are aware of as a text. See also Narrative Audience, Ideal Narrative Audience.

Autodiegetic Narration. A narrative with a protagonist-narrator.

Consonant Self-Narration. This narration occurs in either a homodiegetic or autodiegetic voice. It communicates the thoughts of a character who is employing no corrective judgment to the actions of his/her past. It is a level of consciousness in which the emotions of the speaker in the present are identical to what they were in the past. In other words, it is as if time has stood still for this narrator (Cohn).

Dialogic Narrative. A narrative with two or more competing voices. The competition can be within a single narrator's discourse when the narrator presents, re-accents, or parodies someone else's language, or when the pressure of the narratee shifts the narrator's natural voice and tone (Bakhtin). See also Monologic, Heteroglossia.

Dialogue. An exchange of direct discourse between two or more characters. Also an exchange of direct discourse within a character's interior consciousness that takes the form of questions and answers.

Deictic. Literally "pointer": a word that identifies persons, places, and times, whose meaning depends on who uses them. "I" refers to the person speaking, "here" to his spatial, and "now" his temporal location. Deictics determine the temporal movement of the narrative enabling the reader to know if the events happened in the past, are happening in the present, or are anticipated in the future. (Pronounced "dike-tick.")

Didactic. A narrative designed to convey some truth about the outside world. An apologue or fable (Crane).

Diegesis. Telling. The (fictional) world in which the situations and events narrated occur (Prince). See Diegetic Level.

Diegetic Level. The placement of embedded narratives within the overall framework of the primary narrative. For example, a character's recounting of a story told to him/her by another, or a story from the character's own past that does not play a direct role in the primary narrative. See also Extradiegetic, Intradiegetic, and Metadiegetic (Genette).

Direct Discourse. A character's thoughts, emotions, actions, etc. that are expressed through a first-person, grammatical voice. In a heterodiegetic narrative this voice is quoted by the narrator.

Discourse. Whatever belongs to the way the story is told, as opposed to the story itself. Sjuzet, as opposed to fabula (Shklovsky); raconte, as opposed to récit (Brémond); the treatment, as opposed to the subject (Henry James).

Dissonant Self-Narration. A level of consciousness in which an autodiegetic or homodiegetic narrator retells the events of his/her past employing a perspective that has changed over time (Cohn).

Distance. The difference in moral, intellectual, or emotional perspective between the implied author and narrator, or narrator and characters (Booth).

Embedded Narrative. Narratives that are incorporated or interwoven into a larger narrative world, a diegesis that is separated by narrative agent from the main or frame narrative. The episodes in an episodic narrative that are held together by a primary narrative can be called embedded narratives.

Epilogue. Elements of narrative discourse that occur after the plot itself is completed, often telling what happened to major and minor characters in later years.

Episode. A sequence of scenes leading to a climactic scene.

Episodic Plot. A narrative whose events seem randomly connected, with little causality linking one episode to the next; minor characters characteristically do not recur from one episode to another.

Expectations. The reader's sense of where the story is headed. These can be generic (we can have a sense that we are reading a comedy that will have a happy ending before we know who the protagonists are) or specific to the particular story. Conversely, expectations operate with narrative desire to give us a sense of the genre of the narrative.

Exposition. Elements of the narrative discourse that are presupposed by but not included in the plot itself.

External Focalization. A narrative in which the narrator voices less than what the characters know (Genette).

Extradiegetic. In a framed narrative, the level of the frame. All subsequent embedded narratives are defined in relation to this first level of diegesis (Genette).

Fabula. See Story.

Focalization. Related to point of view, focalization identifies the governing perspective of a scene, episode, or entire narrative and the ways in which that perspective is created and manipulated. One needs to distinguish between who speaks (Voice) and who perceives (Focalization) and the effect this has on the narrative. See Voice, Zero Focalization.

Free Indirect Discourse. A heterodiegetic narrative mode in which the language is read as that of a focalizing character. In effect what the character would be thinking in the first person present tense is expressed in the third person past tense. Also called the *style indirect libre* in French and *erlebte Rede* in German.

Heterodiegetic. A term invented (along with homodiegetic and autodiegetic) to move the focus of a narrating voice or agent away from its emphasis on "person" or "character." This voice narrates in the third-person grammatical form and its source is typically not a character in the narrative (Genette).

Heteroglossia. Interaction between different dialects and linguistic levels within a single utterance (Bakhtin).

Homodiegetic. Character-bound narration in the first person (Genette).

Hypothetical Focalization. A narrative that presents what a person in a particular situation might have seen or heard—if such an observer had existed (Herman).

Ideal Narrative Audience. A hypothetical audience that implicitly believes everything the narrator says; like the narrative audience, it does not know it is reading a text (Rabinowitz).

Implied Author. The image of the author implicitly created in the rendering of the narrative. The implied author may or may not resemble the real author (Booth).

Implied Reader. The reader whose expectations are addressed within the text. This is the reader for whom the narrative determinacies of the text are selected. This term incorporates both the prestructuring of the potential meaning by the text and the reader's actualization of this potential through the reading process" (Iser). The implied reader is also the audience of the implied author.

Indeterminacies. The details left out of a text that readers must supply for themselves to make sense of the narrative (Iser). See Narrativity.

Indirect Discourse. The thoughts and speech of characters expressed in a third-person grammatical form by someone other than the character whose words, etc., they represent. See Free Indirect Discourse.

Internal Focalization. The narrator communicates only what the characters themselves can possibly know (Genette).

Intradiegetic. The narrative embedded within another framing narrative: Sinbad, relative to Sheherezade. This embedded narrative is often unrelated or only tangentially related to the primary narrative (Genette).

Intrusive Narrator. A heterodiegetic narrator who interrupts the direct discourse of the narrative's characters (a narrative metalepsis); a narrator who passes judgment over his/her characters.

Limited Determinacies. The middle ground between indeterminacy in a narrative and total authorial control of the narrative determinacies (Booth).

Metadiegetic. The third level of narrative. For example, a character-bound narrator who had taken over narration from a heterodiegetic narrator and who quotes or narrates the monologue of another character.

Metalepsis. An intrusion from one narrative level into another (e.g., Sheherezade commenting on Sindbad's tale), which serves to make the reader conscious of the various narrative levels and the fictionality of the discourse (Genette).

Mimetic. Imitative, particularly of real life. A character's mimetic functions lead the reader to view him or her as lifelike (Phelan).

Minimal Narrative. A narrative in which almost nothing happens with the exception of a single event, e.g., "The marquise went out at five o'clock."

Monologic Narrative. A narrative expressed through a single voice without any sense of pressure from an audience (Bakhtin).

Multiple Selective Omniscience. A narrative technique in which the inner lives of different characters may be probed, one at a time. See Variable Focalization.

Narrated Monologue. A narrative voice that takes on the idiom of the character while maintaining the third-person grammatical form (Cohn). See also Free Indirect Discourse.

Narratee. The implied recipient within the text of the narrator's discourse. Sometimes the narratee is a definite character within the story (the recipient of a letter in an epistolary novel, for instance); at other times the narratee may be defined as a certain sort of person (the "gentle reader" of Victorian fiction), or (in the case of the "zero-degree narratee") may be undefined except by the information the narrator needs to impart (Prince).

Narrative. The recounting (as product and process, object and act, structure and structuration) of one or more real or fictitious events communicated by one, two, or several (more or less overt) narrators to one, two, or several narratees (Prince).

Narrative Audience. The audience implicit in a text participating in the illusion created by the world of the story. The narrative audience inhabits the same hypothetical world as the narrator (and thus does not know that it is reading a text) but may not necessarily believe everything the narrator tells. See also Ideal Narrative Audience, Authorial Audience (Rabinowitz).

Narrative Determinacies. Conscious selections on the part of the author: narrative level, narrative voice, time sequence, the presentation of consciousness, etc. When one discusses a narrative determinacy, a specific event is taking place. For instance, when the focalization shifts from one character to another. See Narrativity.

Narrative Strategy. The narrative choices made by an author to construct his/her narrative world, e.g., diegetic level, diegetic voice, temporal factors (order of the events), etc.

Narrativity. A text's narrativity is the result of its narrative indeterminacies. It must possess neither too much detail, which will bore and/or alienate the reader, nor too little detail, which will require that the reader "invent" his/her own narrative in an effort at coherence. Robert Scholes defines narrativity as "the process by which a perceiver actively constructs a story from the fictional data provided by the narrative medium" (Scholes). See Writerly Text and Readerly Text.

Narrator. The teller of a story. A narrator should be thought of as a strategy for disclosure rather than as a person or agent—although sometimes characters are used as narrators. A narrative strategy reflects the author's choice of what elements of the fictional world are to be represented in what order in what language.

Omniscience. A narrative technique in which the narrator can report what is going on in the mind of any character at any time. See also Zero Focalization, Multiple Selective Omniscience.

Plot. The events of a story in their causal arrangement. Plots may be episodic (q.v.) or reticulated, with interconnections between the episodes. See also Story.

Plural Text. A text in which the reader constructs meaning by bringing all of his/her outside knowledge into the reading process (Barthes).

Preterite. The past tense in which, by convention, most narrative tends to be written. In some languages, such as French, a special tense is used for written narrative (the *passé simple*).

Privilege. What the narrator can tell. Some narrators can invade the consciousness of every character in the text (including, in biblical narratives, the mind of God); others may be restricted to what a single character knows and feels, or even to what a camera-eye might see and hear (Booth).

Progression. The movement of the narrative from beginning through middle to end. Broader than plot or story, progression can include the piecemeal revelation of a static situation, or incremental changes in the way a story is narrated (Phelan).

Prolepsis. A segment of narrative past intruded into the present; a flashback. See also Analepsis, Metalepsis.

Psychonarration. A heterodiegetic summary of a character's thoughts, feelings, and emotions in the narrator's rather than the character's voice (Cohn).

Quoted Monologue. A speech presented in direct discourse within a heterodiegetic narrative. In other words, the heterodiegetic narrator quotes the character's words (Cohn).

Readerly Text. A text in which the reader constructs coherent meaning by bringing outside knowledge into the reading process (Barthes).

Récit. One of the two French words for "novel." A mid-length first-person narrative, such as Alain-Fournier's *Le Grand Meaulnes* or Camus's *The Stranger*. Longer narratives usually with a third-person or multiple focalization are referred to as a *roman*. Also, in Claude Brémonde, what is narrated, as opposed to how the narrative is structured (*raconte*).

Self-Narrated Monologue. An autodiegetic or homodiegetic narrator who wavers between his/her position of cognitive privilege and a full identification with former feelings, beliefs, etc.

Sjuzet. The way a story is told. See Discourse.

Skaz. A written narrative with the characteristics of oral narrative (e.g., *Huckleberry Finn*).

Story. The events of a narrative; what happens, as opposed to the way it is told. See also Discourse.

Synthetic. (1) Putting something together, as opposed to taking it apart (analytic). (2) A character's "synthetic" components and functions have to do with his or her part in conveying or narrating the story (Phelan).

Thematic. Referring to the themes or discursive meanings of a story or character. A character's thematic components and functions suggest some ideological or moral significance (Phelan). See also Didactic.

Unreliable Narrator. A narrator whose statements of fact or (more frequently) moral and aesthetic judgments differ from those of the implied author. (Booth)

Variable Focalization. A narrative that is focalized through more than one perspective (Genette).

Verisimilitude. A narrative's rendering or representation of "truth" or "reality" in a fictional text.

Voice. Any speaker in a narrative. Voice needs to be considered along with focalization, since at times the language of the narrative can be inconsistent with the character from whose perspective the narrative is presented (focalization).

Writerly Text. A text that possesses so many narrative gaps that the reader must "write" his/her own story to make sense of the narrative (Barthes). See Plural Text and Narrativity.

Zero Focalization. A narrative in which the heterodiegetic narrator provides more information than the characters can possibly know (Genette). This is similar to the "omniscient narrator" point of view.